Reconceiving Experience

SUNY Series in Logic and Language
John T. Kearns, editor
and
SUNY Series in Philosophy
George R. Lucas, Jr., editor

Reconceiving Experience

A Solution to a Problem Inherited from Descartes

JOHN T. KEARNS

State University of New York Press

Published by
State University of New York Press, Albany

Printed in the United States of America

For information, address State University of New York Press,
State University Plaza, Albany, N.Y., 12246

Production by Marilyn P. Semerad · Marketing by Dana E. Yanulavich

Library of Congress Cataloging-in-Publication Data

Kearns, John T., 1936–
Reconceiving experience : a solution to a problem inherited from Descartes / John T. Kearns.
p. cm. — (SUNY series in logic and language) (SUNY series in philosophy)
Includes bibliographical references and index.
ISBN 0–7914–3071–5 (alk. paper). — ISBN 0–7914–3072–3 (pbk. : alk. paper)
1. Experience. 2. Descartes, René, 1596–1650—Contributions in notion of experience. 3. Language and logic. 4. Language and languages—Philosophy. 5. Knowledge, Theory of. I. Title. II. Series. III. Series: SUNY series in philosophy.
B945.K393R43 1996
128′.4—dc20 96–1082
CIP

Contents

Introduction

There are different ways of understanding philosophy and what it is to do philosophy. My own understanding is that doing philosophy is solving problems, figuring things out. To understand a historical philosopher, it is necessary to identify the problem or problems he was addressing, and see how his view was developed in response to them. This isn't always easy. Even though philosophers are primarily concerned to solve problems, they haven't always understood this themselves. In presenting their solutions, they often camouflage or conceal the problems that got them going. They don't do this deliberately, at least not very often. But their writing has this effect, especially on readers at a historical remove from the philosophers. When the problems that concerned a philosopher are no longer a concern of ours, it is doubly hard to understand what he was up to.

I think Descartes is a historical philosopher who is very difficult for us to understand properly, a philosopher who is in fact usually misunderstood. He is commonly taken to be primarily concerned with certainty, with determining what can be known for sure, and with actually knowing for sure as much as possible. Included in his drive toward certain knowledge is a concern to establish the existence of God and the (possible, probable?) immortality of the soul/mind. Descartes wasn't uninterested in these things, but they weren't his primary motivation. They didn't constitute his main problem.

What I understand to be Descartes' most pressing problem, the problem I am naming for Descartes, is that of coping with the conflict between two conceptual frameworks or *conceptions*: the ordinary conception of sense experience and its objects, and the mechanical, causal understanding of the way the world, including our own bodies, works. As we ordinarily talk and think, we directly and immediately experience our own bodies and things around us. But we also believe that experience comes down to events happening in our heads, though these events are caused by things around us. Descartes realized that we cannot consistently retain both the ordinary conception of experience and the mechanical, causal conception of physical processes. His problem is to make sufficient changes to our conceptions to make sense of both our experience and the world.

A philosophical problem is a kind of puzzle. Its solution is an explanation that removes or overcomes the puzzle. Thomas Kuhn has described science, in particular, normal science, as a kind of puzzle-solving activity. I don't think there is a radical difference between the kind of puzzles that scientists attack and those addressed by philosophers. Though at present there is no normal philosophy in the way that there is (sometimes) normal science. Even in a non-normal period, scientists are solving puzzles; they are simply less confident about finding solutions when they aren't doing normal science.

As things have worked out historically, different problems and problem areas have been assigned to different fields. At one time, almost all intellectual problems were philosophical problems. Those problems whose solutions require specialized or hard-to-get data, or which call for specialized apparatus or techniques, have been assigned to (taken over by) specialized scientific fields. Philosophy has been left with problems of explaining phenomena which are readily accessible, problems which can be solved without employing sophisticated apparatus and elaborate techniques. Philosophical problems, or their solutions, tend to be more conceptual than "empirical." We don't need to amass new data to develop or support philosophical solutions. We need instead to come up with new conceptions to make sense of (more or less) familiar phenomena.

Philosophical problems and philosophical research are quantitatively rather than qualitatively distinct from scientific problems and scientific research. Philosophical solutions, philosophical accounts are no less precarious than the scientific solutions to scientific problems. Philosophy, even when done right, has no privileged access to fundamental truths, or privileged means of supporting its claims. But philosophical results need not (in principle, anyway) be more precarious than scientific results. It is probably unreasonable to hope to get things right, once and for all—at least when we are attacking large problems calling for comprehensive and systematic solutions. But we can hope to settle, for the time being anyway, how a problem will be conceived, and what kinds of solution are appropriate. Isaac Newton didn't settle things once and for all, though many of his contemporaries and successors thought that he had. But he did determine what counts as natural science, and how this is to be carried out. That determination has outlasted his actual physical theory. There is no reason in principle why a philosophical theory could not accomplish similar results.

When a solution having a large conceptual component is presented for an intellectual problem, there is no proving that the solution is correct. We can't expect to derive the solution from evident first principles or even from other well-established theoretical knowledge. We can't look for evidence that provides inductive support to the solution. What a philosophical solution has going for it is that it *is* a solution. It must solve the problem it is designed to solve, without conflicting with our other knowledge and beliefs, and without giving rise to problems more difficult than the one(s) it solves. For a philosophical solution to fully solve the problem it addresses is actually a rare event. But to be worth anything, a philosophical solution must clearly solve at least a large portion of the problem. We must be able to simply "see" that it solves that part of the problem. And this much of the solution must promise a solution to the rest of the problem, if we work on it with sufficient diligence. The effective solution can even conflict with our other knowledge and beliefs, so long as it provides promising ways to revise the knowledge and beliefs. The Empiricist tradition which dates from Berkeley and Hume is a good example of a partial solution that seemed promising enough to attract adherents over a substantial period of time, though that tradition is now dead beyond all hope of resuscitation.

The present book is my attempt to solve a problem I associate with Descartes. This problem was addressed by Descartes, but without success. He didn't provide an account which solves the problem, which account we simply don't find acceptable. He just failed to solve the problem. Descartes also failed to provide an attractive partial solution. Many of his contemporaries did find his efforts promising for a while, but no one delivered on the promise, and these efforts were abandoned. The problem that Descartes addressed has remained one of the fundamental intellectual problems of the modern period. This problem has been attacked by philosophers, psychologists, and, more recently, cognitive scientists, though none has been any more successful than Descartes. I think it is about time someone put an end to all these false starts and failed attempts. The present book points out the direction we must take to overcome this hurdle that Descartes stumbled over.

My solution to Descartes' Problem involves new conceptions and reconceptions of familiar phenomena. It provides new ways of thinking and talking about experience, thought, and action, and about language and linguistic activity as well. Rather than introducing lots of new expressions, I commonly provide new meanings to old expressions by applying the old expressions in new ways and supplying them with new semantic relations. One can't tell simply by considering a new conception and the theory which accompanies it that the conception and theory are correct. But one can see that they do the jobs they are designed to do. And one can develop the sense that the conception and theory lend themselves to further developments that will solve other problems than those addressed initially. Selling such a solution is more a matter of persuasion than it is of proof, but this is rational persuasion, and is not a matter of either bullying or bribing.

In developing my solution to Descartes' Problem, I found I needed to attack a number of other problems. After this project was underway, it frequently happened that coming up with a solution to a new problem required me to rethink or modify a solution to a problem I thought had been settled. Everything didn't simply fall into place once I had fastened on fundamental concepts and principles. The experience of thinking and rethinking problems and their solutions made the preparation of this book an adventure, for I was never sure how things were going to turn out. The adventure was both enlightening and exhilirating. I hope I have been careful enough to revise all those portions of the book that were undermined by subsequent portions.

This is an ambitious book and, I suppose, also an arrogant one. I am writing a kind of book which is out of fashion in the twentieth century. I am trying to provide both a foundation and a framework for what Hume called *moral philosophy* in contrast to natural philosophy. But I am focusing on epistemological and ontological issues rather than moral or ethical ones. I haven't got much to say about those issues. There isn't room anyway. But I do think I have directed attention to the essential feature of human activity, its intentional, conceptual character. I have distinguished what is purposive and intentional from what is causal, and have articulated and developed a conceptual framework for dealing with intentional activity, applying this in particular to mental and linguistic activity. While I have answered some questions, I have left many more problems untouched. In this book I am trying to get something started, not to finish anything other than misconceived efforts to solve Descartes' Problem.

Chapter 1

Descartes' Problem

1. Conceptual Frameworks

In this book, the concept of a conceptual framework is very important. I shall begin with a brief explanation of what I understand a conceptual framework to be. I could as well speak of linguistic frameworks, or conceptual/linguistic frameworks. For I don't believe in abstract, nonlinguistic concepts simply waiting to be grasped. Nor do I count a nonlinguistic ability to "deal" with things of a kind as a conceptual skill. As a first approximation, we can consider a conceptual framework to be a set of meaningful expressions used for talking about objects of certain sorts. These expressions have various semantic properties and relations to one another. The meaningful expressions and their semantic features constitute the conceptual framework. For example, it is a constitutive principle of our color-concept framework that whatever is scarlet must be red, because being scarlet entails being red.

Anyone who speaks a language has mastered a number of conceptual frameworks. Although the totality of a person's conceptual frameworks could conceivably add up to one coherent but very complicated conceptual framework, this is unlikely. I will normally speak of conceptual frameworks in the plural. A conceptual framework is not an arbitrary collection of expressions, but has a certain coherence. It is constituted by expressions used for some particular part or aspect of things, or by expressions for some special field or subject. Its distinctive expressions/concepts are characteristic of a conceptual framework, but some expressions belong to many frameworks. Some conceptual frameworks overlap, some are included in others. Different frameworks can also be incompatible alternatives to one another.

While a collection of meaningful expressions with their semantic features is a reasonable first approximation to a conceptual framework, it isn't a conceptual framework. For expressions aren't the primary bearers of meaning. Since nothing "has" a meaning, in the sense of being linked to some kind of meaning object, what I should say is that expressions aren't the primary meaningful objects. That distinction belongs to linguistic acts—acts performed with expressions of a language. The word 'red' isn't itself meaningful, but it is/can be used to perform meaningful acts. The word can be used to represent a certain color or an object of that color. It can be used to acknowledge an object to be of that color. Various kinds of linguistic act are conventionally associated with an expression—the expression is conventionally used to perform the acts. Semantic features of linguistic acts are commonly attributed to the expressions used to perform these acts. A conceptual framework is actually constituted by certain kinds of linguistic acts (by act *types*, not tokens) and by semantic features which can be explained in terms of *commitment*. For example, propositional acts $A_1, \ldots, A_n$ *basically entail* propositional act B if performing, and accepting, $A_1, \ldots, A_n$ commits a person to performing and accepting B, should the occasion arise. Acknowledging Socrates to be a Greek and all Greeks to be mortal will commit a person to acknowledging Socrates to be mortal, if the question comes up.

Although linguistic acts are the primary bearers of meaning, and conceptual frameworks are constituted by act-types and semantic features based on commitment, it is often convenient to speak as if words and their semantic features made up these frameworks. I will occasionally indulge in this loose talk myself. I may, for example, speak of some sentences entailing another, understanding that it is really acts of using the first sentences to make statements that entail an act of using the further sentence to make a statement. The principles which govern—which constitute—the framework can be expressed either by sentences which explicitly describe the framework or by sentences which state fundamental truths about the objects with which the framework is concerned. As a simple example, we have both "Anything correctly labelled by 'scarlet' will be correctly labelled by 'red'" and "Anything which is scarlet is (necessarily) red." Some governing principles are inferential; these authorize inferences from acts performed with certain expressions to acts performed with others. For example, an inference from a statement "*A* is scarlet" to "*A* is red" is valid.

Philosophers sometimes claim that two people (or cultures) who employ different conceptual frameworks to deal with the same things, or in similar situations, cannot understand one another. Their views are incommensurable—the two people are doomed to "talk past" one another. I don't accept this position. It is true that different people might employ different, and conflicting, conceptual frameworks in the same or similar situations. It can even happen that statements in one conceptual framework have no exact or even approximate translations in the other. If the two parties don't realize what is happening, their attempts at communication may not succeed. But conceptual frameworks aren't prisons. A person employing one conceptual framework can "step back" and consider the two frameworks with their similarities and differences. Each person can understand how his view differs from the other's. If he can't express this with words he already knows, he can introduce new words to serve this purpose. What makes it possible for one framework's owner to understand the other framework is not a common experience which the two frameworks package differently. It is instead the common semantic features which structure each framework. The persons may not recognize the same basic entailments. But each recognizes the same kind of entailment, and each can determine how the entailments constitutive of the other framework differ from those of his own framework.

Conceptual frameworks provide resources for talking and thinking about the world, or part of it. But a conceptual framework need not be a neutral, noncommittal scheme for classifying and describing objects. Conceptual frameworks typically incorporate substantive information about those things with which they are concerned. A person who accepts and uses a framework is committed to certain views, by virtue of employing the framework. Learning how to talk about some objects is also, in part, learning what those objects are like. Fundamental scientific theories usually have distinctive conceptual frameworks. But we also have conceptual frameworks for talking about sense experience, about (ordinary) physical objects, and about persons.

A conceptual framework with substantive principles is a theory. It may be an implicit theory, for its principles may never be spelled out. It may also be an explicit theory. The theories incorporated in conceptual frameworks are partial and incomplete. They provide information about features essential to the framework's objects. They don't determine everything that is essential to these objects. As well as telling us what certain kinds of objects are like, the framework provides the resources to say new things about these objects. When the principles of a merely implicit conceptual framework/theory are spelled out, they will frequently seem obvious, or trivial. But conceptual frameworks, even the "obvious" parts of them, can be mistaken. The "fundamental truths" of a conceptual framework may not be true at all.

Deductive systems in logic can serve as models of conceptual frameworks. Deductive systems model spelled-out conceptual frameworks, for the axioms, rules, and results belonging to a deductive system are usually written down, at least in part. In a deductive system which is an adequate model, the theorems will include arguments or argument sequences as well as single sentences or formulas. (I write an argument sequence, or inference sequence, like this: $A_1, \ldots, A_n / B$. The slant line separates the premisses from the conclusion.) Consider a system of classical propositional logic based on the connectives '$\sim$' and '$\supset$'. There are different deductive systems which can present or express the same conceptual system. Some are axiomatic deductive systems with finitely or infinitely many axioms. Others are natural deduction systems. Semantic tableau systems are still another kind. But natural deduction systems make the most appropriate models of conceptual frameworks. For in a conceptual framework, one both makes statements and proceeds by inferential moves from some statements to others. An axiomatic deductive system doesn't accommodate ordinary statements and inferential moves. Neither does a semantic tableau system.

There are two important kinds of expressions/concepts, and two corresponding kinds of conceptual framework. The first kind is *independently significant*. Such an expression doesn't owe its significance to other expressions, and its significance doesn't consist in its relations to other expressions. For an independently significant expression (an independently significant kind of linguistic act), its significance is prior to the semantic relations linking it to other expressions—these relations are consequences of the prior significance. The fundamental criteria for using an independently significant expression might involve sensible appearances. Expressions for sensible qualities like colors appear to be independently significant. Its being independently significant doesn't preclude an expression's being explained using other expressions, but the significance of the expression must finally "come down" to appearances. A conceptual framework whose characteristic concepts are independently significant is *merely classificatory*.

An expression/concept that isn't independently significant is *essentially systematic*. A conceptual framework for which some of the characteristic concepts are essentially systematic is an *essentially systematic* framework. The significance of an essentially systematic concept depends on semantic relations to other concepts. Concepts of unobservable theoretical entities appear to be essentially systematic. An essentially systematic concept must have some ties to experience, but these don't consitute its whole meaning.

What kinds of conceptual frameworks there are is a controversial topic, though the controversy doesn't often surface exactly in terms of concepts and conceptual frameworks. It clearly isn't true that all expressions/concepts are independently significant, but someone might maintain that the fundamental expressions for objects in the world are independently significant, and that systematically significant expressions ultimately owe their significance to their ties to the independently significant expressions. This would presumably make the systematically significant expressions dispensible in favor of independently significant ones, or reducible to independently significant expressions. This issue about concepts and conceptual frameworks has an important bearing on whether there is such a thing as objective knowledge of the way things are independently of us. If certain fundamental concepts or conceptual frameworks are irreducibly systematic, this may show that our knowledge of the world isn't objective—that incompatible accounts of what things are like might be equally successful, so that there would be no basis for claiming that either is incorrect.

What kinds of concepts and conceptual frameworks we actually employ is a topic that will be explored at length in the course of this book. We won't approach these topics in the abstract, but on the basis of our having taken close looks at actual conceptual frameworks.

2. The Ordinary Conception of Sensation: Vision and Touch

We shall first look at the ordinary conceptual framework for dealing with sense experience and its objects. This conceptual framework contains such words as 'see', 'hear', and 'feel', as well as 'table', 'tree', and 'apple'. It is structured by such principles as the one which sanctions the inferences from a sentence 'α sees β' to 'β exists' and 'β is where α can see it.'

Let us begin by asking what kinds of things we see. A quick answer is that we see physical objects. But in *Sense and Sensibilia*, J. L. Austin has reminded us that we see more than substantial physical objects. We also see physical stuff, like water and sugar. We see physical events, like explosions and collisions. We see surfaces, lines, and points—the limits of physical objects and physical stuff. We see light. We see rainbows and shadows. Everything we see is physical: we see physical phenomena. It is difficult to find one word which fits all the objects of vision. For some of these objects, such as rainbows and shadows, we are hard pressed to say what kinds of things they are. (We can provide scientific explanations of these phenomena, but the ordinary conceptual framework does not provide familiar categories into which to place them.)

As well as seeing objects, stuff, events, and so forth, we also see some of their properties and relations. We see color, shape, size, motion, and spatial relations, among others. We never see just a color, or a shape; we see a colored, shaped object. (We do occasionally talk about a color as if it were a kind of stuff, but we aren't then treating it as a property that can be seen in isolation.) And we never see an object without seeing some of its properties and relations—we can't.

The customary verb for vision is 'see'. As well as using this verb for what we literally see with our eyes, we also use it metaphorically; but we ordinarily have no trouble distinguishing literal from metaphorical uses. Our talk about what we touch is more complicated. The verb 'to touch' does not normally indicate a kind of awareness. When the chair touches the wall, no sensation is involved. And I can touch something without feeling it. The verb for reporting what we sense by touch is 'feel', but this verb serves many other purposes as well. We use 'feel' for beliefs—"I feel Sandra is a better student than Bob." We use 'feel' for emotions, though the sense of touch isn't involved when we feel happy or sad. (These various uses of 'feel' aren't metaphorical.) There are some cases where it is difficult to tell whether or not a feeling belongs to touch. If we put our hand on something, and feel it, this is definitely touch. So is it if we feel the chair we are sitting in, or the shoe which pinches our foot. It is even a matter of touch if someone swallows a marble, and feels it going down. In these clear cases of touch, we are in contact with the thing, and feel it on its outside. These cases are examples of what I will call "feeling from the outside."

If I poke my arm with a stick, I feel the stick from the outside. This is clearly touch. But I also feel pressure on my arm. I feel this pressure *from the inside*—of my body. It isn't clear to me whether people generally regard what we feel from the inside as belonging to touch. My students frequently insist that it does belong. Feelings from the inside invariably accompany those feelings from the outside which belong to touch. Feelings from the inside at least deserve to be considered together with those feelings that clearly belong to touch. But the feeling of pressure on my arm surely goes in the same category as my feeling heat in my hand or head. I feel heat from the inside when I am in contact with something hot, but also when I am sick. And I feel tickles, twitches, aches, and pains from the inside, when I am not feeling a corresponding object on the outside. We shall understand sensory experience broadly enough to include feelings from the inside, regardless of whether they are a matter of touch.

We feel from the outside pretty much the same kinds of things that we see. We don't feel exactly the same things. Not light, or shadows, or rainbows. Nor do we see everything that we feel. What we feel from the inside is harder to pin down. We feel our own bodies. These are physical objects. We feel physical events, like being hit in the head. It is more difficult to find categories for tickles, headaches, and the various pains that we feel. We have a dual conception of such things as pains. Sometimes we think of them as properties. In this sense, two people might feel the same pain. Or one person might feel the same pain on different occasions, possibly even in different parts of her body. Sometimes we think of pains as concrete individuals, located in time and place (the place is a bodily location). In this sense, two people couldn't have the same pain. And one person couldn't have the same pain on different occasions—she can only have two pains which are qualitatively identical. Whatever the objects of feeling from the inside are, they aren't immaterial or "spiritual". They are physical phenomena.

Some features we feel from the outside are also visible. We can feel size and shape and spatial relations. But it doesn't seem that we get the same information about these features from touch that we get from vision. It is difficult for me to imagine a miraculously surviving blind race of people inventing geometry. Our feelings of shape and spatial relations don't amount to very much. Properties like warmth and coldness, hardness and softness, and texture are proper to touch. Although we can feel warmth from the inside as well as the outside, the properties of being pleasant (feeling) and painful seem proper to feeling from the inside. (We call something painful either because it feels that way or because it causes pain. It is only the painfulness we feel that belongs to feeling from the inside.)

3. Hearing Problems

Our ordinary conception of hearing is unlike vision and touch in admitting a fundamental and central distinction between direct and indirect objects. *Directly* we hear sounds and noises. *Indirectly* we hear the things that make them. Directly we hear the sound of the car door slamming. Indirectly we hear the car door slam. We hear the indirect object *by means of* the direct object.

We can easily make direct/indirect distinctions for vision and touch. We might say that we see a thing directly when we look right at it, and indirectly when we see the object via its reflection. And we directly feel what contacts our body, and indirectly what we probe with a stick or other rigid object. But these direct/indirect distinctions are not fundamental and central to the senses involved. And for these distinctions, the indirect and direct objects are the same kinds of thing. (Other direct/indirect distinctions can be drawn for vision and touch, which are like the hearing distinction in having different kinds of direct and indirect objects. But these distinctions don't now play an important role in our ordinary conceptual framework.)

When we discuss hearing, my students often claim that, strictly speaking, we hear only sounds and noises. We merely infer the existence of the so-called indirect object. When asked to defend this claim, they usually point out that we can hear a sound without knowing what made it. So in those cases where we do know the origin of a sound, we are making an inference based either on past experience or on what we presently hear. Their argument isn't successful. For we can also see an object without knowing what it is. Not knowing what something is doesn't prevent us from experiencing it in sensation. As far as the way we talk is concerned, we hear both sounds and the events that produce them. To save the claim about what we hear strictly speaking, we must either reconstrue it as a proposal to talk differently than we now do, or understand it to be the consequence of some other theory than the ordinary theory/conceptual framework for sense experience.

Our conception of sounds is like our conception of pains in having a dual character. We treat sounds as properties when we speak of two pianos making the same sound, or of one piano making the same sound on different occasions. We also treat sounds as particular individuals located in space and time. These individual sounds are the bearers of ordinary (i.e., not higher level) features like pitch, timbre, and volume. One of these sounds travels from its source to our ears, where we hear it. I have a conjecture as to why sounds are treated in this incoherent fashion. I think that originally sounds were conceived as properties of events (and, possibly, also of other things). A number of different factors might have contributed to sounds being reconceived as individuals. For one thing, if we simply hear events, it is hard to understand why we see distant events before we hear them. Unless we can hear events in the past, the event must send something our way, which we (directly) hear when it reaches us. It is more difficult to conceive of hearing events in the past than it is to conceive of hearing individuals produced by past events.

It isn't consistent to treat sounds both as properties of events and as products of events. It takes only a small modification to fix this inconsistency, but no such modification has been incorporated in our ordinary conceptual framework. Philosophers have frequently attempted to develop consistent conceptions/theories of sense experience and its objects, sometimes by modifying the ordinary conceptual framework, and sometimes by coming up with a replacement for it. Anyone who wishes to make sense of her own experience needs a consistent conception. With respect to the ordinary conceptual framework for sense experience, which framework we all employ, it seems reasonable to develop a modified, "cleaned-up" version of this framework. This cleaned-up version should be only modestly different from the ordinary framework, incorporating changes needed to remove inconsistencies and bad fits with experience. I will sketch the outlines of a revised conceptual framework, and call it *the* cleaned-up version of the ordinary framework, even though different cleaned-up versions are possible. In my cleaned-up version, sounds are not properties of events. Sounds are objects produced by events. We can continue to speak of sound and sounds as we always have. But from the standpoint of the cleaned-up version, it is correct to say such things as this: Strictly speaking, two pianos don't make the same sound; though they might make sounds which are acoustically indistinguishable.

The cleaned-up version of the ordinary conceptual framework eliminates an inconsistency of the ordinary framework. But it still leaves many things to be determined about sounds. For one thing, how are sounds to be identified, and counted? Does an event like the car door slamming make one sound, which occupies a lot of space, and spreads out in all directions from its source, or does it produce many sounds? And what kinds of things are sounds—objects, stuff, events? Or perhaps they are nondescript entities, like rainbows and shadows. I won't develop the cleaned up version in full detail, though I will make several contributions to this theory. The task of filling in the details can be regarded as a philosophical exercise.

With the cleaned-up version of the ordinary conception of sensation in mind, it makes sense to say that, strictly speaking, the same sound doesn't occur twice. I don't think there is a theory/conceptual framework which makes sense of my students' assertion that, strictly speaking, we only hear sounds, not the events that make them. Such a theory might be developed, but the students haven't done so. They seem to feel that the scientific understanding of things calls for a theory which makes such a claim. But this isn't apparent to me.

4. Double Vision

Directly we hear sounds and their properties and relations. Indirectly we hear events that make sounds, but we don't hear many of their properties. We hear these events begin and end. The other properties of sounds don't also characterize the events. The sense of smell resembles hearing in having direct and indirect objects. Directly we smell aromas, scents, odors, stenches, and smells. Indirectly we smell what give these off. But it seems that the properties of smells, which we don't have many words for, may also belong to the objects that produce them. For the properties we smell resemble those we taste, and the ones we taste belong to the objects we taste. Some objects smell like they taste, although many smell better than they taste. In spite of the connections between smell and taste, we conceive taste like touch, not hearing. We must contact (with our tongues and mouths) the things we taste.

Our conception of vision may not be modeled on our conception of touch (of feeling from the outside), but it surely resembles touch more than it does hearing. We talk of vision as if our eyes made contact with their objects. And there is no central direct/indirect distinction for vision, in spite of the fact that the physical situation when we see something is similar to that when we hear. We both hear and see distant items. With hearing we do this by means of objects which travel from the items to our ears. Why don't we think of vision this way? After all, doesn't light from the objects have to reach our eyes before we can see?

Let us briefly consider an alternative to the present conception of vision, one which treats vision analogously to the way we treat hearing. On this alternative, the distant objects that we see are indirect objects of vision. We need a word for the direct objects of vision. We might press the noun 'sight' into service for this job. Then just as we directly hear sounds, so we will directly see sights. This would be a new meaning for 'sight', since, at present, the sights that we see are simply the distant objects. We might also say that the direct objects are images (optical images). But if we choose this word, we must take care not to confuse the images we see directly with either neural or mental images that we apprehend with "the mind's eye." To fully develop this alternative conception of vision, we must determine whether the direct objects of vision travel from the distant objects to our eyes, or the light traveling from the distant objects produces the image(s) when it contacts our eyes. In either case, the direct object of vision must resemble the indirect object far more closely than the direct object of hearing resembles its indirect object. For, presumably, both images and their objects will have colors, shapes, sizes, motion, and so on.

When it comes to talking about the objects we see around us, the alternative conception of vision would be more trouble to employ than the ordinary conception. And it offers few conversational advantages. But our understanding that light has a finite velocity, and the possibility of "seeing" stars after their demise, shows that the ordinary conception of vision doesn't fit our experience very well. (It makes no better sense to presently see past stars than it does to presently hear past events.) This is reason enough for incorporating the alternative conception of vision in the cleaned up version of the ordinary conceptual framework.

5. Illusory Appearances

Some philosophers have criticized the ordinary conceptual framework for being unable to accommodate the distinction between appearance and reality. In many situations an object appears different than it really is. In a blue light, a yellow grapefruit appears green. Water in a bowl can appear colder to the left hand than it does to the right hand—if the left hand has just been immersed in a bowl of warm water and the right hand has been immersed in cold water. Lines equal in length can appear unequal if oppositely aimed arrowheads are drawn at their ends. Even when the grapefruit looks green, it is still yellow. We can explain that the yellow grapefruit reflects green light, but we see the grapefruit, not the light.

On the ordinary conception, we don't see anything green, only something which appears green. In *Sense and Sensibilia*, J. L. Austin made clear that this is not an inconsistency or fatal flaw of the ordinary conceptual framework. But why should it have ever been regarded as a difficulty?

On the ordinary conception, the yellow grapefruit looks green in blue light. Yellow appears to be green in blue light. But nothing we see in that situation is green. Compared to a different framework which holds that something we see really is green, the ordinary framework is at a disadvantage. The framework which has us really seeing something green is more explanatory. The grapefruit looks green because something other than the grapefruit is green, and we see this something other. The ordinary framework doesn't explain the grapefruit's looking green, it just "tells us" that the grapefruit does look that way. Appearing green in blue light is an ultimate fact about yellow objects—as far as the ordinary framework is concerned. A framework which "reduces" this fact to some others is more explanatory with respect to this phenomenon. And more explanatory theories are better than less explanatory ones.

Once we accept the alternative conception of vision, so that we see both direct and indirect objects, the grapefruit situation will be described differently. Now we will say that the yellow grapefruit produces a green image. Yellow objects produce green images/sights in blue light. The cleaned-up version of the ordinary conceptual framework is more explanatory than the original version when it comes to appearances involving color. But the cleaned-up version won't similarly accommodate all cases of the appearance-reality distinction. When the one line looks longer than the other, its image also looks longer than the other's. The water still feels different to the one hand than to the other. An object with one property can appear to have a different property. One property can appear to be a different property. In such cases it isn't necessary that anything really have the property the object only appears to have.

An illusion occurs when an object appears to have a property it doesn't really possess. An hallucination occurs when a person appears to sense an object that doesn't exist. The line between illusions and hallucinations may not be sharp. The heat-crazed wanderer in the desert who spots an oasis which turns out not to be where he thinks it is may be subject to an illusion. Some features of the way light is reflected may cause a real oasis to appear to be in a different location than it really is. But if the oasis is all in the wanderer's head, he is having an hallucination. Although *he* thinks differently, he isn't seeing anything.

The facts of there being illusions and hallucinations don't require that the ordinary conceptual framework for sense experience and its objects be abandoned. The presence of words like 'looks' and 'appears' gives this framework the resources to describe what goes on without requiring us to claim that when α looks ϕ to John, there must really be something ϕ which John experiences. The ordinary framework is not undone by illusions and hallucinations. But it doesn't provide explanations for these phenomena either. The ordinary framework is at a disadvantage with respect to frameworks/theories that do provide explanations. This disadvantage isn't in itself so important that a person should be eager to abandon the ordinary conception of sense experience and its objects.

In *The Problems of Philosophy*, Bertrand Russell exploits the appearance-reality distinction to launch a more sophisticated argument against the ordinary conceptual framework. He questions this framework's ability to certify those (sensible) features that objects really have. An object may appear to have many different colors in different situations. Since every apparent color has an equally good claim to be the true color of the object we see (and so on for all other sensible features), we must simply abandon the view that we can tell by sensing what the true properties of a thing are. The features we sense must not even belong to external objects, which leads us to abandon the claim that we sense independent external objects and their features.

The ordinary conceptual framework is equipped with principles enabling us to determine the true properties (and relations) of a thing. Russell challenges the ordinary framework to justify itself with respect to merely potential alternatives. But as addressed to a conceptual framework/theory which is a going concern (which is widely accepted and employed), Russell's criticism is idle. We don't need to show that the theories we accept are the best of all possible theories. We must accept certain fundamental theories and their conceptual frameworks if we are to make sense of our experience and the world where we find ourselves. We cannot simply abandon our most fundamental theories/conceptual frameworks. We can "trade in" one for another. But we should only do this if the one runs into difficulties which its replacement solves. Russell has not uncovered a true difficulty, and the replacement he proposed is unworkable.

6. Sensible Activity

As far as our ordinary conceptual framework is concerned, when we have a sensation—when we see, or hear, or feel something—we are *doing* something. Seeing a tree is an act or activity which we do with our eyes. I feel the surface of the table with my hand. We talk about our sensings in much the same way we talk about other instrumental acts. Just as I drive nails, or fasten boards together, with a hammer, so I hear music with my ears. The sense organ is the instrument I use to perform my sensing acts. Each of the five external senses has a sense organ that we employ to enjoy (to perform) the relevant sensings. But for feeling from the inside, there seems to be no sense organ. I feel the door with my hand, but I don't use anything to feel my headache, or to feel the pressure on my arm. When I feel from the inside, I am aware of a state or condition of my body, and I don't need an instrument to accomplish the awareness. This is probably a decisive reason, if one is needed, for saying that feeling from the inside does not count as touch.

Although we conceive sensings as instrumental acts, they differ in certain respects from acts performed with "external" instruments. I drive nails with a hammer and I see with my eyes, but I have less control over my seeing than I do over my hammering. I can be in the presence of a hammer without using it. I can just let it lie on the table. Or I can hold it but refrain from pounding anything. When my eyes are open in the light, I can't help seeing. And so long as I am facing a certain direction, I can't determine what I will see. (Of course, I can cause certain things to be present, and so seen. I can't, simply by using my eyes, determine what I will see.)

If there is something I don't want to see, I can look the other way. Or I can move myself to a new location, from which the original sight isn't visible. I can also shut my eyes. But these strategies don't "shut off" my eyes. They either block my seeing a particular object by keeping that object out of sight. Or they block seeing by imposing a barrier between my eyes and their objects. So long as my eyes are open in the light, I can't help using them. I have even less control over hearing and touch. I am not equipped with earlids. I can't help hearing the sounds in my vicinity. And I can't help feeling things that touch my body—to keep from feeling them I must stay out of their way.

When the circumstances are right, I can't keep from using my sense organs. But I do have some control over the manner in which they are used. As well as simply seeing and hearing, I can also look and listen. I can do something analogous for the other senses, though there are no special words to describe this. I can direct my sensing in various directions, and can focus attention on this or that aspect of what I am sensing.

I do have some control over my sensing, but less control than I have over my hammering (or sawing, etc.). Many philosophers have given the absence of control as a reason for saying that we are passive in sensation. According to them, sensing is not something we do; sensing happens to us. However, the active-passive distinction is basically a linguistic distinction. The agent acts on the patient because this is how we describe (and conceive) it. The agent verbs the patient. The patient is verbed by the agent. The agent typically initiates and sustains the action. There is no requirement that the action result from choice or be voluntary. Nor that the agent make some special effort. The claim that in sensing we are passive isn't one that can be supported by introspection or rational analysis. This claim is (in part) constitutive of a certain conception of sense experience, one that is incompatible with the ordinary conception of sense experience. The way we talk about sensing reveals, and constitutes, the ordinary conception of sensation. There are some circumstances in which we have a different way of describing sensing. For vision, the verb 'show' can be used so that the object seen is the "agent," as in "The wallpaper shows through the paint." If we conceived of seeing as passive, we would commonly and customarily talk of things showing to us instead of being seen by us. And similarly for the other senses. We don't normally talk in this passive fashion. If we spoke this way in a normal conversation, we wouldn't be understood. As we ordinarily talk and think, when we sense we are doing something, as opposed to having something done to us.

There is also a linguistic argument to the effect that in sensing, we aren't performing actions. This argument works best for languages that resemble English with respect to sentences about what is going on at present. In English, the simple present tense isn't used for describing events currently taking place. Instead we use a form of the verb 'to be' with an '-ing' attached to the main verb:

> The clock is ticking.
> The sun is shining.
> David is jogging.

A sentence formed with the simple present tense is normally used to indicate that an event (action) is repeated or habitual. To say "David jogs" is to say that he frequently or regularly jogs, not that he is jogging at this moment. And similarly with the other sentences. There *is* a "play-by-play" use of the simple present, as in:

> He takes a long lead off first base. He runs to second. He slides.

But this is not the customary, conversational way to represent current events.

With verbs for states or conditions, we can use the present tense for the present time:

> The pillar supports the roof.
> Mary has the measles.

Chuck owns a BMW.
The branch touches the wire.

Sometimes we can also use the '-ing' form:

The pillar is supporting the roof.
The branch is touching the wire.

(There is no difference between what goes on at present and what goes on habitually.) Sometimes we can't:

Mary is having the measles.
Chuck is owning a BMW.

Some verbs associated with sensation—such as 'look' and 'listen'— behave like normal verbs for events/actions. But the principal verbs associated with each sense do not. To talk about what is going on right now, we say:

Carolyn sees the two birds.
Ken hears what Jim is saying.
Dick feels a rock in his shoe.
Barry smells the dead skunk.
I taste oregano in the spaghetti sauce.

With 'see', we use the '-ing' form for habitual encounters:

Mary is seeing Bob.

Though we can also use the '-ing' form for what is taking place right now:

We are seeing a beautiful sunset.

We can represent habitual occurrences for the sense of hearing like this:

I am hearing good reports about Carol.

Though we can also say, "I hear good reports about Carol from everyone I talk to." With touch, we use both the simple present and the '-ing' form for current events:

> Dick feels a rock in his shoe, and he is feeling the surface of the desk with his right hand.

We wouldn't say that Dick is feeling a rock in his shoe, though we can say that he feels the surface with his right hand.Taste is like touch:

> Jorge is tasting a wine from Burgundy. He tastes its characteristic richness.

And smell is like hearing:

> I am smelling dead skunks wherever I drive.

Though I can also say "I smell dead skunks wherever I drive."

The linguistic evidence suggests that English speakers don't conceive sensing to be exactly on a par with other actions. It doesn't show us to conceive sensing as passive. Sensings are to a large extent like actions performed with instruments, though we speak of them as we do states or conditions. Even for states and conditions, we distinguish "agents" from patients. The pillar supports the roof. The roof is supported by the pillar. Though it is also true that the roof rests on the pillar, and the pillar is rested on by the roof. It is interesting to speculate why we describe sensing like a state or condition instead of as an action/event. Whatever the reason, it seems to have no great importance. The actual locutions we use don't reveal how we conceive the world. It is the semantic, inferential relations between saying one thing and saying something else that are constitutive of our conception of sensation. For example, if we accept Leonard Talmy's analysis (1990), we can agree that we speak about seeing as if there were something that came out of our eyes and made contact with the objects we see. This way of talking may reflect an ancient belief. But it has no significance at present. If it did, we would accept the claim that seeing is like this. Which we don't—we *merely* talk that way.

Sensing is conceived as something we do, not something which happens to us. Except for feeling from the inside, sensing is performed with a sense organ. In sensing, we encounter, we act on, an object. My eyes are what I see with. But seeing with my eyes is doing something, doing something to the object of vision. The object acted on is an essential ingredient of a sensation. However, sensing is not intentional. We can look for something on purpose, but we don't see something on purpose. Sensing with our sense organs is similar to breathing with our lungs. We are active in seeing, hearing, and so forth, and also in breathing. We can exert control over our breathing—we can hold our breath, breathe rapidly or slowly. But we don't *intend* to be breathing, we simply find ourselves breathing (and are normally content to be doing it). We don't intend to see or hear, either. We just find ourselves doing these things.

Although neither breathing nor sensing are intentional activities, they are surely purposive—they serve functions. We breathe in order to introduce oxygen into our blood; we sense in order obtain information about ourselves and our surroundings. It seems odd to speak of the purpose of a particular occurrence of breathing, but if we breathe in order to obtain oxygen, then breathing on a particular occasion must also have the purpose of obtaining oxygen on that occasion. (However, taking a particular breath may be an intentional act—one performed to satisfy the doctor's instruction.) It is similar for sensing. (And we can intentionally obey someone's command "Come and see my new dress.")

7. Descartes' Problem

The ordinary conception of sense experience is sometimes described as a commonsense view—and it is. But, among philosophers anyway, 'common sense' has a somewhat pejorative flavor, which 'ordinary conception' does not. And the description fails to highlight the fundamental character of the view. If something is merely a matter of common sense, then we might abandon it without much difficulty if we found a more enlightened position. The ordinary conception of sense experience and its objects is more deeply engrained. Indeed, this conception seems to have been with us forever. Our ordinary conception seems to be about the same (maybe even exactly the same) as the ordinary conception at the time of Descartes. Nothing I have read in Plato or Aristotle suggests that the ancient Greeks had a different conception. On the ordinary conception, which we share with our ancestors, we encounter physical phenomena in sensation. The objects of sensation don't simply cause us to have sensations. These objects are literally constituents of our sensations, and we act on these constituents in sensing them. Without the objects no sensations take place. Which explains the entailment from the sensation to the existence of its object.

Our understanding of the world we live in owes a lot to both sense experience and our conception of sense experience. We know what space and spatial relations are like because we see them, and because we know how to describe them. Our understanding of the world goes beyond what experience "teaches." But the understanding we get from seeing, hearing, feeling, smelling, and tasting is the basic understanding on which our more sophisticated understanding rests—even when the more sophisticated understanding corrects this basic understanding.

The ordinary conceptual framework for sense experience has various shortcomings. It treats sounds in inconsistent ways. It doesn't "allow" for the finite velocity of light, and the present seeing based on light from past events. Such shortcomings as these can be corrected in the cleaned-up version of the ordinary framework. However, there is a more serious difficulty which confronts the ordinary conception of sensation. This conception conflicts with our understanding of the physical world, and of the way things work. This conflict "surfaced" at the time of Descartes, and I give him the credit for having called attention to it.

During Descartes' time, the understanding of the physical world was changing in a mechanical "direction." This change started before Descartes came along, and continued after he left the scene. But Descartes was a major "player" in developing and promoting the change. On the mechanical understanding, the same fundamental principles govern the "operation" of all things, both sublunar and otherwise, both natural and artificial. The principles that cover nonliving things also cover at least a large part of the functioning of living things. The mechanical, causal principles that apply to natural and artificial things, and to living and nonliving things, don't provide a role for final causes. We explain what is going on in one place in terms of what has gone on in this and other places, and not in terms of future goals. The mechanical conception of physical processes is called "mechanical" because its early proponents often compared natural processes to the workings of machines. But the conception doesn't depend on these comparisons.

Early mechanists thought of physical processes exclusively in terms of such things as pushes, pulls, and vibrations. Thomas Kuhn (1977) identifies mechanism with the first two kinds of scientific explanation (causal explanation) in the modern—post-Aristotelian—period. The first kind of explanation invoked mechanical efficient causes. The second made use of mechanical (and mathematical) formal causes. These mechanical explanations (and conceptions) gave way to explanations which invoke formal mathematical causes that no longer count as mechanical, because they depend on neither forces nor contact. However, I want a word to cover the whole modern period, in contrast to the period when Aristotle's conception of physical processes was dominant. I will use 'mechanical' in such a way that it is correct to say that Descartes' and Newton's conceptions, and our own conception of physical processes are mechanical, but Aristotle's was not. Our current mechanical understanding has developed from the earlier mechanical understanding, and is much more sophisticated than that earlier understanding. The early and late mechanical understandings are recognizably similar to one another, in a respect in which neither is similar to Aristotle's view.

So what is characteristic of broadly mechanical physical processes? These mechanical processes are uniform: the same processes, developing in the same ways, are found throughout the natural order. And mechanical processes are driven by the past. When objects having certain characters are related in certain ways, they produce or tend to produce a specific outcome. The same antecedent conditions give rise to the same results. But in a mechanical process, specific initial conditions don't simply produce a subsequent event. The initial conditions yield a process which develops in time. It is characteristic of such processes that events which belong to the process can themselves serve as initial conditions producing that part of the process which comes after them. An essential feature of the broadly mechanical understanding of causality is its mathematical and "computational" character. Mathematical, numerical expressions are essential for giving precise descriptions of events in the world. Calculations performed with these mathematical expressions yield new expressions which allow us to precisely describe subsequent events. We can derive (deduce) the results of initial conditions, and can often use effective mathematical procedures to trace the unfolding of the causal order.

In mechanical processes, the past drives the future. Mechanical explanations appeal to what has gone before to explain what comes later. Mechanical processes can be contrasted with purposive (or teleological) processes, which are goal-directed, and mechanical explanations can be contrasted with purposive explanations, which invoke future goals to explain past actions. Although a mechanical process can be used to achieve a certain goal, there is nothing intrinsically purposive or goal-directed about a mechanical process. It is instead an intrinsic characteristic of (broadly) mechanical causal explanations that a complete explanation leaves no "room" for purposive elements.

Once we conceive of physical processes in mechanical terms, we can "apply" this conception to the workings of our own bodies. When we apply this conception to the "process" of sensation and the workings of our sense organs, we get a *mechanical conception of sensation*. This expression does not mean a conception according to which a machine can have sense experience, although perhaps that is possible. The mechanical conception of sensation is what we get when we think of the sense organs (and nerves, brain, etc.) in a mechanical way. The mechanical conception of sensation could conceivably "make room" for other than physical items. And the mechanical conception of sensation might be supplemented (complemented?) by other factors; it might leave a role for purposive elements, for example.

The mechanical conception of physical processes leads us to think of sensations like this: In order for a sensation to take place, an object of the appropriate sort must contact a sense organ. For eyes, light is the appropriate sort of object. For ears, sound is what it takes—or vibrations of air or some other medium. Once the organ is hit, a causal process is initiated which leads from events in the sense organ to an event or sequence of events in some part or parts of the brain. The event or events in the brain I will call the *central neural event* or *events*. For convenience, I will customarily speak in the singular of the central event.

If the appropriate kind of object contacts a sense organ, but something prevents the sense organ from initiating the normal causal process, or something prevents that causal process from reaching the brain, no sensation occurs. It is also possible for the central neural event to occur when no object of the appropriate kind has contacted the sense organ. Perhaps the sense organ or the brain simply "misfires." Or perhaps some other source brings about the central neural event. In Descartes' time, it was natural to think of this eventuality in terms of dreams or demons. Now we think of electrodes implanted in the brain, and connected to some external source. In such a case, the subject will believe, with reason, that she is sensing an external object, when there is no object. She will be "aware" of something that doesn't exist.

My students sometimes think that the mechanical conception of sense experience simply supplements the ordinary conception, filling in details missing from the ordinary conception. But the mechanical conception is incompatible with the ordinary conception. On the mechanical conception, the object which we take ourselves to see, hear, and so on, is not an ingredient of our sensation, and we do not act on this object in sensing it. We can see this most clearly by considering the possibility of there being a central neural event in the absence of a suitable external object. From the event's owner's perspective, her experience is not distinguishable from her experience in the presence of the "real thing." Reflection on this possibility supports the conclusion that in sensation we are normally experiencing our body's responses to an external object, while in the abnormal case we are experiencing the same bodily condition brought about by a nonstandard cause. In comparing the ordinary and the mechanical conceptions of sense experience, we can say that on the ordinary conception we have direct access to the external world. While on the mechanical conception, our access is, at best, indirect.

The mechanical conception of physical processes leads to the mechanical conception of sense experience. This conception/theory conflicts with the ordinary conception/theory of sense experience. They aren't both right. They can't both be right. But we all do conceive of physical processes mechanically (in my rather generous understanding of 'mechanically'). And we all routinely employ the ordinary conceptual framework for talking and thinking about sense experience. It would be legitimate to employ the ordinary conceptual framework, but not "take it seriously" if we had an equally well articulated replacement conception to which we actually gave our allegiance. But I don't think any of us do.

The problem of resolving, or coping with, the conflict between the ordinary and the mechanical conceptions of sense experience is what

I call *Descartes' Problem.* Descartes probably wasn't the first philosopher to realize that the mechanical conception conflicts with the ordinary conception. And he certainly wouldn't have described this as a conflict of conceptions or conceptual frameworks. Descartes may have been the first philosopher who realized how important, and how serious this conflict is. He certainly is the philosopher who deserves credit for having brought the conflict, and the importance of resolving it, to the world's attention. Solving or resolving this problem was one of the fundamental aims of Descartes' own philosophy, though he didn't succeed. No one has succeeded. I think that Descartes' Problem has been the fundamental problem of the modern period of philosophy, and remains one of the fundamental intellectual problems of modern times. The ultimate goal of the present book is to lay the problem to rest.

Chapter 2

The Larger Problem: *Sensing and Thinking*

1. Propositional Sensations

What I have just described as Descartes' Problem is really a proper part of a larger problem. This larger problem, Descartes' *whole* Problem, has two parts. The first part has already been described: To develop an adequate conception of sense experience, one that makes clear what is going on in sensation, and how sensations are connected to objects in the world. The second part of the problem is to provide an account of the role of sense experience in thought and knowledge. For sense experience is only important to us because of the access it affords to the world we live in. If sense experience is not what we have taken it to be, then our thoughts about the world may have a different basis than we thought. Our beliefs about the world will be undermined.

To situate sense experience with respect to thought and knowledge, we need an account of these things, not simply an account of sense experience. This total account must not only accommodate the mechanical conception of sensation, but we now think it reasonable to insist on an explanation of how thinking and knowing can be carried out with neural processes, though Descartes himself didn't accept this constraint. Descartes' whole Problem has been of great concern to philosophers from Descartes' time to ours. And also to psychologists. Recently, the field/discipline of cognitive science has come into existence largely in response to this problem. Dissatisfied with the philosophers' failures, most cognitive scientists attempt to use the understanding of computers and computational processes to explain the mental lives of people. Their efforts so far have been no more successful than the philosophers'.

To understand and evaluate historical attempts to solve Descartes' whole problem, we must first consider what we understand to constitute thought and thinking. The ordinary conception of thought is not so well developed as the ordinary conception of sense experience. This may be because we find it sufficient to express our thoughts, and have little need to talk about the thinking of them. However, in this chapter I do need to deal with thought and thinking; I will develop a very much expanded version of the ordinary conception of thought. This conceptual framework is not undermined as the ordinary conception of sense experience and its cleaned-up version are undermined; the expanded conception of thought has first claim to our allegiance.

We do not ordinarily count sensing as a form of thinking, but the two are clearly connected. A link between sensation and thought may be provided by what I shall call *propositional sensations*. As well as describing ourselves as seeing various things and various of their features, we also say we see something *to be* this or that, and we say we see *that* something is the case. We see Mary to be sitting down and we see that Mary is sitting down. Propositional sensing is reported with sentences (with propositional acts). Two characteristic kinds of sentences to use for this task are *sensing to be* sentences and *sensing that* sentences. Sometimes when I speak of *seeing that*, my eyes aren't involved. I may see that the right thing to do is get more exercise. Here I am using 'see' to mean *understand*, or *recognize*. It is often awkward to use the 'to be' form when I mean understanding. Though I can, I suppose, see the right thing for me to do to be getting more exercise. It sounds better when I see the solution to the problem "to be twelve".

The propositional seeing that interests me is seeing that does involve the use of my eyes. When I see the door, I also see the door *to be* open—or closed, as the case may be. Even when my eyes are involved, I frequently use 'see that' to report what I have read in the paper or newsmagazine. This counts as propositional seeing. With all propositional sensing, there is an important and central direct-indirect distinction. Directly I can see that something is the case. When I indirectly see that something is the case, this is *based on* what is presently before my eyes. Looking at today's paper, I may see that the Buffalo Sabres have obtained a new manager. Looking at the evening sky, I can see that tomorrow will be a nice day. And looking at withered corn fields in central Illinois enables me to see that this has been a dry summer. One may be tempted to say that my indirect propositional seeing is inferred from what I see directly. But I will understand an inference to involve propositional premisses and a propositional conclusion, with a move from one to the other. My indirect propositional seeing is not so formal or so complicated. I *immediately* see that tomorrow will be a nice day—I don't reason to that conclusion from a premiss. I will leave it that what I indirectly propositionally sense is *based on* what is actually present to my senses. (The basis for an indirect propositional sensation need not itself be propositional.)

It is more common to speak of directly seeing something to be so, or directly seeing that something is the case, than it is to speak of direct propositional hearing. Most commonly, when we say we hear (or heard) that something is the case, we are reporting what we have been told. But I can also hear one sound to be higher-pitched than another. I can hear that this sound succeeded that one. When I speak of *feeling* one thing to be this, or feeling that such and such, I am usually reporting my beliefs or attitudes. But I can with my hand feel one knife to be sharper than another. I can feel that the sandpaper is coarse. I can *taste* this pie to be sweeter than the other one. And I can *smell* that this odor is more pungent than that.

In considering propositional sensing, I have been looking at the "first-person" case. I am describing *my* propositional sensing. We also report other people's propositional sensing. I can say that Mary sees John to be sitting down. When we make third-person reports, there is a distinction between 'to be' reports and 'that'-clause reports that isn't of great importance in the first-person case. I might say I see a priest to be cutting grass or I see that a priest is cutting grass. In either case, the expression 'a priest' is *my* expression for the grass cutter. In neither case would we think the person's being a priest is part of what

I see—I am using the expression 'a priest' to (partially) identify the object of vision. If I say that Mary sees a priest to be cutting grass, 'a priest' is most naturally understood to be *my* expression for the mower. But if I say Mary sees that a priest is cutting grass, there is a strong suggestion that Mary identifies the person as a priest. It is *only* a suggestion. In the following sentence the suggestion is cancelled:

> Yesterday when Mary went to the rectory, she saw that one of the priests was cutting the grass, though at the time she didn't realize he was a priest.

This difference between the speaker's identifying expression and Mary's expression isn't important for determining the status of propositional sensations. It depends on conventions for determining whose point of view an identifying expression should reflect.

In a nonpropositional sensation, a thing can appear as it is or as it isn't. A yellow grapefruit can look yellow or green, depending on the light. These sensations aren't true or false, correct or incorrect. (Though we can speak of them as accurate or inaccurate, reliable or unreliable.) A propositional sensation has a truth value, but its value is invariably truth. For sensing something to be so, and sensing that something is the case are instances of knowing. If I see that *p*, then *p*. From a distance I might claim to see that the door is open. If, when I get closer, I determine that it is actually closed, I will withdraw my claim. I merely thought I saw that the door is open, but I was mistaken.

In a nonpropositional sensation, I can experience various kinds of things and various of their features. I can't sense all of their features. I can see colors, shapes, and spatial relations. But although I can see existing objects, I don't see existence. I don't sense similarity either, though I surely do sense similar features and similar objects. However, propositional sensations give me access to features I don't sense nonpropositionally. For I can see that one thing is similar to another. (And I can hear, feel, taste, and smell that things are similar.) Though it sounds awkward to say so, I can also see that something exists.

There are reasons for saying that propositional sensations are sensations. These "sensations" require us to use our sense organs. We report them with unqualified verbs of sensation. There are reasons for denying these "sensations" to be true sensations. For propositional sensations are a form of knowing. They "cover" or deal with features not accessible to our sense organs. Propositional "sensations" may actually be veridical judgments based on genuine sensations. Perhaps it does not matter whether we say that propositional sensations are, or are not, "really" sensations. But that depends on what we understand by *really* being a sensation, which is an important issue. In any case, the ordinary conceptions of sensing and thinking don't determine the status of propositional sensations.

If we took the line that propositional "sensations" are judgments and not sensations, these judgments would have false counterparts. But once we knew a judgment based on sensation to be false, we wouldn't report it with a verb of sensation. Taking this line would require us to solve the following problems: (i) How do we come to understand features not accessible to the senses? (ii) How are we able to recognize that a sensible object is an instance of a nonsensible feature? Aristotle's account of abstraction solves both of these problems, but it is not an attractive solution. Descartes' hypothesis of innate ideas solves the first but not the second. If admitting genuine propositional sensations yielded attractive solutions to these problems, this could be a reason for adopting such a conception.

2. Memories are Made of What?

Propositional sensations involve both sensation and thought. Memory seems to fall more squarely in the domain of thought, though we can remember past sense experience. There are two kinds of memory; it may be better to say there are two uses of 'remember'. We remember past situations and events, things we have experienced and things we have done. This kind of remembering is probably what most people think of first when the topic of memory is introduced. We also remember how to do things. I remember how to ride a bicycle, and how to make my bed, but I no longer remember how to play bridge.

My first inclination is to say that remembering past events is *memory proper*, but remembering how to do something isn't. After all, I don't need to use 'remember' to report my skills. Instead of saying that I remember how to ride a bike, I can simply say that I know how to ride a bike—that I am able to do this. I once knew how to play bridge, but I can no longer do so. However, the way we talk doesn't support this inclination. We use 'remember' in both cases. And the other verb of memory, 'to memorize', applies most naturally to cases of remembering how to do something. We memorize at present to be able to remember in the future. The remembering that we memorize for is remembering how to recite a poem, or how to get from here to there.

When I ask students, many without previous instruction in philosophy, to describe what remembering is like, they almost always use the same model to understand/explain the workings of memory. They claim that to remember something, they "call up" internal images of past events and scenes. To remember is to attend to these images. I don't know what to call the internal image model of memory. Its near universality might lead us to say that this model constitutes our ordinary conception of memory. But we don't normally talk in terms of this model when we say what we do or don't remember. I either remember that man's name or I don't. I simply remember what movies I saw last week. I don't have occasion to speak of images when I describe my past experience. This leads me to deny that the internal image model constitutes our ordinary conception of memory. Instead we have a widely shared belief that the internal image model accurately explains the workings of memory. This is a commonsense view which is not incorporated in the language we speak. But if we don't talk that way, what accounts for the belief?

An easy answer would be that the model is accurate. That would be the best possible explanation for thinking that internal images are central to the working of memory. However, the internal image model can't be accurate. An internal image might conceivably be helpful in remembering a poem or a speech. An image would be totally useless in remembering how to ride a bicycle or swim the breaststroke. Anyway, I am not ordinarily aware of images when I remember things. Most people whom I have asked are able to remember what they had for breakfast, but report that images play no role in this remembering. (Though some troublemakers do claim to be observing images of their breakfasts.) If everyone doesn't always remember via internal images, then the internal image model doesn't explain how *the* memory works.

At this point students sometimes suggest that we all do employ internal images to remember past events, but that some of us aren't consciously aware of these images. This won't work. An image is an object we use to represent another object or objects. The only images that we understand are images that we are conscious of, and that we use to become "representationally aware" of a further object or objects. In order to justify talking of unconscious images, we first need a careful account of conscious images, and a careful explanation of the respects in which unconscious images resemble conscious ones. Without such accounts, to invoke unconscious images is to trade on our understanding of conscious images, and to substitute the empty shell of an explanation for an explanation that gives us understanding. And if there are such things as unconscious images which play some role in our mental lives, these will surely be very different from images we are consciously aware of. It is implausible in the extreme that unconscious memory images function for some people in the same way that conscious memory images function for others.

But suppose our memories did invariably produce (conscious) images of past events. So that when I remembered the croissant I had for breakfast, an image of a croissant would appear before my mind's eye. Now suppose that when I turned my attention to this morning's breakfast, my memory produced an image of a bagel. If this happened, I would recognize the mistake. Whatever picture appeared on my "inner screen," I would know that I had breakfasted on a croissant. The key skill involved in remembering is the one that enables me to send back the wrong picture, and call for the right one. That skill doesn't depend on internal images.

We surely do produce internal images of past events. This is just one thing our memories enable us to do. Another thing that memory makes possible is using words to describe past events. But these skills that exhibit memory don't explain how memory works. We don't first produce an image, and then discover what happened. Knowing what happened allows us to produce the right images and avoid the wrong ones. In remembering we must make use of stored information. The internal image model doesn't explain this. There is no ordinary conception or commonly held belief which enlightens us as to the way our memories work.

Remembering how to do something doesn't require present awareness. I remember how to ride a bicycle whether I am asleep or awake. Actually riding a bicycle involves awareness, and possibly thought, but this active remembering is not a kind of thinking. Perhaps I function better if I think about what I am doing (though I can certainly overdo this). In any case, the thinking is a different activity from the doing. However, remembering past events *is* thinking. This kind of memory isn't "decaying sense," and it may or may not produce images, but it is primarily directed toward what I have experienced and done in the past. Sense experience is a major input of this memory. My past experience enables my present thinking about the past.

3. Images

Philosophers and nonphilosophers agree that internal images play some role in our thinking. To understand and explore this role, we need a general understanding of images and of representation. For mental images are not the primary sort of image; we presumably call mental images images because of their resemblance to whatever images *are* primary. And all images, whether mental or otherwise, are thought to represent objects. As it turns out, the ordinary conceptions of images and of representation are not adequate. We must supplement and extend the ordinary conceptions if we are to know what images and representation are like.

The most fundamental kind of image is an external one: something like a statue or a picture. These images are visual, we can see them. In this fundamental sense, we do not speak of auditory or tactile images, or gustatory or olfactory images. As well as considering images which are artifacts, we also speak of optical images: the reflection of an object in a mirror, lens, or pond. I don't know if a hologram is an optical image, but it too is surely an image. While paintings and statues are made by someone in order to represent something, optical images are caused (at least in part) by the things they are images of. Representing is essential to both kinds of images—they wouldn't be images if they didn't represent. (Nonrepresentational works of art aren't images, though pictures of them are.) These fundamental kinds of image represent objects which they resemble: they look like the represented objects.

It isn't easy to determine what it takes for one object to represent another. Similarity isn't sufficient, for not all similar objects represent one another. The fork with which I eat dinner does not represent other forks, for example. It is sometimes proposed that similarity plus causality produces representation. So that *A* represents *B* if *A* both resembles and is caused by *B*. This proposal probably results from reflecting on optical images, which are caused (in part) by the objects they represent. But it isn't sufficient either. Offspring don't represent their parents, no matter how much they resemble their parents.

Nothing represents intrinsically. A picture is a physical object, made out of some material. A picture has various properties, and it has a structure. We could describe a picture in complete detail, giving enough information to construct a faithful copy, without mentioning the fact that our object is a picture. The description wouldn't entail this, either. To see a picture as a picture, we must notice various components and their properties and organization. We must "interpret" these as the properties and organization of represented objects. *Representing is something that some agent does with a picture.* I will say that she *uses* the picture to represent its object(s); she uses it to become *representationally aware* of its object(s).

We must be careful to distinguish merely seeing an image from using the image to "see" its objects. Any animal that can see can see an image. But being able to see the image is not sufficient for being able to see it *as* an image. It seems likely that many sighted animals are unable to use images to become representationally aware of the images' objects. My cats, for example, surely belong to this category. They show no interest at all in pictures or mirrors or television. Seeing an image as an image is different from merely seeing the image. It is also different from mistaking an image for its object(s). The fundamental kind of image looks like its objects. It isn't uncommon to mistake one thing for something it resembles. An animal which isn't able to use an image to become representationally aware of its objects might still be fooled by an image, and respond to it as if to the image's objects. But this animal isn't using the image to perform a "substitute" act of perceiving the image's objects. To use an image as an image, an agent must perceive the image, become representationally aware of the image's objects, and be aware of the difference between the image and its objects.

Representing is what we do with an image in becoming representationally aware. The *representation* is the object we use to become representationally aware. To qualify as a representation an object must be intended for representing (as a drawing or statue), or especially well suited for representing (as an optical image), or both (as a photograph). Not every drawing or painting is a representation. Much abstract act is nonrepresentational. And if I draw a triangle, there is no reason to consider it a representation. The drawing *is* a triangle, it isn't supposed to represent one. Though I can draw one triangle to depict another. ("Here is a picture of the Great Triangle of Alexandria.")

The "basic idea" of representing is to use one or more items and their features to become representationally aware of other items and their features. Representing is *iconic* if perceptible features of the representation are interpreted as features of the represented objects. In the simplest case, which I will call *directly* iconic representing, the features of the representation that get interpreted are the same as or else look very much like the features of the represented objects. We use photographs and realistic pictures and statues to engage in directly iconic representing. In *indirectly* iconic representing, we provide conventional interpretations for some features. Using halos in a painting to indicate holiness or sanctity yields (slightly) indirect iconic representing. Using graphs and charts to represent the economy is also indirect iconic representing. For the present, I will confine my attention to simple cases of direct iconic representing.

A picture of a man need not be a picture of a particular man. A picture of no man in particular is a picture of an *arbitrary* man. The man may not be completely arbitrary. We might have a picture of an arbitrary bald man with a dark beard, for example. Arbitrary objects are not amazing, unexpected elements of the world, additional to the objects with which we are familiar. I speak of arbitrary objects to characterize certain occurrences of representational awareness. When we use a picture to become representationally aware of its objects, there need not be actual or possible objects apart from the picture, to which the picture, and our awareness, are directed. Representational awareness is not a relation of a subject to objects, it is a condition (or activity) of the subject. Using a picture to represent a man is something like seeing a man. Being representationally aware of a man in a picture is something like being visually aware of a man in real life. But it is the picture, not its object, which stands apart from the experiencing subject.

We can have pictures of arbitrary men. But many pictures are pictures of specific individuals or situations. In such cases, I will say that these pictures are used to *identify* those objects. This use of 'identify' is a technical one which has some connections to some ordinary uses of the same word. But this technical identifying must not be confused with the identifying involved in picking a suspect out of a lineup, or the identifying where someone names or usefully describes a previously unidentified individual. A picture might be used to represent two objects, while being used to identify only one of them. We might have a picture of Napoleon on a horse, which horse is no horse in particular. The painter didn't intend some actual horse that Napoleon rode;

he didn't intend any real horse, but represented an arbitrary horse. The picture is used to identify Napoleon but not the horse. A picture might be used to both represent and identify a number of objects, but represent them in a situation which never occurred. A picture might also be used to represent and identify the individuals taking part in an historic event, and to represent and identify that event as well.

Suppose there is a picture of Napoleon wearing a cape and a tricorn hat. Let two viewers see this picture as a picture, where the first understands it to be a picture of Napoleon and the second thinks she is looking at a picture of no one in particular, a picture of an arbitrary man. Both viewers, if they have normal vision and see the painting in similar circumstances, will become representationally aware of a small man wearing a cape and a tricorn hat. The two viewers won't have different kinds of representational awareness. Both viewers carry out the same kind of representing act. But the first viewer's representing act is also an identifying act, while the second's is not.

Identifying is not essential to representing; only some representing acts are identifying acts. What is essential to representing is that the image is used to become representationally aware of objects with the features shown. In using an image to carry out directly iconic representing, we exploit a similarity between the image and the kind of things represented. (A picture of mythical objects like unicorns resembles the way unicorns would look.) Representing is not identifying, but in representing one can also identify. The similarity which is essential for directly iconic representing also plays a role in identifying. We can sometimes use a picture to identify the right object simply because of the picture's resemblance to the object. But the similarity doesn't produce the identifying. We can use a bad likeness to identify a particular person, and not use a much better likeness for that job. ("This is a picture of David's brother, not of David." "This is not a picture of a particular person, but the person in the picture looks exactly like Anne.")

Using a picture to identify a particular individual is a matter of intention and knowledge. If I see a picture that very much resembles someone I know, I will use my knowledge of that person and what she looks like as a basis for using the picture to identify her. But I may be mistaken. The artist may have intended a different person, and I also intended to identify his subject. After I learn of my mistake, I can continue to use the picture to identify my friend, but I am more likely to use it to identify whomever the artist had in mind. At first, my knowledge of my friend allowed me to intend to identify her with the picture. Afterward, my knowledge of the artist's intention allowed me to intend to identify his subject. The same sort of difficulty could be occasioned by a photograph as well as a painting. But in looking at what I know to be a photograph, I normally intend to identify whatever was the source of the image captured on the film, not whatever the photographer intended.

As we ordinarily talk, an (external) image is visual. We view the image to "see" the objects it represents. Is it possible that the objects of the other senses could serve as images? We certainly do use sounds to represent. But in speaking we aren't carrying out directly iconic representing, for the acoustic features of our utterances don't often resemble features of the things the utterances stand for. In order to use a sound to represent in a directly iconic fashion, so that the sound can be considered to be an image, we must use it, or be supposed to use it, to represent something which it resembles. It seems that a sound could only be an image of a sound. Do we ever use sounds to represent similar sounds? If I say, "The bird made a noise like this: . . . ," and then produce a good or bad imitation, this doesn't seem to be representing. I am trying to make a copy—another token of the same type—not an image. The sound effects in a radio drama have a better claim to be representations. So does an actor's speech in a play: it represents the character's speech. We *can* enlarge our concept of an image to include occasional sounds. We could also do this for objects of the other senses, though we will have few occasions to use these objects as images.

4. Methodological Considerations

In the preceding section, I have enlarged the ordinary conception of representing—this could also be regarded as the introduction of a new conception. The expanded/new conception does not employ novel words. Existing expressions have been given new uses. So what is introduced by this framework? Representational awareness has not previously been recognized, certainly not nonrelational representational awareness. The distinction between representing and identifying has not been marked by either our vocabulary or our concepts.

To develop a new conception is at the same time to develop a theory. Such a theory or conceptual framework is not one we can simply "see" to be correct or adequate. We may be able to see that such a theory accommodates certain phenomena or solves certain problems. We can see whether it is possible to employ the framework in talking/thinking about our own experience of using images and other representations. For the framework to prove itself, the framework must turn out to be useful for understanding the phenomena, it must solve puzzles or problems associated with these phenomena, it must not introduce worse problems than it solves, and it must show promise for being further developed to achieve greater understanding. Such a "proof" would not measure up to the standards of some philosophers, but it would be more than sufficient.

This new conception of representing is disappointingly sketchy. It does not consist of certain key elements on the basis of which everything simply falls into place. Reflection on the framework so far does not produce the conviction that now everything makes sense. A new conception will not generally spring to life in a fully developed form. It is an abstract framework, an idea of how we should proceed. It is subject to further development and refinement. To reach a point where this was no longer possible would be a sign of inadequacy, not success. The perpetual promise of future development is what makes such a framework/theory worth accepting.

What else needs to be determined about representing? Too many things to try to list. A number of further developments will be carried out in the present book. At this point, let us consider the status of objects "in" pictures. We might say that the man in a certain painting is Napoleon. Or that the woman in a different picture looks very much like our friend Joan. We know that neither real nor arbitrary people are in pictures, in the spatial location sense of 'in'. For Napoleon to be in a painting, it is enough that the painting is intended to be used to identify Napoleon. Here identifying Napoleon is using the picture to direct one's attention to Napoleon. The arbitrary woman who looks like Joan has not got sufficient status to be the object of attention. We can attend to the picture itself, and concede that our representational awareness is quite similar to the plain awareness we have when Joan is present. But who is this woman we talk about so freely?

I shall approach this problem by considering fictional objects. These objects have sufficient status that we can attend to them—different people can talk about the same Sherlock Holmes, for example. This status is conferred by the authors who dream the objects up, not by residence in a possible world. Fictional identifying is different from plain (or real) identifying, but it needs to be accommodated. When a person "sees" the object in a picture, she might be using the picture to identify a real object. She might be using it to fictionally identify someone like Sherlock Holmes. She might also construe the picture as a kind of story about a fictitious world, and be fictionally attending to/identifying objects in that story's world. This is a very common way to look at representational paintings.

5. Imagining

Internal images are called internal to contrast them with ordinary images, which are outside ourselves. People often say that internal images are in our minds or in our heads. The reason for calling them images must be that being aware of these images has some similarity or analogy to being aware of ordinary, external images. Such a similarity would make the most sense for visual images, since we don't ordinarily consider other kinds. We actually speak of internal images both in cases where representing is involved and in cases where it isn't. For example, an imagined triangle could simply *be* a triangle. One need not use it to become representationally aware of anything. When I wish to be careful and precise, I will use the word 'design' for the objects of internal sensory awareness. The imagined triangle is an internal design. Some internal designs are used to represent, and so serve as images, and others are not. Being aware of a visual internal design is what resembles seeing. Instead of being careful and precise, I will often use 'image' for both images and designs.

Although most external images are visual, we have occasion to speak of internal designs for all the senses. Oddly, the internal designs for the other senses can more easily be used to represent than can their external counterparts. When I "hear" my voice as I think, I am not using it to represent my voice spoken aloud. I am just attending to that auditory pattern. But when I imagine the sound of something else, an internal design is being used to represent an external sound. Similarly, to the extent that I can imagine tastes, smells, and feels, my mental designs will serve to make me representationally aware of objects of the external senses.

Internal designs/images belong to our mental life. Producing and attending to these designs is a kind of thinking. Our ordinary conception doesn't require that this is all there is to thinking. Some philosophers insist that our being able to produce an internal design depends on a previous sense experience. We can only produce an image/design with quality ϕ if we have previously experienced an object with quality ϕ. While this claim is plausible for "simple" qualities like colors and tastes, it does not seem to be a fundamental principle of the ordinary conception of thought.

Philosophers have often used 'imagination' for the faculty that produces internal images. But this philosophical usage doesn't correspond to the extraphilosophical ways we use 'imagine', 'imagination', and 'imaginative'. Ordinarily, when I say "I imagine that *p*," I could just as well say "I believe that *p*." Though as an illocutionary force indicating device, "I imagine" may be weaker than "I believe." When we speak of being able to imagine certain situations, we aren't usually considering the possibility of producing internal images. An imaginative person need not be good at producing internal images, and an imaginative proposal does not result from particularly ingenious internal images. However, whatever they call it, most people claim that producing and attending to internal images/designs constitutes part of their mental lives.

I must confess that I don't make much use of internal designs. If someone directs me to imagine (to think of) a red triangle, I guess I can do it. But my imaging power is so "weak" that if I didn't know what I had been directed to do, I would not be able to say that I was attending to a red triangle. I'm not really convinced that I can produce visual images at will. I think that when I imagine a red triangle, I do much the same thing that I do when I look for a red triangle. I am disposed to see a red triangle, I am *ready* for a red triangle. But I don't actually produce one. It is different for auditory images. Not when I imagine music, or other people talking. But when I think in words. And when I imagine myself humming, or singing, or making any vocal noise. My awareness of the sounds I am thinking really is analogous to hearing them when I make them aloud. I believe that everyone is really like me when it comes to internal designs. But most other people I have asked about this don't agree. So perhaps I am simply deficient in imaging power.

With an external image we can determine what are its physical properties: what it is made of, its shape, size, and so on. An external image can be completely described without revealing that it is an image, since we call it an image with respect to an activity we perform with it. We can't say so much about internal images as we can about external ones. We don't know what they are made of or how big they are. Though we could fully describe an internal design without indicating whether it is used to represent. We speak of internal images because we have found (someone has found) that apprehending such images has something important in common with apprehending external objects and images.

Although I am dubious about my own ability to produce internal images at will, I have dreams. And internal images are important to the ordinary understanding of dreams (but dreams aren't produced at will). It is common to think that dreaming is like apprehending a movie on an inner screen. Though in a dream, apprehending internal images is mistaken for being (nonrepresentationally) aware of the represented objects. Internal images must be involved in dreams, but do we confuse the images with the objects they resemble, or do we use the images to represent objects, and confuse this "process" with apprehending the objects? When a real picture fools us, we aren't aware that it is a picture. We simply think we are seeing what it resembles. Once we realize it is a picture, we can (and usually do) use it to represent its object—which it also resembles. If someone is to use a real picture to represent, she must be aware of the picture as an object distinct from *its* object. When we confuse seeing a picture with seeing its object, we are mistaking the picture itself for the object. If the case is the same for dreaming, then we confuse internal images with external things. I find it amazing that we could do this—even when asleep.

Although internal images must figure in dreams, having a dream isn't completely analogous to watching a movie. For we are *in* our dreams. And not in the way that we are in movies taken of us. In dreams, we don't see ourselves from the outside. We see things around us. And we make decisions and perform actions. Neither our ordinary conceptual framework nor our common sense beliefs explain what goes on when we dream. Though perhaps this conception/these beliefs more adequately account for dreams than for memory.

6. Propositional Thinking

We don't ordinarily think that thinking consists in attending to internal images. And we shouldn't think this, for it doesn't seem to be true. It certainly isn't true that we only think about objects which we can directly iconically represent with internal images. For some parts of mathematics, such images would be of little help. And there is no way to form images which resemble democracy or justice.

There are philosophers who have claimed that there is no thinking without images. Such a claim can be interpreted in different ways. If it means that our thinking is limited to internal designs/images, and we can only think about objects which are directly iconically represented with these images, then the claim is false and uninteresting. But the claim might mean that we are always aware of internal designs/images. Even when engaged in thinking which doesn't use images, we are *also* aware of images. This view doesn't make images to be essential for all thinking, since it allows for thinking that makes no use of images. On this view, images would provide a background for the thinking that doesn't use images. The view leaves that other thinking unexplained.

The claim that there is no thinking without images might also mean that we need designs/images to think with, but allow that we can use them in other ways than direct iconic representing. For example, we may use language to carry out representing, but the expressions we use don't resemble objects represented with them. Perhaps we need verbal or other designs for thinking, where these designs are not the objects we think about, and don't need to resemble the objects we use them to think about. This understanding would make the claim that we always think with images more modest and less explanatory than some philosophers have thought. But the claim might then have some chance of being true.

There may be many different kinds of thinking—many different activities that should be counted as thinking. But the thinking that matters most for belief and knowledge is *propositional thinking*, which can appropriately be evaluated in terms of truth and falsity, and is typically either expressed by or carried out with declarative sentences. To determine whether there might be a need for internal designs/images in all thinking, we must investigate propositional thinking and the role of internal designs/images vis-à-vis propositional thinking.

Classical philosophers recognized only three fundamental mental operations: simple apprehension (conception), judgment, and reasoning. They assimilated all propositional thinking to judging, the mental counterpart of asserting. Judgments *are* propositional thoughts. But we also think propositionally when we wonder if something is so, or doubt that something is the case. We can propose, or suggest, or wish that things are/were this way or that, making use of propositional thoughts to do so. What is crucial to propositional thinking is that there is a "core" or "content" which can appropriately be evaluated as correct or incorrect, true or false. Propositional thinking is expressed by (carried out with) sentences; the sentences aren't all used to say something true or false ("Is it ten o'clock yet?"), but we can evaluate the *propositional content* of the statements.

Ordinary English provides two distinctive forms for reporting/describing propositional thought. These will be used to label two kinds of propositional thinking. The first form of propositional thinking is the *to be* variety. I can believe Paul *to be* the finest person I know. Bill may think Bonnie *to have been* rude. A 'to be' report can also be negative, as when Leonard believes Bonnie not to have been rude—to have been not rude. The second form of propositional thinking is the *'that'-clause* form. I can believe *that* Paul is the finest person I know. Bill will think *that* Bonnie was rude. And Leonard thinks that she wasn't.

'That'-clauses are quite flexible. But 'to be' often becomes awkward. We can think Charles to be a baker, or to be at home, or to be cutting the grass. This thinking concerns what Charles is or is doing at present. We can also think Charles to have been a baker, or at home, or cutting the grass. We are considering Charles at some point in the past. If we think Charles to have cut the grass, we are considering a task accomplished by Charles, one that took a period of time. We cannot smoothly report this with a form of the verb 'to be'. (We thought Charles to have been in a state or condition of having cut the grass.) I will allow the category of 'to be' reports to include some statements that don't contain a form of the verb 'to be'. Our thinking Charles to have cut the grass will be considered a 'to be' report. The infinitive form is characteristic of 'to be' reports.

Not all propositional thinking is reported in one or the other form. I can simply say Bill thinks Bonnie was rude. I have repeated Bill's propositional thought (his belief), but I have not used either a 'to be' sentence or a 'that'-clause sentence. However, most of us would notice only the slightest of differences between my saying Bill thinks Bonnie was rude and saying Bill thinks *that* Bonnie was rude. The two verbal forms are standard or canonical forms. Reports that don't use either form can be recast using one or the other.

Ordinarily, there is not a sharp separation between situations calling for one form and situations calling for the other. English-speakers will probably feel the same fact about Mary can be reported by saying either "Mary thinks John to be honest" or "Mary thinks that John is honest." It is often a matter of indifference whether we use one form or the other. But ordinary usage is merely suggestive. The present account of two forms of propositional thinking is not simply the result of analyzing ordinary language. I am making a new conceptual distinction, and giving new meanings to the expressions used to mark this distinction. But even in ordinary usage, the two forms aren't completely interchangeable. If Mary believes that someone is responsible for Mrs. Miller's death, she may not believe someone to be (to have been) responsible for the death. Mary can believe *that* someone did it without having anyone in particular in mind. If she believes *someone* to have done it, then she is thinking of a particular someone.

Even on the technical usage adopted here, it will often be a matter of indifference whether we use one or the other form. In reporting Mary's beliefs, I am not reporting what is going through her mind at this very moment, but rather what she is *disposed* to think or accept. If Mary is of normal ability, whenever she is disposed to claim *that* John is honest, she will also be disposed to acknowledge him *to be* honest. Carrying out either form of propositional judging will commit her to carrying out the other (if the occasion arises). The fact that both forms describe acts Mary is disposed to carry out allows either form to be used.

The two reporting forms were used earlier for describing propositional sensations. With propositional sensations, we might see Charles to be cutting the grass or see that he is cutting it. But both of these cases are different from the situation where we see Charles cutting the grass. Seeing him cut the grass is not propositional sensing. I see an activity. To say I see Charles cutting the grass is not "short" for saying I see him to be cutting the grass or for saying I see that he is cutting the grass. But if I say the one I will be committed to accepting the other forms. Seeing Charles cut the grass is not propositional sensing, but the plain seeing provides an adequate "basis" for the propositional seeing. However, someone else might see Charles cutting the grass without either seeing him to be cutting the grass or seeing that he is cutting the grass. That person, from Mars perhaps, might not know what a lawnmower is or what it does.

7. Propositional Identifying

Earlier we saw that representing must be distinguished from identifying. Although representing often coincides with identifying, it can also take place by itself. Representational awareness of arbitrary objects need not provide an occasion for directing attention to objects in the world. But if representing can take place without identifying, then perhaps the opposite can also occur. Do we use anything to direct our attention to particular objects in the world, without becoming representationally aware of a kind of object? Once this question can be asked, it is obvious that the answer is "Yes." We use expressions, which are not images, to attend to particular objects. When I use 'Napoleon' to refer to Napoleon, I am identifying Napoleon (in our present technical sense of 'identify'). The word 'Napoleon' has no features that I interpret to become representationally aware of Napoleon, or an arbitrary man like him.

We can attend to a present object by just looking at it. No further object is needed for this, certainly not an expression. But we can use a name to express our attending, and to get someone else to attend to that object. We can also attend to—think of—an absent object. Here we may need the help of a name or an idea. Attending to an object α may set the stage for *acknowledging* α to be ϕ. This use of 'acknowledging' is a technical one (though I have previously employed the word this way), for ordinarily a person is said to acknowledge only what is the case. On the technical use, a person who sincerely applies the ϕ-expression to α has acknowledged α to be ϕ, regardless of whether α is ϕ. Mary's thinking α *to be* ϕ is constituted by her attending and the acknowledging which this makes possible. Acknowledging α to be ϕ is *judging* α to be ϕ. (There are also negative 'to be' acknowledging acts; Mary performs a negative acknowledging act in judging β not to be ϕ—in denying β to be ϕ.)

A picture can be used to both represent and identify. The picture alone is sufficient for becoming representationally aware. But to use the picture to identify an object, the user needs independent knowledge of the target to be identified, and must intend that target. To use a picture to either represent or identify, the perceiving subject must attend to the picture. In using the picture to identify a further object, the subject is using the picture to direct his attention to that object. We not only use words and ideas to attend to objects, we also use images.

Using a picture to identify an object in the world is using the picture to attend to that object. But not all attending constitutes identifying. If in looking at a painting of an arbitrary horse—a painting of no horse in particular—Mary thinks the painter had a particular horse in mind, Mary can direct her attention toward that horse, intending to identify it. She can speculate about the horse, make efforts to learn more about it, even inquire about purchasing it. But while Mary has used the picture to direct her attention toward the world, her attending has no target. And hers is not an identifying act. In attending, Mary attempts to identify, but if her attending has no target, her attempted identifying act fails to come off.

In the 'to be' form of propositional thinking, the subject uses expressions or images or ideas to attend to objects in the world, or else she attends directly to objects in experience. If these acts have genuine targets in the world, the attending acts are also identifying acts. An initial identifying "sets up" an acknowledging. The thinker/speaker who identifies α, giving her a target which she then correctly acknowledges to be ϕ, has performed two identifying acts. The initial attending act is *preliminary*, and the acknowledging act *further* identifies α. Only correct acknowledging acts are identifying, incorrect judgments are failed attempts to identify. The 'to be' form of propositional thinking is identifying (identificational?) propositional thinking. Words are instruments that can be used for this. When words are used to acknowledge, as when Mary uses 'is wealthy' to acknowledge Tom to be wealthy, no feature of 'is wealthy' is interpreted to produce representational awareness. Mary simply applies the criteria for 'is wealthy' in using this expression to acknowledge Tom to be that way. Propositional thinking of the 'to be' form, when carried out with words, is *merely* identifying, as contrasted with thinking which both represents and identifies.

Although only real objects can be identified, fictional objects have a somewhat objective status, and a person who attends to a fictional object need not be trying to identify a real object. In addition to plain identifying acts, we need to recognize *fictional* identifying acts. Mary fictionally identifies Sherlock Holmes when she thinks Sherlock Holmes to be clever. An attending act is an identifying act if its object is real and the subject notices or intends a real object. An attending act is a fictional identifying act if its object has an appropriate status and the subject intends an object with that status. For an acknowledging act to be a plain identifying act, the real object must satisfy the criteria associated with the acknowledging expression/concept. For an acknowledging act to be a fictional identifying act, the authoritative fictional practice (tradition) must assign the fictitious object to the acknowledged category.

This understanding of fictional identifying has interesting consequences for the writing of fiction. In order for fictional identifying acts to take place, there must be some objective story or tradition which provides targets for the identifying acts. The story writer who makes up the story has no basis for performing fictional identifying acts. So what is he doing? He surely thinks about his characters and their situations. While the storyteller may attend to what he is doing, he can't attend to his characters and the events of their world until he has written some of the story. His initial activity must be regarded as a kind of creative, nondeceptive pretending—he pretends to identify his characters and acknowledge them to be whatever. After he is done, the rest of us can fictionally identify them.

Although we can use words (spoken, written, or thought) to carry out propositional thinking of the 'to be' form, it might be possible to use images for this. Instead of using a word to attend to and (attempt to) identify an object, we could use an image of the object to identify it. In that case, our act would be both representing and identifying. But images aren't conventionally associated with objects. To use an image to identify an object, a subject needs independent knowledge of the object, and must intend for his representational awareness to be connected to that object. (The independent knowledge doesn't need to be detailed. One might know only that the artist painted a real person, and intend that person.) In contrast, there are conventional procedures for associating particular expressions with particular objects. One can rely on these procedures in intentionally directing her attention.

It is less clear how we might use an image to perform an acknowledging act. Suppose Mary thinks Tom to be wealthy like this: First she produces an image of Tom and uses this to represent and identify Tom. She can do this with either a good or a poor likeness of Tom. But to acknowledge Tom to be wealthy, Mary must employ criteria for acknowledging someone to be wealthy, and use an expression or image or idea for Tom on the basis of his satisfying the criteria. Expressions are conventionally associated with acknowledging criteria. But suppose Mary uses an image to acknowledge Tom to be wealthy. This might be an image of wealth: gold, money, jewels, whatever. In using her image of wealth to acknowledge Tom to be wealthy, Mary's representing and acknowledging are distinct. She is representing wealth, not Tom, but her acknowledging act identifies Tom, or is intended to (for Tom may not be wealthy). This difference makes Mary's use of an image to acknowledge somewhat problematic. The mere act of representing wealth gives no help in performing an acknowledging act. There are lots of connections to wealth that a person might have—he might own it, protect it, covet it. The representing won't determine the criteria for acknowledging. Mary's use of an image could possibly be of help as a reminder, but the representing would be incidental to the acknowledging/identifying. The acknowledging act is what is true or false, so the propositional part of Mary's thinking is the acknowledging act; her act of identifying Tom is only preliminary. The representational character of an acknowledging act must be irrelevant to the acknowledging. Propositional thinking of the 'to be' form doesn't represent the way the world is thought to be.

Some of Hume's discussions of ideas suggest that propositional thinking might be carried out with a single image: First the image is used to attend to one thing, then it is used to acknowledge the one thing to be this or that. We might think Tom to be existing (to exist) like this: First we form an image of Tom, and use it to attend to Tom. Then we notice what the idea of Tom has in common with all ideas, and use this image as a general idea to acknowledge Tom to exist. While such thinking might be abstractly possible, it would be enormously difficult to carry out. When an image is used to identify a particular object, the image's resemblance to the object doesn't produce or explain the identifying. The thinker must be able to independently intend the right object. And to use an image as a general idea, which is important both for acknowledging particular objects to "fall under" the idea and for identifying collections which are the subjects of general judgments, the thinker must be able to selectively focus on aspects of the image. This is the ability which would enable the judger to select the appropriate criteria when using the image to perform acknowledging acts. The economy of the one-image judgment is more than offset by the behind-the-scenes activity needed to make such a judgment.

To carry out propositional thinking of the 'to be' form, we require words (uttered or thought) or images or some other form of ideas to be used for attending and acknowledging. Since language is conventional, we must be taught the conventions if we are to think with the language. Two kinds of conventions are involved: (1) Those which associate expressions (our acts of using expressions) with particular objects in the world. (2) Those which associate acknowledging criteria with expressions. If images or some other form of ideas are used for thinking which is of the 'to be' form, then conventions or some replacement for conventions are required. The connections linking a particular image or idea to a particular object can't be determined by features intrinsic to the idea or image. Neither can these connections be provided by our innate endowment, for they must be established in experience, on the basis of experience. (We don't have ideas of particular objects that we never heard of.) The connections must be made by the thinker, on the basis of his independent access to the objects he identifies. If the independent access is supplied by linguistic conventions, then the use of images or ideas to identify particular objects will be indirectly conventional. If it isn't supplied by linguistic conventions, the access is simply mysterious.

If ideas or images are used to perform acknowledging acts, these ideas/images must be associated with criteria for objects correctly acknowledged to be one thing or another. Either a thinker has independent access to these criteria, and arbitrarily links images/ideas to the criteria—which is absurd, or the images/ideas are associated in some regular fashion with appropriate criteria. The associations might be conventionally established, which would mean that images/ideas are simply a special class of expressions. Or certain images/ideas might be innately connected with criteria, and these innate connections would take the place of the conventional associations found in language.

So far, in considering the first form of propositional thinking, we have considered only judgments, the mental counterparts to assertions. (But a sincere assertion is also a judgment.) With the 'to be' form, judging is the primary kind of propositional thinking. We understand nonjudgmental propositional thinking by linking that thinking to judging. (Classical philosophers who recognized the three fundamental mental operations were considering only the 'to be' form of propositional thinking.) For example, we can engage in thinking of the 'to be' form in wondering, doubting, and desiring things to be a certain way. Someone who wonders if Tom is wealthy may identify Tom and be curious as to whether she can correctly acknowledge him to be wealthy. She doesn't perform a wondering act which is a counterpart to acknowledging, but she raises the question of acknowledging Tom to be wealthy. She might also doubt Tom's being wealthy by considering whether to acknowledge him to be wealthy, and declining to do so because she is uncertain. (Declining to acknowledge is not the same as denying.)

8. Representational Propositional Thinking

Expressions can be used to identify objects and to acknowledge objects to be one thing or another, which is a further identifying. In using language to perform acknowledging acts, a person is carrying out propositional thinking of the *to be* variety. It may also be possible to use images or ideas to carry out such thinking, but acknowledging criteria must either be conventionally associated with the images/ideas or innately tied to them.

When language is used in a strictly identifying fashion, no representing takes place. But expressions can also be used to represent. Awareness (representational awareness) of arbitrary objects of a kind is characteristic of representing. But this is just what is going on when we use a sentence like "Some man is wealthy" to make a claim about no man in particular. The quantificational use of noun phrases is certainly a representing use.

There is a puzzle which arises when we try to apply our developing conception of representing to language. Both written and spoken expressions (the tokens) have perceptible features. But these don't get interpreted when language is used to represent. The shape or spelling of written expressions, and the acoustic features of spoken ones, make no difference to the representing carried out with expressions. Language is not used to represent iconically—though with some expressions there may be incidental iconic representing. ("The cow mooed.") Language is used to represent *symbolically*. But in any representing, some features of the representation must get interpreted to provide representational awareness. The puzzle is to figure out what are these features in the case of language.

A solution to this puzzle runs as follows. We must first learn to use language in a purely identifying way. Once this happens, the expressions we use come to be associated with criteria. Some criteria link a particular expression to a particular object. Other criteria are for acknowledging objects to be one thing or another. The criteria associated with expressions are nonperceptible features of those expressions. When language is used to represent, the acknowledging criteria associated with expressions are interpreted to provide representational awareness.

A single sentence can often be used either in a purely identifying way or a representing way. The sentence 'Tom is wealthy' can be used to identify Tom and acknowledge him to be wealthy. The predicate "is wealthy" can also be used to represent an arbitrary person as wealthy, and combined with the act of identifying Tom to portray Tom as wealthy. Some sentences may have only a representing use. Propositional thinking of the 'that'-clause variety is representational thinking. Representational propositional thinking requires a language or language-like apparatus (a language of thought, perhaps).

It is characteristic of 'that'-clause thinking that a propositional representing act can be independent of an act of accepting or rejecting the representing. One can perform a propositional representing act and merely consider the represented situation. One can perform a propositional representing act to suppose that things are as represented. To accept a propositional representing act is to judge that things are as represented. A person can represent and accept all at once; she can also represent first and accept later. With the 'to be' form of propositional thinking, there is no separating the "content" of the judgment from the judging. A propositional act of the 'to be' form is an acknowledging act which is inescapably a judging.

Neither form of propositional thinking provides a significant role for images. The present account/understanding of the forms of propositional thinking has been developed by reflecting on how we talk about thought and belief, and by reflecting on how we use language to think and to report our thinking. This account is rooted in our ordinary conception of experience and thought, but goes well beyond the ordinary conception. As we currently have it, images might be used to engage in the 'to be' form of propositional thinking, but the representing performed with the images would be incidental to the propositional thinking. For all the contribution they make to propositional thinking, the images might as well be uninterpreted designs. (Words are just such designs.) Any representing carried out with the images could at best be suggestive or heuristic; it wouldn't determine either the attending or the acknowledging performed with the images. Images are also unimportant for 'that'-clause thinking. Images are used to represent iconically, while propositional representing is symbolic. If images were used to represent symbolically, their iconic representing would be irrelevant to their symbolic representing.

Although images aren't important for the two forms of propositional thinking we have identified, someone might wonder if images couldn't be used to carry out a third kind of true/false, correct/incorrect thinking. We certainly can use a picture to identify (or try to) a particular situation. Used in this way, the picture is accurate or inaccurate, correct or incorrect. But pictures need to be supplemented if they are to be used for identifying situations. Language contains a variety of devices for directing attention to the objects and situations we talk about. There are proper names and various deictic expressions, including tenses. There are prepositions like 'on', 'over', 'above', and 'inside'. Pictures lack such devices. They have no tenses; there are no pictorial conventions for tying objects in pictures to objects in the world. It is our intentions which connect the picture to its situation, and these intentions get insufficient help from the picture itself. The intentions depend on extra-pictorial knowledge about the world and its contents. And pictures are too specific. To use pictures systematically, we would need to adopt conventions for determining what "counts" and what doesn't "count" in the picture used to identify a particular situation. Carrying out true/false thinking entirely with images used to iconically represent situations isn't feasible.

The ordinary conception of thinking recognizes a role for internal images/designs, and each person's experience confirms this. It isn't a principle of the ordinary conception that images/designs are necessary for thinking, or that they are present in all thinking. We have seen that the use of internal images to represent is not important for propositional thinking. At least a great deal of propositional thinking does not employ images. But expressions in languages are designs, not images, and we use them for propositional thinking. It is possible that all propositional thinking uses designs or images, internal or otherwise. But the ordinary conception of thought has no position on this matter.

If we don't use designs/images for all our thinking, what else could we use? Some philosophers have thought we make use of ideas which aren't sensory images/designs. While I have written as if this were a possibility, there are some difficulties with this suggestion. For we are considering conscious thought. Our ordinary conception is concerned with conscious thought. If we use something other than sensory designs in propositional thinking, then we should be aware of these and have a concept or concepts of them. It isn't clear that we are aware of them or have words for them. We do have the word 'idea', and use it in connection with thought and thinking. But we use this word for a large number of things which don't have much in common. Sometimes we use 'idea' for a person's belief. ("Chuck's idea is that the butler did it.") Sometimes we use it for a suggestion or proposal. ("Jane's idea is to go to the zoo if it is a nice day, and to go to the Science Center otherwise.") A person's bright idea can be her solution to a problem. We also use the word 'idea' to talk about what a person does or doesn't understand. Someone might, or might not, have the idea of a black hole or of justice. And some ideas are internal images/designs. We could produce an internal design to comply with the request that we call up the idea of an orange triangle. There is no single, or central, conception of an idea. Our ordinary conception doesn't indicate that, or how, ideas are used in propositional thinking.

In developing the present account, I have assumed that we must use instruments of some kind to think propositionally. We need images or expressions or ideas or something. But while I find it difficult to understand how thinking could be carried on without using instruments, the ordinary conception of thinking doesn't demand that instruments be used. For propositional thinking of the 'to be' form, it is at least conceivable that someone might carry out unassisted acts of attending and acknowledging. Perhaps a person can simply focus on an absent object without using a name or an image or anything else. Acknowledging might be similar. Knowing what it takes to be red could allow a person to acknowledge an object to be red without saying or thinking a word. It is even conceivable that a kind of propositional representing might be carried out without using symbols. Neither images nor symbols represent intrinsically; we must use them to become representationally aware of objects and situations. Perhaps it is possible to achieve something like representational awareness without using a representation.

Although I judge it unlikely that we can think propositionally without using expressions or images or ideas, the ordinary conception doesn't rule this out. The ordinary conception of thought and thinking is radically incomplete.

Chapter 3

The Larger Problem: *Descartes' Best Efforts*

1. Sensory Awareness

Descartes' Problem is generated by the conflict between the ordinary and the mechanical conceptions of sensation. The mechanical conception of sensation is derived from the mechanical conception of physical processes, once the workings of our bodies are conceived mechanically. This is how Descartes conceived them, and we conceive them in much the same way, even though our understanding of physical processes is more sophisticated than Descartes' was. Descartes' Problem is an inherently interesting problem. To find an adequate solution would be an intrinsically satisfying achievement. But there are other reasons as well for attempting its solution. The problem seems to place many beliefs about the world in jeopardy. For if in sense experience we are not directly aware of external objects, but are instead aware of our body's responses to external objects, what do, or can, we know about the world around us? To answer this question we must determine the extent to which our beliefs about the world are based on, or derive from sense experience. And this calls for an adequate conception of sense experience and an adequate understanding of the connection between sense experience and thought, belief, and knowledge.

I will approach my solution to Descartes' Problem, and the problem of bridging the gap between sensation and thought, by considering important historical attempts to solve, dissolve, or resolve these problems. This will help to understand the "hold" that this problem has over us, and will also assist in determining what strategies haven't worked, or won't work. I will start by considering Descartes.

The problem I am naming for Descartes needs a solution which provides a new conception of sense experience, and which explains what place sense experience occupies in our cognitive life. This solution must also include a general account of this cognitive life. Descartes himself wanted to show that, and how, sense experience is a reliable part of a reliable process for obtaining knowledge of the physical world. To do this much would solve the second part of his problem, as he understood it. The second part can be solved without filling in the details of the replacement for the ordinary conception of sense experience. The first part of his problem is to fill in the details.

The earlier description of the mechanical conception of sensation needs to be expanded. That description recognized three elements:

1. An appropriate object contacts a sense organ.
2. The sense organ, in response to the object, initiates a causal process leading to the brain.
3. A central neural event, or events, occurs.

We need to add a fourth element:

4. An *occurrence of sensory awareness* takes place.

The sensory awareness is the awareness of whatever the subject is aware of—an object, or a quality, or a qualified object, and so on. We can't at this point say anything about the relation between (3) and (4). The occurrence of sensory awareness might simply *be* the central neural event or events. The neural event(s) might cause the awareness. There may be some other connection. If sensation were simply a matter of (1)–(3), then it might seem feasible to design a sensing machine.

Cognitive scientists who favor a computational understanding of cognition frequently dismiss consciousness as unimportant to cognition, and sometimes characterize consciousness as epiphenomenal. However, sensory awareness is an essential feature of our experience—the experience wouldn't *be* experience without the awareness. (For a theory to admit epiphenomena is to confess its own inadequacy.)

We didn't speak of sensory awareness in describing the ordinary conception of sensation, but we can do so. This will help to compare the two conceptions. On the ordinary conception, the sensing subject has awareness of the sensed object. The sensing subject acts on the object of sensation. Since the subject of awareness must be acting on the object, the awareness can't take place without the object. The awareness gives us direct access to, and guarantees the existence of, the object. In contrast, on the mechanical conception, sensory awareness does not give us direct access to the external object. The awareness can occur in the absence of an appropriate external object. It isn't clear whether, on the mechanical conception, the experiencing subject could be acting on anything. If she is, what she acts on is not the external object. But the mechanical conception is compatible with either an active or a passive subject.

2. Sensing Qualities

Descartes' most famous philosophical writings (as opposed to his mathematical and scientific works), the *Discourse on Method* and the *Meditations*, are primarily devoted to solving the second part of his problem: to showing that sensation is a reliable part of a reliable process for obtaining knowledge of the world. In his philosophical writings, he was addressing an audience that didn't (in general) conceive physical processes mechanically. So he didn't present the mechanical conception of sense experience, and use this to undermine the ordinary conception. Instead he attacked the ordinary conception by talking of dreams and demons. And he presented only a small part of his new conception of sense experience.

In the *Meditations*, his changes to the ordinary conception of sense experience primarily concern the objects of sensory awareness. Instead of agreeing that we are aware of various kinds of objects with a large number of features, Descartes insisted that in sense experience we are, strictly speaking, aware of nothing but qualities. We aren't aware of a grapefruit, we only see a yellow shape. This change is harder to carry out for sensory relations than for qualities. It doesn't seem crazy to suggest that we just see blue rather than seeing blue things. But it *is* crazy to claim that we can see *to the left of* without seeing one object to the left of another. Like most of his contemporaries, Descartes had a poor understanding of relations. But once it *is* noticed that we see spatial relations, if we continue to insist that we see qualities rather than their owners, we will be driven to claim that the relations we see link *instances* of qualities. And this will push us in the direction of treating instances of qualities as objects in their own right, objects which have sensory properties and relations of their own, objects which supplant the objects we ordinarily take ourselves to experience.

Descartes would presumably have been unwilling to move in that direction, for he conceived of sensory qualities as properties of material objects. One advantage he derived from his reconception of the objects of awareness is this: If sensory awareness were of objects with sensory qualities and relations, then it would surely be natural for people to believe themselves to be directly aware of these objects in experience. This could properly be described as an instinctive belief. But it would be a mistaken belief, and this unavoidable mistake would be due to our very nature—to God's blueprint for human beings. That God would force us into error in this way was incompatible with Descartes' understanding of God. It would also spoil Descartes' argument for the existence of physical objects.

Since a correct analysis of sense experience shows us to be aware of qualities rather than their bearers, we have no occasion to believe that we are directly aware of objects in the world. People do believe this, which Descartes realized, but he didn't think this is how we *conceive* sense experience. Descartes didn't possess the concept of a conceptual framework, but he was aware that we conceive things, and he believed that our fundamental concepts, or ideas, are systematically related. *A priori* knowledge is obtained by tracing the systematic relations among concepts. But the fundamental concepts, which *we* might describe as constituting *the* fundamental conceptual framework, aren't invented, they are simply given. To investigate them, we employ rational analysis. Descartes' own conception allows no room for a mistaken or inadequate conceptual framework. This forced him to misunderstand the ordinary conception of sense experience as a set of mistaken beliefs which we have carelessly acquired.

Descartes claimed that what we are really aware of is sensory qualities, real sensory qualities. And we instinctively believe these qualities to belong to our bodies and objects around us. When our bodies (including our sense organs) are functioning properly, the qualities we experience are located where we think they are. But we aren't experiencing the qualities-located-in-the-objects. We are experiencing qualities which also happen to be located in (to be exemplified by) the world we inhabit. In providing this account of the objects of sensory awareness, Descartes was actually devising a new conception of sense experience. But he thought himself to be discovering the true nature of sensory awareness, by introspection and analysis.

In sense experience, we are aware of qualities. This means that the objects of sensory awareness are not used to represent objects in the world. Descartes does speak of representing in connection with sensation, and talks about neural events/episodes as representations of their causes. But this is not the representing we discussed earlier. For it is not a case where one object (or objects) with its features is interpreted as other objects with their features. We instead "assign" the qualities we experience to objects we don't experience.

3. Ideas

In thinking, we employ ideas. But Descartes' account of ideas and their role in thought is flawed. Descartes doesn't discuss propositional thinking, and explain how ideas are employed. He speaks of judgments as the fundamental elements of propositional thinking. This suggests that he is focussing on propositional thinking of the 'to be' variety. Since ideas are the mental "units," they must be the elements we employ in making judgments. But Descartes has nothing to say about using ideas to attend to particular objects, or using them to perform acknowledging acts. In fact, Descartes has not distinguished propositional identifying from propositional representing. He appears to assimilate the two forms of propositional thinking, which yields an incoherent account.

Descartes also has competing concepts of an idea. He conceives ideas as modes of thinking—as mental acts of thinking about a thing or kind of thing. But he doesn't say enough for us to determine whether these are attending acts or acknowledging acts. If ideas are acts, then they aren't instruments we use to carry out propositional thinking. These acts would be constitutive of propositional thinking, and Descartes' view should be that we don't need to employ instruments in thinking propositionally. But Descartes also conceived of ideas as objects to which the mind attends. In this connection, he regards an idea as a kind of representation, or at least as analogous to a representation. This suggests that Descartes takes propositional thinking to be representational. On the second conception of ideas, one's awareness has a passive character; the idea reveals itself to the attentive mind. These two conceptions are incompatible. But Descartes didn't recognize the difficulty or resolve the problem. He hasn't provided a coherent account of ideas, or thought.

However, a fan of Descartes might try to resolve the conflict between the two conceptions of an idea by arguing that one conception is fundamental, and is the conception to which Descartes owes his basic allegiance. The other conception is superficial, the result of casual and careless thinking. This is the approach I favor. And I maintain that ideas as mental acts are fundamental. Ideas as objects of attention make a number of problems for Descartes' other views. One problem is to understand what these ideas are made of. Minds are immaterial objects, immaterial active objects. Ideas as objects of attention (nonsensory ideas, anyway) would also be immaterial, but not active—inert immaterial objects. Either we find them or else we create them when we attend to them. If we find them, we can ask where they are before we find them, and also, I suppose, where they are once we have found them. They can't be *in* the mind, for minds don't take up space. Immaterial objects of attention aren't the kind of things that can have locations, but they would need locations if they exist before we find them. Even if we create them, they have a standing which is separate from that of the mind attending to them. It is difficult to understand how they can have such a status, or how we might be in a position to confer it.

If ideas are objects of attention, then innate ideas seem particularly silly. But Descartes is strongly committed to there being innate ideas. So either we come into existence as part of a package which includes immaterial objects of attention to which we have immediate access, or else we are naturally endowed with the ability to produce certain immaterial objects when the occasion calls for it. (And how might the occasion do that?) If we conceive of ideas as mental acts, then to entertain an idea is simply to think about something. We don't use an instrument for doing this. We don't attend to an object that is immediately present to us. Having an idea is having a skill: being able to recognize things of a kind and to think about them when they are absent. An innate idea is not the ability to create inert immaterial objects, but simply the ability to recognize and think about objects and features that can't be experienced by the senses. It would be reasonable to hold that we must use our innate skill for recognizing before we can use it for attending.

Viewing ideas as acts of thinking fits better with Descartes' other positions than does viewing them as objects of mental attention. When Descartes speaks of ideas as representations, we can understand ideas as mental acts of being representationally aware. This is a representational awareness that minds can achieve without using mental counterparts to images. In speaking of ideas as something like images, Descartes would mean only that ideas involve the kind of awareness also achieved with images, which doesn't provide access to an actual object. This interpretation would accommodate the passive character of attending to ideas. We are active in using an image to become representationally aware of its objects, but we must passively recognize these objects for what they are. However, even if we can reconcile Descartes' two concepts of an idea, we won't find a coherent account of thinking in Descartes. He hasn't explained what we do with ideas or how they get fastened to the world. He hasn't distinguished the two forms of propositional thinking.

4. Beyond Repair

In attacking the problem I have named for him, Descartes wanted both to provide an adequate solution and to prove that this is *the correct* solution. In adopting these goals, Descartes was surely attempting too much. It would be more than sufficient to provide an adequate solution (so far no one has), we shouldn't hold out for a proof. But Descartes thought he had provided a solution, and so he attempted to justify it. By proving that God exists, that he is perfectly good, and that he is responsible for our design and our existence. A perfectly good God would not turn out a defective product. So the innate ideas with which we are equipped actually fit the world we inhabit. Our mental powers are adequate to the investigation of these ideas. And since we are naturally inclined to believe that external objects produce our sensations, and possess the primary qualities that our sensations reveal, this must be how things are—in general.

Descartes' solution to the second part of his problem is not successful, and this solution can't be repaired. But it is ironic that most criticisms of Descartes focus on his failure to prove that his is the correct account rather than on shortcomings of his solution. Descartes is commonly charged with not being sufficiently critical, and doubtful, of his own beliefs about reality, perfection, and causality. But these beliefs were fundamental principles of the conceptual framework within which he operated. And its fundamental principles have an *a priori* status within a conceptual framework. The conceptual framework which related value, perfection, and causality (in the Great Chain of Being) was a fundamental given for Descartes and his scholastic predecessors. We no longer accept or employ that framework, which means that we cannot find Descartes' arguments compelling. Not all of Descartes' contemporaries accepted this framework either, as we can see from Hobbes' objections to the *Meditations*. Descartes was on the inside of this framework looking out, and could not recognize that this framework might not be the proper (or best) one to employ. We are on the outside looking in, and need reasons—which no one seems able to supply—for going back inside.

If Descartes had actually provided a satisfactory account of sense experience and its role in our cognitive lives, it wouldn't matter that he failed to provide a rigorous proof. Let us consider some of the shortcomings of Descartes' attempt to solve the second part of his problem. The first difficulty we can notice concerns his reconception of the objects of sensory awareness. We may be able to get away with conceiving colors as a kind of stuff we perceive independently of colored objects. But we can't simply perceive a shape. A shape must the the shape of something. Of an object or its surface, or stuff, and so on. If we conceive of colors as stuff, then color stuffs are objects with shapes. But we don't simply perceive hardness or smoothness, we perceive hard or smooth objects. Similarly, we see spatial relations linking physical objects, not simply occurrences of qualities. Descartes' reconception of the objects of sensory awareness simply doesn't make sense of sensory awareness. His reconception won't work.

Another difficulty with Descartes' solution is his treatment of secondary qualities. These qualities—colors, smells, tastes, warmth, coldness, and so forth—aren't found in the physical world. To account for secondary qualities, Descartes adapts the ordinary conceptual framework's treatment of illusions. In the blue light, a yellow grapefruit looks green, but nothing really is green. Yellow appears to be green under blue light. According to Descartes, when we see a color, we are really seeing something else—some kind of motion, say—which only appears to us to be a color. Secondary qualities can't be clearly and distinctly perceived. Their intrinsic "obscurity" is a sign that in perceiving them, we are not getting an accurate perception of our object. This account is certainly less than satisfactory. It is one thing to say that, in the right circumstances, one color can appear to be another color. It is simply incredible to maintain that a motion can appear to be a color. (It doesn't make things any better if we update, and speak of wavelengths of light.)

And Descartes' inadequate account of propositional thinking and the nature and role of ideas is a major flaw. Although I have suggested a way to resolve the conflict between what seem to be incompatible conceptions of ideas, it isn't clear that this is what Descartes intended. His writing on the subject is obscure, and he was probably confused about it. Anyway, a single, consistent, conception of ideas doesn't explain propositional thinking or the roles of ideas. Without giving such explanations, Descartes couldn't solve his problem.

It may seem that Descartes is in far more serious trouble with his account of innate ideas. But while Descartes' doctrine of innate ideas is frequently the subject of ridicule, it isn't actually a ridiculous view. We should remark that it is difficult to understand the connection between sensation and thought, especially propositional thought. In sense experience we are aware of objects, stuff, events, and various of their features. In noticing the objects, we "take in" the features—we are aware of "featured" objects. At the most basic level, we don't separately notice the objects and their features (we don't notice the objects and separately notice their features). For to separately notice the objects and their features involves propositional thinking. If we can separately notice this ball and its red color, we must notice the ball *to be* red. The ball and its color are not separate in the way this ball is separate from the one next to it.

We do distinguish objects from their features, but our doing this involves propositional thinking, and requires the ability to engage in such thinking. If we can distinguish objects and their features in sense experience, this suggests that we are abstracting the features from the objects and that some sense experience is propositional. Descartes avoided these unwelcome conclusions by claiming that we are aware of certain features in sense experience, but we are not aware of the features' owners. We experience the features and immediately judge them to have owners. We are naturally inclined to judge these features to belong to various objects (including our bodies) in our vicinity.

To judge the features (qualities) we experience to belong to objects, we must understand what it is to be an object with features. But sense experience can't provide this information. We must simply be equipped with this understanding to begin with. We must have the ability to recognize qualities as qualities of something or other. Innate ideas are simply skills needed for making sense of ourselves and our experience. Once we have some such skills, we can develop others on our own. But we need some to begin with. Even if someone finds Descartes' particular candidates for innate ideas to be implausible, it is difficult to avoid the view that we have some innate skills/ideas of the sort Descartes intended. How otherwise can we understand the ability to recognize one thing to be similar to another? This is not simply the ability to respond in similar ways to similar situations. A switch controlled by a photocell does as much. Similarity is not a sensible quality. For the similarity between two shades of color is difficult, impossible, to compare to the similarity between two sounds. And we recognize various degrees of similarity. We clearly understand similarity-in-general, and can recognize instances of it. If the mind doesn't abstract an understanding of similarity from instances of it, we must start out with the ability to judge *X* to be similar to *Y*. No one does, or could, teach us to do this.

Innate ideas are skills we bring to experience to make sense of experience and the world it reveals. But Descartes' hasn't built an adequate bridge over the gap between sense experience and propositional thinking. For if we have the innate idea of *X*, but can't sense *X* in a thing, or sense a quality which is an instance of *X*, how could we ever tell on the basis of sensation that we have actually run into *X*? Aristotle solves this problem by supposing that the mind has access to objects made available by the senses. The mind can "reach in" and "grasp" features which are beyond the scope of the senses. Aristotle's solution is refuted by our inability to discover what things are fundamentally and essentially like, simply on the basis of sensation. And Aristotle's solution is just what Descartes was trying to avoid. For Descartes, sense experience makes qualities, not objects, available to the mind. But then an idea which is not an idea of sensible qualities—

an idea as simple as the idea of similarity or identity—will be an idea we can have no occasion to apply to the material world.

Descartes' solution to the second part of his problem isn't successful. It can't easily be fixed—there is probably no fixing it. For the sake of completeness, let us look at his solution to the first part of his problem. There is no fixing that either. To finish his solution to his problem, Descartes must explain the way that sense organs work, explain the causal processes connecting sense organs to the brain, explain what happens when these processes reach the brain, and explain the connection between the neural event and the occurrence of sensory awareness. Descartes had something to say about all these matters. According to Descartes, when the appropriate sort of object contacts a sense organ, motion is transmitted via nerves to the brain. The nerves are flexible tubes filled with animal spirits. It is the animal spirits which move and transmit motion. The transmitted motions eventually affect a central location in the brain, the pineal gland. Movements of the pineal gland cause an occurrence of sensory awareness, which is a mental rather than a neural event.

Sensory awareness is a mental event, but how are we to understand this? On the ordinary conception, the object of awareness is the external object, which does not depend on the awareness for its existence. Does Descartes think the object of sensory awareness is a mental entity? Does he even think there is an object which is separate from the awareness itself? He must at least agree to a separate object. It is real shapes and real colors that we see. Our awareness isn't shaped or colored—the mind and its acts and states don't have physical properties. But neither can a mental idea be shaped or colored. Descartes maintained that we sense qualities rather than their bearers. But qualities *need* bearers. Qualities are properties of things, they don't float in midair. We are not aware in sense experience of the object to which the instances of qualities that we perceive belong, but a complete account must say what this object is. The primary qualities normally belong to external objects. So do the qualities we perceive obscurely as color, warmth, and so on. But we aren't aware of the instances of qualities located in external objects. The qualities we are aware of in sensation belong to the pineal gland. The pineal gland exhibits various shapes and motions, which are transmitted by the nerves from the sense organs. We are aware of the qualities (some qualities) of the pineal gland, but we aren't aware of the pineal gland itself. We instinctively believe that the qualities we apprehend are (also) located in the various places to which we assign them.

Descartes' understanding of physical processes is crude in comparison with our understanding. But it isn't this crudeness which renders his explanation unsatisfactory. It would be an easy matter to update his understanding of sense organs and causal processes. It is Descartes' understanding of sensory awareness and its immediate objects that spoils his solution to the first part of his problem. The pineal gland doesn't do what he thought it does. Nothing else does either. There is no little stage, or movie screen, in the brain which can serve as the immediate object of sensory awareness. We don't experience the external world by means of a faithful copy inside our heads.

Descartes dealt with interesting and important problems, but he didn't solve them. Descartes' main contribution to Western thought is that he gave us some things to think about—to worry about. This isn't a small contribution. So far, no one has solved his problem. It is important to keep trying.

Chapter 4

The Empiricist Response

1. The Empiricist Conception

In trying to come up with a solution, or solutions, to his problem, Descartes accepted certain constraints. He wanted a solution according to which the physical world is pretty much the kind of place we have always thought. It isn't exactly the same as we have thought. Secondary qualities, qualities like colors, the warmth and coldness that we feel, flavors, and so on, don't belong to physical objects. And the physical world is more mechanical than we realized. But physical objects, physical stuff, and physical events are located in space and time, and they possess the primary qualities (and relations) that we encounter in sensation. A physical thing supports various features, and can support different features at different times. Descartes wanted to provide an account of sense experience and thought that recognizes this kind of physical world, and explains how we fit into it and come to have knowledge of it.

We aren't required to accept these constraints in solving Descartes' Problem. The mechanical conception of physical processes undermines the ordinary conception of sense experience. Our understanding of what the physical world is like depends to a considerable extent on sense experience and our conception of it. Undermining the ordinary conception of sense experience also undermines the ordinary conception of the physical world. But the mechanical conception of physical processes is a development, a refinement, of the ordinary conception of the physical world. Indirectly, the mechanical conception of physical processes undermines itself.

I think it likely that most people would regard Descartes' constraints as reasonable. We aren't anxious to abandon our conception of the physical world. This conception may need some changes, but we aren't prepared for a radically new substitute. I myself would be unhappy with a solution that didn't "respect" Descartes' constraints, as I have described them. But philosophers in the Empiricist tradition didn't accept these constraints. (For present purposes, the capital 'E' Empiricist tradition begins with Berkeley and Hume. Earlier philosophers like Hobbes and Locke shared many views with members of the Empiricist tradition. These earlier philosophers are precursors of the Empiricists, not full-fledged Empiricists.) The Empiricist philosophers gave up both the ordinary conception of sense experience and the ordinary conception of the physical world.

Empiricism was initially a response both to Descartes' Problem and to the development of scientific knowledge. Descartes' Problem needs a solution. Scientific knowledge needs an explanation, one which reveals what the world is like in its essentials and which accounts for our knowledge of such a world. However, the Empiricist tradition endured well into the twentieth century. Empiricist philosophers subsequent to Berkeley and Hume weren't just dealing with the problems that their predecessors tackled. They also responded to contemporary events and developments, especially scientific ones.

The Empiricists provided radically new conceptions of sense experience and of the objects of sense experience. We might say that the Empiricists weren't looking for a solution to Descartes' Problem, certainly not for the kind of solution that Descartes himself could accept. The Empiricists were trying to dissolve Descartes' Problem. If the world around us is totally different from what we think (have thought), then the mechanical conception doesn't apply to it. Without this conception, Descartes' Problem doesn't arise.

The Empiricists' conception of sense experience covers "inner" feelings as well as external sensations. Their conception applies to both visual experiences and feelings of hunger and of anger. Inner and outer feelings are pretty much the same. In what follows, I won't have much to say about emotions, desires, fears, and so forth. But when I speak of the Empiricist conception of sense experience, I mean to include feelings of thirst, pain, lust, hate, and so on.

The first Empiricists adopted Descartes' suggestion that, strictly speaking, we sense qualities rather than individuals with qualities. Instead of seeing a yellow grapefruit, we see yellow—and the yellow we see is round. The Empiricists agreed with Descartes in thinking that the objects of sensory awareness are qualities. They agreed with both Descartes and the ordinary conception in thinking that sensory awareness provides direct access to something real. But for the ordinary conception, the real objects are ordinary physical objects. For the Empiricist, we are aware of real qualities, but these aren't properties belonging to substantial enduring objects.

It doesn't work to claim that we simply experience qualities. We normally construe qualities as properties of things, and a property requires a subject. The same is even more obviously true for relations. Although we ordinarily treat sensible qualities as belonging to physical objects (and stuff, events, etc.), it may seem that we can regard qualities as something other than properties. Perhaps qualities are a kind of thing that can simply occur, without belonging to (inhering in) some further object or subject. This can seem plausible for certain qualities. The ordinary conception of colors is similar in some ways to our conception of physical stuff. If yellow is really yellow-stuff, then we can imagine it existing on its own. And if we "dematerialize" our conception of sounds as physical phenomena, we are left with fairly substantial qualities. But it makes no sense to think of round, or roundness, occurring by itself. We can only experience a round something. Loudness doesn't simply occur either; sounds are loud. Nor can relations occur without something to relate.

Even for the substantial qualities, it isn't sufficient to claim that we simply encounter them in sense experience. We need to recognize occurrences of these qualities, for their occurrences have properties and relations, and different occurrences have different properties and relations. An occurrence of a color will have a shape and a size. I don't know if the occurrence of a color, which has a shape, is also an occurrence of that shape. Could the occurrence of the color be one thing and the occurrence of the shape be something else, two things which happen to coincide? (Or does this occurrence of the color necessarily coincide with this occurrence of the shape?) There is no right answer to this question. Accepting a certain answer is adopting a certain conception. We may have different choices. Once we admit occurrences of qualities, we find that the connection between an occurrence of a quality and that quality is very difficult to distinguish from the connection between the bearer of a property and that property. The simplest course is to grant that all sensible qualities need bearers, and call these bearers something other than occurrences of the qualities. We can call them ideas or impressions or sense data; I shall usually speak of sense data. A single sense datum has both color and shape; it isn't the color which has the shape, or the shape which has the color.

On the Empiricist conception, we are aware of individuals with properties and relations. This much is true of the ordinary conception of sense experience as well. But the individuals are very different for the two conceptions. On the ordinary conception of sensation and its objects, many of the things we sense are solid and substantial and enduring. We are aware of physical phenomena. On the Empiricist conception, the objects of sensation are quite "thin." All they do is support the properties (qualities) and relations we are aware of in sensation. There is nothing else to them. The objects of one sense are not the same as the objects of another sense. We see one thing and feel something different. A sense datum experienced at one time can resemble that experienced at another time. We can't experience a single sense datum at two different times or two different places. We can experience spatial relations—can experience objects related spatially—but objects we don't experience together are not common inhabitants of some wider space.

Sense data we encounter have the properties and relations we experience. Sense data have no hidden features. They have no back sides and no insides. They are just what we experience them to be. On the Empiricist conception, we can't distinguish appearance from reality as we ordinarily do. A sense datum can't appear one way, and really be a different way. It has whatever properties it appears to have. (But we might make an inaccurate judgment about a sense datum. In an optical illusion, we may judge that one line is longer than another, when the two lines are really the same length.) We also abandon the ordinary way of dealing with hallucinations. If a person thinks she experiences a sense datum, then she does. We have no basis for saying she only thinks she sees something, but really there is nothing there. A hallucination is a genuine sense datum which fails to cohere with other sense data in a normal and expected fashion.

On the Empiricist conception, the objects of sense experience aren't independent of our experience. The objects aren't there ahead of time, just waiting to be sensed. The possibility of experiencing sense data may exist before we actually experience them. And it may have been possible for us to experience different sense data than we actually did experience. But sense data don't exist apart from some subject's experience of them. While sense data depend on experience for their existence, this doesn't mean that we make them. We can act in such a way that we have this or that kind of experience, in such a way that we experience these or those kinds of sense data. However, when we are in the right position, the sense data simply appear to us. On this conception we are passive in sense experience. An active sense experience requires independent objects which are there for us to act on in sensing them. This is just how sense data are not.

Sense data are counterparts in the Empiricist conception to ordinary physical objects in the ordinary conception. Sense data resemble those objects in having properties and relations. But the similarities between sense data and ordinarily conceived physical objects are less striking than the differences. If experience is as Empiricists conceive it, then physical objects as ordinarily conceived have no place in this experience. Nor does the Empiricist conception provide some other place for them. For nothing about the objects of sense experience suggests that they are "fronting" for some further objects. The Empiricists can't *prove* that there isn't a physical world "behind" our sense data. But sense experience is self-sufficient and self-contained. The objects of sense experience don't represent some further objects which we can't experience. Since nothing represents intrinsically, it would be more accurate to say that we have no reason at all to use sense data to represent an "external reality." Indeed, it is difficult to understand how it could even make sense to talk about objects behind or beyond sense experience, for the thoughts we have and the significance of the expressions we use must be grounded in our experience. If sense experience is as Empiricists describe, there can be no natural inclination to believe in an external physical reality. Sense experience isn't incomplete.

Even though we experience nothing but sense data, we don't often talk or think about sense data explicitly. We talk and think about trees and flowers, tables and chairs. According to the Empiricists, whether we realize it or not, our talk of physical objects, physical stuff, physical events, and the like is based on our experience of sense data. This experience displays certain regularities. What we see at one moment (usually) closely resembles what we saw a moment before. A certain kind of visual experience is accompanied (or it could be if we do the right things) by characteristic auditory and tactile experiences. Certain kinds of sense data regularly occur together, while others occur in regular succession. The regularities in our experience enable us to use physical object words to describe this experience. One statement about a physical object sums up or "abbreviates" many statements about sense data. Physical object words enable us to talk about collections of sense data instead of attending to them one by one. The physical object statement takes the place of more sense data statements than we could actually make; we don't have enough time or a sufficient vocabulary to make them all.

2. Varieties of Empiricism

In trying to solve his problem, Descartes developed a certain view. This view can be presented by writing sentences that state fundamental principles, and writing sentences which state important consequences of the fundamental principles. We can't write down all the consequences of someone's theory, especially if it happens to be inconsistent, but we can write down enough to convey the character of the theory, enough to enable someone to understand the theory. Unlike Descartes' theory, Empiricism doesn't constitute a view whose essentials can be simply written down. Empiricism is an approach. It is a project as much as it is an explicit theory.

Empiricism involves certain "basic ideas," and these are developed in different ways by different members of the Empiricist "camp." I judge their conception of sense experience and its objects to be what is most characteristic of Empiricist accounts. But different Empiricists conceive experience in somewhat different ways. For example, Berkeley thought that sense experience has a substantial, enduring owner, while Hume did not. For Berkeley, sense data (which he called ideas) are genuinely the objects of our experience. Experience gives us access to these objects. Hume's understanding is harder to explain, because the language we use incorporates the ordinary conception of experience and its objects. As ordinarily conceived, the subjects of experience are substantial, enduring objects. Neither Descartes nor Berkeley abandons this conception, so it doesn't take much forcing to adapt our ordinary language to the task of stating their views. For Hume, sense data aren't exactly the *objects* of experience, for experience has no subject, and objects seem to require a subject. Sense data *take place*, or *occur*. The self that has experience is as much a collection of sense data (and ideas) as is the dining-room table. Hume's and Berkeley's are both Empiricist conceptions because they both understand sense data to be the "thin" bearers of qualities and relations, and they understand sense data to be constitutive of our experience.

Empiricists disagree about the status of the subject, or owner, of experience. They also disagree about the extent to which Empiricism agrees or disagrees with the ordinary understanding of the world. The Empiricists didn't, and couldn't, recognize that their conception of experience and its objects is at odds with the ordinary conception of these things. For the Empiricists were unaware that there are such things as conceptual frameworks. But the Empiricists could have realized that their understanding of experience and its objects is at odds with the ordinary beliefs of ordinary people. Some Empiricists did, but many did not. Empiricists who denied that there is a conflict between their views and the views of common sense claimed that the only conflict was between Empiricism and the views of other philosophers. Berkeley vacillated between seeing a conflict with common sense and denying that there is one. He favored the denial, because otherwise the goodness, and perhaps the existence, of God would be jeopardized. (A good God wouldn't create us as such that we are naturally inclined to believe what is false.)

Empiricist philosophers who denied that Empiricism conflicts with common sense didn't hold that ordinary people actually understand and accept the Empiricist account of experience. They held instead that Empiricist views supplement without contradicting the views of the common man. Some Empiricists did claim that their views are implicit in the beliefs, practice, or language of ordinary people (though, again, ordinary people don't realize this). Regardless of to which of these two camps they belonged, for philosophers who held that Empiricism is consistent with common sense, it became an especially important task to make a connection between sense data and what might be called objects of ordinary experience. Objects of ordinary experience are objects like tables, chairs, and trees. Instead of recognizing that the ordinary conception of such objects is incompatible with the Empiricist account of experience, these philosophers tried to reconstrue the objects of ordinary experience in terms of sense data. Although they regarded themselves as engaged in rational analysis, they abandoned our conception of external, independent objects, and reconceived the objects of experience.

Even those philosophers, like Hume, who agreed that Empiricism conflicts with many commonsense beliefs, found it important to explain in some detail how we "get" from experiencing sense data to dealing with ordinary objects. Bridging the gap between sense data and the objects of ordinary experience was an important Empiricist project.

3. The Empiricist Project

Empiricism isn't a theory which we can simply "spell out." Empiricism is an approach; it is a way of looking at the world, and a strategy for solving certain problems. Their basic conceptual framework for sense experience and the principle that all the materials for thinking and talking must be obtained from sense experience are just the beginning. The project is to start from these beginnings and show in detail that we can actually make sense of our experience and our world on this basis. Once one makes this attempt, various problems emerge—the Empiricist project includes providing solutions to these problems. The real appeal of Empiricism is that it is primarily a project or program. Instead of a list of absolutely compelling statements, we have a challenge that many philosophers felt they were up to.

To successfully "carry through" the Empiricist conception of experience, we must show that it is possible to reconceive the world and the objects of ordinary experience on the basis of this new conception. Berkeley didn't realize the importance of this undertaking, and made little headway in carrying it out. It was Hume who appreciated the extent to which the new conception of experience calls for new conceptions of everything else, and who set about providing them. His successors took up where he left off, though they also tried to correct what they regarded as Hume's mistakes. The program of reconceiving, and reconstructing, the world is the heart and soul of Empiricism.

Given the Empiricist conception, the simplest things become extremely difficult to deal with. Take motion, for example. We see moving things all the time—we see them move. But the fundamental objects of experience don't move, and we can't see them doing it. If we see one sense datum whose different parts are related in a certain way, and then we see these parts change their relations to one another, we must no longer be seeing the same sense datum. Sense data have no permanence. They don't endure. If what we are seeing now has different features than what we saw a moment ago, it is a different object. Two sense data can't change their spatial relations to one another. One sense datum can't have parts that move with respect to one another. When we think we are seeing something move, we must really be seeing a series of similar sense data. Sense data that give us the appearance of motion must pop in and out of our awareness like frames projected on a movie screen. One difficulty with this conclusion is that when we see what appears to be movement, we aren't aware of there being a series of discrete sense data. If we aren't aware of them, then it isn't clear that we are entitled to claim they exist. We shouldn't be allowed to *posit* the existence of sense data—when it comes to sense data, things are as they appear. Another difficulty with the motion picture analysis of apparent motion is that there is in principle no answer to the question how many sense data occur in a particular instance of this motion.

On the Empiricist conception, sense data don't move, but ordinary objects do. For an ordinary object is a collection of various sense data associated with the different senses. When we look at an object at different times, from different perspectives, and in different conditions, the various sense data we see serve to constitute the object. Together with the feelings we have when we touch the object, and its smells, tastes, and sounds. For one object of ordinary experience to move with respect to another can be for the sense data associated with the two objects at one time to have a relation which is slightly different from the relation linking the sense data at a slightly later time, and for this later relation to be slightly different from a still later relation, and on on. On the Empiricist account, a material object, or a quantity of stuff, is a collection of sense data. Though a more careful Empiricist might say that talking about material things is a convenient and indirect way of talking about collections of sense data. It is difficult for the Empiricist to explain just how sense data are clustered. How do we know to associate a particular sense datum with this object rather than that? Although we have no trouble picking out objects in experience, it is a lot of trouble to state principles for grouping sense data. We can in a rough way say that different sense data for one sense and one object resemble each other, that sense data for different senses and one object accompany each other, and that sense data for one object experienced at about the same time exhibit temporal continuity as well as similarity. But this is vague, and can't easily be made more precise. However, if the objects of ordinary experience are really constituted by sense data, then it should be possible to give a clear and comprehensive statement of the principles that govern our grouping of sense data.

For the Empiricist program to be carried out, we must put the world back together, using sense data, and end up with a world that is exactly suited to our successful practices. Not only must we determine which sense data make up which objects, we must also accommodate the practice of identifying one object experienced at different times. If we don't want to explain this by saying that God is looking when we aren't, we seem required to admit possibilities as ingredients of the world. This diminishes the austere simplicity of the original Empiricist conception, by allowing features that can't be observed. Still another problem arises from the practice of classifying ordinary objects into kinds. The defining features for many kinds of thing include dispositional properties. This gives a second entry to properties which are in principle unobservable.

Empiricists must do more than reconstrue objects of ordinary experience. They must also reconstrue relations between these objects. The most important relation affected by the Empiricist analysis is probably causality. As we ordinarily conceive the world, it contains objects of various kinds. To be of a certain kind, an object must not only look a certain way, feel a certain way, and so on, but it must also exhibit certain behavior. For a thing to have the crucial properties and relations, including behavioral ones, is for that thing to have a nature. It is characteristic of objects having certain natures that when brought into specified relations to one another, they interact. It is in the nature of certain objects that one can act on another and bring about a change in the other. A match is such that when it is dry and rubbed against an appropriate surface, it ignites. Physical objects are such that when one strikes another, the impact of the first causes the second to move. On the ordinary conception of the world, when things of appropriate kinds interact, it belongs to their very natures to produce an effect—barring some intervention in the process. The cause necessitates its effect (again, barring some intervention).

The ordinary conception of causality is inconsistent with the Empiricist conception of the objects of ordinary experience. For the Empiricist, there are no independent enduring objects with essential features. The collections of sense data which constitute the objects of ordinary experience are inert, not active. They can't *do* anything. The Empiricists need to reconstrue causality in some such way as Hume's. But then events in the world are "loose and separate," and it isn't clear that such a world is consistent with our success in getting on in it—including our success in developing scientific knowledge.

The accounts developed by Berkeley and Hume were responses not only to Descartes' Problem, but also to the new scientific knowledge. Hume's treatment of factual knowledge seemed to Hume and to many others to accommodate the new science in a satisfactory way. From Hume's perspective, scientists are simply looking for regularities in experience. Scientific progress consists in discovering such regularities; further progress is made when the initial regularities are subsumed under more general and more abstract regularities. We can illustrate this with Newton's theory. Before Newton developed his theory, many different regularities had been discovered. There were regularities exhibited by falling bodies on the surface of the Earth. And regularities displayed by pendulums. The tides move in and out in a regular fashion. Astronomers were aware of regularities exemplified by planetary motion. The descriptions of these regularities are formulated in terms of objects of ordinary experience. But these regularities really come down to patterns exhibited by sense data. Newton's laws of motion provided a uniform account which "explained" all these regularities. What Newton did was to discover a more comprehensive regularity exemplified in the more specific regularities. The scientist simply takes over and refines the ordinary person's practice of noticing regularities in her own experience, and projecting these on all experience. For Hume, science is continuous with common sense. Scientific knowledge posed no special problems for Hume's account. It was, in fact, a plus for Hume's account that it accommodated scientific knowledge so well.

The further development of scientific knowledge posed new problems for Empiricism. As time went on, it became more and more difficult to take the line that science is simply looking for regularities in an experience conceived Empirically. These difficulties provided interesting new challenges to the Empiricist program, but the challenges weren't met successfully. I think the difficulties posed by scientific knowledge had the greatest effect of any factor in getting philosophers to give up on Empiricism. But there were many good reasons for giving up.

Since the Empiricist position, especially at first, seemed to do a fine job accommodating scientific knowledge, we should consider why Descartes' Problem wasn't a problem for Empiricism. Science recognizes many mechanical principles. While the Empiricists didn't think such principles reveal natural necessities, they could admit that such principles describe patterns of experience. Why don't the principles pose a problem for the Empiricist conception of sense experience? Like other physical objects, the human body is a collection of sense data. More carefully, talk about the human body sums up and takes the place of talk about various sense data. We use mechanical principles to describe the operations of the human body, just as we use them for other objects of ordinary experience. The sense organs and their functioning are "governed" by mechanical principles. But experience doesn't take place in, or through, the body. Our experience of sense data isn't carried out by, or by means of, a collection of sense data. A curious consequence of the Empiricist position is that we don't see with our eyes, hear with our ears, and so forth. There *is* a correlation between our eyes and our visual experiences. We don't have visual experiences when our eyes are closed. Similarly, our auditory experiences are "diminished" when our ears are covered. But we aren't using our sense organs to have sense experience. Consequently, the mechanical principles that describe the workings of the human body don't deprive us of "direct" access to the objects of sensory awareness.

4. Conceptual Frameworks

The Empiricist conception of experience and its objects is fundamental to the Empiricist project. This conception was devised in response to both Descartes' Problem and the new scientific knowledge, and was used to make sense of the world we experience. In order to understand how this conception was employed, it will help if we give further attention to conceptual frameworks in general (to conceptual frameworks as such).

A conceptual framework is constituted by types of linguistic acts and by semantic relations which link these. We sometimes talk as if the framework were constituted by meaningful expressions, but it isn't really expressions that are meaningful. Expressions are used to perform meaningful acts. The word 'car' is conventionally used to acknowledge an object to be a car. The 'car'-acknowledging act (the 'car' kind of acknowledging act) is an element of our conceptual framework. In acknowledging an object to be a car, we bring our concept of a car "to bear" on that object. The concept itself can be thought of as the criteria we employ in acknowledging the object to be a car, the criteria the object must satisfy for our acknowledging to be correct. The 'car'-acknowledging act is linked to the 'vehicle'-acknowledging act by commitment. Acknowledging an object to be a car will commit us to acknowledging it to be a vehicle (if the occasion arises). The 'car' act is also linked to the 'sedan'-acknowledging act, for if an object is a sedan, it must be a car.

A person's attending and identifying acts will play a role in determining what his judgments commit him to. If Mark knows Sally to be a politician, then when he acknowledges Sally to be seated at a table in the restaurant where he is eating, Mark is committed to denying that no politician is in the restaurant. However, not all commitments figure in conceptual frameworks. The semantic relations constitutive of a conceptual framework are shared by all language users who correctly speak the language in question. One must understand the 'car' criteria to correctly acknowledge an object to be a car. But one can identify Sally without knowing her to be a politician. Still, there is not a sharp distinction between commitments which are and those which are not constitutive of a conceptual framework. Some commitments generated by attending/identifying acts will be constitutive. An attempted identifying act will commit a person to acknowledge the object of attention to exist. An attempted fictional identifying act will commit the language user to acknowledging the object of attention to have a suitable fictional status.

On the present understanding (the true view of the matter), conceptual frameworks are human products; they are artifacts. Different, and competing, frameworks can be devised for talking/thinking about the same situations. But Descartes, in effect, thought there is only one fundamental framework, which is innate. We discover this by reflection and explore it by rational analysis. Alternative frameworks were inconceivable to Descartes. What I would describe as an alternative framework is for Descartes a misunderstanding or misapplication of the given framework. We may talk, for example, as if we see objects with qualities rather than simply seeing qualities. From Descartes' viewpoint, such talk is careless and misleading. A little reflection/analysis will reveal that we couldn't possibly see anything but the qualities.

The Empiricists agree with Descartes in recognizing what amounts to a single fundamental framework. But they don't think it is innate. This framework is a product of experience, and merely reflects experience. Sense data reveal themselves to us in experience. They give us the ideas or images we use to think with. We can't invent new ideas, though we can "fiddle" with the ones obtained through experience. We consequently can't conceive anything we couldn't, in principle, experience.

The original Empiricists thought they could account for thinking by means of images that people attend to and manipulate. We have already seen that such an attempt won't work. Twentieth-century Empiricists gave up on images and tried to establish direct links between experience and language. But they retained the original Empiricist conception of experience, and also the view that significant statements must describe, directly or indirectly, what can in principle be experienced. Our fundamental conception of experience and its objects (this is our fundamental conception of *everything*) is supplied to us. It is discovered by reflection and explored by rational (linguistic) analysis.

In discussing concepts and conceptual frameworks earlier, I distinguished independently significant concepts from essentially systematic concepts. This distinction is more appropriately made with respect to types of acknowledging acts, or even with respect to meaningful expressions. But it is simpler to speak of concepts, and I will continue to do so, understanding my locution to be a kind of shorthand. Most of us acknowledge objects to be blue on the basis of their appearance. Although we know what blue looks like, there is no describing it. The "look" of blue is all there is to our concept of blue. We may know other things about blue—things about the wave-lengths of blue light, or about what happens when we mix blue with yellow, but if a color had the blue "look" and the other things turned out not to be true, the color would still be correctly acknowledged to be blue. 'Blue'-acknowledging acts (and the concept of being blue) are independently significant. Their significance depends entirely on the appearance criteria used (by normally sighted people under normal conditions) to acknowledge objects to be blue.

We can sometimes explain or define one kind of acknowledging act in terms of others. If we had names for different kinds of animals, we might explain 'animal'-acknowledging acts with respect to particular animal-kind acknowledging acts. So if one has acknowledged or can acknowledge an object to be a dog or a cat or a bird or a fish, then one can acknowledge it to be an animal. Had 'animal'-acknowledging acts initially been introduced in some such way, the concept of an animal would not be *directly* or *immediately* independently significant. Its significance would, in the first place, depend on relations to the particular animal-kind acknowledging acts that entail the 'animal' acknowledging act. But if the particular animal-kind concepts were independently significant, then the concept of an animal would be "reducible" to immediately independently significant concepts. The systematic significance of the concept wouldn't be essential. The concept could also be taught/learned as an independently significant concept. Instead of waiting to acknowledge an object to be a kind of animal, and then performing an 'animal'-acknowledging act, one could simply and directly acknowledge an object to be an animal on the basis of its appearance and behavior.

A *merely classificatory* conceptual framework is one for which no characteristic fundamental concept is essentially systematic. The concepts which are characteristic of the framework (as opposed to, say, logical concepts which are shared with all other frameworks) are either immediately independently significant or reducible to such concepts. So that, in principle, all the characteristic concepts of the framework are/could be independently significant. A merely classificatory framework relates concepts and their extensions by such relations as inclusion, exclusion, and overlap. Principles constitutive of such a framework might be like these:

> All dogs are animals.
> No dogs are birds.
> Some dogs are collies.

as well as principles sanctioning inferences from acknowledging objects to be dogs, cats, birds, fish, and so on, to acknowledging the objects to be animals.

The characteristic concepts of a merely classificatory framework don't depend on one another. From the standpoint of a particular such concept, the other concepts in the framework might as well not be there. A merely classificatory framework shouldn't be self-contained in the sense that it is closed to, or excludes, other concepts of the same kind. So one should be able to combine different merely classificatory frameworks to constitute different parts of a more comprehensive merely classificatory framework. Perhaps, in principle, there is only one merely classificatory framework, the framework made up of all merely classificatory subframeworks, which framework can always be more fully articulated. Although a merely classificatory framework is grounded in experience and doesn't get beyond or "behind" experience, this kind of framework can provide the resources for identifying objects we don't experience. Having a framework for acknowledging kinship relations and identifying people on the basis of kinship relations will allow us to identify one of George's great-great-grandfathers, for example. The fundamental types of acknowledging acts owe their significance to the experiences that call for them. We can afterward use connections we have experienced as a basis for attending to objects outside our experience. However, we can't use the resources of a merely classificatory framework to identify objects of a kind totally different from objects we experience. Recall the Empiricist argument that it makes no sense to suppose or accept material objects which cause our experience, but which can't themselves be experienced and are completely different from the kinds of objects we do experience. From the Empiricist perspective, the only conceptual frameworks that are legitimate—indeed, the only conceptual frameworks there are—are merely classificatory frameworks. According to them, material-object concepts can't be accommodated in such frameworks.

The alternative to a merely classificatory conceptual framework is an *essentially systematic* framework. Some of the characteristic concepts of such a framework owe their significance to semantic relations linking them to other concepts, and the systematic concepts are not reducible to independently significant concepts. If perceptible objects contain nonperceptible components which are unlike perceived objects (in respects other than size), then concepts of these unperceived particles must be essentially systematic. Acknowledging a perceptible object to be this or that may commit us to recognizing the existence of certain components with certain properties. We can identify these components (or groups of them) and acknowledge them to be one thing or another. There is entailment from talk about perceptible objects to talk about the nonperceptible ones, and vice versa. Claims about one type of nonperceptible component will entail some claims and be incompatible with others about different types of component. Concepts of nonperceptible causes of perceived phenomena can also be systematically significant. As can concepts of nonperceptible features of perceptible objects.

It isn't just theoretical entities like electrons and photons whose concepts are essentially systematic. The concepts of the causal and modal features of ordinary objects have this status. If being soluble in water is one of the criteria for being salt, and stuff that won't dissolve can't be salt, then the concepts of salt and water are essentially systematic. While one can observe a quantity of salt dissolve in some water, one can't see the solubility of the salt. And having seen some salt dissolve in some water does not guarantee that the same salt, when recovered from the water, will redissolve on a later occasion. One can't on the basis of appearances decisively determine stuff to be either salt or water. (We can, however, be completely satisfied on the basis of appearances.) Hume was right that we don't and can't see, hear, feel a necessary causal connection linking a cause to its effects. All that our eyes by themselves reveal is the first billiard ball moving toward the second, and the second beginning to move after contact is made. The concepts of the necessary causal properties of things are not independently significant.

Systematically significant concepts include humdrum concepts as well as concepts of scientifically postulated entities. But all systematically significant concepts need to be tied to independently significant ones. Independently significant concepts are (epistemically) foundational both in the sense that they come first in our acquisition of concepts and in the sense that systematically significant concepts must ultimately be linked by semantic relations to independently significant concepts. The essentially systematic concepts are not reducible to independently significant concepts, but they depend on those concepts. Without connections to independently significant concepts, the systematically significant concepts would be cut off from experience.

If a conceptual framework were somehow forced on us by our experience, so that it simply reflected objects we experience and their features, it would be merely classificatory. An essentially systematic conceptual framework must be *brought to* experience, not derived from experience. But even a merely classificatory framework can be developed and brought to experience, to make sense of experience. The early Empiricists were surely wrong in thinking that experience forces our conception on us. Descartes and Kant were right that we bring conceptual frameworks to experience, but there is no reason to think these frameworks are innate. We either acquire conceptual frameworks from other people, or we develop them ourselves. The important difference between the two kinds of frameworks is that essentially systematic frameworks add something to experience, something we don't find there, while merely classificatory frameworks make sense of experience strictly on the basis of what is found in experience. (*Together with whatever is demanded for identifying and reidentifying objects in experience, and acknowledging them to be one thing or another.*) From the Empiricist point of view, essentially systematic concepts are illicit. Worse than that, they are impossible. For the Empiricist framework rules them out.

5. The Framework to End All Frameworks

The idea of a conceptual framework is fairly recent. Certainly no one in the fifteenth through eighteenth centuries recognized such things. At least, they had no words for them. But there is nothing about a merely classificatory framework that poses difficulties for Empiricists. If someone had told the early Empiricists about these frameworks, the Empiricists could have accommodated the frameworks in their accounts. Merely classificatory frameworks simply reflect experience, though they also introduce a certain order by grouping things into various categories.

The Empiricists didn't know about conceptual frameworks (the Rationalists didn't either), but we can use our concepts of conceptual frameworks to describe what they were doing. It is clear that the only concepts they regarded as legitimate were independently significant concepts and concepts reducible to these. For on the Empiricist understanding, we are passive in experience. Experience just *happens* to us. According to Hume, it just happens, period. We are active only in attending or directing our attention, and this is a matter of positioning ourselves with respect to the experience that will come our way. And while we may do things to get knowledge and organize it, the knowledge we end up with simply *reflects* what goes on in experience. Our intellectual resources are too firmly linked to the sense data we experience for us to think or talk about what we don't and couldn't experience. Such thinking and talking makes no sense. From this point of view, there can't be essentially systematic concepts. Nothing can be significant solely in virtue of semantic links to other concepts. Semantic links can't be manufactured out of whole cloth, or from thin air. These links are merely the by-products of experientially grounded significance.

It is clear that the original Empiricists could not accept essentially systematic concepts and frameworks. Indeed, there is only one gigantic conceptual framework and various parts of it. This framework reflects the world as we have experienced it so far. The framework can be further developed either on the basis of new sorts of experience, or on the basis of closer, and new, attention to the old sort of experience. There can't be different and competing frameworks. The only difference is between different parts of the whole. Any attempt at an alternative framework must be confused and incoherent.

Someone might wonder if we could accept the Empiricists' conception of experience while modifying their views about significance and knowledge. We would understand experience to be of sense data, but concede that we are also able to talk significantly about nonperceptible objects, and to make these objects the subject of scientific research. Perhaps someone taking this approach could do a better job of what A. J. Ayer attempted in *Language, Truth, and Logic*. But this is a pointless endeavor. The Empiricist analysis and the Empiricist approach are not independently attractive. They only make sense in response to Descartes' Problem, as a reaction against Descartes' idea of how to provide a solution. To try to gerrymander a theory which combines the Empiricist analysis of experience with a scientific understanding of the material world is neither promising nor interesting. The consistent and thoroughgoing Empiricist position rules out essentially systematic concepts and conceptual frameworks. It rules out conceptual frameworks which are alternatives to its own conceptual framework—any such framework must be essentially systematic.

Although the Empiricist conception of knowledge and experience rules out there being essentially systematic concepts and conceptual frameworks, the Empiricist conception is itself essentially systematic. This conception is parasitic on the ordinary conception of experience and its objects. The significance of the fundamental Empiricist concepts depends on their semantic relations to concepts of the ordinary framework, which the Empiricist account (suicidally) attempts to eliminate.

The ordinary conception of sense experience and its objects is historically prior to the Empiricist conception. The Empiricist conception was devised in response to a crisis for the ordinary conception, the crisis that is (or is part of) what I have called Descartes' Problem. And the Empiricist conception can only be understood in its relation to the ordinary conception of sense experience, it can't stand on its own. Being an alternative to the ordinary conceptual framework is part of the very idea of the Empiricist framework. From the Empiricist perspective, identifying an ordinary object, and acknowledging it to be something or other commits one to there being ideas or impressions or sense data which are the *real* objects of attention, and the acknowledging act *really* pertains to those real objects.

No one adopts the Empiricist framework for her "starting" position, but if the Empiricist position were right, once she learns the framework or develops it for herself, a person will presumably recognize that the framework reflects things as they are. She will then be in the position where judgments about ordinary objects commit her to making sense data judgments. Even if she simply makes judgments about sense data in describing her experience, these judgments will be understood as replacements for judgments about the ordinary objects recognized by the ordinary conceptual framework. The person who accepts the sense-data framework can't actually drop the ordinary framework. The semantic relation between the ordinary-object judgments and the sense-data judgments is similar to entailment, but isn't quite entailment. For making ordinary-object judgments will commit the judger to making sense-data judgments *and to viewing these as the adequate replacement for the ordinary-object judgments*. Similarly, sense-data judgments will commit her to accepting that the judged situations might improperly be described by making ordinary-object judgments. The significance of the sense-data attending and acknowledging acts depends on these peculiar semantic relations to ordinary-object attending and acknowledging acts.

But why can't the Empiricist framework stand on its own? Even if it is, historically, a response to Descartes' Problem, why can't this framework be adopted without reference to the ordinary conception of experience and its objects? (Note that no one has ever done this. The ordinary conception of experience and its objects is *still* the ordinary conception.) The reason why the Empiricist conception can't be adopted "from scratch" depends on the requirements of the fundamental form of propositional thinking, 'to be' propositional thinking. (But 'that'-clause thinking wouldn't be enough to make the Empiricist conception self-sufficient. And 'that'-clause thinking depends on the more fundamental form of propositional thinking.) The account of propositional thinking that was presented earlier describes what propositional thinking is like no matter how experience is conceived. New forms of propositional thinking have not been produced as accompaniments to new conceptions of anything. The trouble with the Empiricist conceptual framework is that its basic objects, sense data, have not got a sufficient "presence" to be identified and reidentified, which is necessary before they can be acknowledged to be this or that.

Sense data are fleeting objects of attention. They won't stand still to be closely scrutinized. Sense data are what we *must* really see when we see tables and chairs, people and trees. A present sense datum wouldn't ordinarily last long enough to be acknowledged to be red or round or warm. Even if that were occasionally possible, we would have no access to single sense data less recent than a second or two ago. We are unable to identify particular sense data in our past experience. This means we are unable to think propositionally about particular sense data outside our immediate experience. And we couldn't learn, from scratch, to pick out particular sense data in our present experience, which could serve as subjects for acknowledging acts. We must, from the beginning of propositional thinking, attend to groups or clusters or structured arrays of sense data, and acknowledge them as wholes to be one thing and another. Sense data are merely inferred from the objects we actually identify and make judgments about.

The Empiricists developed an essentially systematic framework and brought it to experience, to make sense of experience. But this conceptual framework rules out there being essentially systematic conceptual frameworks. What is even worse, the significance of fundamental concepts in the Empiricist framework essentially depends on semantic relations linking these concepts to the rejected concepts of the ordinary conception of experience and its objects. The Empiricist account is self-destructive: it rules itself out. Even if we could ignore or modify the self-destructive character of its conceptual framework, Empiricism is not an attractive position. Once we understand that the Empiricist conception is not the inevitable product of rational analysis, it seems unreasonable to adopt such a drastic remedy for our problem. If we aren't forced to be Empiricists, we don't want to be, no matter how challenging it is to develop this view and solve the problems that one encounters. A conception that is closer to the ordinary conception of experience and its objects, one that doesn't require us to give up (or to drastically reconstrue) the physical world is surely more reasonable than Empiricism.

6. The Empirical Self

Although I have pointed out what I think is the most fundamental flaw of an Empiricist account, a flaw that renders the account unacceptable either in itself or as a solution/resolution to Descartes' Problem, I will consider some other aspects of Empiricism. I will be concerned with these aspects either as consequences of the Empiricist approach or as revealing additional problems with Empiricism. I am doing this both because I find it interesting and because Empiricism has been an important, influential position. Many philosophers who don't count themselves as Empiricists have accepted Empiricist principles and tackled problems unearthed by the Empiricists. Our attending to the principles and problems may make it clear that they are essentially tied to an Empiricist position. So that once Empiricism is given up, it will be recognized that there are no reasons to accept the principles and that the problems have been misconceived.

The first topic to be considered is the self. An Empiricist account must provide for the owners of experience as well as the objects of experience. Since there is no difference between a sense datum existing and that sense datum being perceived, the very existence of sense data demands the corresponding existence of perceivers. It isn't clear to me whether the awareness of a red sense datum is also the awareness of perceiving the sense datum, but the awareness of one thing can't, in general, be the same as the awareness of the awareness of the one thing. Nor can my awareness of *X* require that I be aware of being aware of *X*. However, if I am aware of *X*, I can *become* aware of being aware of X. To be aware of being aware is to be aware of the self as being aware. While the object of the lower-level awareness may be a sense datum, the object of the higher-level awareness is not. So experience not only requires an owner, but it also provides some access to that owner.

What should an Empiricist understand by *herself*? She can be aware of herself sensing, thinking, performing various sorts of actions, and in various emotional states or conditions. She can acknowledge herself to be sensing, thinking, and so on, and the concepts she uses for this acknowledging will be independently significant. But how about the self itself, what does she know about it? On an Empiricist account, there can be no direct access to a separate self behind or beneath experience. Just as when we experience a tree being tall or leafy or shaggy-barked, we have no direct awareness to the *essential* tree behind or beneath its appearances. There is only awareness of the self experiencing something or doing something. While true, this doesn't determine how to conceive the self. One choice for the Empiricist is to take the same line with the self that she takes with material objects, and regard the self as a collection of awarenesses and actions. Another choice is to treat the self differently, and regard it as an enduring, active subject of experience.

Berkeley conceived the self as an enduring, active subject. In doing this he was adopting what is pretty much the ordinary conception of the self, although he had reconceived the objects of which the self is aware. There is nothing inconsistent in Berkeley's conception of the self, for Descartes' Problem is brought about by the conflict between the ordinary conception of sense experience and the mechanical conception of physical processes. This conflict needn't affect our understanding of the self, for it only concerns the self's access to the "external" world. Hume's understanding of the self is not more consistent than that of Berkeley, but his total account of the objects and the subject of experience is more *uniform* than Berkeley's. Just as talk about material objects is a kind of "abbreviation" for talk about sense data, so for Hume talk about the self is a kind of abbreviation for talk about sense data, thoughts, awarenesses of awarenesses, and so on. Each self is just the sum total of its experiences.

There is a respect in which Berkeley's conception of the self can be criticized from Hume's perspective. If experience has the fragmented or fragmentary character accorded it by the Empiricist conception, and the materials for thinking are derived from experience, then it is difficult to understand how we could come by the conception of a unitary and enduring subject of experience. From this perspective, it is clear that Berkeley's conception of the self isn't forced on us (on him) by experience. His conception is instead brought to experience, to interpret and make sense of experience. In fact, all conceptual frameworks are developed and brought to experience in this way. But Hume wouldn't admit this. From his perspective, the correct conception of experience, its objects, and its owner must simply be given to us, forced on us. Since Berkeley's conception of the self couldn't be obtained like this, Hume would reject his conception as illicit.

No matter which conception of the self he adopts, an Empiricist will be unable to provide a satisfactory account of physical actions. Suppose I put up a ladder beneath my plum tree, then climb the ladder and pick plums. Consider the act/activity of climbing the ladder. I can acknowledge myself to be climbing the ladder. The significance of my acknowledging act can be fully grounded by the experience of climbing the ladder. But though I can correctly acknowledge myself to be climbing the ladder, an Empiricist account of what is going on will be complicated and implausible. For on that account, the ladder isn't really a single, independent, enduring object. Neither is my body. My awareness of climbing the ladder is an awareness of various ladder data and body data. I experience various hand and feet data in a certain relation to the ladder data. Then I get hand and feet data with different relations to ladder data. And so on. From the Empiricist perspective, climbing the ladder isn't really something I do, it happens to me. I am passive with respect to sense data. They aren't there ahead of time, and I don't make them. They simply occur and I am aware of them. Instead of moving my hands and feet as I ascend the latter, I experience them moving. (And, of course, they don't really move. I experience a sequence of differently related data.) From the Empiricist perspective, my experience of climbing the ladder "reduces" to experience of one or more decisions that I make and experience of various body and ladder data, variously related. On the face of it, that is simply a preposterous analysis of my climbing the ladder and the awareness that accompanies the climbing.

When I point a gun at the target and pull the trigger, this may initiate a causal sequence which results in the bullet hitting the bull's-eye. I hit the bull's-eye as a result of aiming and squeezing. The Empiricist analysis treats a physical action like a causal sequence. I perform decision acts which initiate what we classify as bodily movements. But this won't do. The experience of moving one's foot is actually quite unlike the experience of watching or feeling one's foot in motion. We don't first decide, then watch what happens. We simply act.

The difficulty that any Empiricist must have with physical actions and our awareness of them is a difficulty that Hume has with all actions. Just as objects of ordinary experience are inert collections of sense data, so the self is an inert collection of sense data, thoughts, awarenesses of awarenesses, and so forth. Such a self can't *do* anything. This makes it necessary to conceive all my actions as if they happen to me rather than as if I do them. An intentional action is regarded as a decision event followed by the various experiences I have when I perform the action. This is a ludicrous account which is completely false to our own experience of acting. This account can't even make sense of representing, which is fundamental to our cognitive lives. For representing must be understood as something we do, not as a feature we find. An inert collection of sense data, thoughts, and so on can't use one object to represent another. We couldn't possibly be such collections.

7. Thinking Empirically

On the Empiricist account, the ordinary objects of awareness are sense data. These "thin" bearers of properties and relations are self-sufficient. None of them points to or calls for a further object. Sense data don't represent objects "behind" or "beneath" themselves. Some sense data do represent others. However, since nothing represents intrinsically, we should say that some sense data are used to represent others. When we produce an (external) image, that image is constituted by sense data, but we also use it to become representationally aware of further sense data. Nothing about sense data suggests that they be used to represent objects behind or beneath themselves.

The early Empiricists claimed that in thinking we are aware of ideas which are derived from sense data. An idea might simply be a faint copy of a sense datum. It might also be obtained by manipulating faint copies of sense data to obtain a result unlike anything we have sensed. The ideas are conceived as internal images/designs. Since these ideas are merely copies of sense data, nothing about the internal images/designs will suggest their use to represent further objects. But ideas commonly are used to represent, and the Empiricists talked as if this representing were intrinsic. For while one doesn't usually consider a sense datum to be *of* something—we have a red sense datum rather than a datum of red, it is customary to speak of ideas *of* this and that. We might consider an idea of Napoleon or an idea of Paris. We can be aware of an idea of blue or an idea of a horse. (The early Empiricists may have thought that one thing's representing another is merely a matter of the two objects being similar. We know that view to be inadequate.) By using the word 'idea' for both sense data and ideas, Berkeley failed to mark this difference. Hume gave us two words, and ordinarily saves 'of' for ideas. Since it is customary to use ideas, but not sense data, to represent, we presumably use the ideas to represent sense data, at least most of the time. We can also use one idea to represent another.

We not only use images to represent, we also use them to identify particular objects. Representing isn't the same as identifying. If we simply use an image to represent, we use that image to become representationally aware of arbitrary objects of various kinds. Even when we use an image to identify Napoleon, we use it to become aware of an arbitrary man having a certain appearance. The awareness of the arbitrary man is the same kind of awareness a person would have who didn't know the image to be of Napoleon, or of any other particular person. The similarity of the image to Napoleon (to any man with Napoleon's appearance) is what allows a person, without having any specialized knowledge, to use the image to represent. The similarity doesn't account for the identifying. To use the image to identify Napoleon requires that we have some independent access to Napoleon. The early Empiricists confused representing and identifying. Nothing in their account can explain, or even accommodate, the use of images to identify.

We use expressions to identify particular objects and groups of objects. The expressions we use for this are not images, but only designs. We could employ a picture language in which some expressions/images resembled the objects we identify with them. Other expressions/images might be used both to represent an arbitrary object of a kind and to acknowledge objects to be of that kind. But the representing dimension of a picture language isn't essential to its use for propositional thinking. The images could at best be suggestive. The use of language is conventional, it essentially depends on conventions. Conventions determine the acknowledging use of a given expression—they determine what kind of acknowledging acts are performed with that expression. Conventions determine which expressions are used to attend to/identify which particular objects and groups of them. Identifying conventions are unlike acknowledging conventions, because they require connections which link an identifying act to the identified object. There are all kinds of connections linking objects in the world, but an identifying act exploits some particular connection or connections. The use of a particular expression to exploit a specific connection is conventionally determined. The reason that images don't provide all that we need to identify particular objects is that we have no identifying conventions for images. To establish such conventions would be to move in the direction of establishing a picture language.

We can't use images to identify particular objects without either establishing identifying conventions or having independent access to the objects so that we can intend the right objects in using the images to represent. It would also be necessary to establish conventions in order to use images to perform acknowledging acts. It is a matter of convention that we use 'horse' to attend to horses and to acknowledge objects to be horses. Our use isn't conventional simply in the fact that some other expression could just as well be used to do the 'horse' job. That there is a 'horse' job at all is a matter of convention. We could "lump" together horses and something else. We could consider some horses to be one thing, and other horses to be something else. Perhaps there really is a horse nature that separates horses from other things. One horse does seem more like other horses than it does like other animals or nonanimals. But our language isn't "obligated" to reflect the true natures of things. Focusing on images rather than words, and considering images as if we used them for attending and acknowledging, can make it seem natural to associate the image with things that it resembles. No convention seems called for. Except that one image will resemble hundreds of very different things, in different respects. To be able to fasten on this or that respect, and to use the image to identify objects that it resembles in a particular respect, requires some convention which establishes the appropriate respects.

The early Empiricists didn't understand propositional thinking of the 'to be' form, and so didn't realize how inadequate ideas/images are for such thinking. But they, like everyone else, engaged in the 'to be' form of thinking, and had some appreciation of attending/identifying and of acknowledging. They thought that ideas/images were themselves sufficient for representing and identifying. They didn't recognize the difference between representing and identifying, though everyone realizes that we can represent fictitious objects and events. They took even less notice of acknowledging than of identifying, but the Empiricists' discussions of the use of particular images as general ideas allows for using an image both to attend to a collection of objects of a kind and to acknowledge an object to be of that kind. None of this is possible without developing/adopting linguistic conventions for using images.

8. Significant Language

Since the Empiricists failed to develop a satisfactory account of thinking, especially propositional thinking, they were unable to explain in detail how belief and knowledge are based on or derived from experience. In spite of this, they did recognize some general principles which enabled them to give a partial account of belief and knowledge.

The basic idea of Empiricism provides a principle of significance for language and principles about the way we get and back up our beliefs. Together, these principles lead to conclusions about the scope and limits of knowledge, factual and otherwise. Hume's principle of significance requires a meaningful expression to be linked to experience via ideas. We can only think about what resembles items we have experienced, for the ideas we use for thinking are all directly or indirectly derived from experience. And we can only sensefully talk about the things we can think about. Significant expressions express ideas. While thought may be confused or not, we don't think of thought as either lacking significance or possessing it (in the semantic sense of 'significance'). Language is what possesses significance, but not all language does; we can apparently babble on about various things without expressing ideas.

On the present understanding, it isn't words that are meaningful, and words don't express ideas. Words are used to perform meaningful acts. Which words are used to perform which (kinds of) acts is determined by convention. We have seen that Hume's account can't really accommodate acts, so he needed to have words merely correspond to ideas which they either express or "trigger," and which are the cognitively important items. However, to fully understand the significance of an expression, we must trace the expression to ideas, and the ideas to experience. Since it is experience that really counts, we can more or less ignore the ideas, and simply derive the significance of an expression from the experience on which it is based. But then we can consider the consequences of Hume's understanding of significance for linguistic acts instead of expressions. According to Hume's criterion for significant speaking, many of the things we say turn out not to make good sense. Talk about substantial, independent, enduring objects which support properties and relations is not significant. Neither is our customary sort of talk about causal relations.

Hume's account of thinking isn't satisfactory, but his criterion of significance is more or less independent of that failed account. It can be adapted to apply to significant acts as opposed to expressions. Hume's criterion of significance was a word-by-word criterion. But he didn't really consider all words or the acts performed with them. His criterion, taken strictly, would disqualify acts of using 'the' or 'all.' To rescue Hume's criterion, we need to understand it as applying to attending and acknowledging acts, which are often performed with phrases or clauses instead of single words. So adapted, Hume's view is that we can only attend to objects which have been experienced or are linked by relations of a kind we have experienced to objects we have experienced. For an acknowledging act performed with a given expression to be significant, it must be possible to provide or describe the experiences to which we can appropriately respond by using the expressions to perform acknowledging acts. (But we must be careful to distinguish experiences that no one has even though they are similar to experiences we have, from unfamiliar experiences that no one has. It makes sense to use the word 'unicorn', because we have no trouble understanding and imagining an experience for which 'a unicorn' would be an appropriate response. We can't similarly understand and imagine, says Hume, an experience to which "a necessary causal connection" would be an appropriate response.)

Hume hasn't given us a satisfactory account of significance. He has only provided the general idea of such an account. To come up with a thorough theory of significant expressions/acts based on Hume's Empiricist principle, one must consider the different kinds of words in a language, and the acts performed with them, and explain how these function. Given certain expressions/acts connected to experience in suitable ways, we can then combine these in specified ways to obtain/perform complex expressions/linguistic acts. A thoroughgoing account of this sort would be either a semantic/syntactic theory for a particular natural language or a universal framework providing general principles that hold for all languages, and that would be supplemented in providing theories of particular languages. Developing such a theory would certainly be a formidable endeavor, if it were possible at all. In addition to its being hard to provide, a theory based on Hume's ideas would probably have consequences disturbing to later Empiricists. For it looks as if such a theory will disqualify some linguistic acts and activities we wish to count as significant. From the Empiricist perspective, it is all right to disqualify wrong-headed philosophical language. It may even be acceptable to disqualify some common-sense talking. But successful scientific practice has a status which is "Empirically sacred"; Empiricists didn't want to find themselves claiming that some accepted scientific statements lack significance.

In the twentieth century, Empirically inclined philosophers have often focused on experience and language, and pretty much ignored thinking. In *Language, Truth, and Logic*, A. J. Ayer simply ducked the task of presenting an account of thinking, and claimed that giving such an account is a job for psychologists. Ayer substituted an account of language and logic for an account of thought. This was sufficient to allow him to develop a criterion of significance, and also to come up with principles governing knowledge and belief, so that he could determine the scope and limits of our knowledge. Hume's twentieth-century followers have generally not followed Hume in developing a word-by-word criterion of significance. That is probably a job for linguists. Instead they have attempted to determine what it takes for a factual statement to be significant—to determine to what kind of empirical test a statement must be subject before it makes factual sense.

Using Hume's approach there would be a uniform but complicated criterion of significance for all statements. Among those which are significant, we would then distinguish those which are either *a priori* truths or contradictory from the rest. The twentieth-century idea calls for us to distinguish factual significance from *a priori* significance. This split is unwelcome; it opens the door to a host of different kinds of significance without providing an idea or strategy for dealing with them all. Anyway, the twentieth-century approach hasn't worked. No satisfactory criterion of empirical significance has been discovered. Most philosophers have stopped looking for one.

Hume's criterion of significance rules out many statements that make good sense, but it is faithful to the basic Empiricist idea. The twentieth century Empiricists abandoned an independent criterion of significance, instead linking significance to methods for justifying belief. They tried to characterize empirical significance and *a priori* significance, and failed to investigate the general significance of which these are special cases. The twentieth-century Empiricists tried to reconcile Empiricism and modern science, but were not successful in this attempt.

9. Acquiring Knowledge

There is no satisfactory Empiricist account of propositional thinking, so there is no account of the way that experience leads to belief and knowledge. But the belief and knowledge expressed by sentences must be stated with significant sentences, and it must be justified in Empirically acceptable ways.

Hume's expression for *a priori* knowledge is "*knowledge of the relations between ideas.*" That is not an entirely appropriate phrase, because mathematics, for example, doesn't deal with ideas; mathematics is concerned with spatial and numerical relations rather than with psychological or epistemic ones. However, on Hume's account, *a priori* knowledge is gotten by investigating ideas and their relations. Hume thought this knowledge is to be obtained by attending to internal designs/images, but we could as well use drawings on a blackboard or paper. What Hume seems to have had in mind was that we consider a particular triangle as a mere triangle, determine the features it possesses, and conclude that all triangles have the feature. We can consider a particular triangle as merely a triangle, a particular square as merely a square, and a particular array of twelve objects as merely twelve objects. Some features of a mere triangle are obvious: its three angles and three sides. Some require a demonstration before we can acknowledge the triangle to have them: the sum of the interior angles being equal to 180 degrees. It is also a demonstrative move when we proceed from the mere triangle to a conclusion about all triangles, but Hume wouldn't have been aware of this move.

More recent Empiricists have dissociated *a priori* knowledge from images/designs, internal or otherwise. They have attempted to provide a linguistic characterization of *a priori* knowledge. This knowledge states principles constitutive of our conceptual frameworks. These principles may merely define expressions, like the principle "A square is an equilateral and equiangular quadrilateral." They can state other relations: "Nothing red (all over) is green" or "No square has five sides." For *a priori* knowledge that is Empirically acceptable, the conceptual frameworks should be merely classificatory frameworks. Except for the basic Empiricist framework, essentially systematic frameworks are not allowed. *A priori* knowledge does not include the characteristic constitutive principles of essentially systematic frameworks. A merely classificatory framework doesn't add to or otherwise alter our experience. It simply provides a catalogue for objects given in experience. This cataloguing system is built into our language, and *a priori* knowledge is knowledge of the cataloguing system. Some *a priori* knowledge is evident, other *a priori* knowledge needs to be derived, or justified inferentially. But no a priori knowledge provides substantive information about the world. No a priori knowledge is of metaphysical interest, or carries ontological (existential) import.

Factual or empirical knowledge is knowledge of what takes place, or has taken place, or will take place. Factual knowledge reflects goings-on in the world of experience. Although we don't know how experience is transformed into propositional beliefs and propositional knowledge, we are able to classify factual claims in terms of their "distance" from experience. Some sentences are suited to report the "content" of the speaker's present experience or present memory. Of these, some like 'This is red' are suited to report experience "directly," and, when used seriously and carefully, constitute claims nearly immune to criticism. Others like "This is a VCR" can be used to make reports that are partly conjectural, and, when used seriously and carefully, yield claims that can more easily turn out to be mistaken. Reports of memory are also less secure than reports of sense data presently occurring.

Our factual knowledge and belief go well beyond reports of what is happening to us now and what has happened in the past. And we can't dismiss the knowledge/belief which does more than reflect our experience. It isn't mistaken or unjustified, for we couldn't get along without it. In keeping with the idea that the world of experience is simply given to us, so that we in no way constitute this world, Hume postulated a generalizing "instinct" that humans share with other animals. Dogs and children can both learn from a few encounters that fires burn and so should be avoided. It was Hume's view that experience conditions us to have certain expectations and beliefs. We don't understand how these come about any more than we understand where experience comes from. Sense data simply occur. We simply find ourselves expecting fires to be hot, believing that fires are hot.

Hume used the word 'inference' to label the process by which dogs and children come to have expectations about fire, water, bread, meat, and so on. But I will speak of *conditioned* expectations and beliefs instead. On my usage, dogs and children can have expectations. But to have beliefs, an individual must be able to think propositionally. There is no reason for saying that dogs can do this. I reserve the word 'inference' for a rather formal procedure where one moves from propositional premisses to propositional conclusions, which one takes the premisses to support. If experience conditions us to have beliefs as well as expectations, I won't say that we infer the conditioned beliefs. According to Hume, we instinctively accept propositional thoughts that generalize our experience. After experiencing a number of hot fires and no other kind, we believe that (all) fires are hot.

We also reflect on and refine our instinctive practice. We can raise questions as to what the world of experience is like, we can seek out specialized and recondite experiences. We can make inferences from premisses describing particular events to general conclusions which we then accept, either tentatively or wholeheartedly. Inferences which have the form of inductive generalizations owe their satisfactory character to the generalizing instinct from which they arise. There is no showing that such inferences will usually yield a true conclusion if the premisses are true. Anyone who tries to provide that kind of justification for induction simply doesn't understand our situation in the world. Generalizing is our instinctive practice. It is an unavoidable one of our ways of coming up with expectations and beliefs. It is what we understand to justify these beliefs and expectations. It is what we understand to *constitute* empirical justification. Inductive inferences are justified to the extent that they reflect (and refine and enlarge on) our instinctive practice.

Hume's conjecture about our generalizing instinct is a fundamental principle of his version of an Empiricist conceptual framework.

With respect to his framework, it is an *a priori* truth that we have such an instinct. But if we don't accept his framework, we needn't accept this "truth."

It seemed to Hume that he had adequately accounted for experience and our knowledge of it. The scientific knowledge that he knew about could be obtained, and supported, in the way he described. But as science marched on, Hume's successors didn't think Hume's procedures were adequate for getting and supporting their contemporary scientific knowledge. Once objects that can't be observed came to be a scientific commonplace, Hume's principles were undermined. If scientists talk about theoretical entities, then such talk makes sense. But we can't point to experiences which confer intelligibility on concepts of things unobservable. Nor can theoretical entities be regarded as collections of sense data. Further, laws covering such objects can't be extrapolated from our experience. Even if an Empiricist philosopher takes the difficult line that theoretical entities are fictitious, Hume's principles are in trouble. At the very least, they must fail to be the whole story of significance and support.

Logically oriented Empiricist philosophers developed new accounts of significance and factual knowledge. They accepted the hypothetico-deductive method as the fundamental method for getting and supporting knowledge of the world. A factual statement is significant (or: a statement is factually significant) if it can be tested in experience, using the hypothetico-deductive method. A statement is factually supported if the consequences for describing experience that we derive turn out to be confirmed. (And no experiential consequence that we test fails our test.) Empiricist philosophers thought that admitting the hypothetico-deductive method would enable them to reconcile scientific knowledge with Empirical principles. It is true that the hypothetico-deductive method comes closer to the procedures that scientists, and ordinary people too, use to obtain factual knowledge, than do the procedures that Hume describes. But the hypothetico-deductive method was a disaster for Empiricism. If this method provides the criterion of factual significance, then virtually all ostensibly factual statements are factually significant. There is no end to the statements that might receive factual support. The scope and limits of factual knowledge extend to infinity.

The hypothetico-deductive method is incompatible with Empiricism. This method can't be justified, not even in the way that Hume thought inductive generalizations were justified. The hypothetico-deductive method is a method that calls for us to be self-conscious and reflective, it isn't an instinctive procedure for acquiring beliefs and it isn't the refined version of an instinctive procedure. Worse, the person who uses this method is not simply looking for features of experience. The factual knowledge and beliefs that this procedure "yields" don't simply reflect experience or extrapolate features found in experience. The person who uses this method is actively trying to make sense of experience. She can use this method to invent a world in order to make sense of experience. This method allows us to develop essentially systematic conceptual frameworks and to link them via independently significant concepts to experience. In using this method we can confer significance on concepts and statements, as well as "authorizing" ourselves to tentatively accept hypotheses which pass the test. The method doesn't, and can't, discriminate between expressions belonging to merely classificatory conceptual frameworks and expressions belonging to essentially systematic frameworks. The only way one might "rein in" the hypothetico-deductive method, and render it compatible with Empiricism, would be to formulate and accept an independent criterion of significance, and insist that the method be used only with statements which pass the independent test. The independent criterion must certify only concepts which can be accommodated in merely classificatory frameworks. However, that approach will have the effect of disqualifying much of modern science. For Empiricism isn't incompatible simply with other philosophical accounts. Empiricism is incompatible with modern science. (It was already incompatible with Newtonian science, but this wasn't obvious at the time.)

10. Back Where We Started

The Empiricist tradition was started by Berkeley and Hume, and lasted well into the twentieth century. Empiricism has the nature of a program or project, rather than being a fully developed body of beliefs. There is a fundamental (kind of) conceptual framework, and there are fundamental principles. These are used in carrying out the Empiricist project, and in solving various problems. When the Empiricist tradition flourished, it seemed to philosophers in that tradition that they were making headway in carrying out the program. They worked at reconstructing the world in Empiricist terms, at solving new problems that turned up, and at improving on their predecessors' solutions to old problems. But some problems were never solved in a satisfactory way. Other problems had solutions which once seemed satisfactory, but were later seen not to be. Empiricism as a movement didn't encounter a decisive obstacle or challenge. But philosophers in the second half of the twentieth century have pretty much given up on Empiricism. There are still philosophers who qualify as Empiricists. Empiricist principles still influence many philosophers, and determine the character of much research in such fields as epistemology. However, the tradition is no longer dominant, or even prominent, in current philosophy.

The history of the Empiricist tradition has some resemblance to one of the inconclusive Platonic dialogues. In those dialogues, a certain problem is addressed, several solutions are proposed and shown to be wanting, and the dialogue ends with the problem still in need of a solution. I understand those dialogues to be like exercises in a textbook. The reader isn't supposed to solve the problem. Instead she is to uncover the assumption or assumptions which keep the participants from solving their problem. The Empiricist tradition was not intended as an exercise. But it has petered out on the same inconclusive note as one of the dialogues. Looking for the fundamental principles or assumptions which led to the decline of the tradition can be enlightening.

I have called attention to fundamental Empiricist "ideas" and principles, and pointed out various shortcomings of the Empiricist program and the Empiricist outlook. Descartes didn't solve his problem. Neither did the Empiricists. There is no fixing the failed efforts of either Descartes or the Empiricists. We are still faced with Descartes' Problem.

Chapter 5

Acting Intentionally

1. A Kantian Response

Descartes' Problem is to overcome the conflict between the ordinary conception of sense experience and the mechanical conception of physical processes. And, in doing this, to explain the contribution that sense experience makes to our thought, belief, and knowledge—which requires us to have an account of these things. The ordinary conception of sense experience is a conception of sense experience *and its objects*. On the ordinary conception, the objects of sense experience are simply the external (physical) world and the things in it. The ordinary conception of the physical world, physical phenomena, and physical processes, is included in the ordinary conception of experience and its objects. Descartes' new, mechanical conception of sense experience is also a conception of the immediate objects of sense experience. Descartes agreed with the ordinary conception that experience gives us direct access to something real, but he disagreed as to what reality this is. Descartes limited our access in experience so that we only "make contact" with features, not the things which have them.

In addition to a conception of sense experience and its objects, Descartes needed a separate conception of the physical world and the things in it. From the ordinary conception of sense experience and its objects, Descartes retained the conception of the objects of experience, though he no longer regarded them as (immediate) objects of experience. And Descartes modified the ordinary conception of the physical world to a considerable extent, dropping the secondary qualities of objects, while retaining their primary qualities. Descartes also claimed that we bring concepts, or ideas, to experience to make sense of experience and of the objects which give rise to experience. These ideas are adequate to the ways the objects independently are.

Descartes' strategy of keeping our basic understanding of physical phenomena and developing a mechanical substitute for the ordinary conception of sense experience still strikes many as the most attractive strategy to pursue, in spite of the fact that it has been pursued for a long time with no success. The Empiricists abandoned both the ordinary conception of sense experience and the ordinary conception of physical objects and processes. They were initially attracted to Descartes' suggestion that we experience features not objects, but finally settled for the view that we encounter objects with features in experience, though there is nothing more to these objects than their having the features we are aware of. Their new conceptions of experience and of its objects called for the reconstruction of the world we inhabit, a reconstruction that was never satisfactorily accomplished.

Although the Empiricists were unable to explain how experience gives rise to thought, belief, and knowledge, they were sure that experience is the sole source of the materials we think with. They couldn't provide a satisfactory account of thinking, especially propositional thinking, but were able to develop their conviction about the fundamental importance of experience and so provided an account of knowledge and how we get it. Without quite solving the second part of Descartes' Problem, the Empiricists did a reasonable job of responding to further problems posed by the advent of scientific knowledge. Perhaps the most ingenious feature of the Empiricist account is the way it moves the subject of experience outside of the body we experience, so that we don't use our eyes to see, our ears to hear, and so on. Nothing we can find out about the way our bodies are constituted or the way they work can have any effect on our understanding of experience or of the status of its objects.

Descartes gave up our ordinary conception of sense experience but kept our conception of the world and the objects it contains. The Empiricists gave up both conceptions. And Kant chose the third alternative. He retained, in a modified form, the ordinary conception of experience, and he gave up the ordinary conception of the world and its objects. The objects that we encounter in experience are not independent of our experience, and they are not the ultimate objects. Kant agreed with Descartes that we bring concepts to experience, to make sense of it. But he went further than Descartes and claimed that we use our concepts to give structure both to experience and to the objects we encounter in experience. Kant agreed with the Empiricists in separating the subject of experience from the body we experience.

No one has solved Descartes' Problem. No one has provided a satisfactory account of thought, belief, and knowledge, including scientific knowledge. But I think Kant was on the right track. His actual account doesn't work, but it can be fixed, or modified, to do the job that needs doing. In what follows I will develop an account based on Kant's, but without initially considering Kant's mistakes and how to repair them. Once the account is sufficiently well developed, we will ask what can be done with it to adequately solve Descartes' Problem.

I will not be trying to present Kant's own view. Instead I will lay out *a* Kantian view, a view *derived* from Kant's. This view is different from Kant's in many small respects, but a larger difference is that mine has a linguistic character. Kant was concerned with thinking and judging, but not so interested in our using language. I am concerned with thinking and judging and with other mental acts and operations, but I try to understand many of them on the model of using language. In much of our thinking we actually employ language. In order to understand how we use concepts to shape experience, we must understand linguistic acts and activity. We use language to shape experience and its objects.

It is important to the present understanding that we make an active contribution to the world we encounter in experience. To account for this active contribution, we need an understanding of intentional and purposive acts. The remainder of this chapter will focus on such acts, on purposive and intentional explanations and their contrast with causal explanations, and on the special class of intentional acts that constitute linguistic acts.

2. Intentional Acts

An act with a purpose is one done to achieve or obtain or accomplish something. If Chuck flips the light switch to turn on the lights, the flipping has as its purpose *to turn on the lights*. The purpose for stepping on the brakes is *to stop the car*. It is only for acts with purposes that we can talk about success and failure in the strict sense. An act that achieves or accomplishes its purpose is successful. Failing is failing to achieve one's purpose in acting. We *can* say things like "The falling rock succeeded in triggering an avalanche," but we are in this case treating the rock as if it were an agent acting for a purpose—as if the rock *wanted* to start the avalanche.

I will use the following:

> *X* did *Y* in order to obtain (accomplish) *Z*

as a standard form for describing acts done for a purpose. Here *X* is the agent, doing *Y* is the act, and to obtain or accomplish *Z* is *X*'s purpose for doing *Y*. Descriptions of specified acts won't always have this exact form. I might just say that Chuck flipped the light switch in order to turn on the lights, rather than saying he did it to accomplish turning on the lights or to obtain the lights going (being) on. The standard form is convenient for discussing purposive acts in general. With both the standard form and my departures from it, the expression 'in order' serves as a *purpose-introducing* expression. Infinitive phrases will normally be employed to report/designate purposes.

A purpose of an act is a feature of the act. The act has its purpose independently of whether or not it succeeds in achieving this purpose. An act with a purpose will also have an end or goal, but we don't describe/report this in quite the same way we describe/report its purpose. Chuck's purpose in flipping the switch is *to turn on the lights*. His goal isn't turning them on. It is either *having them go on* or *having them be on*. The goal is something one has or has accomplished after the act succeeds. We describe it independently of the act which aims at it. Alternative acts might have the same goal. But if we describe an act's purpose in all specificity, it is "essentially" tied to that act. Chuck's purpose in flipping the switch is not simply *to turn on the lights*, it is *to turn on the lights by flipping the switch*. The purpose of *this* act can only be achieved by this act. Some other act can achieve this act's goal.

Suppose Chuck flipped the switch in order to turn on the lights in this room. But the switch Chuck flipped is for the light on the porch. At the moment Chuck flipped his switch, someone else flipped the right switch and the lights in the room went on. Chuck may have gotten what he wanted, but his act wasn't successful. It didn't achieve its purpose. Nor did the other flipping achieve the purpose of Chuck's act. It achieved (or failed to achieve) its own purpose.

Some acts have goals "beyond" themselves. But some acts are considered to be their own ends, they are performed for their own sakes. Such an act might be one the agent enjoys performing. It might be an act which satisfies a fundamental need of the agent. Or it might be an act which realizes a fundamental value of the agent. Suppose Jorge plays tennis because he likes it. We can on a particular occasion say Jorge is playing tennis in order to be playing tennis (on this occasion). His activity has a purpose, but the purpose isn't a "further purpose." We might also say that Jorge is playing tennis in order to gain or obtain enjoyment. But gaining enjoyment isn't like gaining ten dollars. One can have the money after he has gained it. The enjoyment doesn't outlast the gaining. Jorge may play tennis without enjoying it, if he gets thrashed. But when Jorge gains enjoyment from playing tennis, his playing tennis is the same as his gaining enjoyment. So playing tennis in order to be playing tennis is the same as playing tennis in order to gain enjoyment. Stating Jorge's purpose as "to gain enjoyment" rather than "to be playing tennis" makes it clear how Jorge's activity can fail to be satisfactory. It is a more complete or more adequate statement than is "to be playing tennis." With an act which is its own end, the goal and purpose seem to coincide. Different acts couldn't achieve this same goal.

Someone who eats in order to satisfy her hunger may not enjoy eating. But her eating is the same as her satisfying her hunger. This act can also be its own end. So can Edwin's act of paying Jane the money he owes her. Paying one's debts is a fundamental value that Edwin accepts. He doesn't like paying Jane, he would rather have the money to spend. He pays Jane in order to realize the value he accepts (in order to meet his obligation); paying Jane *is* realizing this value (on this occasion).

If doing *Y* has the purpose to obtain *Z*, but *Y* isn't successful, then doing *Y* is *trying* to obtain *Z*, trying unsuccessfully to obtain *Z*. If Chuck flips the switch, but the lights don't go on (it is the wrong switch, or the power is off), Chuck has nonetheless tried to turn them on. If he flips the switch and they do go on, he has also tried to turn them on—he has tried and succeeded. But we more commonly speak of trying in cases of failure than in cases of success.

It doesn't belong to the very idea of a purposive action that the agent who performs the act must be aware of the act's purpose. Both Freudian theory and common sense recognize that people sometimes act to achieve purposes of which they aren't (consciously) aware. Self-deception may be deception about the purposes one is trying to achieve. The abusive parent who thinks he is punishing his child in order to help the child may be acting primarily in order to gain a certain gratification for himself at the child's expense. If his self-deception is culpable, we can hold him responsible for his ignorance of his primary purpose in punishing the child. But he may really be unaware of this purpose.

An act can be done for a purpose without the agent's being aware of the purpose. But it is conceivable that a purposive act might be performed by an agent that lacks awareness of anything. It isn't inconsistent to suggest that a plant might do something for a purpose—turn in order to face the sun, perhaps. But surely plants aren't aware of either themselves or their surroundings. A purposive act is one we understand on the basis of where it is going rather than on the basis of where it comes from. A purposive act is directed toward achieving its purpose.

Purposive acts are understood in terms of purposive explanations. To give the purpose of an act is to provide an explanation for the act. We don't understand the act as a particular instance of a general law, and we don't understand why this act occurred rather than any other. But we do understand what is going on with the act, it makes sense to us. Purposive and mechanical causal explanations are fundamentally different kinds of explanations. Perhaps they are the fundamental forms of explanation. To give the purposive features of an act is to explain it. Similarly, we can explain a situation or event by locating it in a causal context. Aristotle seems to have thought that a single occurrence could, and should, be given both purposive and causal explanations. But we now take these kinds of explanations to be rivals. The difference between the two kinds of explanations will be explored in more detail later, once we have developed a fuller understanding of purposive and intentional acts. For now we can note that an agent which lacks awareness might exhibit purposive behavior. But if someone succeeded in providing a complete causal explanation of that behavior, which explanation came to be accepted, the causal explanation would leave no room for a purposive explanation of the same behavior.

An agent can act with a purpose without being aware of that purpose, but an *intentional* act is a purposive act where there is awareness. An agent which performs an intentional act must be aware of what it is doing, and must intend to be doing this. There are two kinds of intentions that can be associated with an intentional act. The agent's intention *for* her act is what she intends for her act to be, what she intends to be doing. The intention *of* an act is its purpose, which the agent must also be aware of. A person who is unable to swim might flounder in the water, intending to swim. Her intention *for* her activity is that it be swimming. The intention of her activity is whatever she intends to accomplish by swimming. It is essential to an intention that the agent be aware of it. If an agent acts for a purpose without being aware of it, that purpose is not the agent's intention. It is possible that an act will have more than one purpose, where one purpose counts as an intention and the other doesn't. The abusive parent might intend to help his son by punishing him, and unintentionally act in order to achieve a certain gratification. Unless there is an intention for an act, there cannot be an intention of the act. The agent must be aware of what she is doing, and intend to be doing it, before she is in a position to intend to achieve some goal or other. While it is essential to an intentional act that there be an intention *for* that act, there need not be an intention *of* every intentional act. A relatively idle act like scratching one's head when it doesn't itch, or plucking a blade of grass can be done on purpose without having a further purpose.

Since we have allowed the possibility of purposive acts that aren't intentional, we should probably distinguish two kinds of purposes that can be associated with an act. The purpose *of* an act is what we usually have in mind when we speak of purposes. We can also recognize the purpose *for* an act; this purpose determines the kind of act the agent is performing or trying to perform. It would be convenient to say that an act is done on purpose if the agent has a purpose for the act, regardless of whether the agent is aware of this purpose, but this appears to conflict with ordinary usage. When we accuse someone of doing something on purpose, we normally mean that he acted intentionally. Even if it were correct to say the plant turned in order to face the sun, we wouldn't say the plant acted on purpose.

An act can be purposive without being intentional if the agent lacks awareness. But purposive acts can fail to be intentional when the subject has awareness. The owner of sensory awareness need not be *self-conscious*. To be self-conscious is to be aware of oneself as having experiences and doing things. Sensory awareness is awareness of objects with various sensible features. The subject is aware of its body and neighboring objects. The subject can be aware of aches, pains, and tickles in various limbs. It can be aware of parts of its body, or the whole body, being in motion. Sensory awareness does not include awareness of the subject as *doing* the moving. It seems entirely possible that an animal which experienced sensory awareness might fail to be self-conscious. Such an animal would act purposively, but would not be a position to act intentionally. It isn't even clear that the self-conscious agent must be capable of performing intentional acts. For to act intentionally, the agent must be aware of what she is doing. There are two senses in which we speak of an agent being aware of something. In the first sense, our word for the object of the agent's awareness need not express a concept the agent understands. A member of a newly discovered tribe in the South American jungles might see a radio without knowing what it is. The native is aware of the radio, but not of its being a radio. In the second sense, we speak of awareness of what a thing is. The agent who performs an intentional act must be aware of what she is doing in the sense of knowing what this is. Such awareness is *conceptual* awareness. To be conceptually aware of doing such and such, one needs a concept of such and such, and must view her action in the light of this concept.

To act intentionally, an agent must be capable of conceptual, propositional thinking. But even agents who can think propositionally will perform some nonintentional purposive actions. We conceive sensing as acting. I see things, and I am aware of seeing them—I am aware of myself as seeing them. I also have the concept of seeing and I experience my own seeing with respect to this concept. My seeing is purposive, which (fact) I am aware of. But the conceptual awareness of the purposive character of the activity of seeing is not sufficient to render this activity intentional. For I was seeing before I learned to think conceptually. I simply found myself to be seeing, and I found my seeing to have a certain character, as well as learning to intentionally direct my seeing. For an act to be intentional, the self-conscious intention I give to the act must be what makes it to be the particular act and kind of act that it is. But seeing is seeing regardless of anyone's intentions. As breathing is breathing, purposive but not intentional.

The two intentions, and the two purposes, associated with an act or activity give us two kinds of trying. An agent can try both to realize the intention of her act and to realize the intention for her act. The person who intends to swim but only flounders is (merely) trying to swim. The person who actually swims is also trying (successfully) to swim. She may also be trying to reach the raft, or to reach the other side of the river. The two intentions/purposes also give slightly different concepts of success (and failure). For an agent to be successful in performing an act, she must achieve the purpose of the act. She can do this well or poorly, she can just barely succeed or succeed with ease, but to be successful is simply to reach the goal. We don't so often speak of success when a person achieves her purpose for an act. (But we can. "After weeks of trying, Mary finally succeeded in swimming.") Instead we speak of performing the act correctly, or in the right way. We do commonly speak of failure when the agent does not realize the purpose for her act.

Because intentional acts require agents to have some conception of what they are doing, intentional acts are the purposive acts we understand best. Most of our act-concepts are suited to intentional acts. We understand purposive acts that aren't intentional by omitting features from our understanding of intentional acts. We even understand some nonpurposive events on the model of intentional acts with features omitted. If Ray falls asleep while driving, and his car leaves the road and strikes a small tree, we will describe Ray as hitting the tree with his car, just as he might hit a ball with a racquet. The tree isn't simply flattened as a result of its contact with the car, but the event is something Ray *did*.

Even though intentional acts are a subcategory of purposive acts, we cannot noncircularly account for the difference between intentional acts and other purposive acts. For we first understand intentional acts, and derive our understanding of purposive acts from this more fundamental understanding. If there is to be an intentional act, the agent must have a conscious awareness of her purpose for the act—a conscious awareness of what she is doing or trying to do, she must act with this awareness, and her conceptual awareness of this purpose must explain the occurrence of the act. She performs this act because this is her intention, her intention *for* the act, although other intentions and goals will usually be part of the picture.

We cannot always tell by looking that an agent has performed an intentional or purposive act. Even if we are confident that the agent is acting purposively, we cannot always tell the purpose for the act or the purpose of the act. The purposive and intentional features of an act are not directly observable—they are not sensible features. Since we can't observe purposive and intentional features, we can provide a description of an act which fails to reveal that the act is intentional or purposive. A *brute-fact* description is one that does not give any purposive features. A brute-fact description of an intentional act might be sufficiently complete that one could imitate or copy the act, though the imitation would have different purposive characters from the original. This is like a description of a picture that is sufficient for making an exact copy of the picture, but does not reveal that the picture *is* a picture. (In constructing the exact copy it wouldn't be necessary for the agent to know that it was a picture being copied, but the copy would be suitable for being used to represent.)

The possibility of giving detailed brute-fact descriptions of purposive and intentional acts has seemed to some philosophers a reason for denying either the reality or the importance of purposes and intentions. It makes little sense to deny their reality, since the denial is itself an intentional act. It might seem to make more sense to deny the importance of intentional and purposive acts, especially vis-à-vis a scientific account of things; I will later discuss some attempts to deny their importance. Other philosophers have objected to intentional acts because the same act can be intentional under one description but not intentional under another. (Mary's trying to swim is intentional, her floundering in the water is unintentional.) This suggests that the category of intentional acts is somehow spurious. But not every feature of an intentional act is intended. Citing unintended features of an intentional act doesn't undermine the act's intentional character. Nor does a brute-fact description of human behavior provide an adequate account of that behavior. Purposes and intentions, success and failure are essential features of the human condition. We need to understand these features, not pretend that they are of no account.

Although intentional and purposive features are real characters of acts, Fodor and others have suggested that these features are not causally effective. Of course, it isn't features that cause effects, it is things which possess features. The acts which possess purposive features (and which also possess brute-fact features) are causally effective. To understand how a feature might possess or lack causal efficacy, we need to consider causal laws and causal explanations. The features that "come into" a causal law or that figure in a causal explanation are causally efficacious. Since causal explanations are fundamentally different from purposive explanations, and the two kinds of explanations seem to be incompatible when it comes to explaining a single event, it may well be that knowing the purposive features of an act cannot help us understand (or predict) the effects produced by that act. If this is so, the importance of purposive features with respect to scientific explanation will depend on whether there can be a complete, correct, and completely causal account of the world minus its purposive features.

3. Complex Intentional Acts

In investigating purposive acts and their relations to one another, we will focus on intentional acts. And we will presume that purposive acts in general resemble intentional acts in all respects that don't involve the more-than-purposive aspect of intentional acts.

When an act with a purpose succeeds, we can often use our expression for the purpose to form a label for the agent's act. When Chuck flips the switch, his purpose is *to turn on the lights*. If his flipping causes the lights to go on, then Chuck has performed the act of *turning on the lights*. But flipping the switch is not the same act as turning on the lights. Both flipping the switch and turning on the lights are intentional acts. The intention *of* the first act is Chuck's intention *for* the second act. The flipping is, in part, constitutive of the turning on. But there is another constituent: The causal process initiated by the flipping, which culminates in the lights going on. The flipping "points" toward the event of the lights going on—this is a *completing event* with respect to the flipping.

Chuck's switch flipping is different from Jorge's playing tennis, which we considered earlier. Jorge plays tennis in order to gain enjoyment. He can play tennis for this purpose without enjoying it. But if he succeeds, if he enjoys his tennis match, the playing is the same activity as the enjoying. Chuck flips the switch in order to turn on the lights. Chuck can flip the switch for this purpose without the lights going on. But if Chuck succeeds, his flipping is not the same act as his turning on the lights. For Chuck's act initiates a causal process which results in his purpose being achieved, while Jorge's activity does not initiate a process which culminates in a later enjoyment event—Jorge simply enjoys his tennis match.

When agent *A* performs act *X* in order to obtain *Y*, and does obtain *Y*, then performing *X* is a *component* of obtaining *Y*. The complex act *obtaining Y* must contain another component than *X*, for otherwise performing *X* would be the same act as obtaining *Y*. The other component need not be an intentional act. However, some complex intentional acts do contain two component acts. Jane, who is target shooting, might act like this: Jane holds the rifle steady, taking careful aim in order to hit the bull's-eye. And Jane squeezes the trigger with a slow, steady motion in order to hit the bull's-eye. As Jane conceives of what she is doing, she performs two distinct intentional acts at the same time, with a common purpose. The aiming and the squeezing, together, initiate a causal process which culminates in the bullet striking the bull's-eye. (The process continues as the bullet passes through the target and becomes imbedded in the dirt mound behind the target, but this continuation isn't part of Jane's intentional act of hitting the bull's-eye.) Jane's complex act of hitting the bull's-eye has two intentional act components and one causal sequence component.

A philosopher I know claims that it is senseless to speak of one act being a component of another. As a follower of Wittgenstein, he probably thinks his claim reflects the "logical grammar" of the way we speak. But I am not now trying to conform to or capture ordinary usage. I am developing a theory and conceptual framework for purposive and intentional acts, and my conception of the relations between intentional acts is a novel one. It is both helpful and enlightening to conceive Chuck's switch-flipping as a constituent of his turning on the lights. No further argument is required to defend the practice.

If an expression for the purpose of act *X* can be used to form a name for act *Y*, I will say (informally) that *Y* is *defined by* the purpose of *X*, or by the purpose expression for *X*. If act *X* has a purpose which defines act *Y*, and *Y* has a purpose of its own, that purpose is also a purpose of *X*. Intentional acts often have several purposes, but we can distinguish these as immediate and remote. Jane's immediate purpose for taking careful aim and squeezing the trigger is *to hit the bull's-eye*. If she hit the bull's-eye in order to please her father, an army officer, the purpose *to please her father* is a (slightly) remote purpose of the first two acts.

It will be important later to have a scheme for representing complex acts and their components. I will use the following for the light switch act:

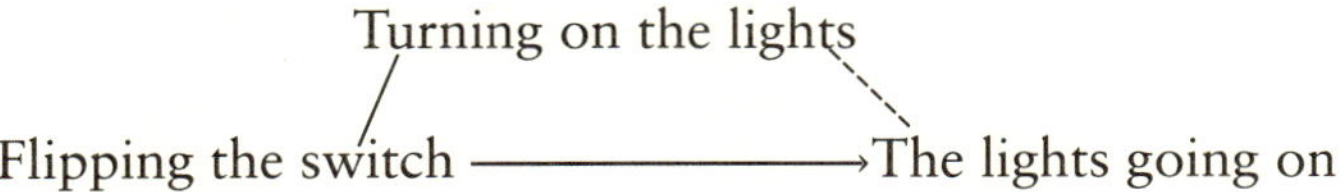

The act labelled by the top node is the complex act. The lower nodes label components of the complex act. The label for a component whose purpose defines the complex is connected by a solid line to the label for the complex act. The flipping which is directed toward the event of the lights going on is *completed* by that event. The flipping is a *completable* act and the lights going on is the *completing event* for that act. In diagrams, an arrow will connect the label for a completable act to the label for its completing event. In this case, the arrow might also be taken to represent the causal process initiated by Chuck's flipping the switch. But completable acts are not always linked by such processes to their events. Since the completing event brings to a close Chuck's act of turning on the lights, and this event is also a component of Chuck's act, a line connects the label for this event to the top node. The use of a broken rather than a solid line indicates that the completing event is not itself an act whose purpose defines the complex.

In the diagrams, left-to-right order corresponds to temporal order for temporally distinct acts. An arbitrary order is used for simultaneous acts. Jane's target shooting act has this structure:

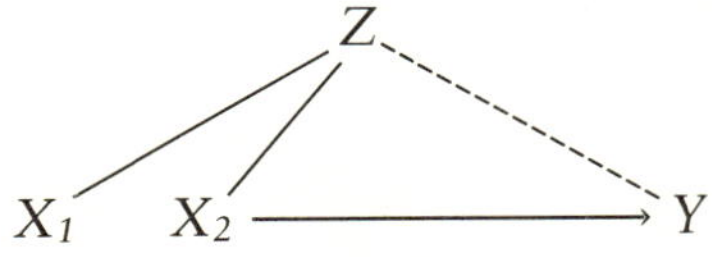

If Jane shoots at the bull's-eye and misses, we will treat her missing as an act she has performed. But unless she missed on purpose, her missing isn't an intentional act. We won't be concerned to analyze or diagram such acts.

If *Z* is a complex intentional act, and *Y* is a component of *Z* whose purpose defines *Z*, then *Y* can be either a simple or a complex intentional act. A simple intentional act might actually be quite complicated, and have several parts. For a simple intentional act is merely one which contains no intentional components whose purpose defines that act. If *Z* has a complex component, we might get an act with a structure like this:

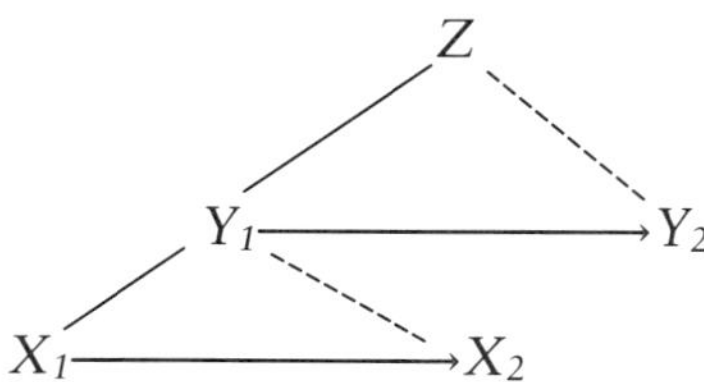

And, then, X_1 might itself be complex, or *Z*'s purpose define still another act.

The examples considered so far are acts intended to cause a completing event. Let us consider somewhat different complex acts. Suppose Miriam mails a letter to her parents in order to get them to send her money. Miriam's act is completeable, pointing toward the completing event of her parents sending money. If she is successful, it would be conversationally acceptable to describe Miriam as causing her parents to send money. But I want to save the word 'cause' for mechanical causality as I described this earlier. And I will leave open the possibility of there being other ways to bring about events than causing them. When Miriam's parents give in and send the money, their action should receive an intentional rather than a causal explanation. Although Miriam didn't cause her parents to send her the money, I am perfectly content to say that she *got* them to do it. To represent Miriam's act, we use the same form of diagram as we did for the earlier acts:

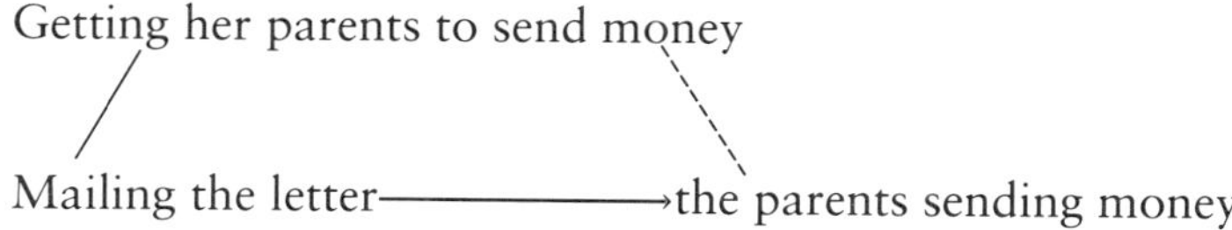

In this case, the arrow doesn't represent a causal process. Miriam's act *does* initiate a process, but it is a process which contains a mixture of causal and purposive ingredients. The intended *outcome* of the process is its completing event. Although Miriam's parents perform an intentional act when they send her money, the purpose of the parents' act does not define Miriam's complex act. So a dotted line connects the label for the parents' act to the upper node.

Now suppose that Karen runs in a race in order to win it, and she does win it. Her running is more naturally described as an activity than as an act, but the activity has the purpose *to win*. The running is a completeable activity, and winning (= crossing the finish line ahead of the other competitors, without cheating or being otherwise disqualified) is a completing event. In this case, the running does not initiate some further process which leads to the winning. The running is itself the process which culminates in (which *becomes*) winning. But now we have some difficulty identifying the complex act (activity) and its components. Since Karen runs (as hard as she can) in order to win, we might expect winning to be a complex act. But winning is the event which completes the running, not an act which has the running as a constituent. To represent this activity we need to supplement ordinary language:

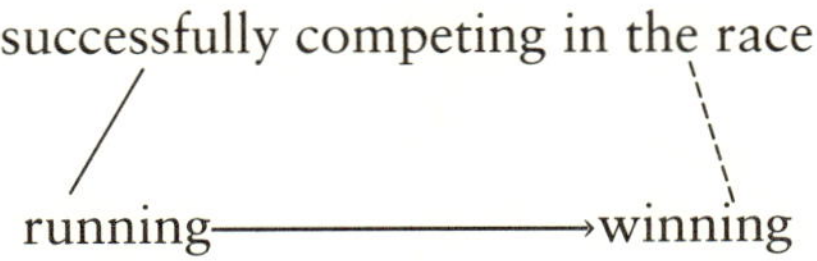

We don't have a convenient short expression for competing successfully. Instead we make do with the two expressions 'running' and 'winning'. The winning is really the completing event. But Karen doesn't get this event to occur, she performs it. We have used the completing-event expression in place of an expression for the complex act (activity).

The complex acts we have considered have all had component acts which initiate (or constitute) a single process designed to bring about the completing event. But there might be complex acts in which distinct processes lead to a completing event. Suppose Miriam, in order to get her parents to send money, first sends them a letter. After enough time has elapsed for the letter to reach her parents, Miriam reinforces the letter with a (collect) telephone call. The intention of the letter is the same as the intention of the phone call, to get the parents to send money. But unlike the two acts which make up Jane's target shooting, these two acts work on Miriam's parents independently. If they are both factors in getting the parents to send money, we will represent Miriam's act like this:

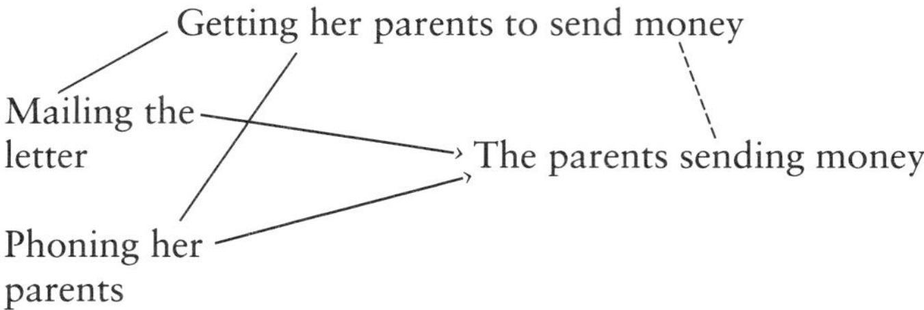

If an act is its own end, the intention for the act is the same as the intention of the act. In that case, the act isn't a component of a further act. We don't use a diagram to represent the relation between an act which is its own end and itself. But the act which is its own end may have various components. When Michelle skis down the hill in order to enjoy skiing down the hill, her run will have various maneuvers as components. But the whole trip down the hill is not a constituent of a further enjoying act.

4. Enabling Acts

The complex acts we have considered contain completable acts or activities and completing events as components; they also contain the processes or sequences which lead up to these events. Component acts belong to acts which they "define" by their purposes, and they "point to" their completing events. But there are other relations between intentional acts. Recall Chuck and the lights. Chuck flipped the switch in order to turn on the lights. His act was successful: he turned on the lights. But why did Chuck do this? Because Chuck wanted to read, and having the lights on was helpful (perhaps essential) to this end.

Although it would be conversationally acceptable to say that Chuck turned on the lights in order to read, this description does not fit the theory/conception being developed. In our current technical usage, this would mean that *to read* was Chuck's purpose for turning on the lights, and that the turning on was a component of the reading.

But turning on the lights sets the stage for reading. It facilitates or enables the reading, it isn't constitutive of reading. We will recognize *enabling acts* as a special category of intentional (and purposive) acts. And we will understand enabling to include merely facilitating as well as literally making possible. Turning on the lights is an enabling act. The reading is enabled by turning on the lights. Chuck had an intention for his act of turning on the lights, but we will say there is no intention of the act. Incompletely stated, Chuck's intention for his act is *to turn on the lights*. A more complete statement is *to turn on the lights, enabling himself to read*. Chuck's turning on the lights is not an act with a purpose, but it does have a goal: reading. Any (further) goal of the reading will also be a goal of turning on the lights.

The way Chuck's act of turning on the lights is directed toward his goal of reading has some similarity to the way his flipping is directed to the event of the lights going on. But his turning on the lights is not a completable act. In turning on the lights, Chuck is not trying to bring about his reading or to get himself to read. If Chuck's reading has some further goal, his turning on and his reading may go to make up some larger activity, but this is not a complex defined by their common purpose. Suppose Chuck is preparing for the class he will teach tomorrow. By reading (completing) chapter 7 in the text, Chuck is preparing for class. So is he when he outlines his lecture and photocopies a handout. The various preparatory acts and activities constitute preparing for class—both the turning on and the reading are preparing for tomorrow's class, where the preparing is broadly conceived. But Chuck prepares in different respects, and prepares for different aspects of teaching. The different preparatory acts and activities are so many enabling acts which put Chuck in a position to teach effectively tomorrow.

One act may facilitate or make possible a second act without the agent having this in mind. In such a case the first act will not be counted as an intentional enabling act. For the agent's intention for such an act must be to make possible a further act or range of acts. The goal of the enabling act must be the agent's goal at the time she performs the act. This goal may be specific or vague. Chuck turns on the lights to enable/facilitate his reading chapter 7 of the text for his course. Someone else might turn on the lights to enable herself to read without having anything definite in mind. She might also turn them on to enable herself to perform actions she will decide on later. Whatever acts she chooses will be acts enabled by her turning on the lights. But the specific goals of these later acts are not directly associated with the enabling act.

Because of the similarity between the way Chuck's flipping the switch "points" to the event of the lights going on and the way his turning on the lights is directed to his reading, we will represent his illumination and his reading like this:

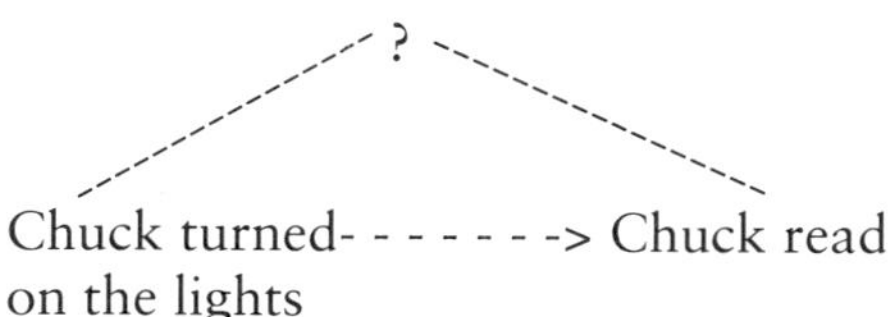

The broken-line arrow distinguishes the enabling relation from the relation between a completable act and the completing event it brings about or contributes to bringing about. That broken lines connect the lower nodes to the upper node indicates that the two lower acts don't have a purpose which defines an act with these two components. But it isn't clear what expression should replace the question mark. The combination of turning on and reading does not constitute a single intentional act, but it can be counted as an activity in the same way that building a house is an activity. Since both the turning on the lights and the reading are ingredients of Chuck's preparing for tomorrow's class, we will replace the question mark with a label for his preparations:

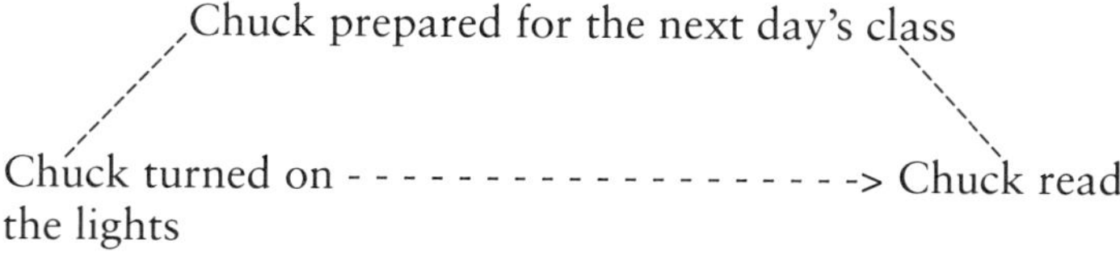

The turning on the lights and the reading are ingredients of Chuck's preparing. In doing these things, he *is* preparing for class. The diagram is not to be understood as showing these two components to exhaust Chuck's preparations. Chuck's turning on the lights enables Chuck's reading, and Chuck's reading enables his teaching. Both the reading and the teaching may also depend on further enabling acts.

The diagram above gives a relatively complete analysis of some of Chuck's activity of preparing for class. An abbreviated representation will be constructed as follows:

Chuck read

Chuck turned on the lights

The abbreviated form does not indicate the activity composed of the enabled and enabling acts, but we frequently don't need to name the activity. Any purpose of the activity will be a purpose of the enabled act.

Although an enabling act may have a vague goal, this goal must be realized by specific, detailed acts. If Miriam turns on the lights so that she can see to do whatever she later chooses to do, and then chooses to write a letter to her parents, the turning on enables her letter writing. But the following representation seems misleading:

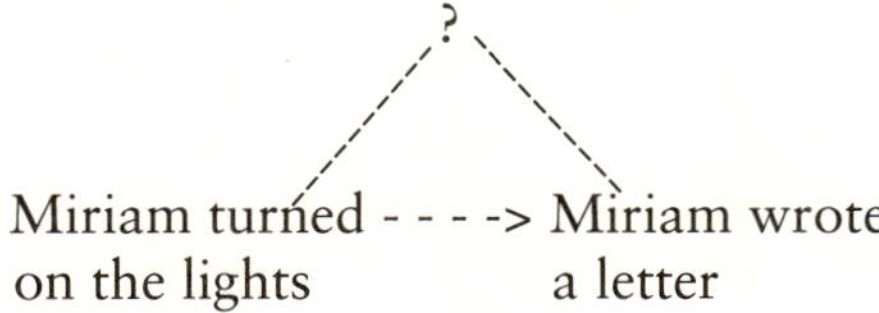

The arrow can appear to suggest that Miriam was thinking about writing when she turned on the lights. To cancel that suggestion, we might leave the broken line connecting the enabling and enabled acts, but omit the arrowhead, or adopt some other notational device. It is harder than in Chuck's case to think of a suitable replacement for the question mark. Although we might describe what Miriam is up to as preparing to communicate with her parents, we could as well say that the enabling and enabled acts don't add up to a single intentional activity.

5. A Third Structural Relation

The relation between a component act and the complex act defined by the component's purpose, and the relation between an enabling act and the enabled act are fundamental relations linking intentional (and purposive) acts. I will call them *structural relations*, although only the relation between a component act and the act defined by the component's purpose is constitutive of a complex act. (In this case, the structural relation provides the structure, or part of it, to the complex act.) There is a third structural relation linking intentional (and purposive) acts.

For an example of this third relation, consider the following situation. Marsha sells real estate, and conducts much of her business by telephone. At a motivational lecture sponsored by her firm, Marsha learned that a cheerful, confident tone of voice is important in doing business over the phone. The lecturer advised his audience to make a conscious effort to smile while talking on the phone, because this will help them to come across as confident and cheerful. At the moment, Marsha is talking with Brian Smith, and is trying to persuade Brian to give her the listing for his house. As she talks, Marsha deliberately, rather self-consciously, smiles.

Marsha is talking to Brian Smith in order to persuade him. If she does persuade him, and this conversation helps, then it is a component of Marsha's persuading Brian. But what about the smiling? Marsha is smiling on purpose—she doesn't smile as a matter of course, she is aware of smiling, and intends to be doing it. Marsha's smiling is intended by Marsha to give her talking a special character. This is her intention *for* the smiling. The intention *of* the smiling is the same as the intention of the talking, *to persuade Brian Smith to let Marsha list his house*. Marsha's smiling is not an act (activity) on an equal footing with her talking. In case this conversation persuades Brian, the talking and the smiling will not be separate components of persuading him. It is Marsha's talking-with-its-special-character that persuades Brian.

Marsha's talking is one activity. Her smiling is another. But the smiling serves to give a special character to the talking. It is the talking with its character that is effective or not. It is the talking with its character than can be a component of further acts. The third structural relation links an intentional act which gives (and is intended to) a special character to the intentional act which receives the character. I will represent Marsha's activity like this:

Marsha talked to Brian Smith (+ Marsha smiled)

In case Marsha is successful, we have:

```
          Marsha persuaded B. Smith to let her list his house
           /                                               \
          /                                                 \
Marsha talked to (+ Marsha smiled)→Brian agreed to let
Brian Smith                          Marsha list his house
```

When one act is performed to give a special character to another, the act with its character is a complex act. Both the character giving act and the character receiving act are components of the complex. The case where one act is performed to give a special character to another act will turn out to be important to some linguistic acts. But an act which is given a special character on purpose need not receive this character from a separate act. Suppose Victor turns on the radio early in the morning in order to learn if school has been cancelled because of the snowstorm. His immediate purpose is to learn whether school is closed. Victor turns the radio on at a low volume because he doesn't want to wake his wife. The act of turning on the radio has the special character of being a low-volume turning-on. Victor doesn't perform a separate act to give his turning on its special character. His turning the radio on low is a simple intentional act. But Victor has a different reason for turning on the radio than he has for turning it on low. The intention of this turning on the radio is one thing: to learn whether school is cancelled, and the intention of his giving the turning on its low-volume character is something else: to not disturb his wife. (This is a completable act which is completed by the "event" of his wife's staying asleep.)

When an act is performed for a certain purpose (this is the purpose of the act) and is given a special character on purpose, this character may contribute to the purpose of the act. The purpose of the act with its intended character is the purpose of the act considered apart from this character. But when the purpose associated with the character is different from the purpose of the act considered apart from the character, the situation is more complicated. In the case of Victor and the radio, both of his purposes are purposes of his act of turning on the radio. Both purposes are features of this act. But some features belong to objects apart from the objects' other features, and some features characterize objects-with-features—temporal properties and relations are like this. The cherry-with-the-property-green precedes that cherry-with-the-property-red. The property of being low and the property of having the purpose *to learn whether school is closed* characterize Victor's act of turning on the radio. The purpose *to not disturb Victor's wife* is a feature of the turning-on-with-its-property-of-being-low.

An act which gets a special character on purpose need not have the character bestowed by a separate act. But if one act is performed to give a special character to a second act, the intention *for* the character-giving act is *to give that character*. There is not a distinct intention *of* the character-giving act. Instead there is an intention of the character receiving act-with-its-special-character. What would have been the intention of Marsha's smiling is the intention of her talking while smiling.

The possibility of performing an act for one reason and providing that act with a special character for a different reason reveals that there are (at least) two ways in which an intentional act can have multiple purposes—there are two ways in which there can be more than one intention *of* an act. The first way involves an act which is (intended to be) a component of a second act, which second act is a component of a third act. For if we do *X* in order to obtain *Y*, and obtain *Y* in order to accomplish *Z*, then *X* has both the purpose *to obtain Y* and the purpose *to accomplish Z*. Any further purpose of *Z* will also be a purpose of *X*. When an act has multiple purposes in this way, the purposes form a chain. One purpose will be the *immediate* purpose of the act, and the other purposes will be more and more remote. The act with multiple purposes need not be successful. If it is not, the multiple-purpose act will not be a component of further acts defined by its purposes. If the act is entirely successful, it will be an *immediate* component of the act defined by its immediate purpose. It will also be a component of the act defined by the immediate purpose of the act in which it is an immediate component. And so on. When an intentional act has a chain of purposes, it seems likely that the chain will be relatively short. A person can only have so many things in mind. The last purpose in the chain might be one which defines (one which is *suited* to define) an act which is its own end. It could also be a purpose which defines an enabling act.

The second way in which an act can have multiple purposes is a way of having more than one immediate purpose. An act might simply be one which (on purpose) kills two birds with one stone. But more commonly a basic act will be performed to achieve one immediate purpose (one chain of purposes) while that act is performed with a special character in order to achieve a different immediate purpose. As in the case of Victor turning on the radio.

The three structural relations that I have explained are the most fundamental relations linking intentional acts. Understanding these relations and their distinctive characters is essential for understanding and analyzing intentional acts. I have no argument to the effect that there are only three such relations. But I am aware of no further structural relations, and I have found these three to be sufficient for my analyses of intentional acts and activities.

6. Two Kinds of Explanations

In this chapter, I have developed a rudimentary theory/conceptual framework for intentional and purposive acts. It provides resources for analyzing and representing acts and their relations. There are three fundamental structural relations and two kinds of intentions/purposes. The three structural relations have distinctive representations. Acts of great complexity result from combining simple acts by these relations, and the tree diagrams perspicuously represent the structures of the complex acts.

The present theoretical understanding of purposive and intentional acts is different in important respects from the understanding provided by typical scientific theories. Unlike a theory in physics or chemistry, say, the present account lacks predictive power. While we can analyze and understand what someone has done, we aren't in a position to say what he will do next—unless we know his long-range goals and purposes. Even then, our account won't provide very detailed predictions. This difference between the present theory and theories in the physical sciences is to be expected, for there is a fundamental difference between purposive acts and activities on the one hand and mechanical causal processes on the other. This is reflected in the difference between two kinds of explanations: mechanical causal explanations and purposive explanations.

I conjecture that these are *the* fundamental kinds of explanations for events and things in the world we encounter in experience. Mechanical causal explanations—from now on I simply call these causal explanations—make sense of what is going on in terms of what has gone before, while purposive explanations make sense of what is going on in terms of what is (supposed) to come. Not all explanations are exclusively one kind or the other. Some explanations have a mixed character. Purposive explanations frequently make reference to mechanical causal processes. For example, to explain Chuck's turning on the lights, we cite his flipping the switch and the causal process this initiated. We also cite Chuck's intention for his act (to turn on the lights, enabling him to read chapter 7) and the goals of the activity which he enabled. In addition to causal and purposive explanations, some explanations are conceptual. An explanation why the sum of the interior angles of a Euclidean triangle is equal to a straight angle would be conceptual—it might be little different than a demonstration of the statement. (But the fact that the sum of the interior angles is equal to a straight angle is not a thing we encounter in experience.)

A causal explanation gives us understanding of something by relating it to the mechanical causal order (to *a* mechanical causal order?). This order contains various sorts of things, belonging to various ontological categories. There are substantial objects, stuff, events, limits of substantial objects and stuff, properties, relations, and so forth. Most things we know about belong to some such category, though we find things that prove hard to place. For things in virtually every category, we can speak of causes and effects. But the category of events is an especially flexible category. Things in other categories can often either be construed as events or understood as components of events. For a substantial individual or quantity of stuff, we might consider its having or coming to have some feature to be an event. We can even do this with its existing or coming to exist. For properties and relations, we can consider the event of having or coming to have that feature. That causes and effects are events is not something we discover by examining the world. The mechanical causal order is not an independent system which reveals itself to us in experience. Causal concepts are human constructions, produced in order to make sense of the world we encounter in experience. The mechanical causal order involves entities in every category, but in talking about causes and effects we decide, as a matter of convention, to highlight the role of events.

To give a mechanical causal explanation, we must identify an event in which things of certain kinds, perhaps having certain features, come together in a specified manner. Given such an event, the items involved behave in characteristic fashion. It is part of what it takes to be these kinds of items, with the features they possess, to behave in this manner. The causal event necessitates a certain process. We consider the whole process to be the cause's effect. We also single out events in the process and call them effects. In a mechanical causal process, what goes before explains what comes after. Mechanical causes operate impersonally, with a certain inevitability. No intentions or purposes or goals figure in the causal order of things. However, a mechanical cause need not be guaranteed to have an effect. It produces its effect unless something intervenes. If we release an egg six feet above a concrete surface, we will initiate a process which ends with the egg breaking. But the causal event can have its effect frustrated (at least in part) if someone intervenes and catches the egg. And we will understand the mechanical causal order to include statistical behavior. If things of kind *A* have a specifiable tendency to behave ϕ-ly in circumstances of kind *B*, then this *A*'s being in a *B* circumstance is part of the cause of the process in which this *A*'s behaving ϕ-ly is an essential part.

A causal explanation does not always explain one event by citing a preceding event or events which gave rise to it. A causal explanation can cite only laws or principles, and be formal in Aristotle's sense (Kuhn 1977). A causal explanation might call attention to an important contributing factor rather than to a causal sufficient condition. What is characteristic of a causal explanation is that it provides understanding of an object, event, or feature by locating the item to be explained with respect to the causal order. This order is our contribution to the world we encounter in experience. At least, that is the *epistemic* status of the causal order. In experience, we encounter various kinds of objects, and various properties and relations. Some events occur simultaneously, others at different times. We don't experience any compulsion which certain events "employ" in giving rise to other events. But we understand the world to contain objects of various kinds, which exhibit characteristic behaviors essential to—definitive of—objects of those kinds. Our knowledge of objects and their behaviors is conjectural and theoretical. We understand the world, we even experience the world, through the conceptual structures we create to make sense of that world.

In order for cause *A* to explain event *B*, there must be some connection between *A* and *B*. The objects and their features which constitute *A* must be such that they characteristically give rise to a process which includes an event like *B*. For a person who knows the relevant facts about the ingredients of *A*, citing *A* provides a satisfactory explanation of *B*. To a person without such knowledge—the person with an inadequate grasp of the relevant concepts and theories—being told about *A* won't serve to explain *B*. To make that person understand why *B* took place, we need to mention *A* and give information about laws connecting *A*-like events to *B*-like ones. The covering laws (which may be statistical) aren't simply accidental regularities which link loose and separate events. In a successful causal explanation, the covering laws are a priori principles of the relevant frameworks/theories.

Of course, it often happens that we find a law-like correlation between *A*-events and *B*-events, when we don't know of theories/conceptions which explain the correlation. We may endorse a statement of the correlation as true, and say that *A*'s cause *B*'s. But the statement of the correlation won't have an *a priori* status. This situation admits of different possibilities:

1. There may be currently accepted theories/frameworks which do enable us to derive a statement of the correlation, but we haven't figured this out yet. Then the statement is already *a priori*, and *A*'s do cause *B*'s.
2. There may be no currently accepted account which entails the correlation. Our situation is such that we believe, or we ought to believe, that either we are in circumstances (1) or else a theory/conception in which the statement has an *a priori* status will be forthcoming. We believe that the statement *deserves* to be a priori, and that further work will give it that status.

To say that *A* caused *B* is to say that there is or there will/can be an adequate theoretical account of the way things behave and work which connects events of *A*'s kind to events of *B*'s kind so that knowledge of *A* gives us an appropriate understanding of *B*. (This might be an understanding of why *B* had to occur or was likely to occur or occurred in just this fashion.) An adequate theoretical account does not always involve deep or recondite scientific knowledge. A fairly low-level understanding of electricity is sufficient to allow flipping the switch to explain the lights going on. An even lower-level understanding of living things will back up the claim that breaking a chicken's neck causes the chicken's death.

Since a causal explanation depends on conceptual systems we deploy to make sense of experience (and the things encountered in experience), a causal explanation can also be conceptual in the sense that it includes principles of a conceptual framework. The explanation of the interior angles of the Euclidean triangle being equal to a straight angle is conceptual without being causal. But if we explain the approximately elliptical orbits of planets by appealing to principles which are constitutive of our conceptual framework for physical objects and their behavior, we have an explanation that is both causal and conceptual. An explanation of one event which merely cites a preceding event will be causal without being conceptual.

Causal claims are relative to theoretical accounts, actual or potential. Theoretical accounts are artifacts, human creations produced in order to achieve various goals. The primary goal of such accounts is *making sense of the world we encounter in experience*. This making sense contributes to our survival and to our flourishing, but it stands on its own as a goal to be pursued. I conjecture, following Aristotle, that there is a fundamental human need to make sense of things, though in many cases it doesn't seem to be an insistent need—certainly not for most students in my classes. A theoretical account of the causal order is a human creation, but such an account aims at getting things right. Epistemically, causal explanations are prior to causal connections, but metaphysically, ontically, the relation is reversed. An adequate and true theoretical account should reflect the way things are and the way things work. Still, any causal claim or causal conjecture can only be judged by the contribution it makes to our making sense of the world.

7. Purposive Explanations

An explanation provides understanding of the item to be explained. Causal explanations provide understanding in terms of the causal order. Purposive explanations make sense of things with respect to acts, purposes, goals, and structural relations. Although it seems clear that purposive explanations are essentially different from causal explanations, Hume tried to reduce purposive to causal explanations, given his diluted understanding of causes and 'cause'. He did this by locating a decision event or a motivation event prior to each purposive act. Since such events are regularly followed by acts appropriate to the decision or motivation, the prior events could be regarded as causes of those acts. But even with respect to his watered-down conception, Hume's effort is unsuccessful. Motivation events that aren't also decision events will be too loosely connected with their effects to constitute a detailed and specific regularity. Feelings of hunger may be regularly followed by attempts to obtain food. But it seems unlikely that specific sorts of feelings will be followed by specific sorts of attempts to obtain specific sorts of food. And decision events that produce actions will be too closely connected to their effects to suit Hume's account. We can, after all, by analyzing the decision determine what is the effect it aims at. Anyway, Hume's conception of causal explanations and the causal order is unsatisfactory. Causes do "necessitate" their effects—if nothing interferes.

The conceptual framework/theory that we have developed for intentional and purposive acts makes it clear that causal and purposive explanations are different from one another. They are both explanations, but neither is a special case of the other. Purposive explanations provide understanding of things by situating them in the purposive order. We understand actions by knowing what they are and what they aim at. We understand other objects and features in terms of their contributions to purposes and goals. However, we should note that purposive explanations frequently include causal components. In acting purposively, agents exploit the causal order; they do things to cause the effects which they want to occur. The purposive order is not complete and self-contained.

The difference between purposive acts that are and that aren't intentional will be explored in subsequent chapters. For now we can remark that it is awareness that makes the difference. The intentional agent is aware of herself as acting—she acts self-consciously. And the intentional agent is aware of her purpose(s) in acting. An agent that isn't self-conscious couldn't be aware of its purposes, but it is also possible for a self-conscious agent to act for a purpose of which she isn't aware. If an intentional act is performed by a language user, this act has an objective character which we can (in principle) discover. The intentional acts that she performs are determined by her intentions and her conception of what she is doing. Two people apparently going through the same motions may be performing different kinds of acts. Suppose two skiers make turns that appear very much alike. But one of them is an accomplished skier, and the other is still learning. To the accomplished skier, the turn may be a simple intentional act without internal structure. The less accomplished skier has to think about what to do with her poles, how to move her feet (and skis), and ends up performing a number of distinct simple acts which are combined to constitute the turn. There is an objective matter of fact about intentional acts and their structural features when these are performed by the owners of concepts. We might discover what this is by asking the person who acts—if she tells us the truth.

Intentional acts are our paradigm of purposive acts, and intentional explanations are the paradigm of purposive explanations. We understand intentional acts "from the inside." Purposive acts that aren't intentional are only seen "from the outside." In giving purposive explanations for acts that aren't intentional, we delete the agents' understanding of what they are up to from our explanations. We can still utilize the structural relations uncovered in exploring intentional acts. All three relations are suited for linking every kind of purposive act. Explanations of purposive nonintentional acts have a more conjectural character than explanations of intentional acts. For the agent performing a purposive nonintentional act doesn't know the purpose of its act, and so can't tell us the purpose. (A non-language-using agent can't tell us anything.)

A purposive explanation can provide understanding of an act or some feature of the act. We can explain what someone is doing—digging for worms—and why: to go fishing tomorrow morning. We can explain why he is digging so fast. We also provide purposive explanations for objects other than acts, and for features of such objects. Consider these proposed explanations:

1. The metal bar attached to the handle of my lawnmower is there in order to prevent the motor from running when the handle is released.
2. An animal has lungs in order to provide oxygen to its blood.
3. A certain harmless snake is colored similarly to a poisonous snake in order to frighten off potential predators, and so protect the snake.

Purposive explanations of nonacts and their features make sense of these by relating them to some agent's intention for them, or by showing how they contribute to some purposive act or activity. In the case of (1), we have the designer's intention for making the bar part of the lawnmower's design. But I can also achieve my own goal of stopping the motor by letting go of the handle (and bar), on various occasions. So (1) gives a general form of explanation for what I am doing on those occasions. Finally, (1) explains how the bar functions in the purposive activity of using the lawnmower; it explains the bar's contribution to this purposive activity.

Explanation 2 might be intended to give the reason why the animal's designer included lungs in his design. We can understand this explanation, but if we think the animal to be the result of evolutionary processes, we will reject the explanation as misguided. Even someone who believes that evolutionary processes are designed to produce a variety of organisms which have a good fit with their environments will not think that a particular object or feature was introduced to serve some specific purpose. Explanation 2 might also be intended as a functional, nonpurposive explanation. Such an explanation provides understanding of the way an object or feature contributes to the existence or the flourishing of an object or kind of object. It does not give understanding of how the object or feature came to be introduced. However, as a merely functional explanation, (2) is misleading. For the expression 'in order' customarily signals some agent's purpose. It would be more appropriate to say that the (a?) function of lungs is to provide oxygen to the blood.

Explanation 2 can also be used to give the animal's purpose in using its lungs to breathe. If this sounds wrong, one may be thinking of purposes as intentions or, at least, thinking of them as associated with awareness and expectation on the agent's part. But that isn't essential to a purpose. In this example, breathing doesn't *happen* to the animal, the animal *breathes*. Although it breathes automatically and instinctively, in breathing the animal is actively contributing to its own continued existence—by introducing oxygen to the blood.

In the animal lungs example, it would also be possible to regard the lungs as agents, and their activity of breathing as having the purpose of providing oxygen. We don't ordinarily conceive of body parts as agents that perform actions. But this is to some extent arbitrary. We have no absolute standard for determining what is a true agent. It is our conception which determines what are the agents in a given situation. It is unlikely that someone would use explanation 2 to explain what the lungs, regarded as agents, are up to in breathing. But we can imagine circumstances in which that would be the right interpretation.

We can interpret explanation 3 as giving the snake's designer's intention for its color or as an inappropriately phrased merely functional explanation. But we can't sensibly speak of the snake's purpose for being colored as it is. Being colored like that isn't an act or activity. This contrasts with a soldier wearing a camouflage uniform. He can do that on purpose and for some purpose. Similarly, if the snake could change colors like a chameleon, that could be construed as purposive. But the snake simply *is* the color it is, and doesn't come to be that color for a purpose.

Purposive explanations provide us with understanding of certain acts, objects, features, and so on, but they don't normally make clear why things aren't some other way. We can understand that David is digging for worms, which he plans to use for fishing tomorrow, but this doesn't explain why David is digging rather than working on his book, or why David plans to fish tomorrow instead of doing something else. If David considered various alternatives and then chose fishing, we might be able to explain his deliberation and choice. But choosing *A* over *B* and *C* is just one more purposive action, and its explanation is like all the rest. ("*X* chose *A*, from alternatives *A*, *B*, and *C* in order to maximize his short-term pleasure.") However, David's deliberation didn't touch on all the things he might have done. And he may have simply decided to fish without considering alternatives. It is characteristic of purposive explanations that they help us understand what is going on and why, without making clear why things must be this way rather than some other. In contrast, deterministic causal explanations do make clear why things aren't some other way.

Nor do purposive explanations provide us with much in the way of predictive power. Purposive explanations are characteristically "after the fact" explanations. With respect to the future, our understanding of purposive features is more useful for planning than for predicting. But purposive explanations can be supplemented by other principles. We may know that agent *X*, or agents of kind *A*, when in circumstances of kind *B*, always, or almost always, or usually, or often, or occasionally act(s) ϕ-ly. Situations where purposive explanations are employed are not by virtue of this fact situations where accurate predictions are impossible.

We might give a detailed purposive explanation of a particular act or kind of act, and we might give such explanations for sequences of particular acts. But where there are a large number of agents acting purposively, we don't expect to be able to integrate all this activity into a single purposive structure. Maybe God can do this. Maybe Hegel could. But most of us can't, and don't try—it probably isn't possible. A purposive explanation of the activity of a population over a period of time will typically take the form of a narrative. The narrative explains what various agents were up to, and how things worked out. The narrative is characteristic of historical explanations. But this isn't confined to human history; according to Hull (1989), the narrative form is also characteristic of evolutionary biology.

Purposive explanations have a normative character in the sense that these explanations support judgments about success and failure. Causal processes don't succeed or fail. But an act is successful if it achieves its purpose, and fails otherwise. Intentional explanations have a further normative character, for intentional acts are characterized by commitment, while merely purposive acts are not. Failure to honor the commitments of one's intentional acts, which is to act and believe inconsistently or incoherently, is a shortcoming peculiar to intentional agents.

8. Causes or Purposes?

Aristotle's four causes aren't causes in my sense, the mechanical causal sense, of 'cause'. Aristotle's four causes were intended to be the four appropriate explanatory factors for a thing. But he didn't recognize a mechanical causal order. However, an Aristotelian explanation of a physical phenomenon in terms of efficient or formal causes is analogous to a mechanical causal explanation, and an explanation in terms of final causes is analogous to a purposive explanation. It might seem that explanations in terms of final causes just are purposive. But I think Aristotle had a somewhat more general understanding of final causes. Explanations in terms of intentions or purposes *are* explanations in terms of final causes. However, just as intentional explanations are a special case of purposive explanations, so I think Aristotle viewed purposive explanations as a special case of more general, teleological explanations. Not all such explanations involve purposes. It was probably medieval philosophers who construed Aristotle's teleologically ordered universe in terms of God's conscious intentions.

What is most interesting about Aristotle's account with respect to the present discussion is his view that a single thing might admit of four explanations. If we adapted his idea to the present account, we might claim that a single event could have both a causal and a purposive explanation, where each explanation is correct and gives us part of the whole story about the event. Let us consider the extent to which the different kinds of explanations leave room for one another.

We shall begin by asking whether purposive explanations are a special case of some more general, noncausal, type of explanation. We can use 'functional' as a label for this more general category. There do appear to be functional explanations which aren't purposive. Such an explanation would give us understanding of how an object or feature or operation contributes to a thing or kind of thing. With respect to living things, we usually think of a contribution to what is *good* for that thing or kind. I understand the most basic concepts of good and evil to be relative. A thing isn't simply good, it is *good for* X. And what is good for X may be bad for Y. For a living thing, the most fundamental good is existing or continuing to exist in a reasonably healthy condition. It is also good for a species to exist and continue to exist. In the earlier example, the snake's coloring contributes to the continued existence of the snake, which is good for the snake. The "construction" of dandelion seeds and the way these are easily dispersed by the wind contributes to the continued existence of dandelions, which is good for the species. So we have functional explanations for the snake's color and for the construction of dandelion seeds.

In a nonpurposive functional explanation, to give understanding of the contribution something makes to what is good for X, that something must really be good for X. Purposive and intentional explanations are special cases of functional explanations. But in an intentional act, the agent may carry out an action which isn't good for the agent, and isn't good for any other object the agent "favors." A young man, for example, might try to impress a young woman by doing something that is wildly inappropriate. Zack's haircut and the clothes he wears may make Anita think Zack is a real jerk, when they were intended to produce an opposite reaction. A purposive act may not even contribute to achieving its own purpose. For a purposive act aims at what appears good to the agent (though the good aimed at may be for some individual other than the agent), and the agent's act is *supposed* to contribute to that good. With a nonpurposive functional explanation, if what is accomplished isn't really good for the object in question, the explanation wouldn't provide understanding. But that an agent aims at a certain goal is all it takes for the act to *function* as a means to that goal.

While functional explanations are typically invoked with respect to living things and "communities" of them, the same pattern of explanation can be used to explain a contribution to what we don't regard as good or bad. We could give a functional explanation which shows how something contributes to the stability of a certain arrangement of objects, for example.

In moving from intentional to merely purposive acts, we omit the agent's awareness of his purposes. With merely functional explanations, we leave behind all notions of trying, expecting, and awareness. And goals or ends don't figure in merely functional explanations. This last distinguishes nonpurposive functional explanations from the most general kind of teleological explanations envisaged by Aristotle (as I have interpreted him). From Aristotle's perspective, I think it would be a mistake to say that the falling rock is *trying* to reach its natural place. But the rock's motion toward its natural place is its natural motion—and its natural place is the *goal* of its falling motion. On my conception, goals are not essential to the functional explanations of which purposive and intentional explanations are special cases. And I do not think there are goals in the world apart from the goals associated with purposive acts and activities. For Aristotle, the appropriate general class of explanations to which purposive explanations belong is a class of teleological explanations. Recognizing this broader class of explanations constitutes the *Aristotelian alternative* to the present account.

Let us consider whether a nonpurposive functional explanation can "cohabit" with a causal explanation. Functional explanations are characteristically given of machines and their parts and features, of living things and their parts and features, and of communities of living things and their parts and features. A functional explanation of a machine is not a purposive explanation of the machine's operation, for a machine does not act purposively. But functional explanations of machines are relative to the purposes and goals of the machines' designers. A merely functional explanation does not give understanding of how the machine or the part or the feature came to be, but only of the contribution it makes. Similarly, a merely functional explanation of an organism or organic part or feature does not provide understanding how this came into existence, or why, but only of the contribution it makes to the continued existence or the flourishing of an individual organism, an individual ecosystem, or a kind of organism or ecosystem. Such functional explanations are relative to the purposive activity of one or more of the organisms.

Since a functional explanation gives understanding of the contribution a thing makes, but not of how the thing came to be, a functional explanation is surely compatible with a causal explanation of how the thing came to be. This doesn't apply to machines, which result from the purposive activity of human beings. But we might combine mechanical causal explanations of the evolution of organisms with functional explanations of what things are good for. As well as giving understanding of the contributions that things make, functional explanations can show why certain organisms and parts and features are stable. ("Sharks have existed virtually unchanged since long before the appearance of mammals.")

A nonpurposive functional explanation of what something is good for is compatible with a causal explanation of how the something came to be. The something might also functional causally in producing its good effects, although the goodness of the effects belongs to the purposive rather than the causal order. A functional explanation of the contribution made to something not regarded as good or bad might simply be a mechanical causal explanation.

Functional nonpurposive explanations are compatible with both causal explanations and with (functional) purposive explanations. A thing can contribute to purposes and purposive activity without itself acting for a purpose. And a thing can causally contribute to a stable order without introducing a noncausal factor. Although functional explanations subsume purposive explanations and some causal explanations, the category is too abstract to be considered a fundamental category. Functional causal explanations are only superficially similar to merely functional explanations on the purposive side. But causal and purposive explanations *are* fundamental, and fundamentally different.

But what about the compatibility and/or complementarity of causal and purposive explanations? It is clear that intentional and purposive explanations leave room for causal explanations. Consider the earlier example where target-shooting Jane performs two intentional acts with a common purpose. Jane takes careful aim in order to hit the bull's-eye. And she squeezes the trigger with a slow, steady motion in order to hit the bull's-eye. A closer look at what Jane is doing calls for a more detailed description. Jane's squeezing the trigger causes the rifle to fire. She squeezed the trigger in order to cause this firing: Jane fired the rifle. But she didn't simply fire it, Jane fired the rifle in the direction where she was aiming. Jane aimed and squeezed in order to perform a certain kind of firing. She performed this kind of firing in order to hit the bull's-eye. So:

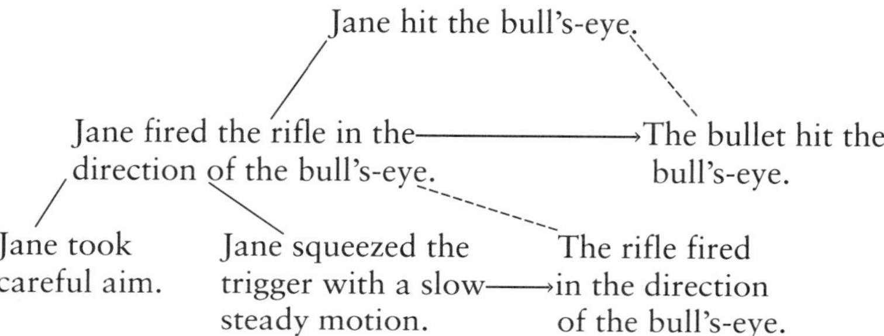

Jane's act of firing the rifle causes the process which includes the bullet striking the bull's-eye. Although Jane deliberately aimed at the target, and intended to hit the bull's-eye, her intention is not essential to the mechanical cause. What matters in the mechanical causal explanation are such things as the construction of the rifle and bullet, the location and orientation of the gun, its distance from the target, and so on. Jane's act of firing the rifle is characterized by her intentions. Those intentions are irrelevant to the mechanical causal explanation of the bullet's hitting the bull's-eye. As well as an intentional act being a cause, an intentional act can incorporate a causal sequence. Jane's act of hitting the bull's-eye is an intentional act. This act is constituted by the completable act of firing the rifle in the appropriate direction, together with the causal process which this initiates, which culminates in the bullet passing through the bull's-eye.

An intentional explanation can cite causal factors, and an intentional act include causal processes. A complete explanation of Jane's target-shooting activity must present both her intentions and the mechanical causes at work. But for Jane to perform her acts, she doesn't need complete knowledge of the causal processes involved. It is enough for her to believe that loading the gun and pulling the trigger will result in the bullet going in the direction she points. An agent can act to bring about a certain effect when causal principles have not been discovered connecting the mechanical causal component of the act to the desired effect. But the agent must believe there is some causal connection (either known or to discovered) if she is to intend to accomplish the effect by performing the action. In acting intentionally, we exploit the mechanical order.

Not all purposive actions are intentional. The agent that performs such an action may not be able to think or even have sensory awareness. But purposive actions of all sorts will typically "take advantage" of the mechanical causal order. Act *A* can be performed in order to accomplish goal *B*, where achieving the goal is an effect of the action. Knowing about the goal makes the agent's action intelligible, while our knowledge of the action may make us understand that achieving the goal was (then) inevitable. Nonintentional purposive explanations also incorporate or presuppose mechanical causal explanations.

A purposive act can be a mechanical cause, but the purposes associated with the act are not "causally operative." Intentions and purposes do not figure in the causal laws which characterize the mechanical causal order. A brute-fact description of a purposive act is sufficient for explaining the causal role of the act. But a brute fact description is incomplete, leaving out real features of the act. Since purposive and intentional explanations are different in kind from mechanical causal explanations, and essentially involve features which are not causally operative, someone might think that intentions and purposes are immaterial components of acts. The mechanical causal order is the physical order. The purposive order has an otherworldly character. But this is a misconception. An act like firing a rifle (for Jane) or catching a mouse (for Jane's cat) is a physical event. The agent's intentions and purposes are not immaterial individuals. They are instead properties of the agent's actions. The distinction physical/nonphysical, or material/immaterial, does not apply to properties and relations. Properties like size and shape are mechanically causally operative, while purposes are not. The causally operative properties and relations are more directly observable than intentions and purposes. But this doesn't make them more real. Indeed, the purposive order is epistemically prior to the causal order, for we introduce causal structure in order to satisfy our need to make sense of experience.

An intentional act isn't caused, because its intentions are constitutive (and characteristic) of the act, and intentions don't belong to the mechanical causal order. Neither are purposive acts caused. A causal explanation makes sense of an event by telling us where it came from, but only in terms of its mechanical causal features. A purposive explanation makes sense of an event by telling us where it is headed. However, intentional and purposive acts do have antecedents. Suppose the phone rings, and Helen answers it. The phone ringing is part of Harry's act of calling Helen. But it isn't an act of Helen's. Her answering the phone is an intentional act performed in response to the phone ringing. It is prompted, even brought about, by the phone ringing. But the ringing phone doesn't cause Helen's answering. Instead, the ringing phone provides an *occasion* for Helen to act. (Helen may or may not rise to this occasion by answering the phone. The occasion is there whether she answers or not.)

To give an intentional explanation of an act, it may not be sufficient to indicate the structure of the act and its purposes and goals. We may also need to identify the occasion which prompted the act. The occasion for an intentional act might be an external event, like the ringing of a phone or doorbell. It might be a perceived need, like hunger. It might be a desire, or a feeling of pain. But for the occasion to play an explanatory role with respect to an intentional act, the agent must be aware of the occasion and its relevant aspects.

The occasion for an intentional act is like a cause in preceding what it helps to explain. But for an occasion, the intentional features of the act are not superfluous. It is the intentional act that is occasioned. This difference between occasions and causes has nothing to do with predictability or determination. Even if there were a kind of occasion that invariably called forth a specific kind of act, the occasion wouldn't thereby become a cause. Occasions and causes belong to the explanatory order. The difference between them is constituted by our different conceptions of them and the different uses we make of them. Purposive acts that aren't intentional can also be occasioned. Animals which may not be self-conscious surely respond to various occasions. However, it is difficult to understand how agents without any kind of awareness could act purposively in response to an occasion. (So if the plant acts purposively in turning toward the sun, and the plant possesses no kind of awareness, then it must always be *try-*

ing to face the sun. Various causal factors would then impede or facilitate the plant's efforts.)

9. The Irreducibility of the Intentional Order

A purposive act can't be given a causal explanation, for the purposive features of such an act do not belong to the mechanical causal order. An event without purposive features can be given a purposive explanation. A purposive explanation will provide us understanding of why the event took place, or why it was given certain features. Such an event might be given both a purposive and a causal explanation, but the two explanations won't give understandings of the same features of the event.

We know that the purposive order is not self-sufficient or self-contained. Purposive explanations incorporate and presuppose mechanical causal explanations. But what about the mechanical causal order? Is it or could it be complete and self-sufficient? Purposive features aside, could we have a mechanical causal account of everything that takes place in the world? Kant thought so. In fact, he thought that *everything* that happens in the world of experience could be given a mechanical causal explanation. Put this way, Kant can't be right. Intentional and purposive acts are performed in the world of experience, and they aren't caused. So let us try to give a careful account of what it might be for the mechanical causal order to be complete and self-contained.

To discuss this adequately, we must distinguish causes that invariably produce their effects from causes that yield their effects x percent of the time—where $x<100$. Let us call these *invariable* and *statistical* causes. To begin with, we will focus on invariable causes and proceed on the assumption that all causes are invariable. And we will consider a fairly abstract example. Suppose act *F* is performed in order to accomplish *Z*. So act *F* is purposive. Investigation reveals that act *F* is constituted by three events: *A*, *B*, and *C*. At least one of these events must have purposive features, since the three events constitute purposive act *F*. Let us distinguish mechanical causal event *A* (*B*, *C*) from plain event *A* (*B*, *C*). The mechanical causal event is the plain event minus its purposive features, if it has any. In the present case, mechanical causal event *A* invariably causes mechanical causal event *B* which, in turn, invariably causes mechanical causal event *C*. (It might be more realistic to say that *A* causes a process which includes mechanical causal events *B*, *C*.) Since *F* is a purposive act with purposive features, so must be *A*. For there is no "room" for purposive features in either *B* or *C*. Once *A* occurs, the mechanical causal order adequately accounts for *B* and *C*. Any purposive features which they contained would be idle. (Act *A* is performed in order to cause the process which includes *B* and *C*. The process initiated by *A*, and extending as far as *C*, is what act *F* amounts to.)

Now consider the question whether mechanical causal event *A* has a mechanical causal explanation (where *A*'s cause is invariable). It isn't necessary that *A* have such an explanation. *A* makes sense (*we* can make sense of *A*) whether or not some previous event causally brings *A* about. The question whether *A* (mechanical causal event *A*) is invariably caused is related to the issue of whether the mechanical causal order could be complete and self-sufficient. If the mechanical causal order were self-contained and self-sufficient, then *A* would have an invariable cause. In cases like this, the initial event would always have such a cause. Which is to say that the mechanical causal components of purposive acts would always have invariable causes.

The scenario for act *F* considered above isn't the only way to approach the issue of whether the mechanical causal order is complete. We could imagine that the progression from *A* through *B* to *C* is simply the mechanical causal aspect of *F*. In that case, *F* wouldn't be constituted (solely) by *A*, *B*, and *C*. The progression from *A* to *C* is simply the "scaffolding" in which purposive features are hung. On this scenario as on the first one, the issue of whether the mechanical causal order is self-sufficient and self-contained depends on whether *A* has an invariable cause.

It isn't possible to prove that the mechanical causal order is complete and self-sufficient. Though if this order isn't self-contained, we might be able to prove that it isn't. Philosophers who oppose uncaused events frequently roll their eyes and wave their hands, claiming that uncaused events must be mysterious and unintelligible. Admitting such events is regarded as tantamount to giving up the attempt to make sense of the world. This is certainly an overreaction if causes are understood to be mechanical causes. For mechanical causal explanations are only one kind of explanation. It would be mysterious and unintelligible to admit events that cannot be explained. Events with purposive but not causal explanations are events we can understand and make sense of.

The claim that the mechanical causal order is complete and self-sufficient has the character of a fundamental framework principle. To the person who adopts a framework constituted (in part) by this principle, the principle will seem obvious. But we don't need the principle in order to be "scientific" or "rational." That a person accepts the principle tells us how that person wants the world to be, how she hopes things will turn out.

Suppose the mechanical causal order were self-contained and self-sufficient, where the causes were invariable. Then, apart from purposive features, it would in principle be possible to provide a mechanical causal explanation of everything that takes place. If things were like this, and we realized it, we could continue to employ purposive language. But we couldn't take it seriously. Such talk must be one of:

1. informal as opposed to "sober and scientific";
2. provisional in that we use it to describe situations for which we haven't yet uncovered the mechanical causal account;
3. indicative of a belief in a designer who constructed (created) the mechanical causal order in such a way that it would realize his intentions.

If the mechanical causal order is complete and self-sufficient, then acts don't have purposes of their own. We attribute purposes to various acts in order to make sense of them. But as we have imagined things, there would be nothing to make sense of by attributing purposes. Purposive explanations would be idle, redundant—worse than that, they would be mistaken. The only purposes there could be in the imagined situation would be a designer's purposes, and these would be dubious in view of the fact that we introduce causal structure to make sense of the world we experience, and would have little reason to introduce additional purposive structure.

Someone may think I am too quick to conclude that causal completeness eliminates the purposive character of acts. Couldn't it simply be the case that the causal and purposive orders coincide? So that for every purposive explanation there is a corresponding causal explanation of the brute-fact component of the purposive act. Why can't there be two equally legitimate ways of looking at a given situation or event, and two equally legitimate kinds of explanation for that situation or event? But if the acts for which we successfully provide purposive explanations were also, when considered apart from their purposive features, fully explicable by means of mechanical causal explanations, this would be a kind of miracle. The parallelism of the two orders would be neither a causal nor a purposive fact, but a different kind of fact, one crying out for an explanation. This parallelism is as striking, and as mysterious, as any parallelism between mind and body in a Cartesian account. Nothing less than divine providence could account for the perfect match between the purposive and causal orders. But this would be a divine providence that undermines the purposive order. Purposes and goals would be "hitchhikers" that attach themselves to the causal order, without playing a role in determining how that order unfolds. A complete, completely sufficient causal order with invariable causes leaves no room for purposes. The purposive order would be a "ghostly" accompaniment to this order.

If we consider statistical causes rather than invariable causes, the situation is more complicated. A statistical causal explanation might very well be the only explanation there is for a given event. But statistical explanations leave "room" for other explanations—even other kinds of explanations. If we know that *A* events bring about *B* events 75 percent of the time, we have some understanding of why this particular *A* event led to that *B* event. But the *A* event might also be equipped with the purpose *to bring about a B event*. The purposive explanation would supplement the causal explanation, so that we understand why this particular *A* event belongs to the majority rather than the minority of *A* events. Purposive explanations could also be appealed to for minority *A* events. There might be a domain in which invariable and statistical causal explanations are available for every event that occurs (are available for the mechanical causal components of every event). It is conceivable that no other explanations are or will be forthcoming. But so long as some causes are statistical rather than invariable, we cannot show that the causal order precludes the purposive order.

I think there are purposive acts that aren't intentional. Dogs and cats don't seem to possess the kind of awareness (self-consciousness) required for acting intentionally. But they certainly act to accomplish this or that goal. They succeed in some of their attempts and fail in others. If all their movements could be adequately and completely explained in causal terms, their purposes and goals would play no role in determining what they do. It could only be a mistake to suppose that they have purposes and goals; they would instead be the kind of automatons Descartes thought they were. If the purposive order is not reducible to the causal order, then there are some events, some motions, which don't have a causal explanation—or, allowing for statistical causes, which don't have a completely causal explanation. There are some motions that occur without an (adequate) antecedent cause, some motions which can only be accounted for in terms of an agent's goals. If it is just living things that act for purposes, and living things are (ultimately) composed of nonliving components whose behavior is completely a matter of causal principles, it is a puzzle to understand/explain how purposive activity "enters" the world. That this is a puzzle is no reason for denying that it takes place.

It seems preposterous to deny that there are purposive nonintentional acts, purposive acts that can't be adequately explained in causal terms. But someone might consistently maintain this position. However, the case is different with intentional acts. It makes no sense at all to suppose that the intentional order can be reduced to the causal order. For we don't discover the causal order, we invent it and introduce it to the world we experience *in order to* make sense of that world and our experience of it. If we are right, the causal order is there independently of our invention. But we know about this order only because we have thought it up, and have found that we can appeal to it to make sense of things.

The intentional order does not have a similar status. We are aware of ourselves acting intentionally. We are aware of our intentions and intentional actions from within, we don't just suppose the intentional order so that we can make sense of things. Suggesting that we do is self-defeating, for making sense of experience is itself intentional activity. If the mechanical causal order were complete and self-sufficient with respect to all human acts, then it would in principle be possible for a person to give a causal explanation of her activities at the moment she gives the explanation. If she did this, she wouldn't really explain what she is doing, for intentional acts wouldn't be explained, they would be explained away. She would both explain and fail to explain what she is doing—a clear impossibility.

Epistemologically, the intentional order is prior to the causal order. But it sometimes happens that if *X* is epistemically prior to *Y*, then

Y is prior to *X* in some other sense—perhaps *Y* makes *X* possible, and so is ontologically prior to *X*. It isn't clear whether this is the case with the causal and intentional orders. If we are right in rejecting the Aristotelian alternative to the present account, and if the initial production of living things is entirely brought about by the mechanical causal order, then the causal order will be *historically* prior to the intentional order. (Someone who adopts a religious perspective can hold that the intentional order is ultimately prior even historically, while admitting that in the created world the causal order comes first.) And our intentional acts surely depend on and exploit the causal order. But the very idea of intentional activity doesn't seem to presuppose or demand mechanical causes. At all events, given the irreducible status of the intentional, we are required to admit that there are intentional acts which—when described in mechanical causal terms—don't have invariable causes. They either have no causes at all, or they have statistical causes. If they can be given statistical causal explanations, these explanations will be essentially incomplete. The statistical explanations provide less understanding of the acts than we get from intentional explanations. For the statistical explanations can only show how the causal order leaves "space" for intentional acts and activities.

Even though it isn't possible, I wouldn't say that it is inconceivable that every intentional act has an invariable cause. This impossibility is conceivable in the same sense that time travel is conceivable: there are stories about time travel, and someone could write stories in which all actions have invariable causes. Since it isn't possible, the stories must ultimately be incoherent.

10. Linguistic Acts

There are a great variety of intentional acts. Some intentional acts are performed solely with one's own body, while others require instruments. We use tools to make things and to fix things. We use bats, balls, racquets, and so forth to play various games. We can regard words as tools or implements, even though we make some of them with our bodies, unaided by further utensils. But whether expressions are spoken or written (or thought), we use them to perform various tasks. If we produce the words ourselves, we produce and use them all at once. When we listen with understanding or read, we use someone else's expressions to perform our acts.

An act of using an expression, whether we produce it or simply encounter it, is a *linguistic* act. If we used the words literally, a *speech* act would be the act performed by someone who utters an expression aloud. But I will regard speech acts and linguistic acts as the same. So even a person who thinks with words is performing speech acts, though in such a case I will normally use the more apt expression 'linguistic acts.'

The "reality" of language is not constituted by words, phrases, and sentences, but by the linguistic acts and activities of a language community, together with dispositions and skills for performing these acts. This understanding is unorthodox, for ordinarily a language is taken to be constituted by simple and complex expressions, having syntactic structures and semantic meanings and truth conditions. The language may also contain "hidden" expressions, and rules or principles or procedures for transforming the deeply hidden expressions into those which appear in books and newspapers, and come tripping off people's tongues. We even talk as if language does some things by itself. Expressions mean this or that, for example. So to use language, we must select the expressions which do what we want, and try to get them to serve our further purposes. The fit between the structures and meanings of expressions and the tasks we perform with them is studied in pragmatics. But syntax and semantics are concerned with language before we get our hands on it.

On the present account, neither words nor longer expressions *do* anything. They don't *mean* anything either. It is people who mean things. Linguistic acts are meaningful. A given simple expression will conventionally be used to perform acts with a certain meaning—the meaning of the acts is often attributed to the expression itself. But it is common for expressions, even simple expressions, to be used to perform different kinds of acts, with different meanings. We must distinguish the acts performed from the expressions used.

The primary bearers of (linguistic) meaning are linguistic acts, which are intentional acts. There are simple and complex linguistic acts; acts performed with sentences are typically complex. Complex acts have structures which can be analyzed in terms of the relations we considered earlier. A complex linguistic act is organized by its *semantic structure*. To give a complete semantic account of a complex linguistic act, we must identify and explain the component acts; we must also identify semantic structure and its effects. For someone to understand an expression, simple or complex, is for that person to understand what meaningful acts he can perform with it. The expressions we use don't dictate the acts we can perform; we adapt the expressions to serve our purposes, some of which are semantic.

Linguistic *acts* have semantic features, including structural features. It is linguistic *expressions* that have syntactic features. To be a noun or noun phrase is a syntactic feature of an expression. So are such features as gender, number, case, and word order. Syntactic features serve as clues to the semantic structures of acts of using expressions which have these features. What is commonly understood as syntax lumps together both (what I am calling) genuine syntactic features and semantic structural features. In this book I will be careful to disentangle the two elements of what commonly passes for syntax.

Linguistic acts can be performed by oneself, for oneself, but they are frequently directed by a speaker (or writer) at an audience. The later Wittgenstein was so impressed by the variety of things that can be accomplished in communicating with language that he despaired of finding an "essence" common to all language or linguistic acts. He despaired of there being such an essence. But the variety that Wittgenstein remarked is a variety of kinds of acts that can be performed by means of sentences and longer segments of discourse. There is a considerably smaller number of kinds of acts that can be performed with single expressions, and a relatively small number of ways of combining simple linguistic acts. By fastening on these, we can identify a common core of linguistic acts and activities.

Austin and Searle have been responsible for the modern study of speech acts. Since they are the founders of speech act theory, the way they do/did things has been taken as the right and proper way to proceed. (In much the same way that Frege's work, and his deductive systems, determined how modern logic was to be carried out.) One unfortunate feature of their work is their failure to distinguish a speaker's intention to mean something from his intention to communicate. Indeed, Searle has taken a principle from Grice, and further refined it to constitute an enormously complicated and unsatisfactory explanation of what it is to say something and mean it:

> *S* utters sentence *T* and means it (i.e., means literally what he says) =
>
> *S* utters *T* and
>
> (a) *S* intends (*i*-I) the utterance *U* of *T* to produce in *H* the knowledge (recognition, awareness) that the states of affairs specified by (certain of) the rules of *T* obtain. (Call this effect the illocutionary effect, *IE*.)

(b) *S* intends *U* to produce *IE* by means of the recognition of *i*-I.
(c) *S* intends that *i*-I will be recognized in virtue of (by means of) *H*'s knowledge of (certain of) the rules governing (the elements) of *T*. (Searle 1974, 49[–]50)

The trouble with Searle's analysis is that he is conflating what the speaker means with what the speaker is trying to accomplish in addressing *H*.

A person can produce language and mean what she "says" whether she is talking to someone else, talking out loud to herself, or just thinking with words. Some kinds of linguistic act demand an audience—commands and promises, for example. But saying/thinking a statement can be done at home alone. Even with a command, what a speaker means is different from what she intends to accomplish in making her utterance. And communication is less formidable than Searle suggests. The speaker's complicated intention and the audience's recognition of this intention don't really need to be invoked. The speaker uses her expressions to mean things. She intends to be understood by her audience. But their understanding is constituted by their using her expressions in appropriate ways. Understanding a speaker's statements is doing something with a speaker's words, not looking into her mind, or head.

That an act is directed at an audience is a feature of the act. This feature is connected with the purpose of the act. Knowing the act's purpose is knowing the (speaker's) intention *of* the act. This is not the speaker's intention for the act. In general, when a language user directs her language to an audience, her acts "point" in two directions. She might, for example, use the expression 'Napoleon' to identify the French military leader and emperor. If her identifying act is directed to an audience, she performs the act in order to get her audience to understand her. For her audience to understand her is for her audience to use her utterance to identify Napoleon. So our speaker identifies Napoleon (out loud) in order to get her audience to identify Napoleon. Her communicative act is a completable act. It will be successfully completed by her audience's performing the appropriate act. The speaker has identified Napoleon no matter whether or not her audience understands her. If she does succeed in communicating, she has performed a *consummated* identifying act.

The speaker's identifying act is directed toward her audience. But it is also pointed in another direction: she is concerned to relate this linguistic act to other linguistic acts she has performed or will perform. The speaker may go on to say that Napoleon was a tyrant. She first identifies Napoleon, then acknowledges him to have been a tyrant. As well as being directed to her audience, the speaker's identifying act is directed to her acknowledging act. In performing her identifying act, the speaker attends to, she focuses her attention on, Napoleon. This gives her the subject of her acknowledging act—it *enables* the acknowledging act by providing the subject matter of the act. The speaker's intention *for* her identifying act is that it be an identifying act. But there is more to it: she intends that her act be an identifying act which enables a further acknowledging act. The intention *of* her act is that it will get her audience to understand.

Not all linguistic acts aim at communication. Those that do will normally have (at least) two orientations. To provide an account of language and linguistic acts which accomplishes what traditional studies of syntax and semantics have been looking for, the audience-directed intentions are less important than the intentions which organize linguistic acts with respect to one another. In discussing linguistic acts, I will focus on intralinguistic intentions rather than extralinguistic ones. But the two kinds of intentions don't constitute separate and self-contained systems. It is impossible to achieve a complete understanding of the one kind of intention without considering the other.

11. Coming Up

In the next chapter, I will begin carrying out Kant's strategy (as I understand this), by tracing a way that we might come to learn language to deal with experience. Learning language does not enable us to communicate propositional thoughts which are independent of language. In learning language, we learn to think conceptually and propositionally. It is necessary to trace a path into language and propositional thinking both to show that doing this is possible (as against language of thought theorists), and to show how the ordinary conception (or a cleaned-up version) of experience and its objects is inevitable and inescapable.

What I will say about the way we might come to use language is not intended to provide a detailed account of steps children go through in learning language. My account is based on logical or conceptual analysis, as well as on informal observations, and provides a means to understand both language and experience. If I am successful, I will have provided a framework within which controlled studies of language learning can be carried out. But my account must initially be judged on the basis of the amount of sense it makes of both our mature linguistic practice and the connection between language and experience. Once we know what it is we actually do, and we realize that we weren't always able to do this, we can be sure that there is some process or other by which we have come to be able to do it.

Chapter 6

Learning to Use Language: *Getting Started*

1. Preverbal Experience

The strategy of retaining a cleaned-up version of the ordinary conception of experience and its objects is suggested and supported by taking a close look at language, and the way in which a person can learn to perform linguistic acts. Tracing a path by which a child might gain entry into the language-using community shows how language is based on experience, and how it serves to structure our experience and the world we experience. The phrase 'the world of experience' will be used to label the object and objects we directly encounter in experience. The world of things as they are in themselves is the *real world*. There are disadvantages to this terminology, for our experience is real, and we really encounter the world of experience. But I prefer using plain English expressions to adopting more traditional and abstract terminology. I will take pains to minimize the misleading aspects of my chosen expressions.

The overall goal of our close look at language and language-acquisition is to solve Descartes' Problem, Descartes' whole Problem. I want to understand the connection between experience and thought, especially propositional thought. I want to accommodate belief and knowledge, and to provide an adequate conception of experience and its dependence on or independence from our bodies. That it solves Descartes' Problem will be an important reason to accept the account that gets developed. But, as it turns out, this account explains other phenomena and solves other problems. These successes provide additional reasons to favor this account.

In what follows, I will devote considerable space to showing how the developing account sheds light on other issues than Descartes' Problem. But I will try to retain an overall focus on that problem. I will refrain from discussing some very interesting topics at great length, even though I take delight in exploring those topics. I will restrain my inclination to give detailed analyses of a wide variety of linguistic acts, though some readers may feel that even more restraint would have been in order. And I will not present the philosophy of logic to which this account leads, for that provides enough material for another book.

The language we speak and the concepts we employ are important to the experience we have. But not every experience is affected by language and concepts. Before they learn to talk, children have experience. Animals that never learn to talk have experience. What can their experience be like? How can we describe it? We must use words and concepts to do this. We wish to develop a conception of their experience. But on my view, its owners have no conception of anything. For concepts and conceptions are language-based. No one who hasn't mastered some language has concepts or thinks conceptually.

To conceive preverbal (nonverbal) experience runs the risk of distorting or falsifying this experience. But even apart from this difficulty, it isn't easy to say what preverbal experience is like. For learning to use language transforms experience. Since we can no longer "enjoy" preverbal experience, our attempt to reconstruct it must involve conjectures and hypotheses. These will be guided to some extent by our current conception of experience—which we are in the process of revising. Our mature experience must have some similarity to the experience we had before we began to think conceptually and propositionally.

I will not characterize the subject of preverbal experience as seeing something *to be* the case, or seeing *that* something is the case. I will not credit the subject with any awareness *that* something is one way or another. To begin with, I will simply speak of the *world* of experience. The overall object of the child's or animal's experience is the world of its experience. Various sensible qualities are "housed" in various parts of this world, and the parts are spatially organized. The world of experience changes, develops, in time.

One might wonder whether it is merely occurrences of qualities that are encountered in the world of experience, or whether it is qualified (perhaps 'qualitied' would be a more apt expression) parts of the world. But this conceptual distinction is out of place in describing the world of preverbal experience. Some parts of this world are red, others are green. Some are hard and some are soft. The world of preverbal experience is neither substantial nor phenomenal. To even raise this question is to try to conceive the world of preverbal experience "from the inside." In describing it from the outside, we must not conceive or imagine ourselves as being on the inside.

The owner of preverbal experience can be aware of a red or a hard or a sweet part of the world. She can notice or attend to such a part on the basis of a quality which it possesses, which she is equipped to detect, and does detect. She is aware of both the part of the world and its quality, but it is probably better to say she is aware of the part of the world *with* its quality, or she is aware of the part of the world *being* its quality. She is aware of a part of the world being red, for example. She can do this without judging that part to be red. She attends to a part of the world on the basis of its qualities, but she doesn't simply or separately attend to the qualities.

Some parts of the world of experience have internal spatial structures. The owner of experience can be aware of such a part, and be aware of how the different parts are arranged with respect to one another. She isn't aware simply of the arrangement in abstraction from the arranged elements, she is aware of the elements in their arrangement—she is aware of the elements *being arranged* (this does not mean *in the process of* being arranged). She does not see them to be arranged. It requires a concept to see or judge the objects to be arranged, and our subject does not possess concepts.

The world of preverbal experience has both spatial and temporal structures. Spatially, the owner of experience is aware of *how* parts of the world are situated with respect to one another, she is aware of their *being situated* with respect to each other. Each subject uses her own body as her primary spatial location and frame of reference. A person is normally aware, even without looking, of her body and the way its parts are arranged with respect to one another. The body and its parts provide locations for what is felt from the inside. A feeling of pressure or pain, an itch or a tickle, or warmth or cold can be felt in a hand or a foot. The part of the subject's world which constitutes her right hand is experienced as *being* painful or hot or whatever. The body is a primary location, and its owner can attend to the body or a part without detecting a quality which sets it apart from the rest of the world of her experience. The body itself is a location for feelings from the inside. It is also a reference point for attending to other parts of the world. These parts are in front or in back of, to the right or left of, or near or far from the subject's body. Since the other parts of the world of her experience are located with respect to the subject's body, her body is also located with respect to them. But she will have little occasion to use these other parts as reference points for attending to her own body.

The subject's own body is a part of the world of her experience. It serves as a reference point for constituting other parts. What is directly to the front of a person's body is one spatial part of the world of her experience. This is normally a constantly changing part, especially if she is moving around. As well as attending to her body and to other spatial parts of her world on the basis of their situation with respect to her body, she can also attend to a part on the basis of one or more qualities occurring there. A spatial location (part) can just be empty space. It can also be a discrete object or a quantity of stuff, though from the preverbal subject's point of view it is a location marked by one or more qualities. A spatial location marked by qualities or by an ongoing process can serve as a reference point for attending to parts situated with respect to it; the subject's body is not her *only* spatial reference point. A spatial location marked by its features can have sufficient integrity to move with respect to other parts of the world of experience. When this happens, different parts of the world of experience can come together, or converge, so that they coincide, and they can separate. A multicolored beach ball which moves from left to right in front of a person may constitute a part of her world which for a moment coincides with a directly-to-the-front part of that person's world.

Immediately before and after this, the beach ball part coincides with other locations/parts.

When one spatial part coincides with another, the subject can be aware of this. For the two parts coinciding constitute a single part with different features. The part to which the subject attends might be multicolored, round, and directly in front of her face. To be aware of the one part being all these features *is* to be aware of the ball part of the world coinciding with the directly-in-front-of-her-face part. But the subject's awareness is not static, she is also aware of parts changing.

I will use the word 'situation' for a part of the world being qualified or organized in some way, or for parts being situated in a particular way with respect to one another. The cherry being red (its being red) is a situation, and so is the cherry being on the branch of the tree. A spatial location having a feature constitutes a situation. But situations have features of their own. The cherry being red is a situation which occurs after the situation of the cherry being green. The cherry being green is a situation which has a certain duration, and can be dated. A situation having a feature, or situations being situated with respect to one another constitute further situations.

Those situations which constitute temporal locations are *events*. The cherry being green and the cherry being red are events. So is John being happy on some occasion or the ball being on the table. Events are temporally situated with respect to one another. Some events take place at the same time. Some are earlier or later than others. Some events are temporally included in others, and some temporally overlap others.

Not all situations seem to be events. The event of the cherry's being green precedes the event of the (then ripe) cherry falling from the tree. The being green is situated by precedence with respect to the falling; the two events so situated themselves constitute a situation. But this situation doesn't seem to be an event. For it isn't clear that there is an answer to the question when this situation occurred. It probably isn't important whether we decide to call all situations events, or say instead that some situations are events and others aren't. In any case, situations are constituents of the world of experience, and some situations are constituents of others. Both situations and their components can be objects of attention.

A spatial location described abstractly ("the doorway") doesn't "sound" like a situation or event. But real locations have a variety of features, many of them changing. The location as having those features is a situation which qualifies as an event. "Full-blooded" spatial locations are also temporal locations. An event can be short, even momentary, or quite long. But the temporal locations that figure in the preverbal subject's world are those she is aware of, so most of her events are relatively short-lived. Each subject's primary reference point for situating temporal locations is her present awareness. The things she is aware of at present constitute her "now."

Philosophers who favor phenomenal analyses sometimes claim that the qualities experienced by different senses belong to separate domains which simply develop in tandem. So that the shape that someone sees is not located together with the sensation she has when touching what she is looking at. The feeling and the seeing simply take place at the same time, and she is aware of their temporal coincidence. This understanding falsifies the world of preverbal experience. The different senses experience qualities within a single spatiotemporal framework. The subject of experience can be aware of this yellow part being soft, and this soft part being yellow. The hand which feels hot to her may also be this red part of the world of her experience. She can be aware of this red hand being hot and this hot hand being red. The hand with its qualities is the single focus of her attention.

Each experiencing subject has her own world of preverbal experience. But one person can occupy a place in another person's world. The owner of experience is aware of her own body from the inside. She can also see parts of her body, and can use her hands to feel parts of her body from the outside. She can as well be aware of the part of her world taken up (constituted) by someone else's body. She can attend to the someone else and his activity, she can imitate his movements and sounds, she can interact with him. If both parties are in the preverbal stage of development (or if they are animals that will never learn a language), then their worlds of preverbal experience overlap. They contain some of the same parts.

The preverbal subject is aware of various spatial/temporal locations, and of their being this and that. She can either innately or on the basis of her experience know how to get around in this world. But she doesn't have any beliefs about it. For I understand a belief to find its natural expression in a sentence. If an agent is to believe something, she must be capable of propositional thinking. And propositional thinking requires language or some language-like apparatus. So the owners of preverbal experience are unable to believe anything. But they have a belief substitute. The owners of preverbal experience can have *expectations*. Hearing a sound get progressively louder and closer, a subject can expect to see a part of the world associated with that sound. A cat sneaking up on a bird will expect to catch the bird. Those of us who use language have propositional expectations. I can expect Jane to be meeting me for dinner. And Jane will expect that I will pay. Propositional expectations are simply a subclass of beliefs. But preverbal expectations are not beliefs. They are the most belief-like thing which the preverbal (or nonverbal) subject possesses.

Many philosophers and scientists are quite willing to use 'belief' so that it covers all expectations. But I am concerned to highlight (and understand) the discontinuity between preverbal experience and thought on the one hand, and verbal experience and thought on the other. To simply impose the same words on both the preverbal and the verbal situations is to arbitrarily favor continuity over discontinuity. If it should turn out that the continuity between the preverbal and the verbal is much greater and more important than the discontinuity, this should be a discovery, not a conclusion forced upon us by our terminology.

Since beliefs demand a propositional formulation for their expression, it seems reasonable to refrain from using the word 'belief' to describe the preverbal subject. But expectations don't require this form of expression. As well as expecting that something will occur, we can simply expect a certain kind of experience. I can expect seeing Edwin wearing a blue shirt. Since I am linguistically competent, if I expect this, I will also expect *that* I will see him and *that* he will be wearing a blue shirt. But the primary expectation is an expectation *of* a certain kind of experience, not an expectation *that*. (It is an expectation of a blue-shirted-Edwin experience.) An expectation of a certain kind of experience can be an expectation of an experience at this very moment or in the immediate future, but it can also be of a certain kind of experience with no "due date." A child who is familiar with the family cat might expect certain behavior on the part of the cat. The child expects to witness familiar behavior from the cat, but doesn't expect to experience a specific type of behavior at any particular moment.

2. Perceptual Frameworks

Sense experience as we conceive it is an activity. The subject *uses* her eyes to see, her ears to hear, and so on. No sense organ is required to carry out feeling from the inside, but the subject is *doing* the feeling of what is going on in her body. It remains for us to determine whether the activity that constitutes sensing is part of the causal or the purposive order.

One reason for thinking the activity to be purposive is that the alternative to sensing being purposive is for it to be a causal process. But it isn't plausibly construed as a causal process. We can imagine a device, a computer or a robot, that is so constructed that light received by an optical scanner causes the device to produce the right expressions for the objects reflecting the light to the scanner. The device might behave in ways immensely more sophisticated, appearing to observers to take account of its surroundings and respond in "reasonable" ways. While we can understand how such a device might be designed, we have no idea what it would take to provide the device with sensory awareness. There are just inputs and outputs, causes and effects. And this isn't just a technical limitation. It scarcely seems to make sense to suppose that we could provide the device with sensory awareness. But all of us enjoy sensory awareness, and we think that animals do too. I take the unimaginability of producing an entirely causal robot with sensory awareness to reflect the purposive character of sensory activity, including sensory awareness. Purposive activity can't be caused, or it wouldn't be purposive. The purpose of some activity is where that activity "is headed"; it is a feature the activity possesses, and serves to explain the activity's occurrence. But the purpose *for* some activity is also a feature of the activity and provides a noncausal explanation of the activity's character. Sensory awareness is an activity depending on the agent's purpose for it.

We are actively and directly aware of things in the world. But we sense things in and with our bodies, and our bodies are involved in the causal order. Our ordinary conception doesn't offer a fully worked-out account of how the body functions in sense experience, but it doesn't rule out causal processes playing some roles in experience of the world. However, given this conception, the activity of sensing is "of a piece" with purposive and intentional acting. We do things, intending to enable or facilitate our seeing, hearing, and so on. We respond to our sensing with various acts that the sensing occasions or enables. While the sensing subject may employ and exploit causal processes, her activity in sensing is not causal. A hurricane acts causally in destroying things in its path. Machines in breweries act causally in filling bottles with beer and putting caps on them. Things which act causally are driven by the past and their operation unfolds in the future. But sensory awareness isn't produced by past events, for it is something we do, not something that happens to us. And it doesn't produce effects in the future.

Although sensing is purposive, sensing isn't intentional. For animals not capable of acting intentionally have sense experience, or so we believe. A person isn't consciously aware of all that takes place in sensation, while to act intentionally one must be aware of doing so. And even a subject of sense experience who can act intentionally doesn't intend for her activity to be sensing. It is like breathing; we find ourselves doing it and are perfectly willing to continue. (However, the subject who doesn't hear or see intentionally might intend to listen or look.) An activity is purposive if there is a purpose *for* it. Usually there is also a purpose *of* it. The purpose for sensing would simply be *to be sensorily aware of things*. The immediate purpose of sensing is probably something like: *to satisfy an instinctive need*. There are lots of benefits that an agent gains from sensation, so sensing will contribute to achieving further purposes, like to survive and to flourish. But the "automatic" and instinctive character of sensing suggests that its immediate purpose is less long-range.

The preverbal subject doesn't just experience different objects with their features, she imposes order on these objects. The subject organizes experience so that objects belong to various categories. The subject either begins by experiencing objects as *representative*, or she comes to experience objects this way. She does not experience them as representative of this or that conceptual category, for the perceptual categories are prior to the acquisition of concepts. The subject will simply experience objects as familiar, as *one of these* or *one of those*. We can get some appreciation of what this is like from an experiment in classifying sounds. From a human point of view, an important difference between 'b' sounds and 'd' sounds (between 'buh's and 'duh's) is the different vocal mechanisms we use to produce them. A mechanical device can produce a sequence of sounds that vary along a single dimension, starting with 'b' sounds and ending with 'd's. Listening to these sounds, a person will experience the sounds as of two kinds, with a fairly abrupt transition from one to the other. The sounds at the transition point can be hard to classify, and different people can disagree as to where the transition point occurs, but everyone does begin by hearing 'buh's (by hearing each sound as representative of 'buh') and end by hearing 'duh's. Even though each successive sound in the sequence is different from all the others, we effortlessly experience them as one or the other of just two kinds.

The experiencing subject may be innately endowed with skills for classifying some objects she senses. Such skills as those for "picking up on" horizontal and vertical edges, or on long thin objects and round objects. But whether or not some such skills are innate, the subject will actively develop new skills. For example, research by Jusczyk and Mehler and their colleagues and collaborators shows that babies do not initially distinguish the sounds of different languages. But long before they are understanding language, babies in English-speaking families develop a preference for English statements and English-like nonsense syllables over statements and similar-sounding nonsense syllables from different languages. Babies in Dutch and in Italian-speaking families show a similar preference for Dutch and for Italian.

Skills to use expressions for talking and thinking about the world constitute conceptual frameworks—the subject who has such skills possesses or has mastered conceptual frameworks. The preverbal subject who organizes her experience to experience certain objects as representative does not possess concepts. But we need a name for what it is she has or can do. I will say that being able to experience an object as representative of ϕ's (of 'buh's, say) is to possess the *percept* of a ϕ. Families of percepts constitute *perceptual frameworks*. The skills for organizing the perception of sounds might constitute one perceptual framework, and skills for organizing smells a different framework. Although one can perceive objects as representative without concepts, when a person acquires concepts, this allows her to use representative perceptions to support universal judgments about all objects of the representative kind. One might perceive triangles as representative without possessing the concept *triangle*. After we are in possession of geometric concepts, we can use a representative triangle to determine features belonging to all triangles—features belonging to triangles *as such*.

The preverbal subject's world of experience is constituted by spatial and temporal locations with qualities and relations. The preverbal subject has no basis, and no ability, for making an ontological distinction between locations and objects in them. Some locations are more "spacey" than others, but an empty space can be as much a part of the subject's experience as a solid, substantial object. However, while ontologically an empty space in the subject's experience is on a par with the dog she sees, the percepts she acquires are bound to favor "filled" spaces over empty ones. She will treat this perception as representative of the family dog, but not perceive that empty space as representative. Some parts with features are more interesting/important to the subject than others.

Percepts and perceptual frameworks help the preverbal and the (permanently) nonverbal subject get along in the world of her experience. They are essential for having expectations and are a necessary prerequisite for learning to perform linguistic acts. An actual experience is always particular and detailed. No one can have an expectation of everything that is to take place. The preverbal subject must have expectations of certain *kinds* of experience. To do this, she must be able to experience them as of this or that kind. Perceptual frameworks inform and organize expectations as well as experience. And percepts are needed in order to learn language, because it is essential that one expression can be used on different occasions, both for the same object, as when we use 'John' over and over again for John, and for a variety of objects, as when we use 'red' for various red things. Language users must perceive the different occurrences of one expression as representative of a single kind of utterance (as representative of one another). If the different occurrences of 'red' were not perceived as representative, then it wouldn't be one word 'red' that is used on different occasions to acknowledge things to be of that color.

Once I am linguistically proficient, I can expect that if *A*, then *B*. But the preverbal subject cannot have this kind of conditional expectation. Preverbal counterparts to such expectations are dispositions to have expectations once certain conditions are fulfilled. A preverbal subject can be disposed to expect a *B* experience once an *A* situation occurs. An *A* situation is a "trigger" activating her *B* expectation. Expectations rather than conceptions inform the conscious purposive activity of preverbal/nonverbal subjects. The cat sneaks up on the bird, expecting to catch it. A preverbal/nonverbal subject in a position where she can do *X* or *Y*, who must choose only one of them, can't expect that if she chooses *X*, then *A* and if she chooses *Y*, then *B*. Even if doing *X* would trigger the *A* expectation and doing *Y* would trigger the *B* expectation, she isn't equipped to think about these alternatives. She can choose either to do *X*-with-an-expectation-of-*A* or to do *Y*-with-an-expectation-of-*B*. When confronted with such a choice, the preverbal subject doesn't entertain each alternative, considering its pluses and minuses, before she chooses. She simply attends to parts of the world of her experience, and chooses to act-and-expect in a manner that suits her desires (and fears, etc.). The choice may be instinctive, it may be a choice she has learned to make in situations of this kind, or it may simply be arbitrary.

It isn't appropriate to attribute beliefs to a preverbal subject. Nor is it appropriate to conceive her as making inferences. I understand an inference to be a move from propositional premisses to a propositional conclusion which they support—to a conclusion which the reasoner *thinks* is supported by the premisses. The preverbal subject may have some instinctive expectations, some instinctive dispositions to activate expectations. She may also be equipped with innate procedures for acquiring new expectations on the basis of her experience. But it begs too many questions to say that someone infers her expectations from her experiences, and to regard this as being roughly the same kind of thing that goes on when we conclude that Socrates is mortal because he is a Greek and all Greeks are mortal.

The subject of preverbal experience doesn't have beliefs or make inferences. Another thing she doesn't do is recognize objects as having been previously encountered. A part of her world or a kind of experience can be familiar. She has experienced it before, and has a well-developed set of expectations concerning it. But she hasn't got sufficient conceptual resources to think that this is the *same* part she experienced previously, for she isn't able to think this object *to be* that one. The preverbal subject can't think that this mother part of the world is the same mother she saw an hour ago. But before her mother appears, she can expect to have a mother experience, or a being-fed-by-mother experience, and she can be gratified and pleased to have such an experience. A preverbal subject can't take this part of the world to be one she experienced previously. And she can't take something to be a kind of thing she has experienced previously, though she can have expectations on seeing this kind of thing.

Each subject of preverbal experience has her own world of experience, though the worlds of different subjects often overlap. A preverbal subject's world of experience is a world of present experience, and extends no farther than her current experience. The past is gone and the future hasn't arrived. Existing but not now present objects have no standing in a world of preverbal experience. The subject hasn't got what it takes to believe in currently existing but absent objects. And nonpropositional expectations aren't sufficient to give status to such objects. The moving subject can expect to see new objects as she moves, but she can't expect those objects to be there ahead of time. While on occasion it may seem natural to describe the subject of preverbal experience as looking for an object of which she isn't currently aware, for example an object which she just dropped, this verbal description isn't appropriate for a preverbal subject. That subject can be trying to achieve a certain kind of experience: an object-locating experience. She is acting with the expectation (which may be strong or weak) of having such an experience, but she does not have the missing object in mind.

3. Identifying Parts of the World

Preverbal children are exposed to language users, from whom they learn to perform linguistic acts. I am not in a position to speculate about the invention of language, and the steps by which this came about. And I shall have very little to say about the equipment one must possess to learn a language, and the strategy employed in first learning to speak. I am concerned instead with what one can do when he has finally learned to use language: with the basic skills that one acquires and the basic acts he performs. I will explore these by tracing a line of development that could lead from preverbal to postverbal experience. My account is what I have elsewhere called a heuristic model—it is sufficient to help us understand what goes on when we use language, regardless of whether it accurately presents the way real children learn real languages.

But before indicating how a preverbal person might become a language user, I will consider an argument that such a transition is impossible. According to Jerry Fodor, for example, the child learning a language must make and test hypotheses. Before the child can use 'dog' to talk about dogs, he forms hypotheses about which things are and are not dogs. Then he tests these hypotheses in his interactions with other language users. After a series of false starts, the child eventually comes to use 'dog' for just the dogs in the world. But, the argument goes, one must speak or think a language in order to make and test hypotheses: the hypotheses must be framed in some language or other. Fodor claims that the child's first language is the language of thought, with which all humans are innately endowed.

This is not a persuasive argument. The process of learning a language, either one's first language or a subsequent language, is a trial and error procedure. The process of making and testing hypotheses is also a trial and error procedure. But not all such procedures involve hypotheses. A person who already knows a language does have occasion to make hypotheses about language. For example, when I encounter an unfamiliar word while reading, I usually make a guess about the meaning associated with it and proceed on the basis of that guess. If the word is used often enough, I may be able to figure out exactly what the writer means. But the preverbal subject is unable to form hypotheses, if we understand hypotheses to require propositional thinking. That subject can nonetheless make various trials, and respond to corrections provided by other people.

Forming and testing hypotheses is a trial-and-error procedure available only to language users. But even language users carry out trial-and-error procedures that don't involve hypotheses. Learning to ride a bicycle is a trial-and-error procedure. Children normally learn to talk well before they learn to ride bikes, but their talking needn't have much influence on how they learn to ride. The trials in bicycle learning are attempts to stay upright while moving. The errors are falls. It isn't at all plausible, it is on the contrary just plain silly, to describe bicycle learning as a process in which hypotheses are framed and tested. The bicycle learner is trying to acquire a physical skill, not to discover the truth about anything.

A subject in a trial and error procedure must have a goal that he tries to achieve, for he is acting purposively. The subject performs an act to achieve his goal. If the act succeeds, he is done. Otherwise he performs another, presumably an act of a different kind. And so on until he succeeds, is interrupted, or tires of the effort. The language-using subject engaged in a trial-and-error procedure will normally be acting intentionally. He has a certain conception of his goal, and of what he is doing, and acts in the awareness of what he is doing.

The child who has gotten the hang of using language, but is so far able to use only a small number of words, can't formulate hypotheses about what things a new word stands for. He can tentatively affirm the word of certain objects and deny it of others, and learn from more advanced speakers which affirmations and denials are on target. In deciding of which objects he will affirm or deny the expression, the child will be influenced by features of the object which he is equipped to detect. He will presumably affirm the expression of objects that are similar in certain relevant respects, but he need not be able to articulate the criteria he employs. The language user who knows some but very little language and is trying-and-erring to learn a new expression can't adequately conceive the linguistic proficiency at which he aims. But he can form some conception of his goal. For he can use the expression itself to identify the skill at which he aims.

The language learner who has not gotten the hang of using language can't conceive a goal of linguistic proficiency. The trial and error procedures he carries out must be accompanied by preverbal expectations rather than conceptually articulated intentions. He tries things with the expectation of successfully imitating his teacher, or pleasing his teacher, or receiving praise from his teacher. If one trial isn't successful, he makes another. It isn't necessary for the learner to judge or be able to judge that some attempts succeed while others don't. It is just that some do succeed and others fail, and he responds to the failures by further trials.

Now consider how a preverbal subject might acquire the "hang" of using language. That subject already organizes his experience with respect to perceptual frameworks. He experiences various objects as representative of categories to which they belong. The preverbal subject can notice other people and what they are doing. Another person can act in ways, like moving or making sounds, which capture the subject's attention. The language teacher can often tell to what the language learner is attending, and can produce a word for that object. The teacher can try to get the learner to attend to objects on cue—once the expression is pronounced, the language learner is to look for the object, and look at it. If he is disposed to make sounds in imitation of the language teacher, the language learner can be encouraged to say the words for the objects to which he attends. He can learn to use those words to get other people to attend to the appropriate objects.

The language learner who attends on cue can be cued by a word for a single item, like 'Mama', or by a word for a kind of thing, like 'man' or 'dog'. The learner won't appreciate the fact that there is only one Mama while there are lots of dogs. But if more than one dog is present, he can satisfy the language teacher by attending to any of them. The language learner who is trying to follow his teacher's cues will go through two steps in directing attention. If he hasn't already noticed an object to match the verbal cue, he looks for it. He can look for a suitable object without finding one. Perhaps none is present. Perhaps one is present but difficult to make out. If his looking is successful, he completes the looking by attending to the object. While the subject is looking for Mama or looking for a cat, I will say he is *provisionally* attending to the object. One can provisionally attend to either a particular object or to an object of a kind, to an *arbitrary* object of a kind. But it isn't possible to actually attend to an arbitrary object, for there are no arbitrary objects. The adjective 'arbitrary' doesn't signal a category of objects, but rather a kind of act or activity. One always actually attends to a particular object or part of the world.

The language learner who attends on cue will also produce expressions by himself. He will learn to produce certain expressions when attending to certain kinds of objects or parts of his world. Simply producing appropriate expressions in the presence of the right kinds of objects does not constitute using language, but learning to attend on cue and to produce the expressions are natural steps on the route to language use. The language learner might actually break into speech act territory by producing the word for an object, and using the word to classify the object as one for which the word is suited. The language learner already possessed the ability to use language; he starts to use it when he catches on to using words *for* objects, when he *intentionally applies* a word to an object. Intentionally producing the word for an object of attention is acknowledging (in our technical sense of the word) the object to be what he says.

Acknowledging is a fundamental linguistic act. It is subsequent to attending, for one must attend to an object before he can acknowledge it to be anything. But attending need not be a linguistic act. Someone, or some dog, can attend to an object without anyone saying anything. A subject can also use a word to "express" his attending, or to get others to attend to a part of his world. These *are* linguistic attending acts, or linguistic acts closely tied to attending acts. There is very little difference between using a word to express one's attending to an object in experience and using that word to acknowledge the object to be whatever.

Someone who uses a word *X* to express his attending to an object *Y*, or who uses *X* to acknowledge *Y* (to be an *X*-thing), if he has used *X* correctly, has *identified* *Y*. He has identified *Y* as *X* or as an *X*. This identifying is not the same as the identifying discussed earlier in connection with representing. However, we will later see that there is a close connection between the two kinds of identifying. In speaking of the correct use of *X*, some qualifications are needed. When they learn to talk, it isn't uncommon for children to use a word for more things than we do. A child might initially use 'dog' (or 'doggie') for all medium-sized four-legged animals. Rather than writing the child off as mistaken, I shall say that he uses the word 'dog' to express a different concept than we do. So long as the child uses the expression consistently for animals that he groups together, animals that he experiences as representative of their category, he can correctly use 'dog' to acknowledge a cat to be what he calls a dog. He has identified the cat in that case. The child's language is, in this respect, not quite English. Although the child has failed to master the English use of 'dog,' his standards determine which of his acts are identifying acts. However, the child isn't immune from error. If he acknowledges a dog-shaped bush seen from a distance to be a dog, he will not have identified the bush. Similarly, a mature speaker of English might, due to some mistake, use 'magenta' for a certain shade of green. He consistently uses the word for the wrong color. Although he deviates from standard English, this speaker can correctly acknowledge a green object to be (what he calls) magenta. This is sufficient for him to have identified the green object.

Someone who uses a word to express his attending to a present object, or to acknowledge an object to be ϕ, intends to identify the object. If he gets things right, he has identified it. If his attempt fails, he has still performed an acknowledging act. Acknowledging is correct or not, but identifying is like knowing. There is no incorrect identifying.

When *A* utters expression *X* to get *B* (a language user) to direct his attention to a certain object or kind of object, and *B* hears *A* and does what is wanted, then *A* has used *X* to perform a certain act. But *B* has also made use of *A*'s utterance. If *B* first looks for *X*'s object, then *B* has used the utterance to provisionally attend to an object or kind of object. If *B*'s search is successful, and he finally attends to *X*'s object, then he has also used *A*'s utterance to acknowledge the object to be *X*. If *B* actually attends to the right object, or to one of the right objects, then *B* has identified that object.

Acknowledging is positive or negative. One can acknowledge an object to be *X*, and he can acknowledge the object not to be *X*. Acknowledging the object not to be *X* is *denying* the object to be *X*. It wouldn't be possible to learn to perform only positive acknowledging acts. To use expression *X* correctly, we must be able to tell both what are and what aren't *X*. On the present usage, all acknowledging is sincere. Though one can pretend to perform an acknowledging act without really doing this. In addition to positive and negative acknowledging acts, a person can decline to perform an acknowledging act. Declining is different from denying.

A language user who is able to use words to acknowledge objects to be one thing or another, and correctly acknowledges the object of his present attention to be ϕ or a ϕ, has (*conceptually*) *recognized* that object. (Perceptual recognition is experiencing an object as representative of a category to which it really belongs.) Using a word to recognize/acknowledge an object to be ϕ is a fundamental, and simple, linguistic act. These acts will constitute building blocks in analyses of complex linguistic acts. But it may seem that such acts themselves require some kind of analysis. Isn't some kind of computation required before a subject can recognize the object to be ϕ?

Suppose there were a ϕ-device that, given certain perceptual inputs, yielded *yes* or *no* or *undecided* outputs. And that this device enabled the speaker to acknowledge some objects to be ϕ, to deny other objects to be ϕ, and to hesitate about still others. If the subject were aware of the device's outputs, and used them as a basis for acknowledging objects to be ϕ, the device wouldn't explain very much. For now we need to know how the subject is able to recognize the three kinds of output, either perceptually or conceptually. We are still left with fundamental recognition skills. If the subject were not aware of the device's outputs, then the outputs couldn't provide an analysis or explanation of the acknowledging acts and the ability to perform them. Events of which the subject isn't aware may figure in his intentional acts, but they don't provide the occasions for such acts.

4. Simple Sentential Acts

The child who has learned to use words to express his attending to parts of the world he experiences, to influence others to attend to this or that part, and to acknowledge parts to be this or that will not initially distinguish between a word like 'Mama' that is used for a single object and a word like 'dog' that is used for more than one object. However, it shouldn't take too long to learn the difference between words like 'dog' that apply to "discrete" individuals and words like 'water'. Parts of water are also water but parts of dogs aren't dogs. Combining two quantities of water simply yields water, but the same isn't true for dogs. The language learner should learn to use the indefinite article to perform acknowledging acts with some expressions but not others. He would learn to say 'a dog' but not 'a water' or 'a red'.

When a phrase like 'a dog' is used to perform an acknowledging act, the speaker may use two or more words to perform a simple linguistic act. The speaker may also be more self-conscious, more deliberate, about what he is doing. He might use just 'dog' to acknowledge an animal to be a dog, and use 'a' to mark this as a *discrete-object acknowledging*. This gives a special, explicit, character to the acknowledging act, and exemplifies this intentional act structure:

(a +) dog

(The expressions used to perform linguistic acts are used to represent those acts.) Even if the indefinite article isn't used to perform a separate intentional act, the article still provides a special character to the acknowledging act, signaling its discrete-individual character.

A single part of the language learner's world can be the target of different linguistic acts. He might first use 'ball' to express his attending to a ball, or to acknowledge the object to be a ball. He could follow this up by acknowledging the ball to be red. The first act prepares the way for the second, even makes it possible, by focusing attention on the ball. The simplest acts the language learner can perform with sentences will combine an attending and an acknowledging act in just this way. We can represent the acts just described like this:

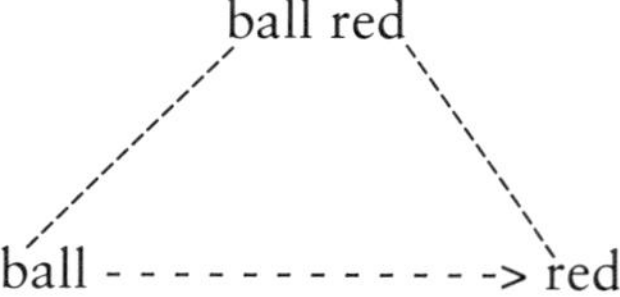

The use of 'ball' to express the attending or to acknowledge the object to be a ball is intended by the speaker to "set up" or enable his use of 'red' to perform an acknowledging act. The two acts together constitute the sentential activity of attending-to-the-ball-and-acknowledging-it-to-be-red; they don't constitute a single act.

Acknowledging an object to be something is *judging* the object to be that something. An acknowledging act has the *force* of a judgment. Following Austin and Searle, it is customary to speak of *illocutionary* acts and illocutionary force. But the standard usage fails to distinguish the intention to perform a meaningful act from the intention to communicate one's meaning. For Austin and Searle, an illocutionary act is a meaningful communicative act. On the present usage, the (plain) illocutionary act is the meaningful act. Illocutionary force attaches to meaningful acts whether or not these are directed at an audience, whether or not these are understood by the audience. An audience-directed illocutionary act which is understood by the audience is *consummated*. For us, then, an acknowledging act is an assertion. The sign '⊢' will be used to mark the illocutionary force of acknowledging acts:

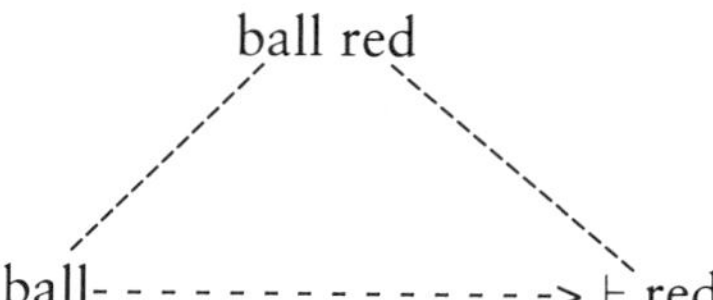

I have not put an illocutionary force marker in front of 'ball', because the language user might use this word to *merely* express his attending. But if one acknowledging act is performed to enable a second, we need this diagram:

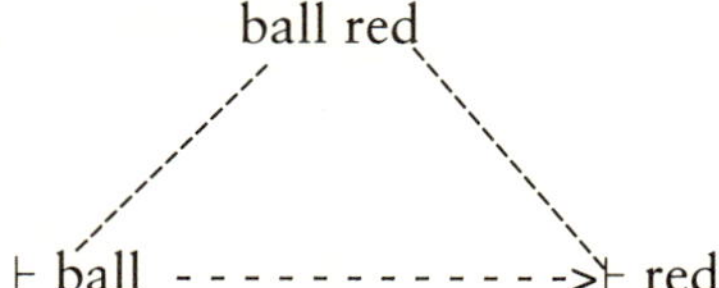

The abbreviated representation for this last would give us:

However, this form of the abbreviation proves inconvenient for linguistic acts. The diagrams will be more perspicuous if they provide the total expression used in a form that is convenient to read. I will represent the acts like this:

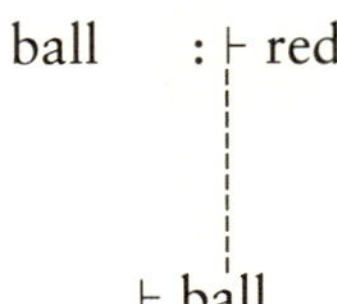

At the bottom is the expression used to perform the enabling act. It is connected by the broken line to the expression used to perform the enabled act. The enabling expression is repeated at the higher node, so that we have the complete sentential expression at that node. But the upper occurrence of 'ball' does not represent a linguistic act, which is why the illocutionary force marker has been dropped. The expression used to perform the act represented by that node is marked by the colon flanking it.

When two acts are combined in the manner just indicated, it is proper in English to use the expression 'is'. So the language learner will be taught to perform these acts:

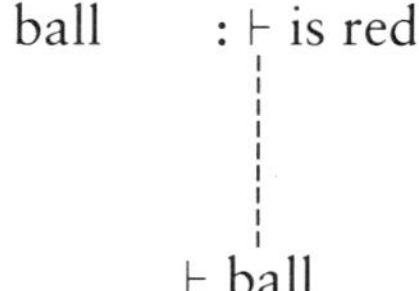

The expression 'red' is the fundamental acknowledging expression here. The speaker might simply use 'is red' as a unit, to perform a simple act, or he might perform these acts:

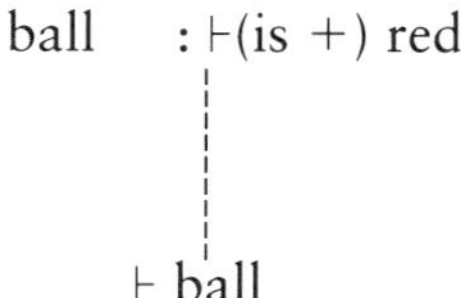

Here the copula is used to make explicit a character the acknowledging act "already" has. The 'is' might be used to signal the enabled character of the act. With a more proficient speaker than our language learner, it might also serve to highlight the present time of the being red.

Once the language learner has gotten the idea of using expressions to perform/express attending acts and to perform acknowledging acts, he will acquire more refined skills. Instead of using 'ball red' or 'ball is red' to acknowledge a present ball to be red, he will say "The ball is red" or "This ball is red." With expressions like 'ball' that can be used for more than one part of the world, it is important to master devices to mark just which part of the world it is that he intends. He will learn to perform linguistic acts like these:

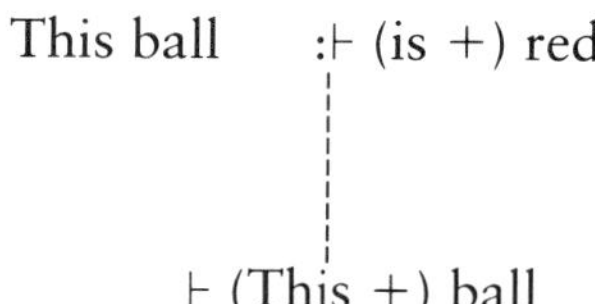

The demonstrative adjective gives a special character to the initial act, which character makes explicit the "direction" of the speaker's attention.

But the speaker can direct his attention without at the same time performing an acknowledging act. He might perform acts like the following:

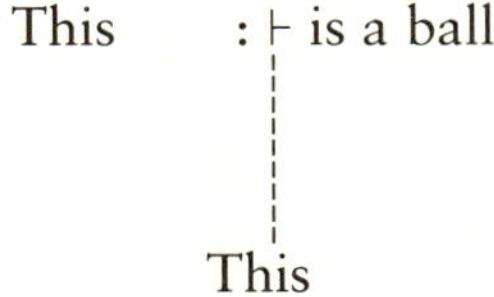

In this case, the initial act is not a propositional act. The predicate is used by itself to perform the propositional act. In the preceding diagram, I haven't shown any structure in the acknowledging act. The speaker might use 'is a ball' to perform a simple intentional act. But the more deliberate language user has several options:

(1) This : ⊢ (is +) a ball
This

(2) This : ⊢ is (+ a +) ball
This

(3) This : ⊢ (is a +) ball
This

(4) This : ⊢ (is +)(a +) ball
This

The differences between these acts would show up in the speaker's intonation and timing. For (1), there is a slight pause after 'is', and 'a ball' is pronounced as a unit. For (2), there would be a slight pause both before and after 'a', and 'a' would receive a slight emphasis. For

(3), it is 'is a' that is pronounced as a unit, with a slight pause before 'ball'. And for (4), there are pauses and slight emphases on each of the words 'is' and 'a'.

Speech-act structure shows up in the intonation, timing, and rhythm of speakers. Because of this, we can tell when someone reading out loud doesn't have a clear understanding of the text he reads. This is fairly common in churches where members of the congregation read scriptural passages. Apart from having trouble with unfamiliar names, the readers often just say things wrong, emphasizing the wrong words, pausing in the wrong places. Mistaken timing, emphasis, and so on is even more noticeable in children who have reading difficulties. Reading with understanding requires more than sounding out or pronouncing the written text. The written text is a script to be performed by the reader, even if he doesn't read aloud.

When one expression can be used to perform acts with different structures, as illustrated in (1)–(4) above, we can try to describe the way these structures show up in speech. But the features of speech are just cues to the structures, they don't indicate the significance of the structures. To explain what is the significance of such structures, or why a speaker would provide one rather than another, it is often helpful to describe circumstances in which the structure would be appropriate. We shall do this with the structures represented above.

For (1), the speaker uses 'is' to perform a separate act. Someone who was teaching language to a young child and was trying the make clear the difference between affirming and denying, by giving examples of what things are and aren't, might perform these acts. ("This is a ball. That is not a ball.") A speaker might perform the acts represented by (2) if she was teaching the difference between acknowledging with nouns and with adjectives. ("This is red. This is round. This is a ball.") A speaker could also perform these acts if she intended to mark a contrast between simply being a ball and being a particular ball, or between one and more than one ball. The structure shown in (3) is the most common of the four structures; the speaker simply treats 'is a' as a unit, and uses it to mark his as an acknowledging act. The structure in (4) is an "emphatic" structure, and might be used to correct someone who had misidentified the ball. The differences between the acts represented by (1)–(4) are semantic differences, for the diagrams represent the *semantic structures* of linguistic acts and activities. However, these semantic differences are slight. For most of the issues that concern me in this book, these differences are of little importance. So I will most commonly use a diagram like this:

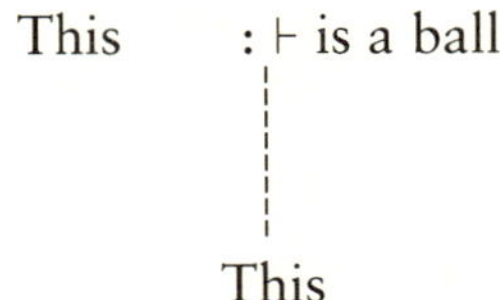

and ignore the finer details of the linguistic acts. However, it is very important to realize that one sentence can normally be used (on different occasions) to perform acts with many different semantic structures. Sentences are scripts which allow (speech-)actors a lot of leeway in the performances they give.

The child will learn to perform both positive and negative acknowledging acts—both affirming and denying acts. For one can't learn what counts as a ϕ without also learning what doesn't. Once the child can use 'This is a ball' to acknowledge a present object to be a ball, he will be able to use 'This is not a ball' to deny an object to be a ball. There are different ways in which a negating act might be structured, but most commonly the speaker will reject the application of 'ball' to the object of attention. I will use the reversed assertion-sign '⊣' to indicate rejection or denial. The speaker's denial will be represented like this:

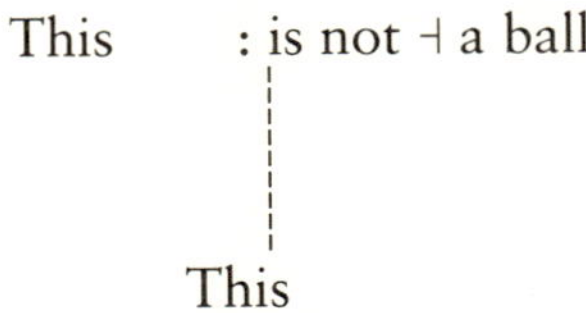

The infixed rejection-sign indicates that it is 'a ball' whose use is being blocked or rejected. (What is being rejected is the use of 'a ball' to acknowledge the object to be a ball.) A more detailed representation shows 'not' used to make the negative character explicit:

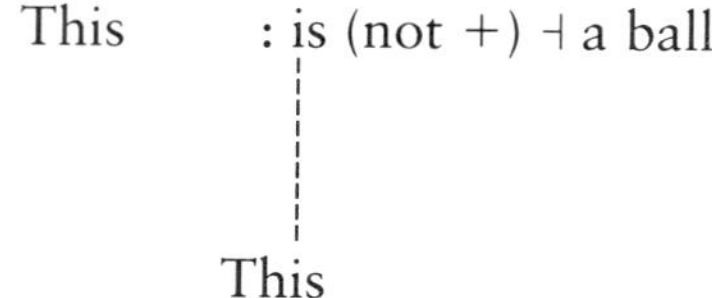

Communication between a speaker and his audience involves linguistic acts performed by both parties. When a speaker produces-and-uses expressions to perform speech acts, his audience, if they understand him, also uses the speaker's expressions to perform speech acts. Consider a simple situation where the speaker acknowledges a present object to be red:

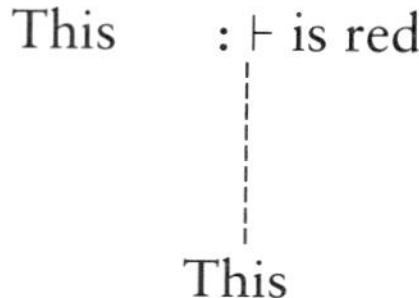

The speaker produces and uses his expressions all at once. But the audience must first hear the speaker's utterances, and then, once they have recognized them, use them. In the situation described, the audience might first hear/listen to the speaker's 'This,' then look for (provisionally attend to) the object of his attention, and finally locate it. By locating this object, the audience has acknowledged it to be the 'This' to which the speaker attends. The audience's acts so far can be represented:

The word enclosed in quotes represents the audience's act of listening to the word. By getting the audience to look for and find the speaker's object, the listening act enables the locating/acknowledging act. Fastening on the object the speaker intends enables the audience to use the speaker's predicate expression. The simplest thing for the audience to do is agree with and accept the speaker's acknowledging act:

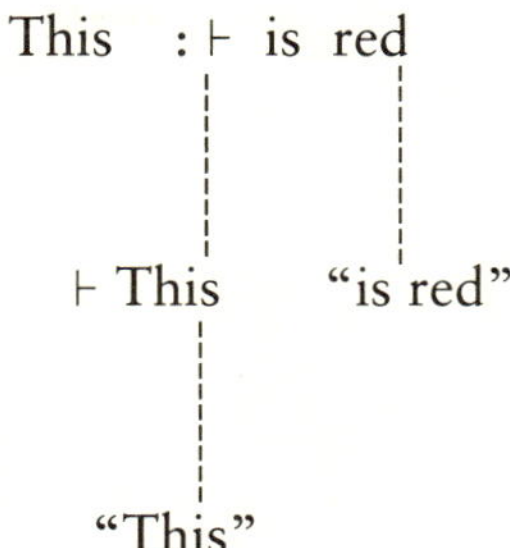

The beginning language learner will be in no position to challenge the linguistic acts of his teacher. If he understands the speaker at all, he must "echo" the speaker's acknowledging act. But speakers sometimes make mistakes. A more proficient listener might hear the speaker's acknowledging act without himself performing that (kind of) act. The proficient language user will attend to the object, attend to the speaker, and use the speaker's utterance to acknowledge the speaker to be situated by *red*-acknowledging with respect to the object:

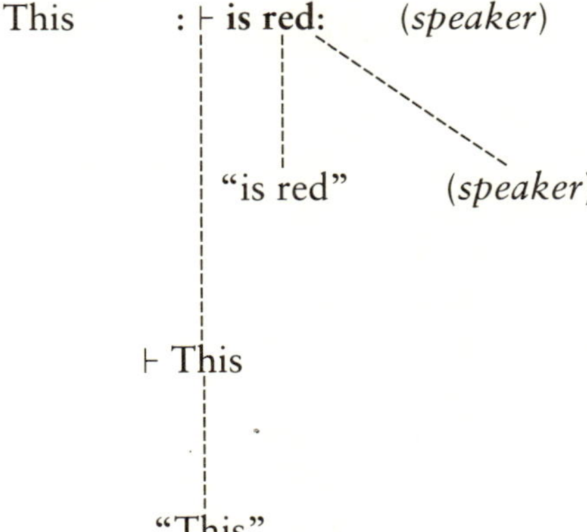

The bold type indicates that instead of being used to acknowledge an object to be red, the expression is used to acknowledge a person to be using the expression to perform a linguistic act. Writing the italicized 'speaker' in parentheses indicates that 'speaker' is not used to perform a linguistic act, but is instead (our word for) identifying the language-using audience's object of attention.

5. Situating Objects

In acknowledging an object to be ϕ or a ϕ, one is classifying the object as ϕ. This is also bringing or applying the concept of ϕ to the object. But the language user isn't thinking about a category or a concept. He simply uses the ϕ-expression for the object. Although the language user employs criteria when he correctly acknowledges an object to be ϕ, he doesn't need to think about the criteria, and he doesn't need to be able to articulate the criteria.

Suppose someone uses the sentence 'Mary is beside Frank' to acknowledge the way Mary is situated with respect to Frank. Following our earlier analysis, he might perform acts like these:

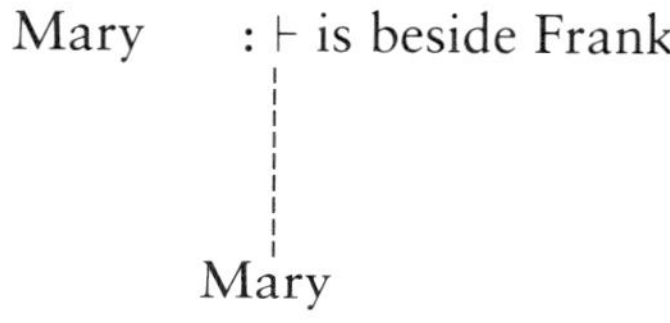

But this diagram is not sufficiently detailed. In using this sentence, the speaker will attend to both Mary and Frank, but his two attending acts play different roles. Mary is the focus, the target, of the speaker's acknowledging act. While Frank serves as a reference point, allowing the speaker to acknowledge the focus to be situated in a certain way with respect to Frank. The act of attending to Mary and the act of attending to Frank are both enabling acts, but they operate on different "levels." (The second enabling act occurs after the act which it enables. The speaker performs the enabled act first by virtue of his knowing what comes next.) The 'Mary' act provides an object of attention, without which there is nothing to acknowledge. But Mary is acknowledged to be *beside Frank*. The Frank-attending act is almost a constituent of the acknowledging act. It isn't actually a constituent, for the acknowledging act is performed with 'beside'. But 'beside' needs help to be suited for performing acknowledging acts. The Frank-attending makes it possible to use 'beside' for acknowledging. With respect to the acknowledging act, the act of attending to Frank is "prior" to the act of attending to Mary. First the expression 'beside' must be rendered suitable for performing an acknowledging act, then it can be used to acknowledge Mary to be beside Frank. I will use the following representation for such acts:

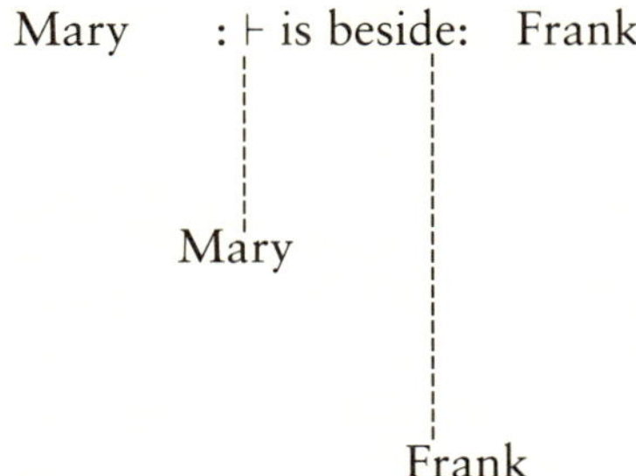

That 'Frank' is written lower than 'Mary' indicates that the Frank-attending act is semantically prior to the act of attending to Mary. The higher node represents the act of attending to the focus/target of the acknowledging act. (I will from now on drop the "complete" diagrams for linguistic enabling acts.)

The acts represented above are appropriate for a speaker addressing an audience that knows where Frank is, but has yet to find Mary. The very same sentence could be used in a different fashion:

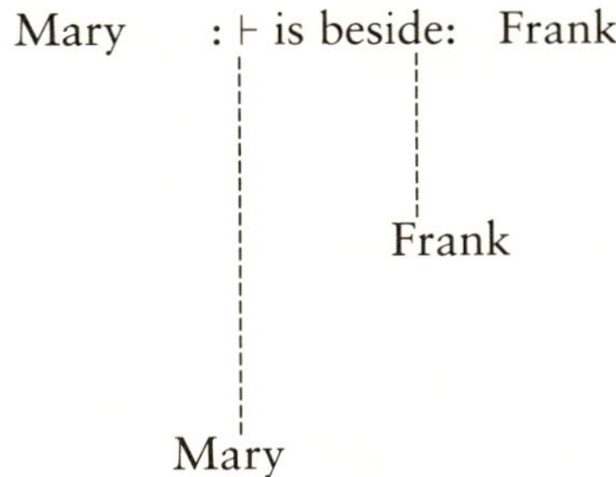

Here Mary is the reference point and Frank is the focus of the acknowledging act. These acts would be appropriate in addressing an audience that knows where Mary is, but is trying to find Frank.

Although it is more unlikely (and demands more linguistic proficiency), the sentence could also be used to perform acts organized this way:

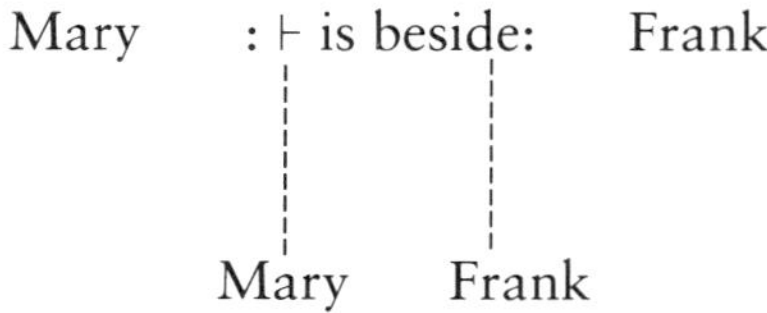

Neither Mary nor Frank is used as a reference point. Instead the pair Mary, Frank is acknowledged to be a beside-one-another pair. The two attending acts pick out the two foci for the acknowledging act.

Consider an audience who knows where Frank is, and is looking for Mary, an audience inclined to simply accept what the speaker says. The audience will use the speaker's utterance of 'Frank' to attend to Frank. (Since they already know where Frank is, their act won't be counted an acknowledging act.) This enables them to use 'beside' to attend to the part of their world beside Frank. And this, in turn, enables the audience to attend to Mary, which amounts to acknowledging the object of attention to be Mary:

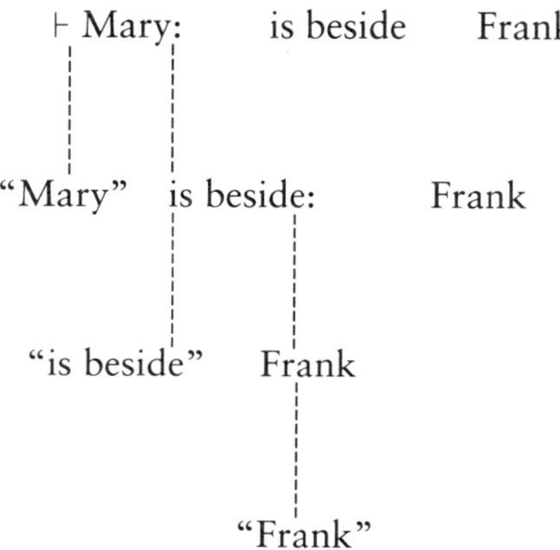

The order in which the audience performs acts using the speaker's utterances is not the same as the order in which the speaker produces the utterances. On hearing 'Mary', the audience will provisionally attend to Mary, but they don't perform the acknowledging act until they find her.

Before he learns language, a subject experiences a world with spatial structure. Its different parts are situated with respect to one another, and the subject has a perceptual framework he uses to organize his spatial perception; this allows him to find his way about. The subject's spatial discriminations and his spatial percepts will be very much increased when he learns to use language. For he will acquire a variety of spatial concepts which inform his perception—although a subject will have percepts before he has concepts, his concepts also function like percepts in determining which objects and situations he experiences as representative. Learning to use spatial prepositions like 'on', 'over', 'above', 'inside', 'outside' provides the subject with new tools for organizing experience.

We normally think one finds the world the way it is, and simply learns expressions for describing the way things already are. But in fact the language learner introduces structure into his world. We can agree that the cat sees the box on the table, the plate on the wall, and the fly on the ceiling, but there is no reason to think the cat sees each situation as representive of a single kind of situation. Language does more than provide concepts for pre-existing percepts, it provides new categories for perception. Someone who insists that regardless of the cat's "take" on things, the fly in the cat's world is nonetheless on the ceiling, is imposing his structure on the cat's world of experience. Each subject's world must have some structure to begin with. But the subject provides more when he develops perceptual frameworks and very much more when he learns language. However, the subject isn't "free" to impose any structures at all, for the world of experience is *suited* to be organized in certain ways but not others. A subject's world never receives all the structure it might. No matter how organized the subject's world becomes, it could always receive more organization. And some available structures preclude others.

Not only are nouns and adjectives used to perform acknowledging acts, but so are pronouns and prepositions. And verbs too. In using the sentence 'Dick is running', we can use the main part of the verb just as we use nouns and adjectives:

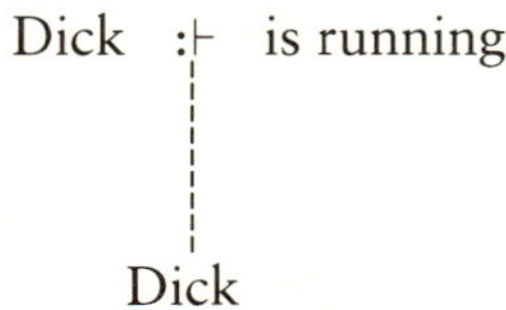

In a language with different verb constructions than English, one might use a sentence like ‘Dick runs’ to acknowledge Dick to be running:

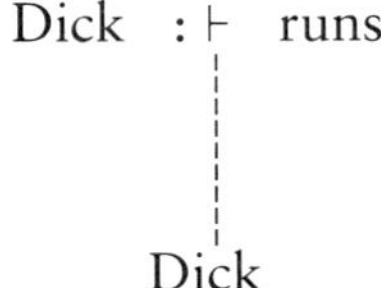

In acknowledging Dick to be running, the speaker is concerned with a short-lived event rather than a permanent condition like Dick’s being a man. But the language learner can identify events and temporary situations as well as enduring individuals and long-lasting situations.

The speaker can both acknowledge Dick to be running and Dick’s running to be fast. There are different ways to do this. The speaker might perform acts like these:

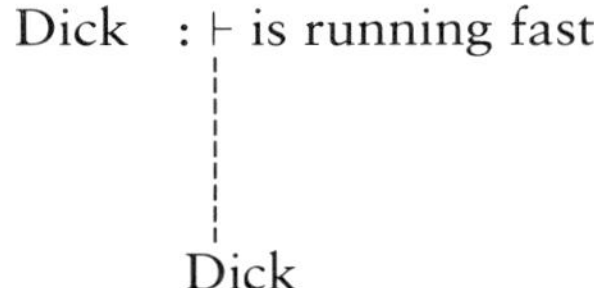

Here ‘running fast’ (or ‘is running fast’) is used as a unit. But the speaker might also say it like this:

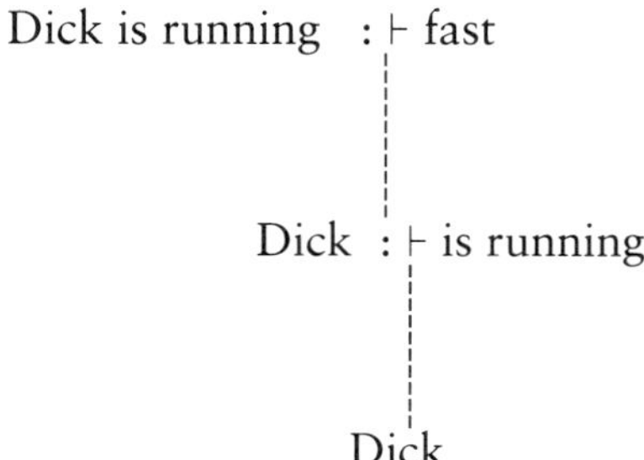

In this case there are two acknowledging acts. The speaker attends to Dick, giving him a focus he can acknowledge to be running. This acknowledging Dick to be running is also an act of attending to Dick running—to Dick’s running. And this gives a target which can be acknowledged to be fast. In performing these acts, it would be natural for the speaker to pause after he says 'running', then throw in the 'fast'. If Dick's running has already been remarked on, the speaker might do this:

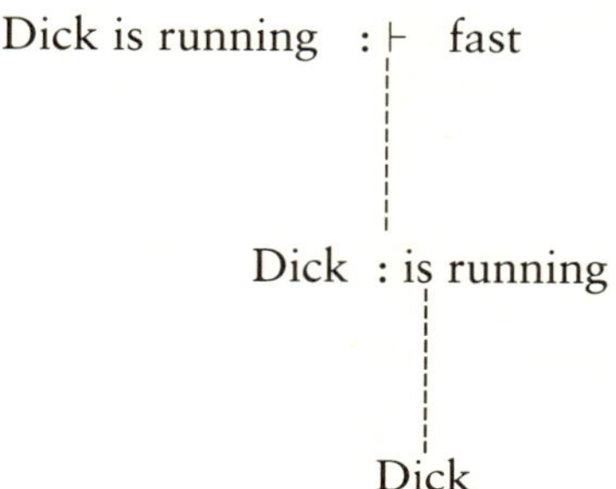

Or even just this:

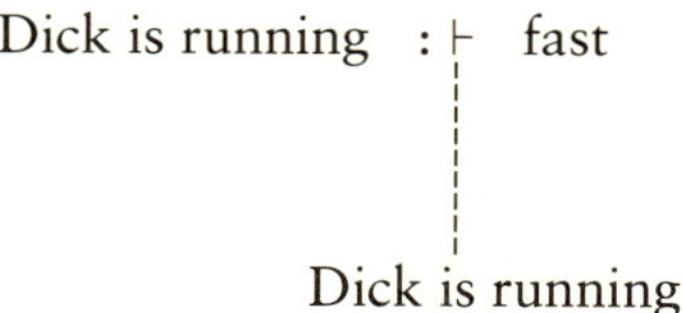

Here the speaker attends to Dick's running without performing an acknowledging act, which enables him to acknowledge that running to be fast.

Consider how someone might use the sentence 'Dick sees Jane'. Even though this sentence does not concern spatial situation, it can be used like this:

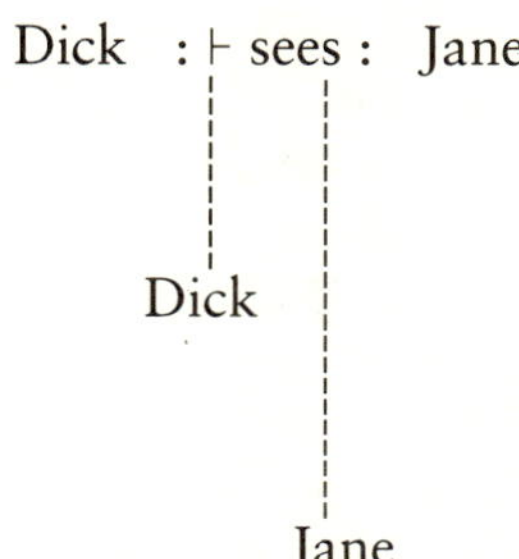

Dick is the focus of the acknowledging act, while Jane is the reference point with respect to which Dick is acknowledged to be seeing. The world of a subject's experience has some spatial structure to begin with. It acquires more when percepts are developed, and still more with the advent of language. But language also brings in nonspatial structures. Not all situations are spatial ones.

The diagram above represents a subject-oriented use of the sentence. Such acts would be appropriate to answer the question "Who sees Jane?" But if the speaker wanted to use the sentence to tell his audience who(m) Dick sees, he might do this:

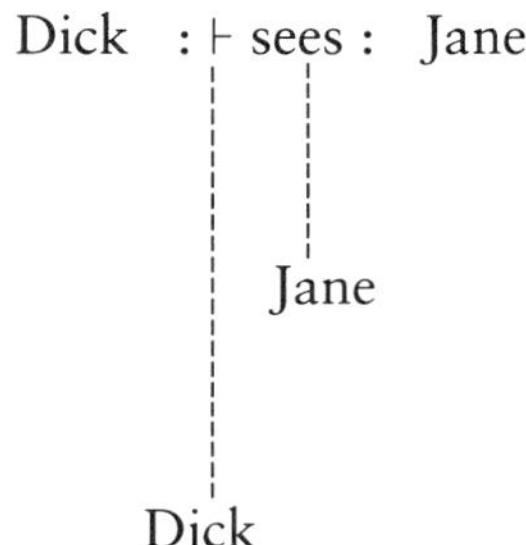

It may seem hard to accept my claim that acquiring transitive verbs introduces new structure to the language learner's world of experience. Wouldn't Dick see Jane even if the language learner wasn't able to say so? The learner's world of experience is different from the world which *we* encounter. So far, the language learner hasn't acquired the idea of a common world which we all inhabit. His isn't that kind of world, being so far confined to his present experience. As well as encountering his own world in his experience, the language learner inhabits our common world, where Dick does see Jane whether the learner knows it or not. The language learner lives in our world, but he experiences only some parts of our world and some of its structure. His world of experience is constituted by his experience. In that world, before the language learner can talk about seeing, Dick is spatially situated with respect to Jane, but Dick isn't situated by seeing with respect to Jane. However, his world is suited to be enriched with the *sees* structure, it has room for that structure.

Learning language changes the world. The world comes to have kinds of things in great profusion. It acquires more spatial structure as well as elaborate nonspatial (and nontemporal) structures. This enriches perception by providing enormously many new perceptual categories. It makes possible propositional thinking, giving rise to belief and knowledge. We have seen how the language learner might introduce nonspatial structure to his world. But nonspatial structures might simply provide new links between objects also situated spatially with respect to one another. However, the child will have occasion to recognize at least one object which isn't spatially situated. For he will learn to attend to his self, and acknowledge the self to be this and that.

People aren't always careful to distinguish different kinds, or levels, of consciousness. But it is essential to distinguish sensory awareness from self-consciousness. Sensory awareness is of variously qualified and related objects. When one sees or hears or feels, one is sensorily aware of, say, a round, smooth, red ball, or a high-pitched whine, or whatever. A person is sensorily aware of feelings from the inside, of pokes, pinches, headaches, and sore throats. Any experiencing subject has sensory awareness. But the subject of sensory awareness need not be self-conscious. To be self-conscious, a subject must be aware of his self as having experience or as acting in some way. It is one thing to see a dog and something else to be aware of seeing the dog. Awareness of seeing is awareness of the self as seeing. Similarly it is one thing to be aware of one's body being in motion, and something else to be aware of doing the moving.

It is difficult to design tests to determine if an animal that doesn't use language is self-conscious. It seems possible that the use of language or some language-like substitute is necessary for self-consciousness. Could a subject be aware of seeing something without having the concept of seeing? Although it isn't clear whether non-language-using subjects are or could be self-conscious, it is completely obvious that language users are self-conscious. Who is there that can understand 'There is a ball' but be incapable of comprehending 'I see a ball'? Who could recognize that his hands and feet are going up the ladder while failing to understand that he is climbing the ladder?

Language users are self-conscious. It seems possible that a person might first become self-conscious in learning to speak. But how does/could this happen? No one can be taught to notice and attend to things, these are skills we must start with. Someone can be taught to attend on cue and to produce sounds in response to various stimuli. But this isn't using language. Each subject capable of using language has whatever it takes to appreciate/hit upon the idea of using words for things: for attending to them and acknowledging them to be something or other. When the subject learns to use an expression to attend to/express his attending to a ϕ and to acknowledge objects to be ϕ, he has acquired the skill(s) for using the ϕ-expression in these ways. But the ϕ-expression is also available to the subject as a label for his ϕ-acts. In acquiring the concept of a ϕ, the language user acquires an expression he can use to attend to and acknowledge (some of) his own acts. Attending to his own acts is attending to himself acting.

Attending to the self is not being aware of a mysterious something behind or beneath one's experience and activity. One always attends to the self with features, the self doing this or doing that. In learning to use first-person expressions, one codifies and organizes his self-consciousness. The language learner will become able to situate his self with respect to the objects in his world. Although it may subsequently be possible, and even a good idea, to identify the self with his body or brain, the language learner won't initially make such an identification. His self is a part of the world of his experience, nonspatially situated with respect to spatially located objects. It is a nonspatial part, though not outside the temporal order.

Chapter 7

Learning to Use Language:
Gaining Proficiency

1. Expanding the Language Learner's Horizons

The language learner begins by using words to express his attending to parts of the world of his experience, to get other people to attend to parts of his world, and to acknowledge parts of this world to be one thing or another. He can direct his linguistic acts at an audience, and he can perform them for himself. The language learner also becomes able to use the utterances of other people to perform acts of his own. In learning to use different expressions and kinds of expressions, the language learner enriches the world of his experience. This world has perceptual structure to begin with, which involves spatial, temporal, and qualitative features. But in learning language, the child introduces much more structure. There is additional spatial structure. There are an enormous number of new categories of things. The language learner comes to recognize dogs, cats, balls, bottles. He distinguishes between stuff and countable individual parts of the world, between short-lived events and enduring, stable parts. Spatial and temporal structures are supplemented by a host of other conceptual structures. Seeing, hearing, liking, owning, are new respects in which objects can be situated with respect to each other. These structures supplant perceptual structure, but they also enrich perceptual structure, for conceptual categories become perceptual ones as well. Conceptual structure organizes the world of experience, and makes possible propositional thinking about this world, as well as knowledge of it.

Before the subject learns language, the world of his experience is the world of his present experience. This world has no place for currently existing but absent objects, or for past or future events. The present time of this world is not instantaneous. It has a certain temporal thickness. The subject experiences one thing giving way to another. He experiences whole sounds, not simply fragments of them. But once an event is over, he no longer has access to it. The language learner whose progress we are tracing has not so far expanded his world beyond his present experience. But the acquisition of language (of linguistic skills) will lead him to do this. Once he learns to use 'Mama' for Mama when she is present, he will find himself able to use the word to attend to her when she isn't present.

To begin with, the world of experience is the world of present experience. The language learner then learns to attend to objects in response to the words for them, to use words to express his attending to present objects, and to use words to acknowledge present objects to be this and that. Having learned to use words for present objects, he finds that he can use these words to think of objects whether or not they are present. This *mental attending* is sufficiently like attending to a present object that we call it attending, though its object can be anywhere.

All attending is mental. Some mental attending is also perceptual. Perceptual attending doesn't take place unless the object is present to the attending subject—the object is, in part, constitutive of his perceptual awareness. But mental attending does not, in general, require the presence, or even the present existence of its object.

Someone like Hume might try to explain the nonperceptual mental attending as follows. The word for an object calls up or "triggers" an image of the object. The subject who attends to the absent object is really attending to the present image of that absent object, so that attending, after all, is always directed to a present object. However, this isn't a successful explanation. In the first place, we aren't always aware of images when we use words to talk/think about absent objects. Even when images are employed, the connection between an image and its object is as mysterious and as much in need of explanation as the connection between a word and its object.

A second try to explain merely mental attending in terms of other mental operations might run as follows. When someone uses a word to attend to/acknowledge an object, there are criteria associated with these uses of that word. An object must satisfy certain criteria to be correctly acknowledged to be ϕ. The language user need not be able to articulate them, but he must *employ* the criteria when he performs linguistic acts. Learning to use an expression to perform certain kinds of attending and acknowledging acts is learning to employ the criteria for these acts. When someone finds himself mentally attending to an absent object, he is employing the appropriate criteria without the object being present.

Although it may be correct to say that the language user employs criteria when using an expression to attend to an absent object, this isn't enlightening. The connection between employing the "Mama" criteria and actually attending to Mama is as mysterious and unexplained as the connection between looking at a picture of Mama and thinking of her. The use of an expression to attend to an absent object is a case of identifying that object; this is the identifying that was discussed in connection with representing, not the identifying carried out in performing acknowledging acts. Being able to use expressions to identify absent objects is a fundamental skill the language learner acquires, and probably can't be explained in terms of anything more fundamental.

Although the use of words to attend to objects can't be reduced to or derived from more fundamental skills, we can investigate this use to see what it involves. That the skill is fundamental and irreducible does not prevent us from characterizing it. To begin with, the child learns to use expressions when attending to particular objects in his present experience. He subsequently finds himself able to use expressions for objects he has experienced to attend to those objects when he isn't experiencing them. And he can use conceptual structures he has introduced to attend to objects situated with respect to objects he is experiencing, or has experienced. If he knows Frank, but not Frank's mother, he can nonetheless attend to Frank's mother, or maternal grandmother. He can attend to the object Mary is looking out the window at. He can attend to the person Frank mentions, even if he didn't previously know about that person. And the language learner will acquire expressions and techniques for talking about the past and future. Once he can acknowledge things in his experience to be before or after other things, he is equipped to attend to what was before or will be after this present experience. Language users exploit the network of structures that language brings to experience to attend to objects situated in one way or another with respect to themselves, their bodies, and their present and past experience.

When the language learner's world acquires sufficient organization, he will use expressions to attend to particular parts of his world, which may or may not be present. He can also acknowledge these objects to be one thing or another. As well as using words to attend to particular objects, the language learner will be able to use images in this way—he will be able to use images to identify particular individuals and events. He can attend to Mama when she is present and acknowledge her to be here. When she is absent, he can acknowledge her to be not here. He can acknowledge her to have been here or to be going to be here. And he can recognize a picture as a picture of Mama whether she is here or not. Nothing in a picture can identify its object. The child is able to use the picture to identify Mama because he has experienced Mama and his world has a network of connections linking him to Mama, and the picture resembles her.

Even if the language learner can attend to absent objects, it may seem hard to understand how he can acknowledge such an object to be ϕ, when the criteria for ϕ-acknowledging involve the appearance of the object. If the object isn't present, how can a language user apply his criteria? There are different possibilities. The language user might produce an image of the object, and use the image as a basis for his acknowledging. He might simply be conditioned by his past experience to acknowledge the object to be ϕ. He could take another person's word for it. Or he could, in using an expression to attend to a particular object, employ the criteria associated with his attending-act expression and, on that basis, find himself in a position to acknowledge the object to be ϕ.

To perceptually attend, one needs only to look at the object, or touch it, or sense it in some way. We can use an expression or an image to attend to an object that isn't currently perceived. But we might wonder if a person could simply direct his mental attention without employing any instrument. On one of Descartes' understandings of ideas, entertaining an idea of something is nothing else than mentally attending to that thing. An idea of a particular thing would then be a skill for recognizing and attending to that thing. I have no argument to show that we must always use an instrument for our attending, but in my own case I always do seem to use an expression or image. Descartes' two conceptions of an idea may reflect an uncertainty (or confusion) on his part about the need for an instrument.

Once the language learner can attend to objects he isn't currently perceiving, it will be common to perform initial attending acts that aren't acknowledging acts. Instead of using the sentence 'Mama is asleep' like this:

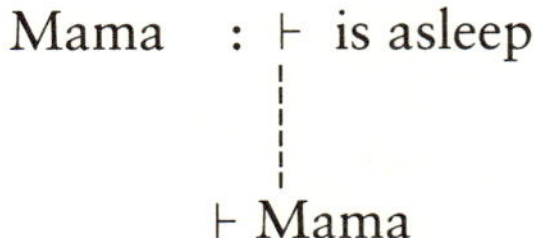

the speaker is likely to perform these acts:

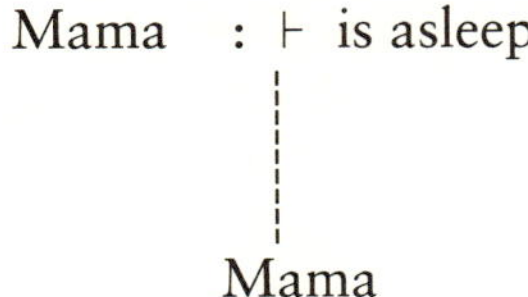

And the audience won't need to visually attend to the speaker's object. The audience might organize their acts in a similar fashion:

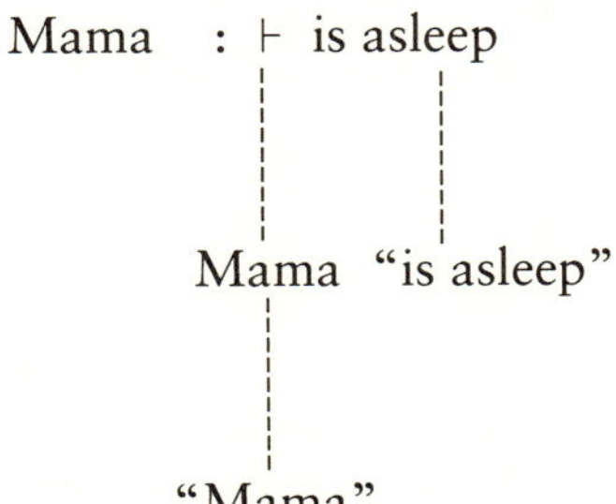

if they simply accept the speaker's claim. An audience that understands the speaker without "copying" the speaker's acknowledging act might do this:

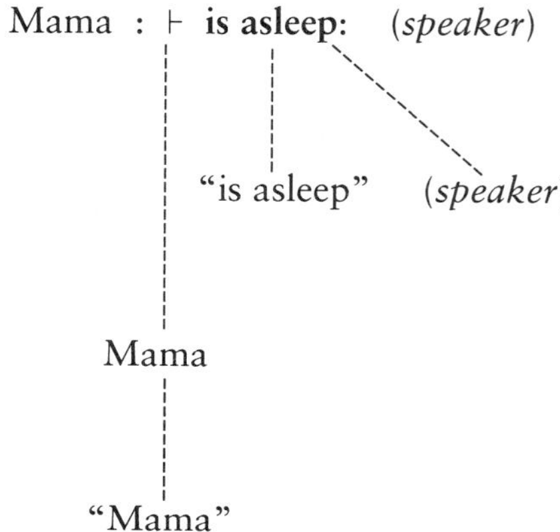

The audience acknowledges the speaker to be situated with respect to Mama by acknowledging (and thinking) her to be asleep.

Once the audience can attend mentally without attending perceptually, they can act differently than before in understanding the following acts (of a speaker):

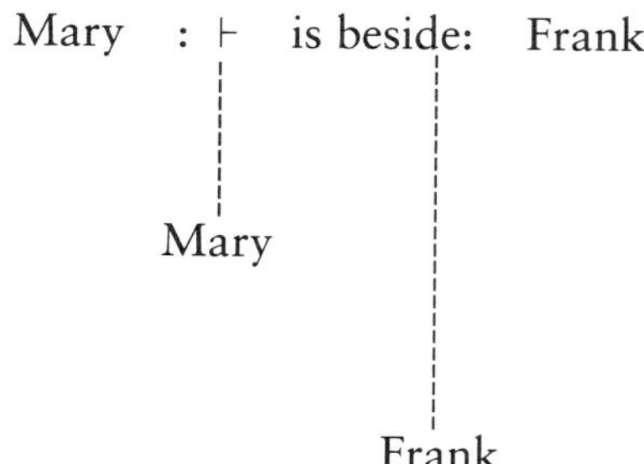

For the audience will understand what is said before they actually fasten their eyes on Mary. If the audience accepts the speaker's statement, their acts may simply "reflect" his:

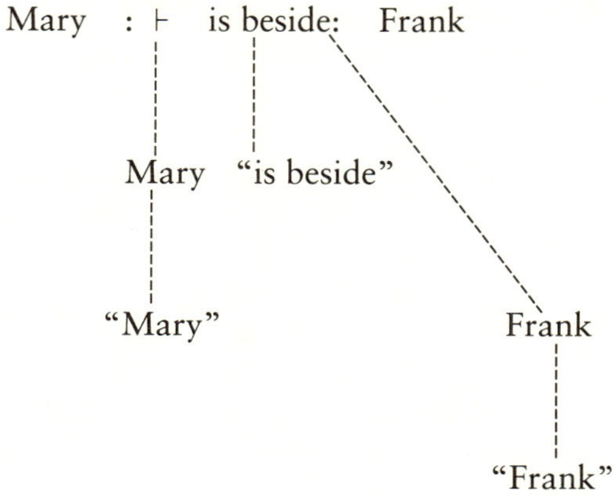

This audience may be content just to know where Mary is, but if they actually want to lay eyes on her, they will also respond to the speaker's acknowledging act by looking beside Frank. If Mary is really there, this should enable them to pick her out, and so to use the speaker's "Mary" act to acknowledge her to be Mary. The one act would first be used to mentally attend to Mary, and subsequently to acknowledge the perceived Mary to be Mary. The audience might also understand the speaker's statement without accepting it (and without looking for Mary). In that case the audience could perform these acts:

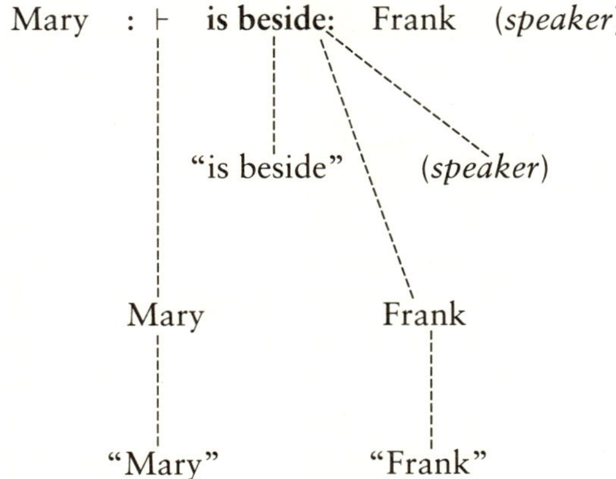

Once he can use expressions to merely mentally attend to objects, the language learner is able to make a new kind of mistake. In normal circumstances, one can perceptually attend only to an object that is really there. But it is easy to come up with expressions for objects that are nowhere to be found. A speaker might tell us, "The man in the next room is my uncle," when no one is in the next room. While it is clear that the speaker has made a mistake, there are different mistakes he might be making. One mistake would involve the failure to attend to any real object. Suppose this failure occurs. How shall we describe what the speaker has done? Has the speaker performed an attending act, or has he merely tried, unsuccessfully, to do so?

We shall say that the speaker *has* attended to the man in the next room, but has not performed an identifying act. Attending depends on the speaker, with his intentions, and on relations which structure the world of his experience. When attending is successful, and constitutes identifying, the speaker is *connected* to the object to which he attends, and he *exploits* his connection in identifying the object. If the speaker attends to an object he currently perceives, his connection to that object is direct, and there is little that can go wrong with the identifying. The speaker who succeeds in identifying an object he isn't currently perceiving achieves this identification via connections linking him to the object. The connections might link the speaker at present via his own history to an object experienced in the past, or they might link him to objects that are merely related to objects of experience.

There are a network of connections—of "paths"—linking the speaker to any given object, but not every connection comes into play when the speaker uses an expression to attend to the object. For the speaker won't know that the various connections have a common terminus. In a particular attending/identifying act, the speaker will *exploit* some but not all of the connections linking him to the object. The connections are objective/empirical features of the world of experience. And when a speaker exploits certain connections to attend to an object, this is an empirical fact about the world (both inside and) outside the speaker's head. A speaker won't know, of all the connections linking him to a single object, that they do link him to one object. But he will commonly know a group of connections to have a common terminus. When he knows/believes this, that group of connections constitutes a *cluster* of connections for him. He will exploit the whole cluster when he uses an expression associated with that cluster. That a speaker has and exploits such clusters is also an empirical fact.

The speaker who attends to/identifies an absent object isn't limited to connections that link presently existing objects. One can attend to objects experienced in the past, and to further objects to which those past objects were connected. My current ability to think and talk about Napoleon is ultimately based on what I have heard and read in the past. But not all my connections to Napoleon traverse that past experience. The knowledge I gained by reading and hearing about Napoleon has given me a large cluster of connections that I can exploit in attending to him. For example, I know about the connection linking me to Napoleon's tomb in Paris, to the earlier event of his interment there, and finally to the man whose lifeless body was subsequently interred.

A subject can only identify an object via connections linking him to that object, but he need not focus on or attend to those connections. Still, the subject can normally attend to those connections if he chooses, and the linguistically proficient subject can articulate them to some extent. While the subject successfully attends to (identifies) objects via connections which are an objective feature of his world, various things can go wrong with his attending. A genuine connection may not terminate the way he thinks. A speaker might say "The person who broke that vase was malicious," when the vase was broken by a careless cat. The speaker is connected to the broke-that-vase part of the world, and attends via that connection. A speaker may also think there is a connection, and attempt to exploit it, when there is none. If someone says "Danny's girlfriend must be attractive," when Danny doesn't, and didn't, have a girlfriend, the speaker is trying to use Danny as a reference point for attending to a particular girl. In both cases, the speaker attends to an object that isn't there. While it isn't necessary for there to be a genuine object of attention, it *is* necessary that the subject think there is such an object. Someone can attend without identifying, but he can't insincerely attend. To *pretend* to attend is not to attend.

Regardless of whether there is a man in the next room, the speaker might use 'The man in the next room' to perform an attending act. Suppose the speaker performs such an act when there is exactly one man in the next room. This fact alone doesn't insure that the speaker has identified that man. The speaker doesn't intend to identify just anything that happens to be the single man in the next room. If he further intends to acknowledge that man to be his uncle, he must have some reason either for thinking some particular uncle is in the next room or one of his uncles is in the next room. Either he believes the path through the next room connects him to the same object as other paths leading to that uncle, or he believes the object at the end of the path he is exploiting satisfies the criteria for being his uncle.

If no one is in the next room, but the speaker intends a particular uncle, he has identified that uncle, but in a mistaken and misleading way. If more than one man is in the next room, and one of them is the intended uncle, the speaker has still identified the uncle, in a somewhat unclear (to the audience) way. The speaker who uses 'The man in the next room' to identify a particular uncle might perform these acts:

(The +) man [+ (in +) the next room]

The speaker uses 'man' to identify the intended uncle. The first 'The' makes explicit that a single man is intended. The prepositional phase does not help the speaker pick out the man he intends; it makes explicit to the audience the person the speaker intends. It provides information to the audience. On the first scenario, this information is incorrect, so the audience may not succeed in performing an identifying act. For the speaker, the connections linking him to the intended uncle will outweigh the mistaken attempt to exploit the next-room-path. For the audience, the path specified by the speaker will be more nearly equal to the other paths linking the speaker to the object he intends.

If the speaker is not thinking of a particular uncle, then the next-room-path is critical for determining the object the speaker intends. The speaker might perform these acts:

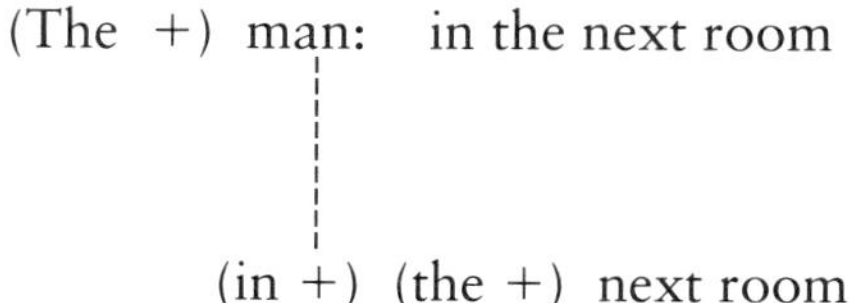

He uses 'next room' (or 'in the next room') to attend to the next room. The definite article indicates that this is an act of attending to an object uniquely determined in the present context. (Lots of rooms are next rooms, but in this context a particular room is intended.) The preposition 'in' makes explicit how the room figures with respect to the identified object. The "lower" identifying act enables the speaker to use 'man' to carry out a further attending act. The speaker is not acknowledging anyone to be a man, but he does intend to attend to an object satisfying the acknowledging criteria for 'man'. The criteria characterize his attending act, which act *presumes* there to be a man in the room. The definite article indicates the kind of act being performed, it isn't used to make a claim.

Attending to a nonexistent object is different from talking about an object when the speaker isn't sure there is (will be) such an object. Suppose someone announces, "The first person on Mars will be American." There are two scenarios to consider. In the first, the speaker confidently expects people to travel to Mars. He is sure there will be a first person on Mars, he is *committed* to there being such a person. This speaker uses 'The first person on Mars' to attend to the first person on Mars. He intends to identify this person. If no one ever reaches Mars, the speaker has made an error, and has failed to perform an identifying act.

In the second scenario, the speaker is not confident about future travel to Mars. His statement has the sense "The first person on Mars, if there is one, will be American." In this case the speaker has not performed an attending act, and has not tried to perform an identifying act. His is a new kind of *provisional* attending act. It points in the direction of a first person on Mars, but does not commit the speaker to there being such a person. Since the speaker has not attended to anyone, he also has not acknowledged anyone to be anything. The speaker has either made or reflected a commitment to acknowledge the first person on Mars to be American, should such a person be brought to his attention. The analysis of this kind of act will be given later. The language learner we are following is not yet in a position to perform such acts.

Once the world of his experience is expanded beyond present experience, the language learner/language user has a great many objects to which he can attend. He can use proper names to do this, or demonstrative/indexical/deictic expressions, or definite descriptions. But these resources are not always adequate or convenient. The child will also learn to use indefinite phrases and 'some'-phrases to attend to/identify particular objects. For example, the sentence 'A dog bit Sally' might be used like this:

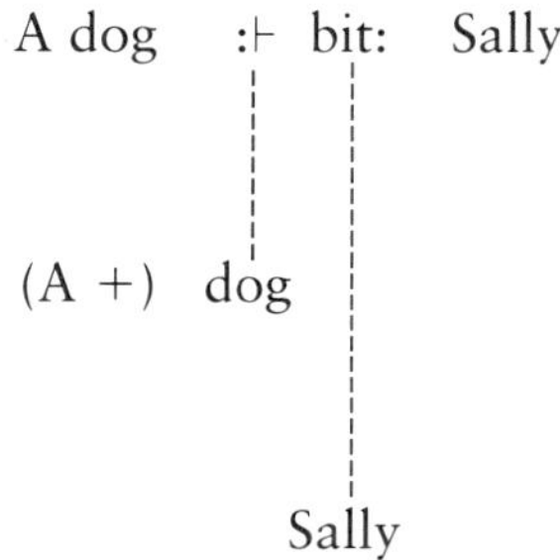

Here, 'A dog' is used to attend to a particular, but unspecified, dog. The dog is *indefinitely* identified. The indefinite article signals the indefinite character of the act. The speaker does not provide his audience enough information to independently attend to the dog in question, but the audience will use the speaker's act as a reference point with respect to which the dog is situated, and attend to the dog on that basis.

Indefinite phrases are used to perform attending acts, and to perform acknowledging acts. Proficient language users also use such phrases *quantificationally*. If the phrase were used that way, the sentence above would be used to say *some dog or other* bit Sally. When used quantificationally, the phrase represents an *arbitrary* dog which is no dog in particular. But the quantificational use exceeds the abilities of the language learner who can so far use expressions only to attend, to acknowledge, and to indicate features of the acts he is performing. Even language users who know how to use indefinite phrases quantificationally commonly use such phrases to identify particular individuals. The indefinite phrase in 'A dog bit Sally' would most naturally be used in this way. So would the subject phrase in 'An aunt left me some money.'

The child who expands his world beyond present experience will learn to acknowledge objects to presently be ϕ, to have been ϕ, and to be going to be ϕ. In using the sentence 'Mama was asleep' like this:

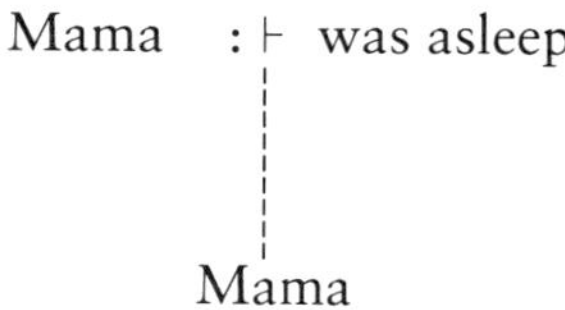

the past-tense auxiliary marks the acknowledging act as concerned with the past. It does this whether or not the speaker separately attends to his use of 'was', so that he intends to perform an act signaling the temporal orientation of his acknowledging. The speaker is not attending to Mama-in-the-past, or to a past "slice" of Mama, he simply attends to Mama. In acknowledging her to have been asleep, he also attends to a past event of Mama sleeping. If he is right, he has identified the event as well as having identified Mama. This observation provides a link between our two senses of 'identify'. In the more fundamental sense, identifying consists of using an expression or image to attend to a particular object. Correctly acknowledging an object to be ϕ is also a way of identifying that object, but this is a less basic sort of identifying. However, correctly acknowledging an object to be (or to have been) ϕ is also a way of identifying, in the fundamental sense, the *situation* of the object being ϕ.

One can attend to an event in the past or present or future. Events can be acknowledged to be one thing or another. Instead of simply acknowledging Mama to have been asleep, the speaker might use 'Mama was asleep for a long time' to characterize her sleeping. He could do this in several different ways. Like this, for example:

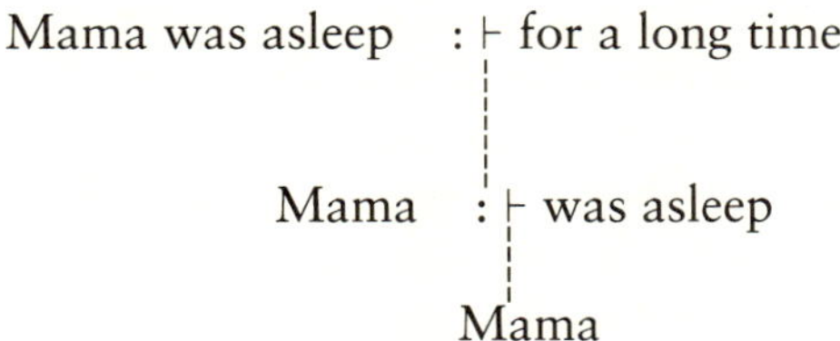

The speaker attends to Mama, which gives him a target he can acknowledge to have been asleep. This enables him to acknowledge the (event of her) sleeping to have gone on for a long time. The phrase 'for a long time' is an idiomatic way to acknowledge an event to be lengthy. It would be odd, even unnatural, for the speaker to use 'a long time' to attend to a particular length of time. In the acts above, there are two "moments": the speaker separately acknowledges the sleeping and the long time.

If the event of Mama sleeping had already been the focus of discussion, the speaker might perform these acts:

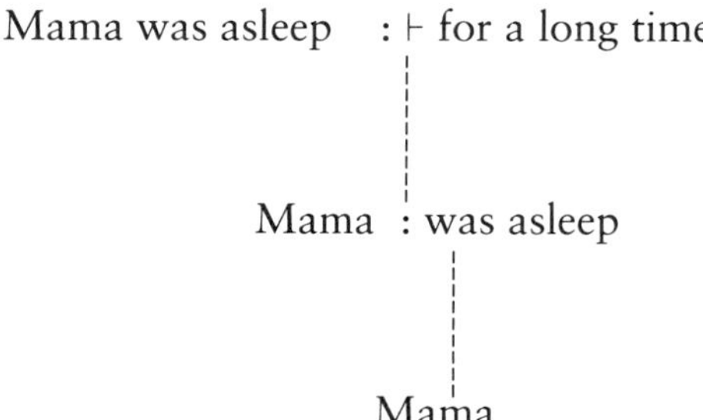

Instead of acknowledging Mama to have been asleep, he simply attends to the event of her sleeping, which is enabled by his attending to Mama. In case the speaker's "Mama was asleep" echoes a previous statement, he might perform acts like this:

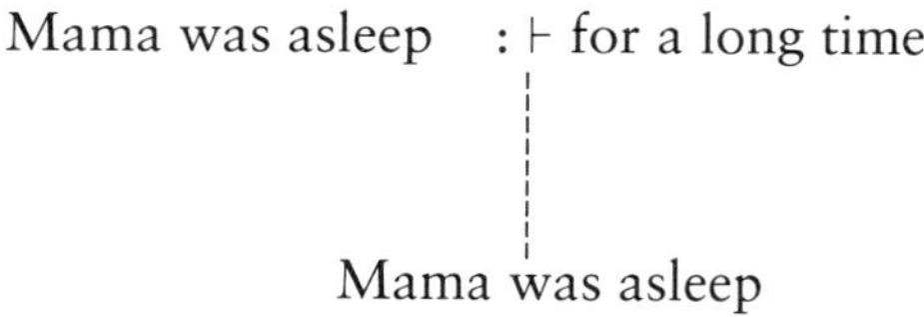

The speaker uses 'Mama was asleep' as a unit to attend to the event of Mama's sleeping.

The language learner who can attend, acknowledge, and make explicit some of the things he is doing is unable to use indefinite phrases quantificationally. For similar reasons, he is unable to use the sentence 'Mama was asleep' to say that a Mama-sleeping event occurred at some time or other in the past. He cannot quantify over future times either. The language learner can attend to particular events and collections of events, he cannot yet represent an arbitrary event of a kind. But this does not mean that when the language learner performs acts like these:

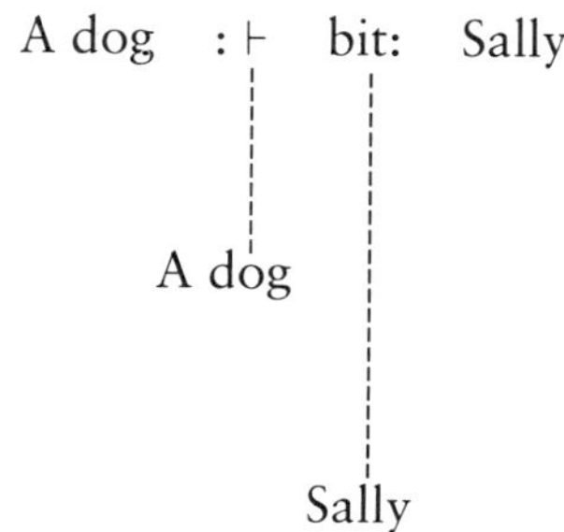

he must be able to give an answer to the question "When?" For this question calls for a day or date, or some finer subdivision (like "Saturday afternoon"). A particular event is itself a temporal location. It also belongs to days, dates, and times, but one can attend to the event even when he can't say what day the event belongs to.

Before he learns to use language, the preverbal subject's world of experience is constituted by his present experience. One subject's world can contain other subjects, but only while the other subjects are being perceived. Two preverbal worlds that overlap in the sense of containing some of the same parts will do so only temporarily. The preverbal subject's world of experience isn't private, but it is limited. Different subjects don't, and can't, experience a common world.

When a child learns to use language, his world expands. It contains things perceived and unperceived. It is a world with a past and a future. The world of the language-using subject is not independent of the subject, for the world is organized and structured by concepts that the subject brings to it. But no language user speaks a private language. Each language user is a member of a linguistic community, and not one limited to speakers of a single natural language like English. A family of intertranslatable languages can provide the basis for constituting a community. When the child becomes a member of a linguistic community, the world he experiences can be experienced by other members of his community. Members of a linguistic community are in a position where it is possible for them to experience a common world.

Although it is possible, members of a linguistic community don't quite experience a common world. For different members speak their language(s) with varying degrees of fluency. Different members have different specialties, and have mastered different technical sublanguages. They also have different values and goals, which leads them to conceive certain things differently. Since the world a given subject encounters in experience is determined by the conceptual structure he brings to it, different people can't encounter exactly the same world.

Putnam has reminded us that there is a division of linguistic labor. Some people know more than others, and this includes linguistic knowledge. Those who know less defer to those who know more. When I encounter a word I understand imperfectly or not at all, I can look it up. Either by paging through the dictionary, or by consulting someone who understands the word. But my world isn't already structured by the experts' concepts. In mastering or acquiring a concept, I give additional structure to my world of experience. Previously my world contained this structure potentially, since I belong to the community and am disposed to defer to experts. My world didn't actually contain the structure. And the disposition to defer to experts won't cure the differences in worlds that are derived from accepting different values.

A world of experience common to members of a linguistic community is an ideal that we strive for, not an actual fact. Although each person experiences a world that is in principle common to other language-using subjects, there are in fact a very large number of (slightly) different worlds that different people experience.

2. Parts of the World

The child learning language constitutes his world, but not from scratch. For he provides structure to the world of experience, and he had a world of experience to start with. The structure not only organizes his present experience, but it also enlarges his world to include parts not presently being experienced, as well as the past and the future. He doesn't invent the structures he imposes, but takes over structures provided by his linguistic community, though his language and his world may have some "twists" peculiar to himself. The ordinary conception of experience and its objects is essential to the language learning we are following. The child must learn to identify and reidentify objects he has experienced or might experience, or objects connected to them in ways he understands. He is in no position to infer the existence of objects which merely cause his experience, nor can he identify objects so fleeting that they can't be experienced twice.

At the start, the part of a subject's world that constitutes a single object, like his mother, won't have a different status from a part with multiple instances. He can't appreciate that there is only one mother but there are (potentially) lots of dogs. But how might he come to appreciate this? If ϕ is a kind with multiple instances, then it is possible for different ϕ's to turn up on a single occasion. The language learner will acquire devices for distinguishing one ϕ from another. He can attend to this ϕ or that one or to the ϕ in the corner. He will also learn to track the different ϕ's, and to acknowledge one to have been that, and now be this. He will come to appreciate that different connections lead to one object. The language learner will also acquire devices for indicating that different attending acts have a single target. He will learn to use expressions like the following:

Some dog bit Sally. It was . . .
Some dog bit Sally. That dog was . . .
Some dog bit Sally. The dog that bit Sally was . . .

Once the language learner has acquired these (linguistic) devices, he is well on the way to having a concept of individual identity. (Being able to perform identifying acts is not the same as possessing a concept of identity. 'Identifying' is our technical term for certain kinds of linguistic acts. To possess a concept of individual identity is to understand what it is for an object at one time to be the same as an object at a different time, and what it is for two attending or acknowledging acts to identify the same object—to identify a single object.)

When he can perform linguistic acts, the language learner can use expressions to attend to the same object more than once. He can acknowledge a single object to be different things (a dog, in the corner, brown, etc.). When the language learner expands his world beyond his present experience, he must not only attend to one ϕ on different occasions, but must also understand the difference between attending to this ϕ and attending to some other. ("The dog in the corner is the dog that bit Sally." "The dog that bit Sally also bit Danny." "The dog in the front yard is not the dog that bit Sally.") To be able to identify and distinguish objects of a kind, at the same time and at different times, is to possess the concept of (individual) identity. The language learner who can recognize a ϕ on one occasion to be (the same object as) a ϕ on another occasion possesses the resources to recognize his various Sally-identifying acts to have a single target. Objects with names are like instances of the dog part of the world. They don't themselves have instances or elements, they are simply found in different places at different times, never in different places at one time.

The objects to which the language learner attends, and which he acknowledges to be this or that, are parts of the world of his experience. A part of the world of experience is a location or (possibly) a situation which isn't a location. The language learner can attend to a spatial location (his right hand, Mama), a temporal location (today, yesterday), a spatiotemporal location (Mama sleeping yesterday), or a location situated with respect to one of the foregoing (the subject's self). Although each subject's own body, and also each self-conscious subject's self, are fundamental locations for that subject, there are no absolute locations. Whenever *X* is situated with respect to *Y*, then *Y* is situated with respect to *X*.

Some parts of the world of experience are relatively stable. Some prominent qualities endure, or the part continues to be organized in a certain way, or its behavior is regular, etc. Some parts are short-lived, like the dog's biting Sally. And some longer-lived parts are unstable, constantly converging with and diverging from other parts which provide its "content." Parts move with respect to each other. Although characteristic parts of the world of experience are locations, they are dynamic locations, not static ones. They are not situated with respect to one fixed frame of reference, but are situated with respect to a variety of frames which are themselves constituted by various locations.

The language learner can also attend to groups or collections of ϕ's. He can attend to *these* ϕ's or *those* ϕ's. He can, for example, attend to these animals and acknowledge them to be dogs:

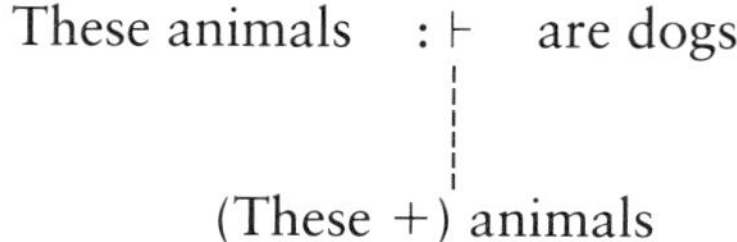

The plural 'These animals' signals that the object to which the speaker attends involves more than one animal. Particular animals which he presently perceives are a *group*. A group of animals is a physical object constituted by the animals and their (constantly changing) spatial relations—other relations may be important as well, as when the animals constitute a pack that has some cohesion. A speaker can also attend to a particular *collection* of objects. A collection is constituted by objects considered together. Animals which constitute a group can also constitute a collection for a person who considers them "in abstraction" from their relations to one another. Collections have some similarity to sets, but they aren't sets. For collections are literally constituted by their elements; there are no null collections, and collections go out of existence when their elements do. Collections are also different from structured wholes whose different parts are organized to constitute the whole. (A group is a structured whole.) A collection is "put together" from the outside rather than unified by some internal structure.

In acknowledging the particular group or collection to be dogs, the speaker is performing a (slightly) different kind of acknowledging act than a speaker who acknowledges a single animal to be a dog. The multiple dog-acknowledging act is marked by the plural form, but its kind is determined by the criteria used in performing it. The criteria for acknowledging one animal to be a dog involve the appearance and behavior of the animal. For acknowledging the group or collection to be dogs, each member must satisfy the one-dog criteria.

The language learner will soon be taught to count, and to use numerals to perform acknowledging acts. ("That is one cat." "There are two dogs." "Here are five fingers.") A numerical sentence might be used to perform these acts:

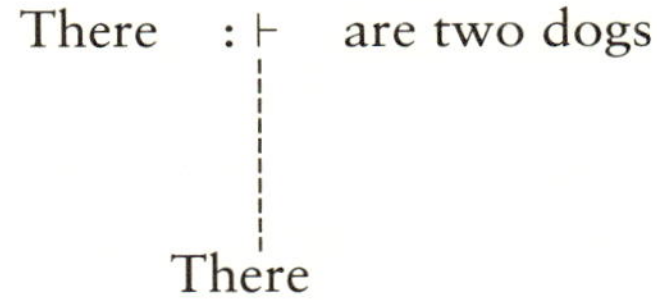

The speaker uses 'There' to attend to the particular group or collection. (From now on I will simply speak of collections rather than of collections *and/or* groups. Most of what I say applies to both collections and groups. If it doesn't, I will say so.) His attending act enables him to use 'two dogs' to perform an acknowledging act. Each element of the collection must satisfy the one-dog criteria, and the collection as a whole must be two-membered. In acknowledging a collection to have a certain number of elements, a speaker performs a different kind of collection-acknowledging act than the speaker who acknowledges a collection to be animals. For the numerical acknowledging act is *collective*, its criteria concern the collection as a whole.

3. Groups and Collections

Initially, preverbally, the world of experience consists of various parts, variously qualified, variously situated, and variously changing. When perceptual structure is introduced, some parts are classified in the sense of being experienced as representative, or typical. It seems likely that this structure favors stable objects and short-lived events of recurring and easily recognized kinds over sporadic events and locations that contain now this, now that. One learns to experience quantities of water as representative, and also dogs and certain sounds. But not the location directly over one's head. While the perceptual framework introduces structure into the world, it doesn't introduce new objects; neither does it introduce *kinds* of objects. A kind is constituted by objects of that kind, and the experiencing subject needs some device to unify the various objects that make up the kind. His perceptual frameworks allow him to experience objects (parts of the world) in new ways, but don't provide unifying devices. When the child learns to speak and understand language—to use language—he acquires indefinitely many such devices.

An object correctly acknowledged to be ϕ may possess the property of being a ϕ. But the language learner isn't yet in a position to talk or think about properties. Being able to use the ϕ-expression to attend to ϕ's and to acknowledge objects to be ϕ doesn't give the learner access to a property, but it does give him the resources for attending to the ϕ part of the world. A particular dog or group of dogs can be a location in the language learner's world of experience. A preverbal subject could attend to such a location when it belongs to his present experience, though he couldn't conceive it to be a dog or dogs. The verbal subject is further equipped to attend to all the dogs there are, which dogs constitute the dog part of his world. This requires that the language learner achieve a new degree of abstraction in his linguistic acts. To attend to an absent object or objects, there must be a connection between the language user and the object of his attention. This connection must be in his world of experience. Things are different when a person uses an expression to attend to all dogs. He isn't attending to just those dogs that he (or someone else) already knows about. He attends to the collection of those objects that *could* be correctly acknowledged to be dogs. This is a collection that contains different dogs at different times, a collection that didn't always exist, and that may someday cease to exist. (But if it did cease to exist, it might reemerge at a later time—for example, on some scenario like that of *Jurassic Park*.) A person attending to the collection of all dogs is not exploiting a connection or connections linking him to each dog. (Although, of course, there are various connections linking him to each dog.) So what is he doing?

Dogs constitute a *part* of the language user's world, and so does water, once the language user knows expressions for dogs and water.

(Dogs are in his world before he understands 'dog', but the dogs don't constitute a *part* of his world before he learns the word.) These parts are discontinuous, or scattered. Parts constituted by discrete individuals are different from parts constituted by stuff, for parts constituted by discrete individuals are collections (they aren't groups), and a part constituted by stuff is like a scattered lump of the stuff. The water part of the world is the quantity of water constituted by all the quantities of water scattered here and there. Both kinds of parts are literally made up of their various instances. The language user attends to one of these parts with respect to a linguistic practice, an acknowledging practice. The practice of acknowledging objects to be dogs (this practice constitutes the concept of a dog) is the basis for attending to the collection of objects satisfying the dog criteria. Instead of exploiting objective paths through the world, the language user "exploits" the criteria for being a dog. The dogs don't constitute an objective item in the world before the language user attends to them, and (consequently) there isn't an objective path linking the language user to the dog part. The language user can consider together all those objects that satisfy the *dog* criteria. His thinking them together "makes" the object of his attention. This isn't a unified or a unitary object. It has no status apart from his attending, and isn't qualified to be a single element of some further collection.

If a language user acknowledges a particular animal to be a dog, he has brought that animal under the concept 'dog'. He has classified the animal as a dog, but he has not acknowledged the animal to belong to the dog part of the world, for he hasn't attended to the dog part of the world. However, if his acknowledging act is correct, the animal does belong to the dog part (whenever the dog part is constituted). Once the child learns to acknowledge objects to be ϕ, then, if there are ϕ's, he has introduced a new object into his world. (We could teach a language learner to use 'unicorn' to perform acknowledging acts, even though he will never have occasion to correctly do so. But his world wouldn't contain a unicorn part.) Before he learns to identify ϕ's, the language learner's world is suited to the introduction of the ϕ part, but for that part to actually belong to his world, he must acquire the concept of a ϕ.

The language learner who can use 'dog' and 'dogs' to attend to dogs and to acknowledge animals to be dogs will learn to use the same words for the entire dog part of the world. He will learn to perform acts like these:

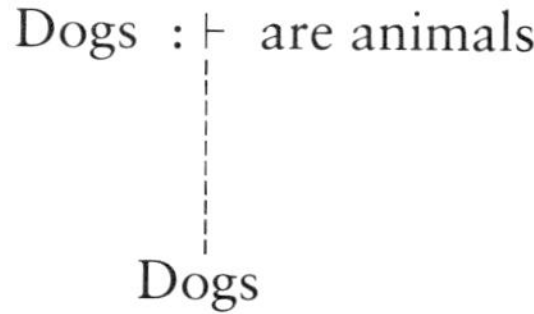

The speaker attends to the dog part of his world, to the dog *kind*. The plural number makes explicit that his is a multi-dog attending act. He uses 'animals' to acknowledge the dog part to be an animal part. Language users also use indefinite phrases to attend to multiple-individual parts of the world:

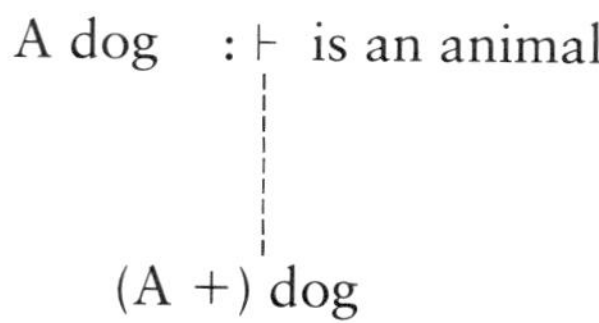

Here the indefinite article makes explicit that a discrete-individual part of the world is the object of attention, though many speakers would simply use the phrase as a unit to attend to the dog part of the world.

The language learner/user who becomes sensitive to scattered, multiple-individual parts of the world might use the sentence 'A dog is an animal' to perform acts different from those represented above. A single sentence can be used to perform acts organized in quite different ways. He might use the sentence as follows:

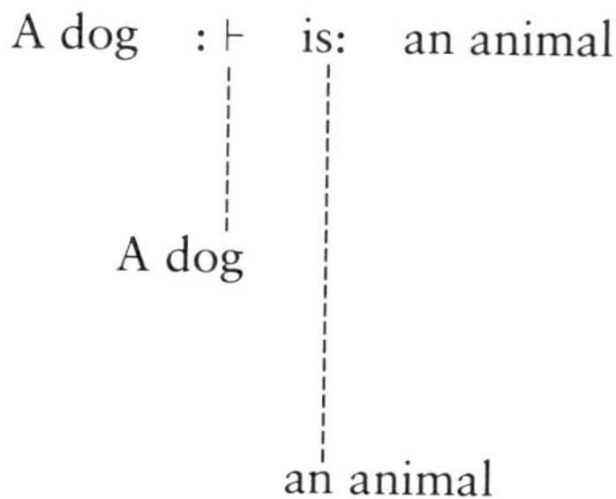

The speaker uses ‘A dog’ to attend to the dog part of his world, and ‘an animal’ to attend to the animal part. The animal part serves as a reference point for his acknowledging act. Here he uses ‘is’ by itself to acknowledge the dog part of the world to be situated by inclusion with respect to the animal part. This last use of the sentence might be marked by a break before and after ‘is’. These acts would be appropriate in a context where the speaker is considering different multiple-individual parts of the world.

If the sentences ‘A dog is an animal’ and ‘Dogs are animals’ can be used to acknowledge one multiple-individual part to be situated-as-included with respect to another, then the sentence ‘Muppet is an animal’ might be used to do something similar:

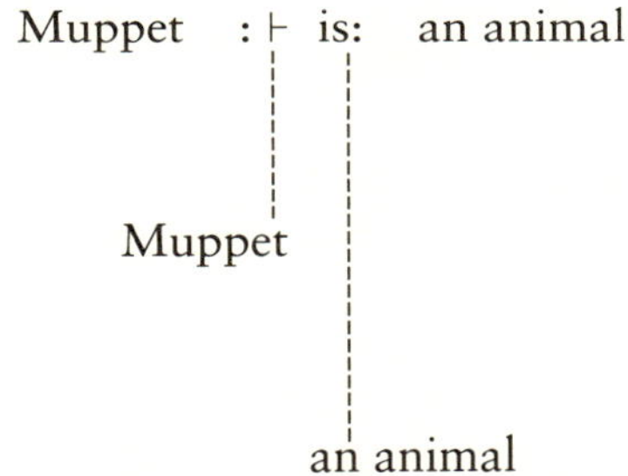

The speaker uses ‘an animal’ to attend to the animal part of his world, enabling himself to use ‘is’ to acknowledge the particular dog Muppet to be situated by inclusion with respect to that part.

When a language user acquires a concept ϕ and becomes able to attend to the objects that fall under ϕ, he has increased his opportunities to attend to objects that aren’t there. He might learn to use words like ‘ghost’, ‘goblin’, and ‘vampire’ without learning that there are no such things. And it is easy to combine words for real things to obtain compounds like ‘round and square’ and ‘healthful cigarette’. A speaker who uses an expression to perform an attending act is trying to perform an identifying act, for he is committed to there really being an object of his attention. However, these expressions can be used to perform negative acknowledging acts without the speaker being committed to the existence of ghosts and goblins and vampires. A speaker who attends to a shadowy figure and performs these acts:

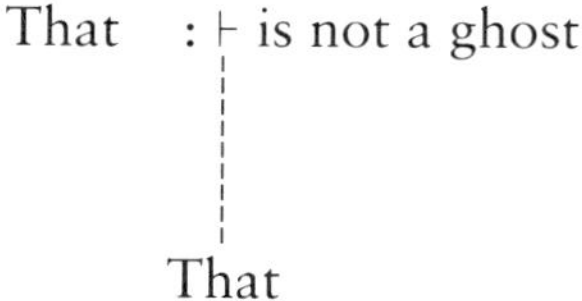

has not acknowledged anything to be a ghost. And, of course, everything *is* a nonghost. As well as denying a particular object to be ghost, a speaker can deny there to be ghosts:

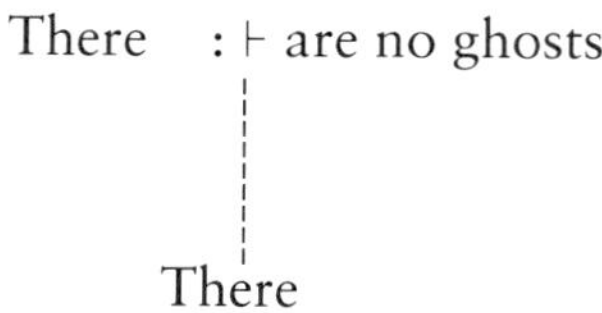

The speaker uses 'There' to attend to the whole world, which enables him to acknowledge it to be wholly (either in the present or at all times) without ghosts.

The language learner can attend to groups in his experience; he doesn't need an expression for this. He needs expressions to attend to collections. He can use an expression ϕ to attend either to a particular collection like the dogs that knocked over the garbage cans or to a scattered multiple-individual collection like the collection of all dogs. It is his (or someone's) attending to them together that unifies the members to constitute a collection. But his attending to and constituting collections is not sufficient for his possessing the concept of a collection of things or a kind of thing. This requires that the language learner become aware of his own practices of attending to objects and of using words for things. The criteria for being acknowledged to be a collection or kind require that the members be collectively attended to either with respect to his own acknowledging and attending practices or with respect to those of his linguistic community. Although the language learner will attend to collections before he understands what a collection is, it shouldn't take long for him to acquire such concepts.

He can then advance beyond acknowledging dogs to be animals. He can acknowledge dogs to be one *kind* of animal and cats to be another, performing acts like these:

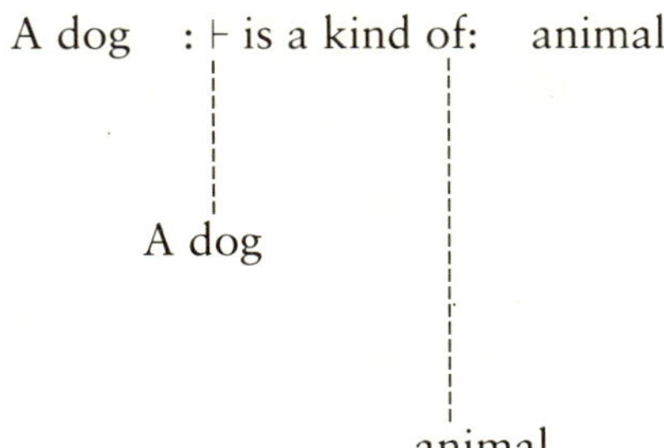

The animal part of the world provides a reference point, enabling the speaker to acknowledge the dog part to be a kind with respect to that reference point. Once the language learner can deal with kinds of animals, he is in a position to admit new kinds when he encounters new animals, even if he doesn't have a word for them. Pointing to an unfamiliar individual at the zoo, he could use the sentence 'That kind of animal is ugly'. Although he can visually attend only to the particular animal before him, he can mentally attend to the kind to which the animal belongs—of which it is representative.

Not every part of the world included in another part is called a kind of that part. But some nonkind parts are treated in ways characteristic of kinds. Talk of colors and shapes is like this. In these acts:

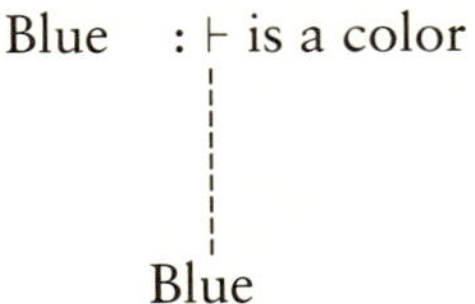

blue is not a quality with multiple exemplifications. The speaker uses 'Blue' to attend to the blue part of the world. He acknowledges this part to be a color part. Just as in these acts:

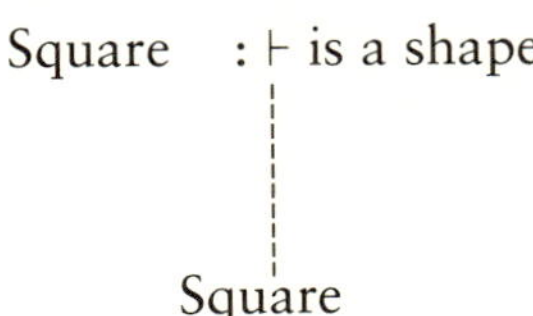

the square part is acknowledged to be a shape part. (But the blue part seems more stuff-like, while the square part is best regarded as a collection.)

Now that the language learner can attend to scattered multiple-individual parts of the world, he can use the sentence 'There are two dogs' to perform differently organized acts than those considered earlier. He might use the sentence like this:

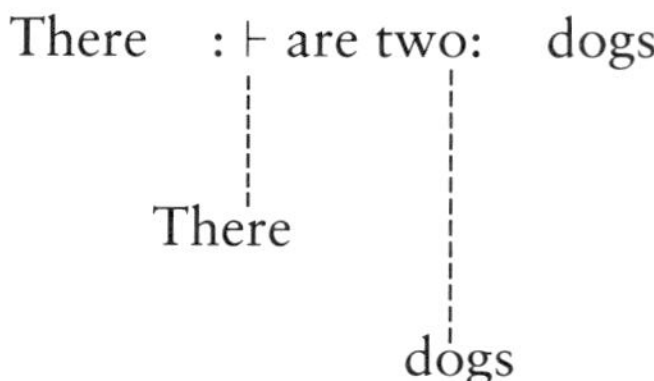

The speaker uses 'There' to attend to a particular collection, and uses 'dogs' to attend to the dog part of the world. He acknowledges the collection before him to be two with respect to the dog part of the world. These acts would be appropriate if the speaker is displaying his ability to use numerals correctly. ("Here are three dogs. There are two dogs. Altogether we have five dogs.")

4. Categorical Statements

In tracing a path for learning language, we haven't so far arrived at very many kinds of linguistic skills. We have considered acts of attending and acknowledging, and acts which confer a character on a further act, usually a character which makes explicit a feature the further act already has. Attending acts have particular things and particular groups and collections of things as objects, as well as scattered, multi-thing parts of the world. Someone can attend to objects present and absent, to objects no longer or not yet in existence. He can also, by mistake, attend to objects with no existence at all.

Of the character-conferring acts, some are performed with expressions designed just for this job. Expressions like 'this', 'that', 'the', 'a', and 'same'. Characters can also be conferred by attending acts. A speaker might perform these acts to attend to a particular dog:

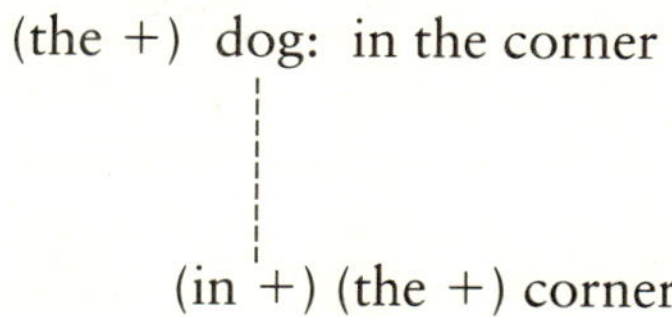

He uses the corner as a reference point, which enables him to use 'dog' to attend to a particular dog situated in the corner. But he might also perform these acts:

(the +) dog [+ (in +) (the +) corner]

Here he simply uses 'dog' to attend to the dog in question. He adds 'in the corner' to make clear to his audience where the dog is. The prepositional act makes explicit the dog's situation with respect to the corner.

When someone uses expressions to attend and acknowledge, the simplest (and most common?) cases are those where he attends to particular locations, to particular events, to particular situations, and then acknowledges them to be this or that. And when the particular thing is acknowledged to be ϕ, or to be situated by ψ with respect to some other thing, nothing is acknowledged to be included in a part of the world. The speaker who acknowledges Sally to be mean is classifying Sally, but he isn't attending to the mean person part of the world. However, if his acknowledging act is correct, then Sally is included in the mean person part.

We can acknowledge things to be variously situated with respect to scattered multiple-individual parts of the world. We can also attend to these parts and acknowledge them to be one thing or another. A part of the world can be acknowledged to be various sorts of things. Dogs can be acknowledged to be animals and to bark. Birds are animals too, and they fly. Cows give milk. Birds are numerous and widespread. Dinosaurs are extinct. In discussing acts acknowledging a collection to be this or that, we have distinguished collective from noncollective acts. But this distinction isn't fine enough. There are importantly different kinds of noncollective acknowledging act. Someone acknowledging dogs to be animals has noncollectively acknowledged the collection of dogs to all be animals. Someone acknowledging dogs to bark, or to make good pets, is also performing a noncollective acknowledging act. But he isn't (or shouldn't be) acknowledging the dog part of the world to be entirely barkers, or potential good pets. In these cases it is sufficient if dogs *characteristically* bark or make good pets.

So far we have recognized more kinds of acknowledging acts than of attending acts. A person can use an expression to attend to:

> a particular location or situation or event;
> a collection;
> a scattered part constituted by stuff—scattered "lumps."

A group is different from a collection in this context. A group is a structured object, and so constitutes a particular location. A collection is slightly more abstract than a group, for it is constituted by objects considered apart from their spatial and other relations. Someone reflecting on set theory might attempt to distinguish two kinds of collection-attending acts, which would constitute two kinds of collection. Consider the difference between:

> Dogs are animals.
> Dogs are a kind of animals.

or between:

> Dogs and cats are animals.
> Dogs and cats are two kinds of animals.

Modelling our understanding on set theory, we might think we could understand the first two like this:

> Dogs $\subset$ Animals
> Dogs $\in$ Kinds of Animal

and the second pair like this:

> (Dogs $\cup$ Cats) $\subset$ Animals
> {Dogs, Cats} $\subset$ Kinds of Animal

However, this set theoretic analogy is a bad one. Our language learner hasn't yet got the resources for thinking or talking about set theory. Nor can he speak this set theoretic analogue. To do this requires new fundamental skills.

It is certainly true that there are different ways, or different respects in which one can attend to a collection. There are also different ways or respects in which one can attend to a particular object. One can attend to a person, and consider her face, or her eyes, or the color of her hair. These different respects don't give different kinds of person, though they do lead to (support) different acknowledging acts. Someone might acknowledge her to be smiling, or to have blue eyes, or to be blonde, for example. Someone can also attend to a collection either "distributively" or as a whole, but that doesn't give us two kinds of collection. The different kinds of attending support different kinds of acknowledging. Attending to cats distributively is appropriate if one is going to noncollectively acknowledge cats to be felines.

A collection is constituted by several items, considered together. While a collection is something in addition to its various members, someone's considering the members together doesn't provide a unifying principle as strong as that which informs a structured whole. A collection isn't qualified to play the role of a single indivisible element of a larger collection. A collection of two collections is no different from the collection of the elements of the two collections, for in considering the collections one is considering their elements. Considering the collections together is no different from considering their elements together. If we perform these acts:

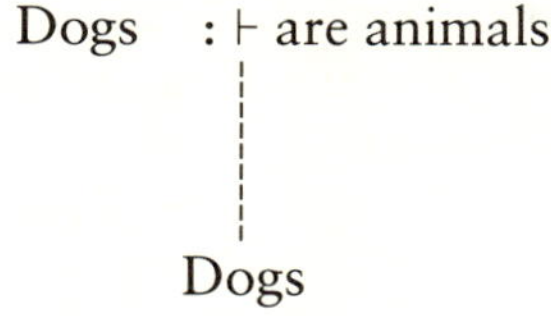

the acknowledging is not collective. But here:

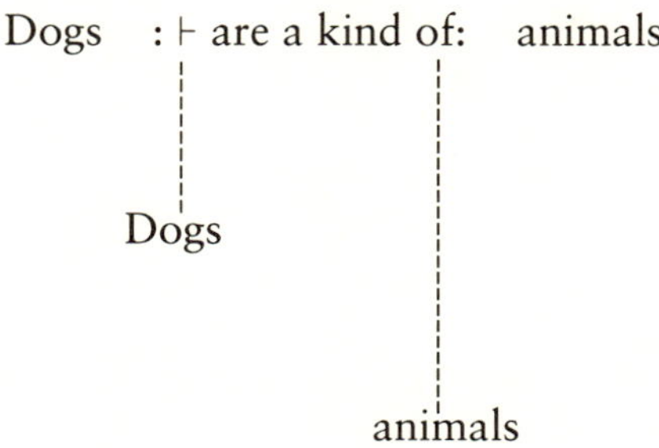

the speaker is collectively acknowledging the dog part of the world to be situated with respect to the animal part of the world. The dog collection is as a whole an animal kind. This collective acknowledging act is of a different sort than that performed using ‘Dogs are numerous’. The criteria for acknowledging dogs to be numerous require us to consider how many particular dogs there are. To acknowledge dogs to be a kind of animals, we needn’t “look into” the dog collection.

The sentence ‘Dogs and cats are animals’ might be used like this:

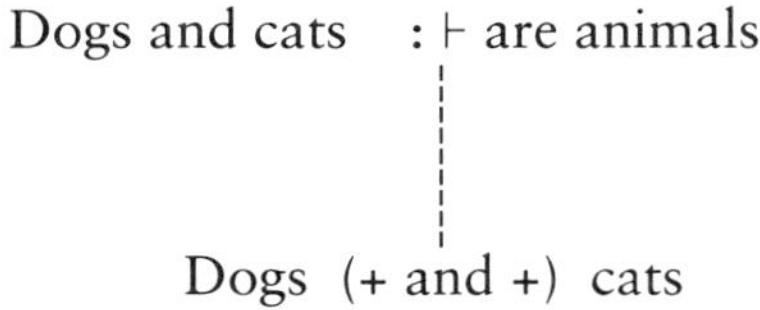

The phrase ‘Dogs and cats’ is used to attend to the part of the world constituted by both dogs and cats; every cat and every dog belong to, and constitute, the collection. In attending to dogs and attending to cats, one has done all the attending needed to attend to dogs-and-cats. What is required in addition is the intention to attend to them together. In the acts represented above, the speaker uses ‘and’ to make explicit that this is his intention.

In using the sentence ‘Dogs and cats are two kinds of animals’, the speaker won’t attend to a different collection than that represented above. There is no two-element collection of the dog kind and the cat kind of animals, which is different from the collection of all cats and all dogs. The speaker could use the sentence like this:

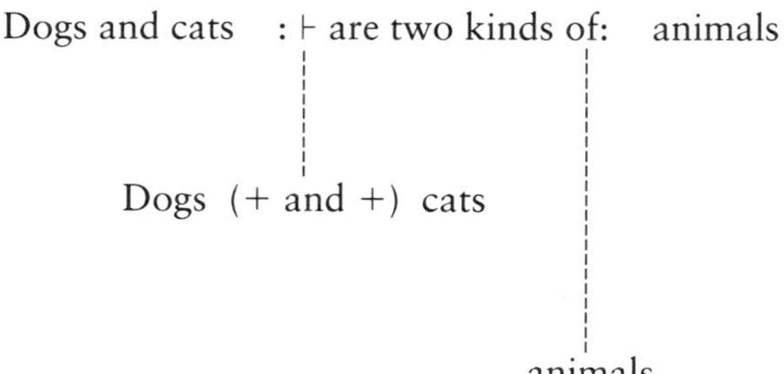

Instead of attending to a different collection, the speaker is performing a different kind of acknowledging act than is represented in the preceding paragraph. The dog and cat collection is collectively acknowledged to be (disjointly and exhaustively) divisible into two animal-kinds.

If someone attends to a collection of collections, he at the same time attends to the collection of elements of the component collections. Collections as tightly knit units have no standing in the language learner's world of experience. The collection of objects of attention might itself be the object of attention, but it is not an element of itself, somehow distinct from itself. Our understanding of collections seems to be the "leading idea" behind Lesniewski's formal system *Ontology*. The fundamental categories of expressions in Ontology contain "words" for this sort of collection and functors for performing different kinds of acts acknowledging collections to be this or that. (Lesniewski construes particular objects as limiting cases of collections, as one-member collections.) Lesniewski's nominalism may be partly due to his thinking (in effect) that the fundamental linguistic acts we have uncovered so far are the only fundamental acts. If we were limited to performing only the linguistic acts considered to this point, we would have no basis for admitting properties, sets, and other abstract entities into our ontology. However, even to develop and investigate the formal system Ontology requires resources exceeding those presently available to our language learner.

Lesniewski's system Ontology is a kind of theory or conceptual framework for collections. His system Mereology is suited to talking/thinking about scattered (and nonscattered) lumps of stuff, though it also accommodates "lumps" of discrete objects. (Sobocinski [1949] speaks of collective and distributive classes, and says that Ontology is concerned with distributive classes while Mereology deals with collective classes. This terminology is unfortunate, for collective classes don't deserve to be called classes.) Lesniewski regarded the concept of a set as illicit and incoherent. He thought it was the product of a failure to distinguish collections from scattered and nonscattered lumps.

For a scattered part of the world to be ϕ, it is often sufficient that members of that part are typically ϕ. But a person *can* acknowledge such a part to be wholly ϕ. While 'Dogs bark' can be used to make a true statement, the sentence 'All dogs bark' cannot. This last sentence wouldn't be used as follows:

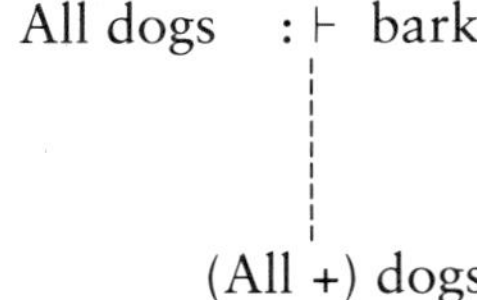

'All' makes its contribution to the speaker's acknowledging act rather than to his attending act. In using the sentence (correctly), he would acknowledge the dog part of the world to be wholly a barking part. He would either use 'bark' to perform this acknowledging act, and use 'All' to make explicit that he is doing so:

(All +) : dogs :⊢ bark

dogs

Or he could use 'All . . . bark' as a single expression to perform his acknowledging act:

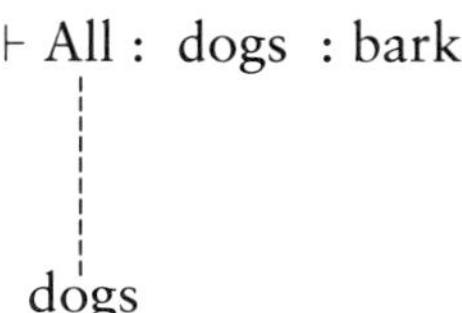

As well as acknowledging a scattered part of the world to be wholly ϕ, one can acknowledge it to be wholly not-ϕ:

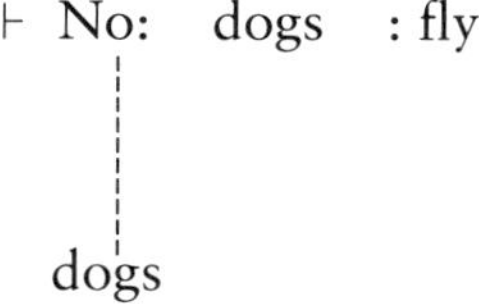

A sentence of the form 'All S's are P's' can also be used like this:

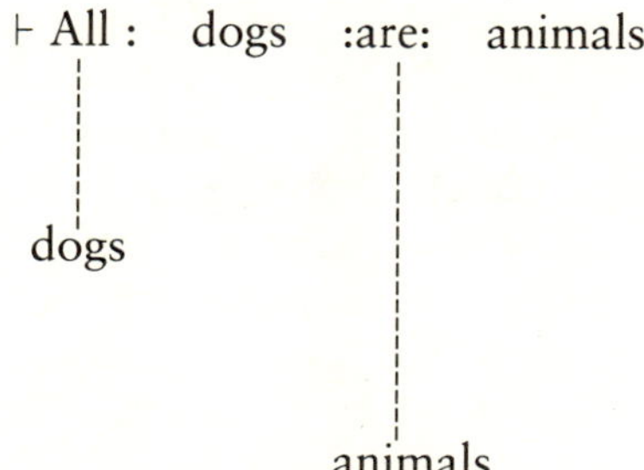

The animal part of the world serves as a reference point, enabling the speaker to acknowledge the dog part to wholly belong to the animal part.

A particular object can also be acknowledged to be wholly ϕ, but in that case being wholly ϕ would be contrasted with being partly ϕ. So we have both:

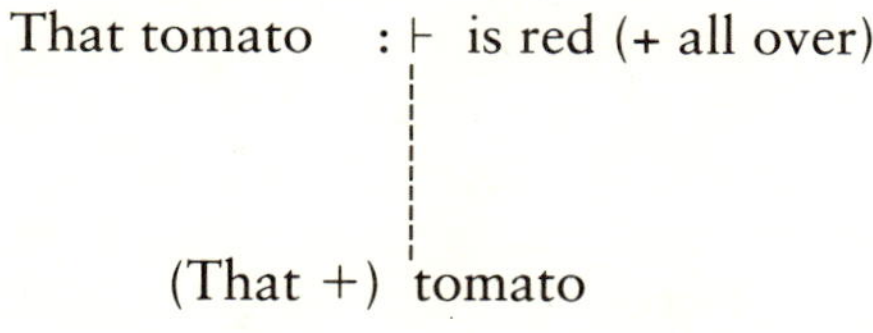

and:

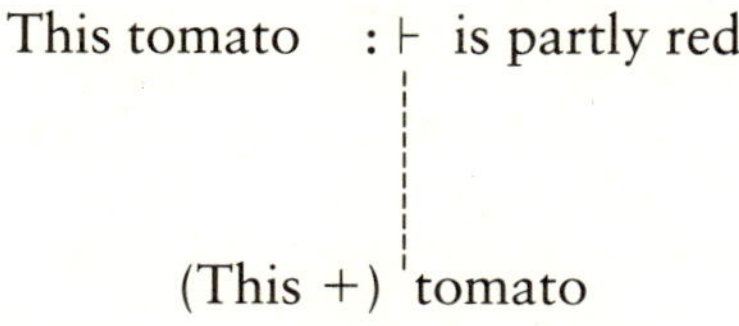

A scattered multiple-individual part of the world can also be acknowledged to be partly ϕ, where this requires that one or more instances be wholly ϕ:

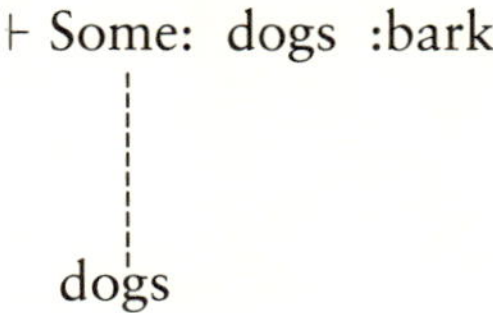

We need 'some' to carry out this kind of partial acknowledging. For example, saying that some dogs are black means something quite different from saying either that all dogs are partly black or that some dogs are partly black. Though 'Dogs are partly black' could probably be used to say that some dogs are black.

In illustrating categorical statements that involve attending and (various sorts of) acknowledging, I have used plural forms because I want to distinguish these statements from those in which expressions are used quantificationally. Although 'Every dog is an animal' and 'Some dog is an animal' can be used similarly to 'All dogs are animals' and 'Some dogs are animals,' it is more natural to use 'Every dog' and 'Some dog' quantificationally. The speaker who says "Some dog is a collie," meaning some dog or other, is not attending to the dog part of the world and he doesn't acknowledge that part to be anything. The quantificational use of expressions exceeds the resources of the language learner who can only attend, acknowledge, and make explicit.

The quantificational use will be explained when we see how the language learner gets beyond the initial stage of language learning/language use. The categorical statements "All S's are . . . ," "No S's are . . . ," "Some S's are . . . ," "Some S's are not . . . ," are equivalent in some important sense to statements which use phrases quantificationally, but not all statements containing quantificational acts are equivalent to categorical statements. So far the language learner can acknowledge boys to like girls, either characteristically or wholly or partly, but he can't acknowledge each boy to like a girl who is too good for him. When expressions are used quantificationally, one quantificational act can "cover" or apply to another (it can include the other in its "scope"). Such relations don't figure in the categorical statements.

The language learner can so far acknowledge the S part of the world to be partly ϕ. Without too much further effort, he can learn to use numerical expressions with respect to multiple-individual parts of the world:

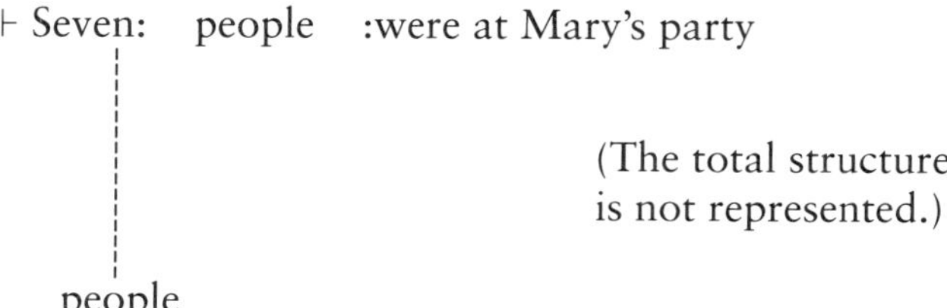

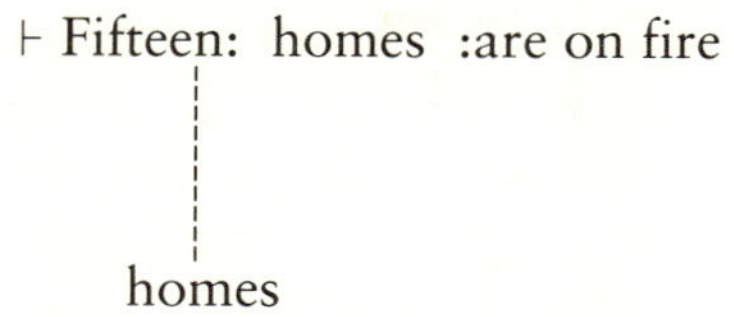

In the second diagram (in the acts that it represents), 'homes' may not be used to attend to the entire home part of the world. It is more likely that the expression will be used to attend to a smaller selection determined by the context of utterance. (Homes in this town, homes in this neighborhood, etc.)

5. Identity

The language learner can use expressions to identify objects and situations, as well as to make explicit certain features of his acts, but, so far, he cannot use expressions to represent. He is in the *purely identifying stage* of language use. Once he learns to use expressions to become representationally aware of arbitrary objects of a kind, he will enter the *representational stage of language use.* In order to understand propositional thinking, as well as belief and knowledge, we will explore the purely identifying stage, to see what kind of experience and understanding are available at this stage. We will then be in a position to appreciate how much of an advance the learner makes in entering the representational stage.

This investigation of the uses of language is necessary to provide a solution to Descartes' larger problem. To understand experience and its contribution to thought, belief, and knowledge, we must understand the linguistic/mental acts that constitute propositional thinking, and give conceptual structure to experience. The investigation will also provide understanding of linguistic and mental phenomena that have an interest independently of Descartes' Problem. In this section we will consider the concept of identity that is expressed by judgments of identity, and determine just what meanings are conveyed by such judgments.

Acknowledging an object to be ϕ is judging that object to be ϕ. This is to judge it to satisfy the criteria for being ϕ, though without (necessarily) giving special thought, or attention, to those criteria. The speaker uses an expression to bring the object under the concept ϕ; it is the same kind of acknowledging act whether there are one or many ϕ's. Although an acknowledging statement is an attempted identifying statement, this is not the same thing as an identity statement. An identity statement involves two acts of attending to (what is claimed to be) a single object; in making the statement, the speaker judges there to be a single object. Sentences like 'Mark Twain is Samuel Clemens' have traditionally been associated with identity statements. But the sentence can be used in other ways, as is illustrated here:

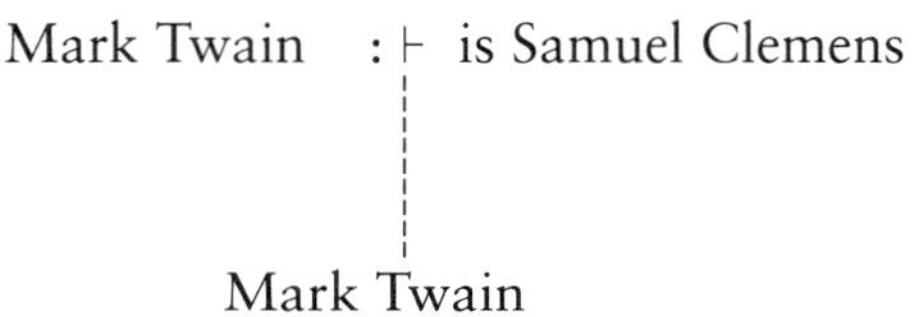

The phrase 'is Samuel Clemens' is used to acknowledge Mark Twain to be Samuel Clemens, much as one might acknowledge him to be human. The speaker judges Mark Twain to satisfy his criteria for applying 'Samuel Clemens'.

The same sentence could be used to make an identity statement. The speaker might perform these acts:

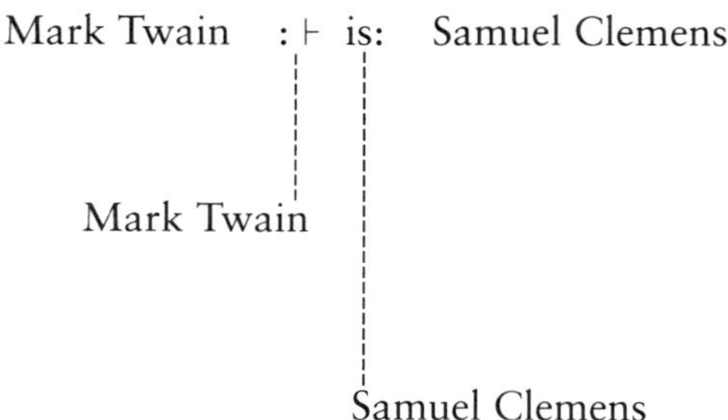

The speaker attends to Samuel Clemens, using Samuel Clemens as a reference point. But what is Mark Twain acknowledged to be with respect to Samuel Clemens? It seems more than odd to say that Mark Twain is situated by identity with respect to Samuel Clemens (with respect to himself). An object being itself scarcely counts as a situation; the object itself would be no different from that situation.

It will help to consider some different examples. Dwight Eisenhower was for a time the president of the United States. At that time, the Dwight Eisenhower part of the world coincided with the president part, and vice versa, but this was only a temporary occurrence. This coincidence is a genuine situation linking different parts of the world.

Now consider the ambiguity of the sentence 'The mayor of Buffalo was a Republican in 1980'. Even this representation is ambiguous:

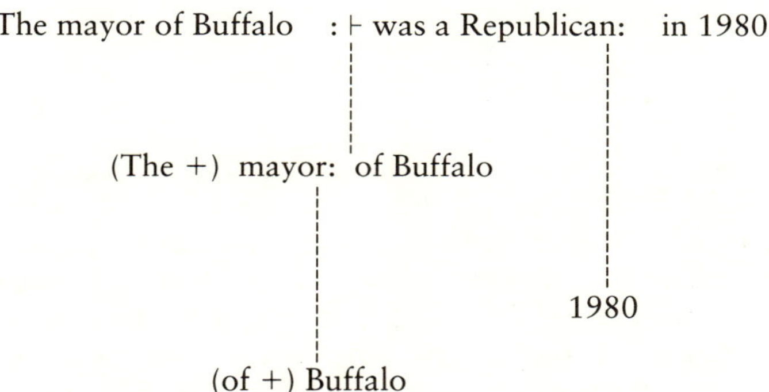

The subject phrase can either be used to identify:

1. The person who is at present the mayor of Buffalo,
2. The person who was mayor in 1980,
3. The mayor of Buffalo part of the world.

If the first statement was followed by 'But he is a Democrat now', then (1) requires the present mayor to have changed parties, (2) requires the past mayor to have changed parties, and (3) requires only that the incumbent in 1980 was Republican while the present incumbent is Democratic. The mayor of Buffalo part of the world changed parties, but no individual person need have done so.

Now consider statements made with 'Dwight Eisenhower is the president of the United States' at a time when he was president:

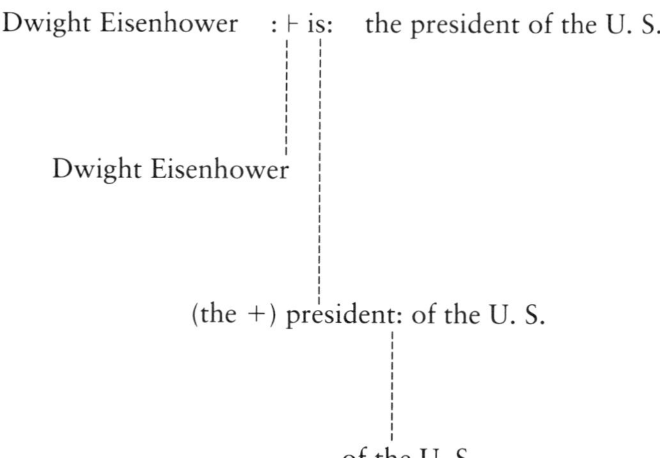

This representation is also ambiguous. For the language user will (most likely) use 'Dwight Eisenhower' to identify the Dwight Eisenhower part of the world. But he can use 'the president of the United States' either to identify that same part, or to identify the United States president part of the world. If he identifies the United States president part, then the identity statement reports the coincidence of two parts. Otherwise, it is the same kind of identity statement as that made with 'Mark Twain is Samuel Clemens.' (But it is conceivable for someone to understand the Mark Twain part to be different from the Samuel Clemens part—perhaps the Mark Twain part begins only when Samuel Clemens starts writing under that name.) Those identity statements are limiting and degenerate cases of two parts coinciding. Trivially, every part coincides with itself simply by being on the scene; there are no identity situations in which one object figures twice.

It is often useful to let someone know that two identifying acts have a single target. In acknowledging Mark Twain to coincide with Samuel Clemens, the language user simply endorses the 'Mark Twain' way of identifying Samuel Clemens. The single object Samuel Clemens/Mark Twain is what makes the statement true, and is the object identified by the correct acknowledging statement.

The subject of an identity statement need not be the primary focus of attention. In the following:

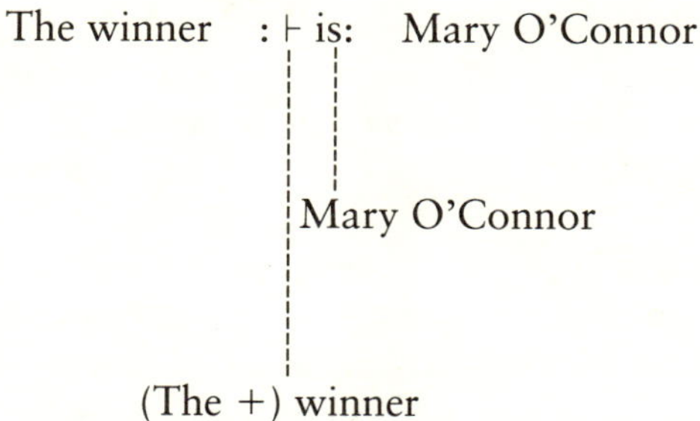

the winner (of the contest made clear by the context) is the reference point which Mary O'Connor is acknowledged to constitute.

An identity statement might also make both objects the focus of attention:

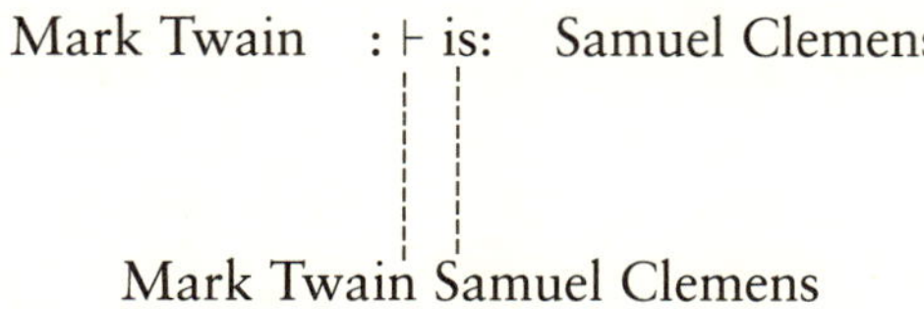

The speaker acknowledges the pair Mark Twain, Samuel Clemens to be a single-object. He still identifies Samuel Clemens/Mark Twain.

Although it is most common to make identity statements about particular individuals, it is also possible to make them about parts of the world. A speaker might use 'That kind of dog is a collie' like this:

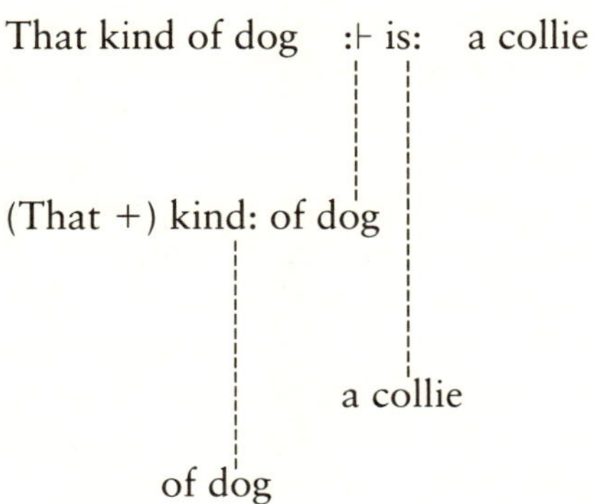

where he uses 'That kind of dog' to attend to the part of the world illustrated by the specimen before him, and acknowledges that part to exhaustively constitute the collie part of the world. (The same sentence could be used in many different ways; not all of them would yield identity statements.)

The identity statements considered so far have been made with simple sentences in which 'is' connects two expressions used to perform attending acts. But in discussing identity statements, it is hard to avoid using the word 'same'. Let us consider some uses of this word. We shall "work" our way into this topic by first looking at sentences which don't contain 'same'. In using this two-sentence sequence:

A dog bit Dennis. That dog also bit Sharon.

the speaker might perform acts with the first sentence similar to acts we discussed earlier. And he could use the second sentence like this:

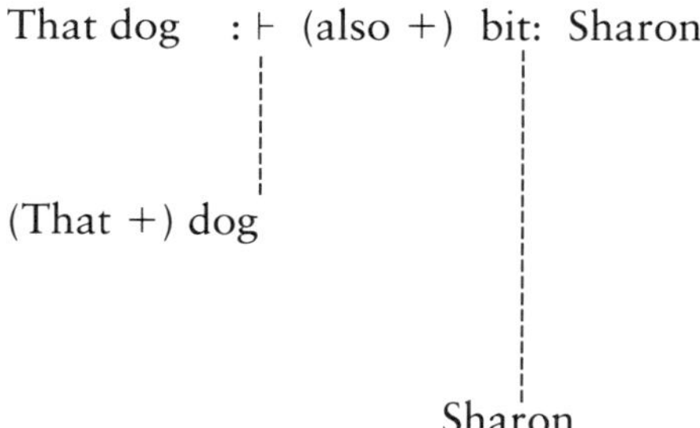

The expression 'That dog' is used to attend to the dog that bit Dennis. This attending is made possible by, it exploits, the acts performed in using the first sentence. But those acts need not be enabling acts with respect to the act of using 'That dog'. For the speaker may not have been thinking of what he would say next when he acknowledged a dog to have bitten Dennis. Indeed, the second sentence would make sense even if uttered by a different speaker than the first. The first statement provides a context in which 'That dog' can be used to attend to a particular dog. In uttering the first sentence, the speaker uses 'A dog' to attend to a particular dog. When he utters 'That dog' in the second sentence, he uses the earlier attending act as a reference point. His use of 'That' make explicit the dependence of this act on the earlier act.

(The word isn't used to *make* this act dependent on that, it simply *marks* the dependence.) The word 'also' makes explicit that this act is an additional acknowledging act concerning the dog in question.

Rather than saying "That dog also bit Sharon," the speaker could as well say "The dog also bit Sharon." For 'The' can be used to mark the dependence of the attending act on the particular context—which is partly constituted by the previous acts. The speaker could also perform these acts:

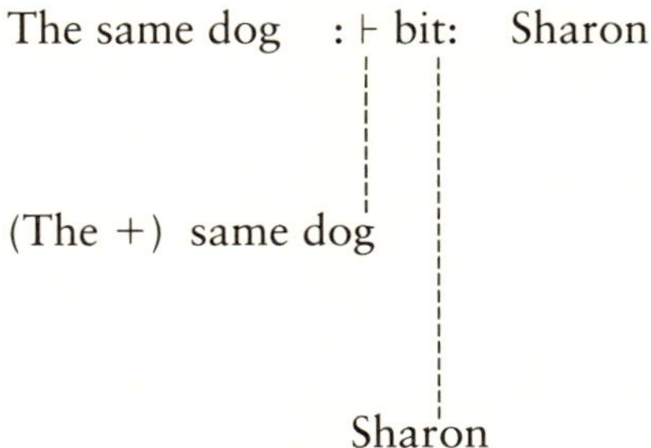

The expression 'same dog' is used to attend to the dog in question. The speaker does not use 'same' to indicate some character of that dog. In saying 'same dog,' the speaker is "reusing" the previous attending act. For the word 'same' or an expression 'same ϕ' is conventionally used to perform a kind of act that has just been performed. The word 'same' indicates the connection between this attending act and the one it repeats. Since the 'same dog' attending act is explicitly linked to the previous attending act, we don't feel the need to use 'also' in making this statement.

Now consider this two sentence sequence:

> Anne has red hair. Sara's hair is the same color.

The first sentence could be used like this:

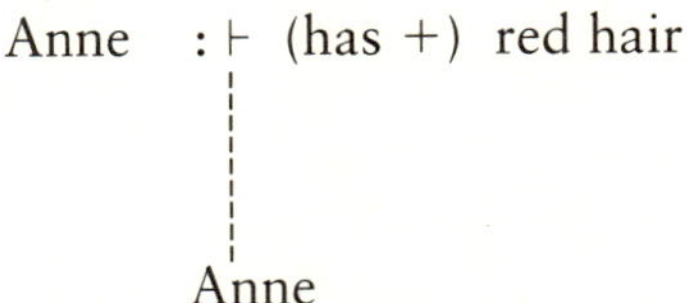

The verb 'has' is an auxiliary. It is not used to acknowledge Anne to be situated with respect to her hair, but to make clear that Anne is acknowledged to presently have red hair. Different auxiliaries also mark different "respects" in which acknowledging acts fit their targets.

The second sentence could be used to perform these acts:

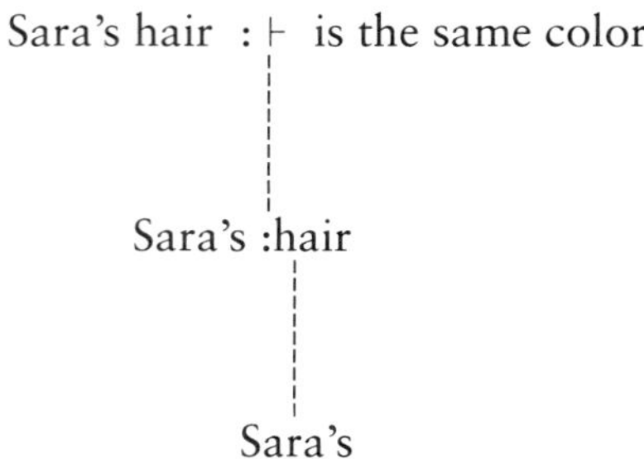

The expression 'the same color' is not used to attend to a color or colored part of the world. It is used to acknowledge Sara's hair to be red. This acknowledging act, in effect, reuses the color "part" of the previous act. The expression 'same color' indicates that this is a color-acknowledging act like that performed with the preceding sentence.

The sentence 'Frank's car is the same color as Joe's car' has some similarities to the sentence about Sara's hair, but its analysis poses a different problem. For the sentence about Frank's car can be used alone; it doesn't require a previous act to serve as a model. As a first attempt, we might try this analysis:

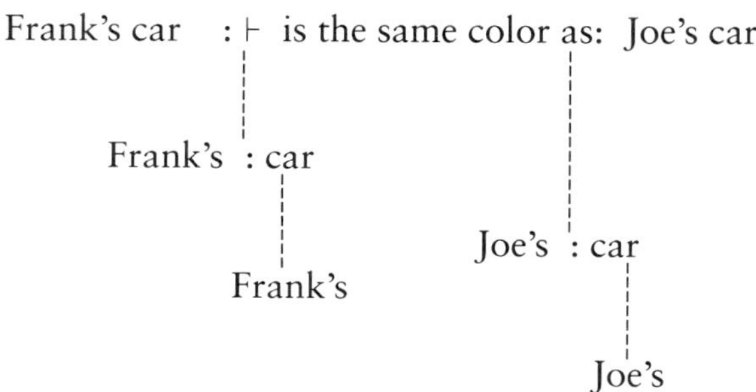

where the speaker attends both to Joe's car and to Frank's car. He uses Joe's car as a reference point, or standard. But one object isn't situated with respect to another by being the same color, so this statement isn't reporting a situation. Each object is whatever color it is. If we know the colors, we can judge the objects to be of the same or different colors. However, our judgments don't reflect "color facts" additional to the one object being its color and the other being *its* color.

We must distinguish two important kinds of acknowledging acts, two important kinds of judgments. A *situational* judgment acknowledges one object to be something that doesn't involve other objects or to be situated with respect to another or others. The acknowledging acts considered so far have been situational. (An identity statement which identifies one object twice is the limiting case of a situational judgment.) We also make *comparison* judgments. We can judge one object to be more ϕ or less ϕ than another. We can judge them to be equal in ϕ. If a speaker uses 'John is taller than Clare' to acknowledge John to be taller than Clare:

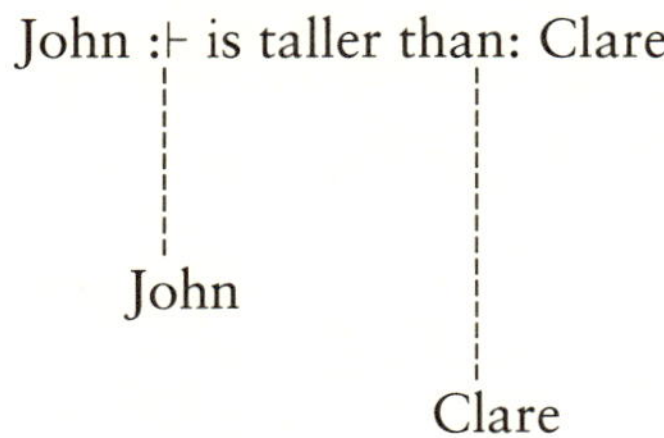

he is indicating how the two compare in terms of height. In attending to Clare, he does not use her as a reference point which enables his acknowledging act. Instead he uses Clare as a *standard* with respect to which he acknowledges John to be greater in height. The sentence 'Frank's car is the same color as Joe's car' is most naturally used to make a comparison judgment. The diagram in the preceding paragraph represents one way to use that sentence. In those acts, Frank's car is acknowledged to be equal in color to the object used as a standard—to Joe's car. The word 'same' indicates that a single kind of color-acknowledging act can be performed for both cars.

The sentence 'Mark Twain is the same person as Samuel Clemens' would not be used to compare two men in terms of humanity or personhood. The sentence might be used to perform a long-winded version of the acts performed with 'Mark Twain is Samuel Clemens':

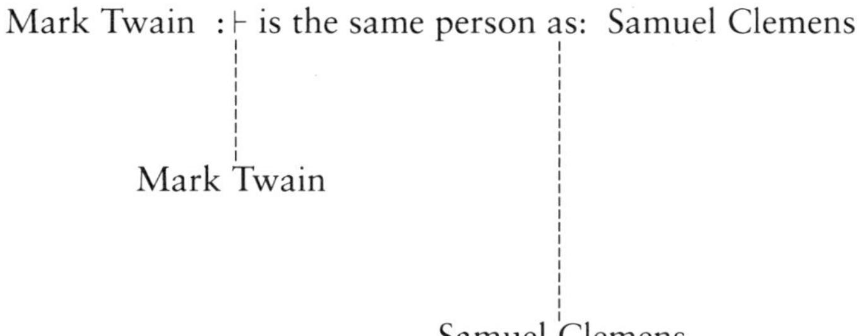

But the additional words also suit the sentence to be used to say something directly about the Mark Twain and Samuel Clemens identifying acts. The speaker can acknowledge the Mark Twain act to identify the target of the Samuel Clemens act. Identifying acts can enable both acts talking about the identified objects and acts commenting directly on the identifying acts themselves. If the identity sentence is used to acknowledge the component acts to have a single target, it will be represented thus:

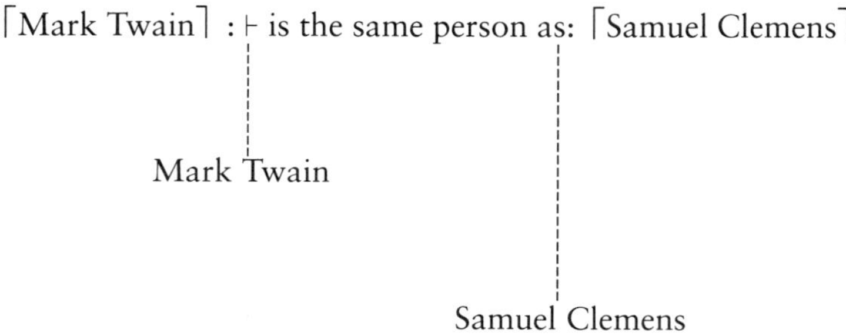

or:

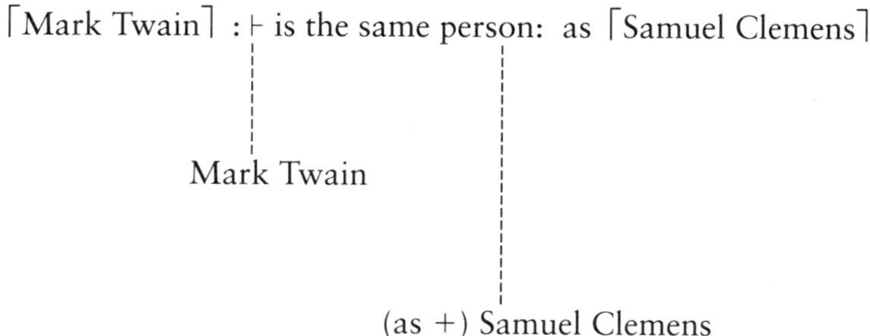

(The placement of the 'as' act is determined by the language user.) The upper corners are a sign that the acknowledging act is concerned with identifying acts (not identifying expressions) rather than with identified objects.

Note that the sentence 'Dwight Eisenhower is the same person as the president of the United States' doesn't sound quite right. If the phrase 'the president of the United States' were used to attend to the United States president part of the world, then this statement:

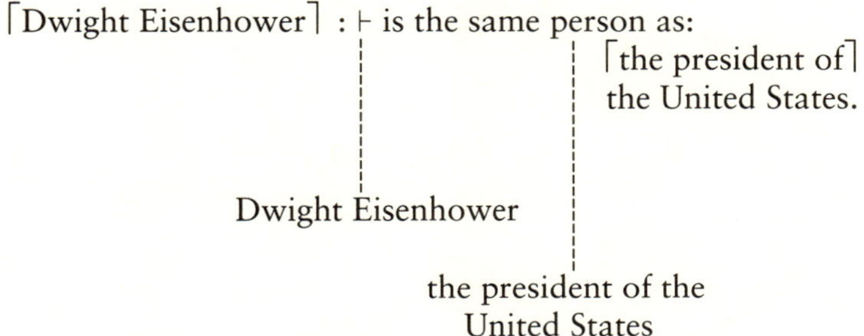

wasn't true when Eisenhower was president. Though the diagram would have represented a true statement if the definite description were used to identify the person who was the president.

Chapter 8

Learning to Use Language: *Theoretical Issues*

1. Names and Their Criteria

In this chapter, I will investigate features of attending acts and of acknowledging acts. I will consider the criteria used in performing acknowledging acts. This closer look at the identifying use of language will improve our understanding of the world of experience and of our access to objects in this world, and will enable us to understand how proper names and other expressions are used to identify particular objects. Following this discussion, I will reflect on consequences that the present approach has for characterizing linguistic phenomena and studies of language. Syntactic and semantic phenomena need to be reconceived. So does logic. Once we have surveyed linguistic phenomena, we draw metaphysical consequences about situations in the conceptually structured world of experience.

When a child first learns to acknowledge objects to be one thing or another, he will employ criteria involving the appearance and behavior (*apparent* behavior) of the objects. This is true whether he is acknowledging an object to be Mama, or Sally, or to be a dog or a tree. The fact that there is, and can be, only one Mama although there are lots of dogs won't show up in his linguistic acts. Once the child expands the world of his experience, and uses words to attend to objects he isn't perceiving, it becomes important to associate some expressions with particular objects. He doesn't use 'Mama' to attend to any object which happens to look or behave like Mama. When the child uses expressions to attend to objects he isn't perceiving, his attending depends on connections linking him to the objects.

The child who acknowledges a changing object α to have (just) been ϕ though it is ϕ no longer is not attending to a past "slice" of α. He is attending to the single object α and the particular event of its having been ϕ. His conception of time and temporal relations provides a connection he can exploit from his present situation to the past experience of α's being ϕ. His remembering α's being ϕ is (among other things) his being able to exploit this connection to acknowledge α to have been ϕ on that occasion.

To attend to a familiar object he is not currently perceiving, the child needs various connections linking him to the object. He will be able to remember objects experienced in the past, as well as many past experiences. But objects experienced in the past aren't confined to the past. A person's knowledge and beliefs apply in the present. Everything is connected to everything else by a great variety of "paths." A person can only exploit a connection to attend to a particular object if he knows about the connection and that it leads to the object. Acquiring new knowledge and belief about an object allows a person to group together different connections to form a *cluster* that can be exploited to attend to the terminus of the connections. For example, the language learner will know Mama to be his mother and Sally his sister. He will know which bedroom Mama sleeps in. He will know which chairs they sit in at meals. And so on. He can attend to these familiar persons on the basis of his past experience of them. He can also attend to them via the kinship and other relations that now structure his world. These last connections are not mediated by his past experiences of the objects.

The same thing takes place when we attend to an object we haven't experienced, about which we have been told. Initially most of us learn about Napoleon in school. We actually experienced utterances or written texts. We were able to use those as reference points for attending to the person intended by our teachers or the books' authors. These early experiences gave us a name for the object "reached" by several paths. Our initial clusters of connections were enlarged as more information about Napoleon came our ways. I can no longer remember how I originally learned of Napoleon (some elements of my earlier cluster of connections to Napoleon have dropped out), but I have plenty of connections to exploit in attending to Napoleon.

Names aren't the only expressions we use to attend to particular objects. Definite and indefinite descriptions, and various other kinds of phrase are also used for this task. A whole sentence can be used to attend to a particular event. Attending acts depend on and exploit connections between the language user and those objects to which he attends. When an attending act succeeds, constituting an identifying act, the object intended is actually found where the language user directs his attention. However, when a speaker uses a word like 'dog' to attend to all dogs, or 'water' to attend to the scattered mass of water, he is not exploiting paths which link him to dogs, or water. He is in this case attending (and identifying) in virtue of a linguistic practice and its associated criteria. As we will see later, this affects the status of acts acknowledging the collection to be this or that.

To begin with, a "perfect imposter" might turn up who satisfies the Mama-acknowledging criteria as well as the real Mama does. From the child's perspective, both women would deserve to be acknowledged to be Mama. Once the child uses names and other phrases to identify long-lasting particular individuals, which is to acquire the concept of individual identity, he will still use appearances in deciding whom to call Mama. But his criteria for correctly acknowledging someone to be Mama now include being the person to whom he is tied by the appropriate cluster of connections. This is the person who is his mother, with whom he has interacted on various occasions, and so on. Even though connection criteria are harder to apply than appearance criteria when it is a matter of recognizing the person in front of him, they count the most for performing correct acknowledging acts. The perfect imposter was initially entitled to be acknowledged to be Mama, but she isn't Mama after all.

For acknowledging acts, I will distinguish *connection* criteria from *feature* criteria. An expression has connection criteria if the expression is appropriately used to attend to a particular object, and its acknowledging criteria involve links between the language user and the object, which links the language user exploits in attending to/identifying the object. Connection criteria will be peculiar to a language user, for the connections must link that user to the object. Although an expression may acquire connection criteria by conventional means, the connections themselves may be completely nonconventional, in the sense that the connections associated with the expression depend on the circumstances in which the language user learned to use the expression, and what she happens to know about the object to which she is connected. A proper name like 'Buffalo' will probably have completely nonconventional connection criteria. The connections they exploit will vary wildly among persons who use the name to identify the city.

Other connection criteria are partly or wholly conventional. The connection criteria that speaker *A* associates with 'the mayor of Buffalo' involve nonconventional connections to Buffalo, and conventionally specified being-mayor-of links between Buffalo and the mayor. For the expression 'my mother', there are completely conventional links between a language user and his mother. An expression has feature criteria if it is properly applied to objects on the basis of features they possess, which don't involve any (other) objects in particular. The words 'Mama' and 'Sally' have both connection and feature criteria. But the connection criteria are the more important. Whoever satisfies the appropriate connection criteria is Sally, no matter what she looks like. But while appearance criteria can fail, not all feature criteria are dispensable. The Sally cluster of connections must link the speaker to an object with the features *human* and *female*.

Connection criteria involve links between a particular language user and a particular object, and so vary from one language user to another. But conventional connection criteria involve links conventionally associated with specific expressions. Even though connection criteria are more important than feature criteria for names of particular objects, we all use appearance criteria—a kind of feature criteria—for applying names to familiar objects. I know Jorge when I see him. I also recognize the skyline of downtown Chicago. But these appearance criteria are second in importance to connection criteria. The person I intend when I use 'Jorge' to attend, the person whom it is correct to acknowledge to be Jorge is the person to whom I am connected in a large number of ways. He is my colleague. We have done things together. I can get to both his office and his home from where I am presently located. I know his wife and children. And so on and so forth. For long-dead historical figures, appearance criteria are even less important than for living individuals. And there may be more similarity in the connection criteria from one informed person to the next. But the connections are still different for different language users.

Both proper names and definite descriptions will have connection criteria which are more important than their feature criteria. It is characteristic of proper names to have almost wholly nonconventional connection criteria, while for descriptions, the connections are either partly or wholly conventional. A context-dependent identifying phrase, like 'that dog' or 'the same dog', doesn't have connection criteria associated with it by language users, for in using the expression either to attend or acknowledge, a language user will exploit or employ connections that she intends only in that particular context. Similar remarks apply when an indefinite phrase is used to identify a particular object.

But are proper names properly characterized as rigid designators? If we consider the two kinds of criteria, connection criteria seem flexible in being different for different people, while feature criteria are "rigidly attached" to an expression, being the same for all language users. However, rigid designation is understood to be characteristic of proper names, while a description like 'the mayor of Buffalo' can be used for different people with respect to different times, and if things had turned out differently in the past, might be used for a different person at present than the present mayor. One proper name is not rigidly tied to one object, for there are several Buffalos and several Chicagos, and a great many John Smiths. A language user may associate different connection criteria with a single name, where the connections lead to different objects, but each cluster of connections must tie the language user to just the object that it does.

The description 'the mayor of Buffalo' can be used for different mayors with respect to different times. If things had been different, it could have been used for still different men. How is it that the connection criteria associated with the description allow this flexibility? When 'the mayor of Buffalo' is used to identify the mayor of Buffalo part of the world, the connection must link the user to just that object. However, the mayor of Buffalo part of the world coincides at different times with different people. Our linguistic practice authorizes us to either use the phrase to identify the mayor of Buffalo part of the world or to identify the person who is at some time mayor. We are not authorized to use proper names to identify parts of the world that coincide for a time with the name's bearer. However, a speaker who uses either a name or a description to identify a particular object/part of the world is connected to and identifies just that object/part. Even if the world had been different in various ways, this very act could not have identified something different.

When a name is used to perform an acknowledging act:

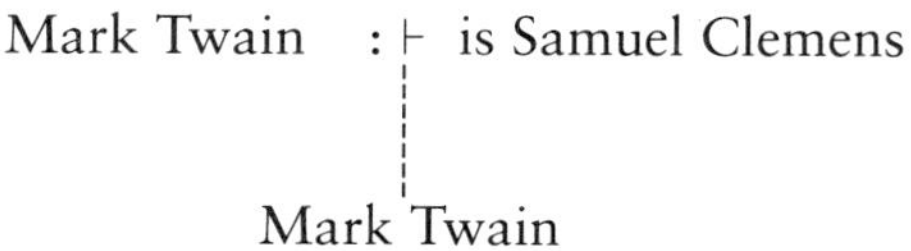

as opposed to figuring in an identity statement:

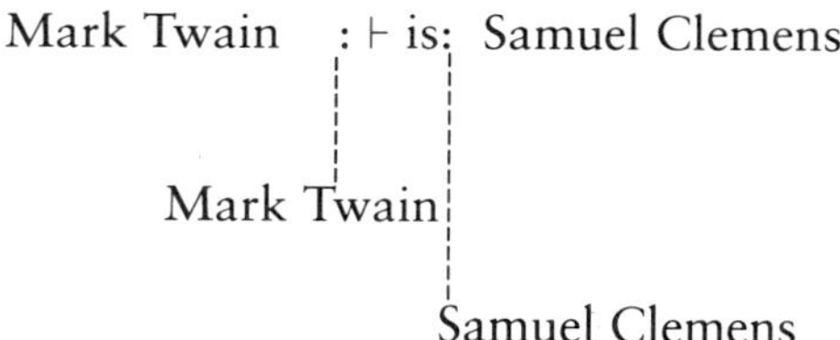

the information conveyed is no different. Satisfying the Samuel Clemens criteria is being reached by the 'Samuel Clemens' connections, and this is coinciding with the Samuel Clemens part. The acknowledging criteria associated with a phrase like 'the mayor of Buffalo' involve connections to the mayor of Buffalo part of the world, not to the person who at some time is/was mayor. So this statement:

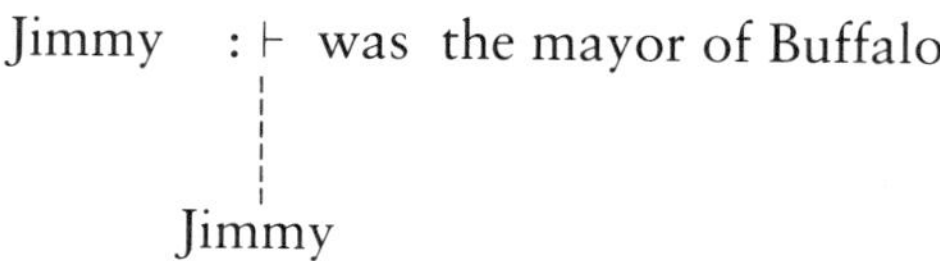

may or may not convey the same information as this:

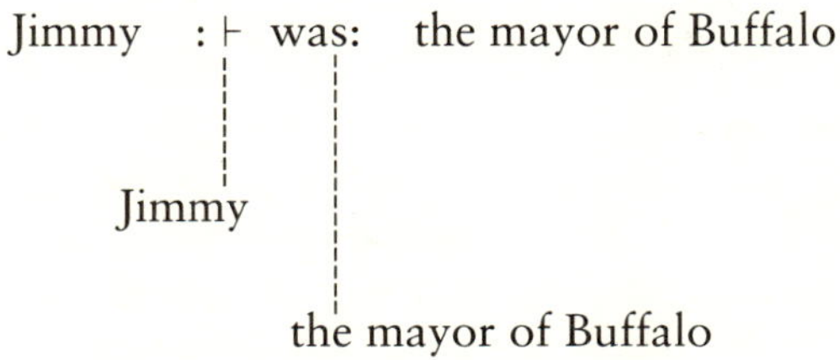

It depends on the speaker's intentions in using 'the mayor of Buffalo' in the second statement. He could simply be identifying Jimmy twice.

Of the two kinds of theory of proper names, I seem to have come down on the "causal" side as opposed to the Frege-Searle side. However, 'causal' is certainly the wrong word for the present account. In using a word for a particular object, the language user exploits/employs actual connections linking her to the object, but these aren't causal connections. And the present account does not recognize a major difference between the identifying-stage uses of names and definite descriptions. The connections associated with descriptions have a more conventional character than those associated with names, and descriptions can be used to identify either "their own" parts of the world or objects coinciding for a time with those parts. But we use both kinds of expression to identify particular objects by exploiting connections linking us to the objects.

The Frege-Searle understanding of names is usually taken to treat names on the model of descriptions. But this is a misleading way to put the matter. For it is the Frege-Searle understanding of descriptions which is most characteristic of that account. From the present perspective, we can say that the Frege-Searle theory understands a description to be representing an arbitrary object possessing a certain property or properties, and also to be expressing a commitment to there being only one such object. The Frege-Searle theory understands language to be primarily representational. But this is a mistake. The fundamental, and first, use of language is the identifying-stage use. The fundamental use of names and descriptions is to either identify or acknowledge. At the representational stage, descriptions and (other) quantified phrases will sometimes be used to represent arbitrary objects of a kind, but the identifying use of names and descriptions never drops out of language and linguistic activity.

2. Natural Kinds

Another issue that has been raised concerning proper names is their similarity or dissimilarity to natural-kind expressions. A natural-kind expression like 'dog' or 'water' can be used to perform acknowledging acts. The original criteria associated with familiar natural-kind expressions must surely have been appearance criteria, which are feature criteria. To be a dog, or a quantity of salt, an object must look or taste a certain way. The animal must observably behave in suitable ways: walking and running and barking are appropriate, but not flying, tree climbing, or swinging by a tail. The stuff must have the expected effect when put on or combined with food. As knowledge of the world increases, additional criteria will be associated with the expressions. As well as looking and tasting, we can use chemical tests to determine that something is salt. With the increase in knowledge, some expressions will acquire additional criteria picking out the same objects. Other expressions will have their criteria refined as well as expanded, so that the new criteria no longer pick out exactly the same things as the earlier criteria. But early and late, the criteria associated with natural-kind expressions will be feature criteria.

When natural-kind expressions are components of phrases used to attend to/identify objects, language users will exploit connections not determined by criteria associated with the expressions. A speaker who uses 'that dog' doesn't identify a particular dog simply on the basis of its being a dog. Even when a natural-kind expression is used to identify a part of the world, either a collection-part like all dogs or a lump-part like all water, the speaker is not exploiting a connection to that part of the world. The speaker is "exploiting" acknowledging criteria; for a natural-kind expression, these are feature criteria.

Since natural-kind expressions are not used like proper nouns (names), we should ask what similarities between the two kinds of expressions have struck some theorists as important. With proper names, the fundamental acknowledging criteria are connection criteria. Feature criteria associated with a name can (often) be overridden by connection criteria. The connections associated with a name can allow a person to attend to/identify the name's object even though her beliefs about that object are largely mistaken. It also happens that people living in different historical periods use the same natural-kind expressions to pick out the same things, even though their knowledge, especially their scientific knowledge, is very different. The people living at different times don't assign the same feature criteria to natural-kind expressions, yet they can use the same or corresponding expressions for the same things. This might suggest that natural-kind expressions function in much the same way as proper names. But we have seen that they function differently. How is it that ancient people, or primitive people, used 'water' (or their word for it) for the same stuff we do?

Suppose ϕ is a natural-kind concept that initially has only appearance criteria, and later acquires other criteria. Different scenarios are possible. The simplest is that the more refined, more "scientific" criteria pick out exactly the same objects that the original appearance criteria selected. But when the original speakers acknowledged an object to be ϕ, or attended to the ϕ part of the world, did they *mean* the same thing as later language users? Were they attending to the same part of the world that later users identify? The more knowledgeable language users employ additional criteria to those used by the earlier speakers. The additional criteria characterize the acts in which they are employed, making them different in kind from acts performed by the earlier users. The later speakers' acts don't mean the same as the earlier ones. The additional knowledge characterizing the later speakers' acts also structures their world. So the later speakers don't encounter and inhabit the same world of experience as the earlier speakers did. Although they don't inhabit exactly the same world, their worlds are pretty much the same. For the later world is merely a more refined and further articulated continuation of the earlier world.

From the perspective of the later language users, the earlier users are included in the more developed world of experience, and were dealing with objects and locations of the later world, though without realizing this. The earlier language users knew less about ϕ's than the later users, and so acknowledged objects to be ϕ on the basis of fewer criteria than the later users employ. The earlier language users attended to the same objects, but their attending acts were characterized by fewer feature criteria than the later speakers' acts. Since the earlier criteria are not incorrect by later standards, from the later perspective, the earlier speakers used their ϕ-expression for the ϕ's and the ϕ part of the world. Without using the ϕ-expression as a kind of proper noun.

We will change the scenario. Suppose the appearance criteria for acknowledging an object to be ϕ are replaced by more sophisticated criteria that yield somewhat different results. Some objects formerly acknowledged to be ϕ are no longer considered to be ϕ, or some objects formerly considered not to be ϕ are now considered to be ϕ. (Whales and dolphins are no longer considered to be fish. And, presumably, some marine animals not previously regarded as fish now count as fish.) It is still correct that earlier and later language users inhabit different worlds. But the later world isn't simply a more refined version of the earlier one. From the later perspective, and perhaps absolutely, the original world was incorrect and (slightly) incoherent. The earlier and later language users don't perform the same kinds of ϕ-acknowledging acts. Nor do they use the ϕ-expression to attend to the same part of the world. This is something like the child who uses 'dog' ('doggie') for more animals than dogs. He can, even from our perspective, use the word to attend to a genuine part of the world. It simply isn't *our* dog collection.

A variant of this scenario is often discussed in connection with water and Twin Earth. Let us skip the Twin Earth part of the story, but use water as our example of a natural kind. Suppose that the water-acknowledging criteria used by long-ago language users were such that what we now consider to be water could have correctly been acknowledged to be water, but some other stuff that doesn't satisfy our criteria would have satisfied theirs. As luck would have it, the past language users never ran into any of the water-like nonwater. They couldn't, because the ersatz water occurs only in places that were inaccessible to those language users—either in a remote part of Earth or on a distant planet. What needs to be determined is what part of the world those people used 'water' to attend to. Was it just what we consider to be the water part, or did they attend to the part constituted by both genuine and ersatz water? We can note that the past language users only knew about connections to particular quantities of genuine water. Even though they would certainly, and correctly, have acknowledged the ersatz water to be (what they called) water if they ran into some, they never actually did so.

The long-ago language users inhabited a different world of experience than we do. Their world was structured by their concepts and conceptual systems, which are somewhat different than ours—the two worlds also exhibit massive similarities. When we ask just what part of the world those people identified with 'water,' there is no determinate answer. Their water-criteria fit both genuine and ersatz water. But they never ran into ersatz water, and they developed their concepts to deal with the things they did run into. Had circumstances brought some ersatz water to their attention, they would have ended up with a generic water-concept that applied to both genuine and ersatz water. As we have told the story, their water-concept evolved into ours. From our perspective, with respect to our story, they were dealing with just our water. With respect to the long-ago people's own setting, there is simply no answer to the question whether they used 'water' to attend to a part of the world partly constituted by the ersatz water. Although we can't determine whether the long-past people used 'water' for our water and other stuff as well, we can determine that real people in the historical past didn't use their 'fish' words to attend to exactly our fish. Their fish part of the world was different from ours.

3. Identifying Situations

The connections exploited in using a proper name for identifying provide the most important criteria associated with that name. These connections are also important when the proper name is used to perform an acknowledging act. Connections are even exploited when feature-criteria expressions are used to perform acknowledging acts. Recall that when the language learner says "Sally fell down," he doesn't mean that Sally fell down on some occasion or other in the past. He isn't able to make such a statement at this point. And we ourselves would normally use the sentence as he does, for a particular occasion when Sally fell down. In acknowledging, the speaker would have attended to the particular event of her falling down. If he were correct, the speaker would have identified that event.

What allows the speaker performing these acts:

```
Sally  : ⊢  fell down
         ¦
         ¦
         ¦
       Sally
```

to acknowledge Sally to have fallen on a particular occasion are his connections to the event in question. The criteria for acknowledging require that Sally did whatever counts as falling down. In using the expression to acknowledge her to have fallen down, the speaker applies the criteria to Sally with respect to some particular occasion. Connections to the particular event of Sally's falling characterize his acknowledging act, without providing the criteria for his act. The connections are preliminary or prior, for without the connections, the speaker would be in no position to perform the acknowledging act. Different people who witnessed Sally fall down will each exploit different connections in acknowledging her to have fallen down. But the different speakers will be saying the same thing, because each employs the same criteria, and each exploits connections leading to the same event.

Suppose Sally fell down on two occasions, an hour apart. If speaker *A* witnessed the first but not the second, and speaker *B* had the opposite experience, then when each speaker acknowledges Sally to have fallen down, they are saying different things. Their acknowledging criteria are the same, but they exploit connections linking them to different events. And what about speaker *C*, who witnessed both events? What he is saying when he tells us "Sally fell down" depends on speaker *C*'s intentions for his acknowledging act. He may intend one or the other particular fall. He may also intend the complex event constituted by the two temporally separated falls. (The components of a complex event need not all be temporally contiguous or overlapping. A game of chess played by mail is a complex event. But not everything the players do between moves is a part of this event.) If he intends the complex event, he could appropriately append "two times" to his statement. Speaker *C* could also perform these acts:

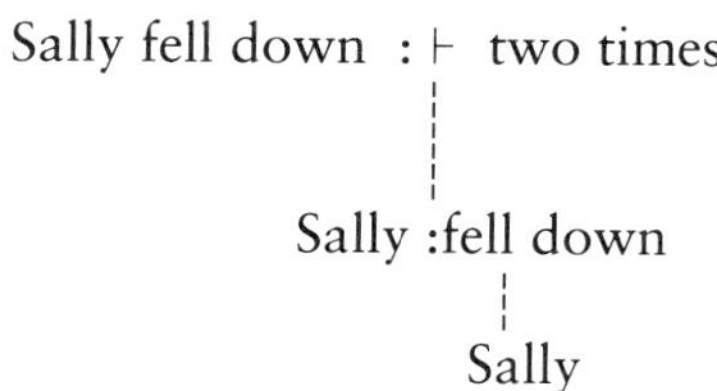

The intermediate act is not in this case an acknowledging act, but an act of attending to a particular group of Sally's falls. Which enables him to acknowledge the group to be two-membered.

Now consider speaker *D* who didn't see Sally fall, but learned of her fall from another speaker. The other speaker didn't fill *D* in on the particular circumstances of the fall, or the exact time. When *D* acknowledges Sally to have fallen down, he also exploits connections. For speaker *D* attends to the fall in virtue of his connection to the witness and the witness's connection to the fall. Had his source provided him more information, speaker *D* might have been able to exploit additional connections to the event.

There is a sense in which simple identifying-stage statements "make contact" with the situations which they describe. This is sufficient to dissolve or avoid some puzzles about belief and knowledge. There isn't space to explore the puzzles, but I shall try to make clear what I have in mind with one more example about Sally. Suppose the speaker saw Mary fall down yesterday, but he was pretty far from the event, and thought it was Sally who fell. Later in the day Sally also fell down. The speaker has no information about that event. When this speaker says "Sally fell down yesterday," he is acknowledging Sally to have fallen down on the particular occasion to which he was a witness. Since there was no such event, the speaker has failed to identify a Sally-falling-down event. Many philosophers would say that the speaker has a true belief about Sally, but not knowledge. They think the speaker was right "by accident." However, the speaker was mistaken and his statement was false. The fact that Sally did fall down may keep his mistake from being discovered, but the speaker has expressed neither knowledge nor true belief.

These discussions have dealt almost exclusively with positive judgments. We should also consider negative ones. If a speaker perceptually attends to a ball directly in front of him and acknowledges the ball to be red, he has attended both to the ball and to the situation/event of its being red. He is connected to these objects in the most direct way possible. The speaker could also use 'The ball is not blue' to deny the ball to be blue. What can we say about the situation/event that grounds his act? Has the speaker attended to a particular event of the ball's not being blue? What kind of event could this be—in addition to the positive event of the ball's being red are there hundreds of negative events for the various shades that the ball isn't? In performing the negative act, the language user is *rejecting* the use of 'blue' for the ball. He is rejecting its use as being inappropriate or incorrect. Applying the criteria associated with an expression is like trying to make an object pass a test. If the object can't be made to pass the test, this failure can be marked by a negative acknowledging act. The ball isn't simply not blue. It is something *instead* of blue—in this case the something is *red*. In acknowledging the ball not to be blue, the speaker who knows the ball's color might be attending to the situation of the ball's being red. If he is, we can represent his acts like this:

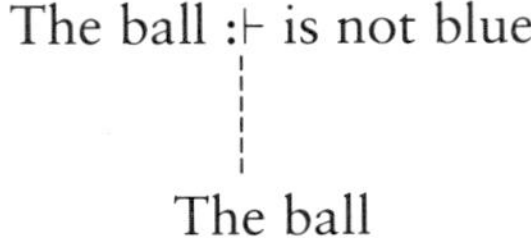

Here the predicate is used to acknowledge the ball to be its color without making clear (to the audience) what color this is. But someone can legitimately deny the ball to be blue without knowing what color it really is. (He might have been told that the ball isn't blue, for example.) He *merely* rejects the use of 'blue' for the ball. We represent such acts like this:

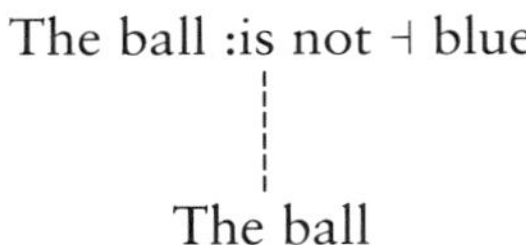

Acts acknowledging an object to presently not be ϕ are simpler than negative acts about the past. The ball can simply be not blue now. But consider the negative counterpart to a statement acknowledging Sally to have fallen down yesterday. The speaker who acknowledges Sally to have fallen down attends to a particular fall or falls, which didn't last all of yesterday. In contrast, the speaker who says "Sally didn't fall down yesterday" is talking about the whole day. The negative statement doesn't just deny or take back what a speaker says with 'Sally fell down yesterday'. A statement:

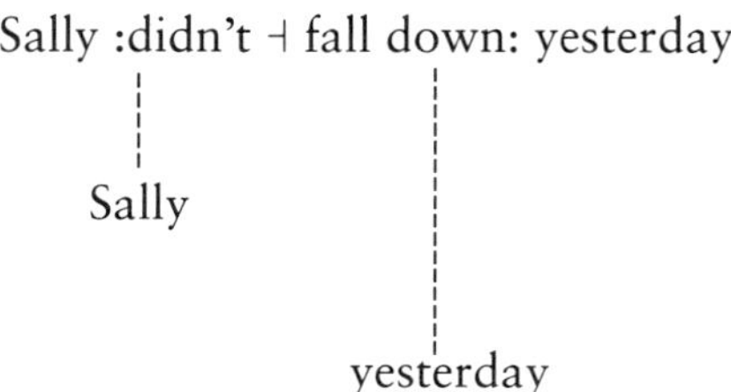

rejects the use of 'fell down' for Sally with respect to yesterday. So how could a speaker exactly deny someone's positive statement? First note that he isn't in a position to do this unless he knows the source of the someone's mistaken judgment. If he doesn't know the source, the best he can do is make the whole-day denial. If he is in a position to correct the someone, he could do it by saying something like: "You are wrong. The girl you saw fall was Mary."

4. Semantic Structure and Truth Conditions

It is difficult to determine which linguistic acts should be taken to constitute a statement. If the sentence 'Sally is asleep' is used like this:

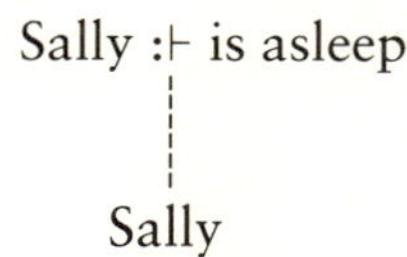

the speaker has performed two related acts. We might decide that just the acknowledging act is the statement. For this is what is true or false, and statements are generally regarded as being one or the other. But statements are traditionally thought to be made with whole sentences, in which case the statement would be the activity constituted by the two interrelated acts. We shall understand the statement to be this activity. We can still classify statements as true or false, though in a derivative sense. For the statement will have the value of its acknowledging component. If a statement has more than one acknowledging component, the statement will be *entirely* true if all such components are correct, and partly true if only some components are correct.

The diagrams that have been developed represent both syntactic and semantic features of statements and their components. The *semantic structure* of a complex linguistic act/activity is determined by the (semantic) kinds of the component acts and their relations to one another. The acts/activities are performed with *syntactic* objects, which have syntactic features. The expressions with their syntactic features constitute the *syntactic character* of a linguistic act/activity they are used to perform. Our diagrams represent both the semantic structures and the syntactic characters of statements.

Even a simple sentence like 'Sally doesn't like Dennis' can be used to perform differently organized acts:

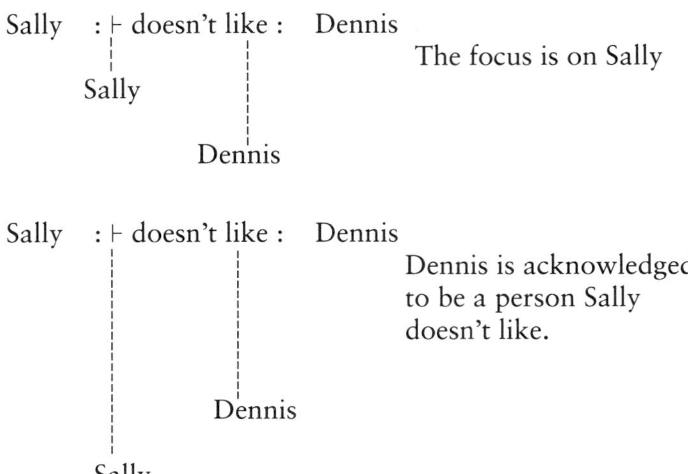

(Even more structures than these are possible.) A sentence doesn't have a meaning or a semantic analysis; the accepted linguistic conventions associate a sentence with a range of possible linguistic acts/activities. (But languages are flexible. Given the fundamental conventions, a reasonably clever person can extend the conventions and the structures in unconventional ways, and still get through to her audience.)

Statements and their counterparts in other forms of linguistic activity (i.e., questions, commands, etc.) are the focus of semantic analysis and semantic theory. In studying syntax, the focus is on sentences, the expressions used to make statements. The diagrams we have developed represent (kinds of) statements. Although they show both a statement's semantic structure and its syntactic character, our diagrams have a semantic bias. Syntactic features are not explicitly identified or labelled. A diagram shows the syntactic character only by displaying the syntactic object used to make the statement. The diagram's organization and special notation are designed to represent semantic structure. The diagrams are only part of our representations of statements. They must be accompanied by explanations of the acts performed with expressions and of the semantic "effects" of structural relations. In addition, to understand the diagrams one needs to understand English—she must know what acts are conventionally performed with the expressions in a diagram.

A diagram which represented more about a statement, and depended to a smaller extent on supplementary explanations and understanding of natural-language expressions, would be *more explicit* than the diagrams I am using. It is possible to develop diagrams that are considerably more explicit than those in this book, but diagrams cannot represent all important semantic and syntactic features. The connections that a language user exploits in performing acknowledging/identifying acts are semantic features of his statements. These vary from one person to another, and are not easily spelled out. Diagrams are suited to represent features common to statements that different language users make with one sentence, and this is the most we will ask of them. A *fully explicit* diagram is one that shows all the semantic and syntactic features that can suitably be represented. Fully explicit representations might be an appropriate goal for some linguistic or philosophical theories, but they are not being pursued in this book. Our supplemented diagrams are well suited to our analyses, and don't need to be more explicit.

Although our diagrams represent both syntactic and semantic features, it is possible to devise purely semantic representations of linguistic acts and activities. For example, we might employ a diagram like this:

> ⊢ An expression is/was used to acknowledge the object of attention to be θ—for which the feature criteria are χ_1 and χ_2, on a specified occasion.
>
> ¦
>
> An expression having feature criteria ϕ_1, ϕ_2, and ϕ_3, is/was used to attend to object α, exploiting particular connections in doing so.

Such a diagram would indicate the kinds of acts performed, and their intentional, structural relation. It wouldn't specify the words used to perform the acts. It wouldn't indicate the order in which the words were produced, nor would it reveal whether these words have a certain gender or number or case.

The possibility of entirely semantic representations of linguistic acts/activities suggests that someone develop an abstract semantic theory which is independent of any particular language. If a system were devised which provides representations for everything it is possible to say, particular languages could then be investigated to determine which possibilities they are equipped to realize, and the manners in which they do this. This abstract theory wouldn't belong to linguistics, an empirical study of actual natural languages, but would instead be housed in philosophy, psychology, or logic.

At present, logic is a largely semantic study of linguistic acts. Sentences of artificial logical languages are not tied to one or another natural language, but can be used for statements in different languages. However, logic is concerned with semantic structure at a relatively abstract level. Many natural-language statements having different specific semantic structures will exemplify a single logical form. Logic does not at present provide a catalogue or a complete classification of the things that might be said. And the project of developing such a classification isn't promising. For people aren't equipped with a substantial array of innate ideas. If they were, these ideas might determine what can be said. People invent and develop language to give shape to experience and its objects. Which specific meaningful linguistic acts a person performs is determined by the conventions and practices that he or other members of his linguistic community has thought up. Which kinds of meaningful acts can be performed can only be determined by investigating existing languages or inventing new ones.

A purely semantic theory for language-in-general isn't feasible. Nor do we want an entirely semantic theory for a particular natural language. Because a purely semantic representation of a linguistic act is not a complete or adequate representation. A statement (or question, or command) has a syntactic character as well as a semantic structure. The stuff, or matter, of linguistic acts is sounds or marks. To completely determine the kind of a linguistic act or activity, one must indicate both its semantic structure and its syntactic character. Although the structure is different from the character, a purely semantic theory of a natural language would be excessively abstract, omitting much of what is distinctive about the language.

There is little interest in a purely semantic theory. But what about syntax? Is an entirely syntactic theory either feasible or desirable? To deal with this question, we must distinguish two kinds of syntactic theory. The first kind deals with *semantically motivated* features and categories. Features like *singular*, *plural*, *past tense*, and *future tense*, and categories like *adjective* and *adverb* are *semantically motivated.* These are to be distinguished from *brute* features and categories which are characteristic of the second kind of syntactic theory. Brute features/categories involve only the shapes, acoustic "contours," and spatial and temporal organization of written and spoken expressions. If there were a system of rules for obtaining some expressions from others, and this system were formulated solely in terms of brute syntactic features, it would then be a brute syntactic feature to have been obtained from brutely specified input expressions by applying a definite sequence of rules (of transformations).

A brute-feature syntactic theory would be for a particular natural language, since the brute syntactic objects and features are different for different languages. An independent, autonomous syntactic theory (a presemantic theory) would characterize well-formed expressions in brute-feature terms. It is conceivable though unlikely that a brute-feature system could be provided for assembling just those sentences of a natural language that are intuitively recognized to be grammatical. If such a theory were developed, it might be developed with semantic structure in mind, as are the syntactic "theories" for artificial logical languages. Otherwise the autonomous syntactic theory would be neither interesting nor enlightening, for syntactic structure would be independent of semantic considerations. In any case, the vague ideal of capturing intuitive grammaticality is not an important goal. None of us have any trouble using intuitively ungrammatical sentences to perform meaningful linguistic acts.

A purely syntactic theory dealing with semantically motivated features and categories is still a theory of a particular natural language. But the basic concepts of such a theory might be applicable to different languages. Just as the present account of semantic structure provides resources for representing statements in different languages, even though all our examples have been English examples. There may be distinctive semantic features of statements in different languages, but a general system of representation will allow us to characterize the differences.

Once semantically motivated features and categories are countenanced in syntax, it becomes difficult to determine whether a theory is syntactic or semantic. While theories of syntax are conceived as dealing with structures of expressions and not acts, the structures assigned to expressions are intended to characterize sentences with respect to (abstractly conceived) statements made with the sentences. If syntactic theories in linguistics were not semantically motivated, they would have no occasion to assign different structures to a single sentence (to a single sentential string of words). But these theories can be regarded as systems of representations of linguistic acts/activities, showing both semantic structures and syntactic characters at an abstract level. They can also be conceived as theories of the syntactic characters of abstractly conceived linguistic acts/activities. Allowing ourselves to recognize semantically motivated syntactic categories and syntactic features opens the way to providing a very rich account of the syntactic characters of linguistic acts. For example, from the perspective of brute syntactic features, the phrase 'pretty little girls' school' is a single syntactic item. But if we admit a syntactic relation *modifying*, the one string of words can be used to exemplify different syntactic characters:

pretty [little (girls' school)]
pretty [(little girls') school]
(pretty little)(girls' school)
and so on

Unless some restriction is placed on what is considered a syntactic feature, a syntactic counterpart can be provided to every semantic feature. Developing such a rich set of syntactic concepts only camouflages the semantic structures of linguistic acts and activities, and leads to a misunderstanding of the relation between the semantic and the syntactic. For example, the procedures involved in producing representations of syntactic characters are easily mistaken for processes that go on "inside" language users. Rather than building a complete account of semantic structure into our syntactic concepts, it is more enlightening to develop an explicit account of semantic structure. I propose limiting what count as syntactic features to what can be detected by looking or listening. This allows semantically motivated syntactic categories and some semantically motivated syntactic features. We can see and hear the difference between different words, and between 'he' and 'him', between 'boy' and 'boys'. Cases, number, and gender are legitimate syntactic features, but modifying relations are not. To say that an adjective modifies a noun is not to make a syntactic statement; it is instead to say how adjective acts are semantically related to noun acts. Similarly, relations between pronouns and their antecedents are semantic rather than syntactic.

Instead of trying for an entirely syntactic or an entirely semantic theory of a natural language, what is wanted is a combined syntactic-semantic theory. This agrees with Montague's remark (1974, 210) that syntax and semantics must be developed "hand in hand." A complete syntactic-semantic theory of a natural language should provide detailed analysis of the semantic structures of statements. While such analyses are certainly semantic, they provide detail that is often thought to be pragmatic. The "pragmatic" character of these analyses is reflected in my finding it most convenient to explain the different ways of using one sentence by describing circumstances in which one or another structure is appropriate. For example, this structure:

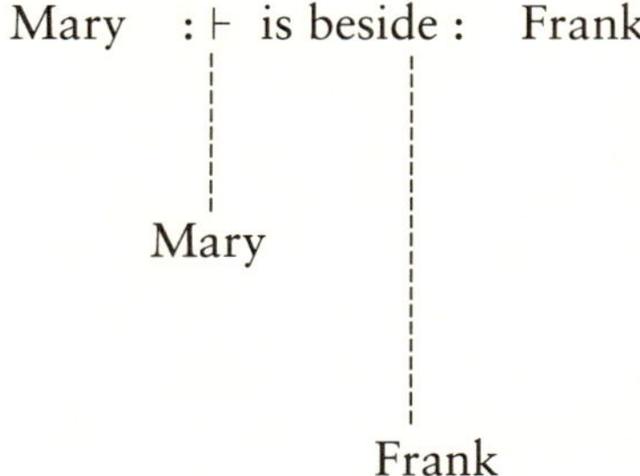

is appropriate when the audience knows where Frank is but not where Mary is, and this structure:

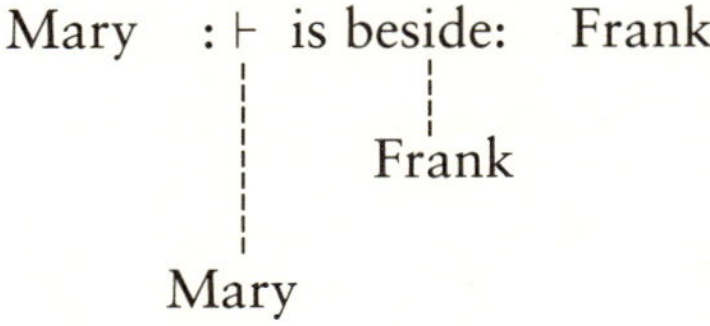

is appropriate in the opposite case. The fundamental linguistic (and semantic) reality is constituted by linguistic acts and activities, organized by structural relations. But certain semantic structures are better suited than others for communicating information to a particular audience. Pragmatics seems best understood as the study of the communicative use of language. It is an appropriate pragmatic problem to determine which semantic structures are suited to various communicative tasks.

If syntax is limited as I propose, modern theories of syntax in linguistics turn out to be syntactic-semantic theories which provide representations of both semantic structures and syntactic characters. But they are not entirely satisfactory theories, for the representations of semantic structure are neither adequate nor perspicuous. Even if my proposed limitation is not accepted, it must still be conceded that syntactic theories are infected by semantic concerns and concepts. Semantic structure doesn't grow out of syntactic character; the syntactic characters are introduced to accommodate the intuitively recognized semantic structures.

From the present perspective, linguistic accounts of syntactic structure are really accounts of semantic structure and syntactic character. But these theories are highly abstract, for they are not concerned with the detailed semantic structures of statements. An abstract theory groups together a number of different statement kinds, and considers them to be instances of a single general kind. It considers different specific kinds to be one kind—what counts as a single statement (kind) for an abstract theory is determined by an abstract level of semantic structure.

Since theories of syntax take account of the syntactic characters of statements, these theories don't lump together statements made with different sentences. Different sentences are different syntactic characters, and one statement cannot have more than one syntactic character. But we have seen that a single sentence can be used to make statements having different structures. Syntactic theories in linguistics are disposed to recognize one statement where we see several.

Consider the sentence 'Joan played tennis yesterday'. A simple way of using the sentence employs these acts:

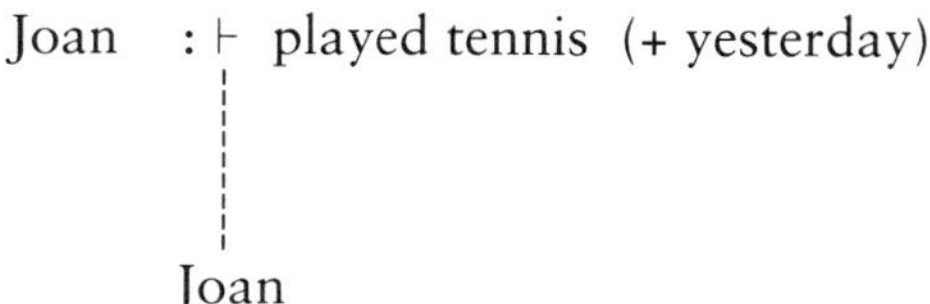

The speaker uses 'played tennis' to acknowledge Joan to have played tennis yesterday, and uses 'yesterday' to attend to yesterday, intending to make clear the time of the event—intending to make explicit that his acknowledging act is directed to an event which took place yesterday. In acknowledging Joan to have played tennis yesterday, the speaker attends to a particular event of tennis playing. We cannot tell from the diagram just which event. The event that is his object is determined by his intentions, by the connections he exploits.

If what Joan did yesterday is being contrasted with what she did other days, the following might take place:

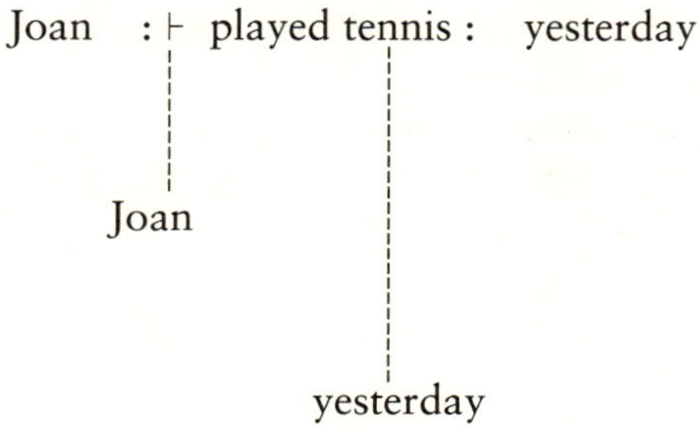

The speaker uses yesterday as a reference point, allowing himself to acknowledge Joan to be situated by playing tennis with respect to yesterday. In performing his acknowledging act, the speaker is again attending to a tennis playing event, which may be the same as the first speaker's event. If it is the same event, the two statements make the same demands on the world, and so have the same truth conditions.

Now suppose that athletic Joan plays different sports on different days, and someone asks what she played yesterday. The speaker might say this:

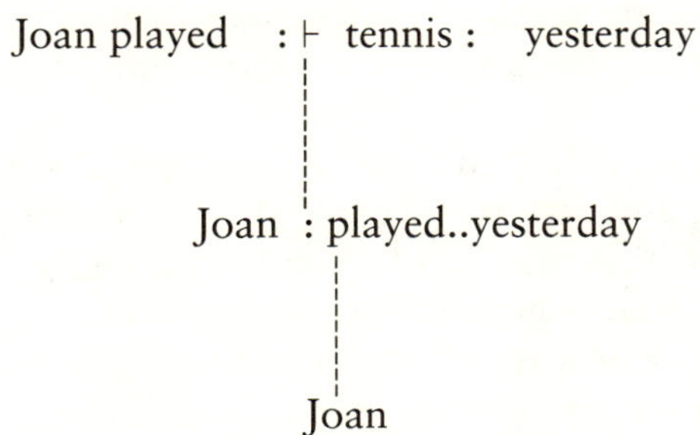

Attending to Joan enables to speaker to attend to a particular event of playing yesterday, and this enables him to acknowledge the playing to be tennis. If the event to which he attends is the same as that intended by the previous speakers, his acknowledging act (his statement) will have the same truth conditions as theirs.

In each of the cases represented, the statement has the same truth conditions, since there is only one "way" the world needs to be for the different acknowledging acts to be correct. If we consider semantic structure "at the level of truth conditions," we can say that each speaker has made the same (abstract) statement. It would be possible to devise a new system of representation, so that a single representation would be used for the three statements.

Such a system would provide representations that are more abstract than the ones we are using. But our diagrams are themselves quite abstract. We can use this diagram:

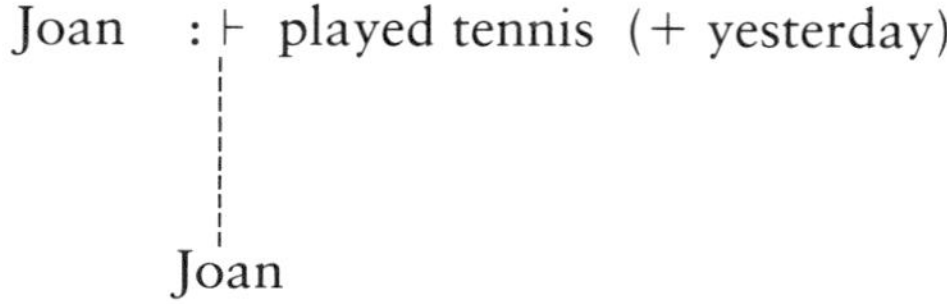

to represent a particular person's statement about a particular Joan and a particular tennis-playing event. This is a kind of statement that can be made more than once. The diagram will also represent a different person's statement about Joan and her tennis playing. And the diagram can be used for a statement about Joan and a different tennis-playing event. It can even be used for a statement about a different Joan and a tennis playing of that Joan. These possibilities for representing constitute different levels of abstraction; they are different possibilities for counting various statements as one abstract kind of statement.

It seems difficult to find a principled basis for selecting an abstract level of semantic structure, and determining that this is the appropriate level for a syntactic-semantic theory of a natural language. Current theories in linguistics group together those statements made with one sentence that have the same kind of truth conditions apart from differences due to connections exploited by specific speakers, and differences due to the particular objects and situations that the speakers are trying to identify. The abstract level at which linguistic theories aim might be the level at which syntactic principles "take effect" in

English or some other natural languages. It seems unlikely that this is the "operative" level for all natural languages, for there are languages which mark the focus of a statement syntactically. Even if there is an abstract level of semantic structure which is appropriately characterized by a theory of language, we also need a theory which explains the detailed semantic structures of natural-language speech acts.

5. Logical Truth Conditions

Although linguists represent statements at a highly abstract level of truth conditions (they group together statements having a single syntactic character and the same relatively specific kinds of truth conditions), linguists don't normally attempt to provide an account of the truth conditions of statements (or the analogous conditions for other kinds of sentential acts/activities). A theory of truth conditions should state how the world must be for a statement or propositional act to be true. The theory should explain the "fit" between a true linguistic act and the part of the world that makes the act true. It is logicians rather than linguists who provide accounts of truth conditions. Such an account is different from a syntactic-semantic theory of a language. But a theory of truth conditions depends on an analysis of semantic structure. Like pragmatics, a treatment of truth conditions is a suitable "companion theory" to a syntactic-semantic theory.

Logicians don't give the truth conditions of natural-language statements. Instead they formulate truth conditions for sentences in artificial logical languages. But it isn't entirely accurate to speak of artificial *languages* (though I am not proposing that we change this usage). Basic linguistic reality is constituted by linguistic acts and activities. Expressions have no "standing" apart from their use by the community to perform these acts/activities. But no one speaks or writes or thinks the "languages" of modern logic. We could regard the sentences of artificial languages as instruments that *might* be used to make statements, and investigate the kinds of statement that *would* be made with them. However, it makes more sense to regard these sentences as abstract representations of linguistic acts/activities. They don't represent particular statements made on specific occasions, for representing isn't identifying. A logical-language sentence represents an arbitrary statement of a kind. For example, a first-order sentence '*F(a)*' will represent a statement constituted by an identifying act and a predicative act.

In logic, it is common to think syntax provides rules for constructing sentences, and semantics gives the truth conditions for these sentences. A deductive system then syntactically characterizes semantically distinguished sentences and arguments. But sentences don't have truth conditions or semantic features. Truth conditions are for statements and other propositional acts represented with the "sentences." Nor are arguments constituted by syntactic objects. The deductive system codifies techniques for constructing representations of proofs (including proofs from hypotheses, or deductions), valid arguments, and logically true statements. Syntactic rules for an artificial language are directions for constructing representations that we can investigate and "manipulate" to find things out about the statements they represent.

Sentences of logical languages represent semantic structures (and the propositional acts that have these structures) characterized by certain kinds of truth conditions. All representations are abstract in the sense of omitting certain features found in particular objects and situations. But some logical representations are more abstract than others, for some represent less detail than others. If we use '*C( )*' to represent predicative acts performed with 'is a callow youth who inherited a fortune from his grandmother', our representing will be quite abstract. Because they also abstract away from syntactic features, the languages of logic are not tied to specific natural languages. One logical-language sentence can represent statements made with different expressions in a single language, and it can represent statements made in different languages. But we should not think that statements in different languages share a syntactic feature called logical form. The forms displayed by sentences in logical languages are artifacts of logical analysis. They represent structures that may be common to statements made in different languages, but the structures need not be marked by the expressions used to make those statements. The languages of logic are so designed that each logical-language sentence/representation is unambiguously associated with specific truth conditions. This is what it is for logical form to coincide with grammatical form in those languages. Syntactic objects in natural languages are not similarly linked to uniquely specified truth conditions.

Because logical-language sentences are commonly taken to have both syntactic structures and semantic features, especially truth conditions, the relation between syntactic structure and semantic features is commonly misunderstood. Semantics is not subsequent to syntax, and added to it. Syntactic structure in logic is devised *in order* to represent semantic structure, which precedes the logical language, and "exists" apart from that language. The correlation between syntactic features of logical-language sentences and the semantic features they represent is entirely conventional. But this correlation is practically important. We can develop techniques for manipulating/transforming representations so that the outputs of the transformations provide important semantic information. The kind of transforming techniques I have in mind are exploited with Venn diagrams. The Venn diagram for a statement is a syntactic object which can be used to represent the statement. By combining representations for different statements, we can obtain a representation that allows us to "extract" statements that were not "entered" in the diagram. Transforming techniques are exploited to greater effect by modern computers.

We don't exploit such techniques when we deductively infer one statement from others, for (1) deduction requires a reasoner to understand what she is doing, and (2) the syntactic characters of natural-language statements are not reliable guides to their semantic features. However, some such techniques might be exploited in storing and remembering propositional knowledge (belief). It isn't likely that we simply store remembered sentences, for remembered propositional knowledge is often stated with new sentences. Perhaps we "enter" propositional knowledge into a memory-analogue of a Venn diagram, which allows us in remembering to perform (kinds of) propositional acts we haven't performed before. This sort of computational account can only be invoked for processes of which we aren't consciously aware.

Logicians and linguists both devise representations of abstract levels of semantic structure. But the logicians' representations are much more abstract than those of linguists. Logical representations abstract away from all or almost all syntactic features. This brings together statements made with different expressions, even in different languages. And logical form links statements about different objects—a French statement about one thing will have the same logical form as a German statement about something else. For the two statements can both be represented (under different interpretations) by a single logical-language sentence.

The way in which logical-language sentences are interpreted can determine what statements they represent. We can interpret a group of expressions by performing linguistic acts of the sort they are used to represent. For example, in order to evaluate this argument:

> If Danny ate any cookies in the jar, he was punished. Danny ate a cookie in the jar. So Danny was punished.

we might give the following interpretations to first-order expressions:

> *C(x)*—*x* was a cookie
> *I(x, y)*—*x* was in *y* on the relevant occasion
> *A(x, y)*—*x* ate *y* on that occasion
> *P(x)*—*x* was punished on that occasion
> *d*—Danny
> *j*—the jar

We could then represent an argument which approximates the original argument:

> $(\forall x)[[[C(x) \mathbin{\&} I(x, y)] \mathbin{\&} A(d, x)] \supset P(d)]$
> $(\exists x)[[C(x) \mathbin{\&} I(x, j)] \mathbin{\&} A(d, x)]$
> *So* $P(d)$

This allows us to construct a formal deduction showing the argument to be valid. However, while the linguistic acts that are represented under such an interpretation have truth conditions, these truth conditions aren't the focus of the interpretations. A different kind of interpretation is needed in order to provide a systematic account of truth conditions. It is Tarski's work that brought a revolutionary change to logic, by spelling out the truth conditions associated with formulas of the predicate calculus.

A Tarski-style semantic account interprets an artificial language by assigning things to expressions. But a Tarski-style interpretation is more abstract than that illustrated above, in the sense of being inadequate to determine which statements are represented by logical-language sentences. To understand this, suppose, borrowing Quine's example, that the creatures with hearts are exactly those with kidneys. It isn't the case that a statement that α has a kidney will entail that α has a heart. But if '*H(x)*' is a first-order predicate that is assigned the set of creatures with hearts, then it is so far qualified both to represent predicative acts performed with 'is a creature with a heart' and to represent acts performed with 'is a creature with a kidney'. If it represented both kinds of acts (if it represented an abstract kind of act which included both more specific kinds), then this interpretation would "validate" the invalid inference mentioned above, for an inference from '$H(\alpha)$' to '$H(\alpha)$' is clearly valid. In addition to a Tarski-style interpretation, additional stipulations are needed to determine which logical language predicates correspond to which natural-language predications. This abstractness could be overcome by adopting a different semantic account. Montague's approach, for example, is to assign a function from worlds to objects in the worlds as value of an expression of the artificial language.

It seems desirable to have a theory of the truth conditions of actual statements in a natural language. But it may not be easy to adapt logical theories to this end. One difficulty is that logical-language sentences don't represent kinds of linguistic acts we commonly and customarily perform. I have argued (Kearns 1979; 1984) that first-order languages don't provide accurate representations of quantificational statements. If we translate a statement made with 'Every child is asleep' like this:

$$(\forall x)[C(x) \supset A(x)]$$

we have represented a quantified conditional statement, though the original statement is not conditional. The first-order sentence represents a statement which is at best an approximation to the original. An approximate translation is still useful, for it represents a statement (statement kind) that has important semantic relations to the original. However, it would be enlightening to accurately represent statements we actually make. (The languages developed in Kearns 1979 and 1984 are steps in that direction.)

If we overlook the fact that familiar logical languages represent kinds of statements we don't often make, there are further difficulties with logical treatments of truth conditions. These semantic accounts are not suited to statements made at the identifying stage of language use. For with respect to a given object (possibly in a given world), a predicate either applies or fails to apply. But a natural-language predicate like 'played tennis' can be used on different occasions to acknowledge Joan to have played tennis on different occasions. I might first acknowledge her to have played tennis yesterday, and then acknowledge her to have played tennis on Monday of last week. The same syntactic predicate is used each time, with the same feature criteria, but different connections are exploited. I can also combine the predicate with a negative expression to deny that Joan played tennis on other occasions (she didn't play last Tuesday, for example). Predicates, or acknowledging acts characterized by specified feature criteria, are not simply true or false of an object (*n*-tuple) unless we confine our attention to predicates used for the present time, or predicates used for a timeless realm like that of mathematical objects. But even with respect to such predicates, standard semantics are still unsatisfactory. The world's independently being a certain way is not sufficient to make an act acknowledging it to be that way true, though it is sufficient to make an act acknowledging it to be an incompatible way false. The truth of an acknowledging act depends on the speaker's acts, not simply on the words he says or the acknowledging criteria he employs. Though the ball *is* red, the speaker may falsely acknowledge it to be red. He may have improperly applied the criteria for being red, or be relying on the testimony of a woman who was talking about a different ball.

Although a statement is surely true if things are as it says, this concession amounts to less than endorsement of correspondence theories of truth. At the purely identifying stage of language use, the truth of a simple acknowledging statement does not amount to correspondence. The language user must identify the situation he is talking about. Even if his statement *corresponds* to the facts, he may not be exploiting a connection to the relevant facts, and so may not have got things right. Truth as correspondence is better suited to propositional representing acts. A propositional representing act might identify specific objects and represent or portray them as this, that, or the other. It might represent arbitrary objects of a kind as doing one thing or another. In representing a situation of a kind, the language user may only claim that there is such a situation. Even if he is in no position to identify one such situation, his claim will still be true.

Although standard semantic accounts are only suited to statements characteristic of the representational stage of language use, they are't completely satisfactory for such acts. Even at the representational stage of language use, we employ the same past-tense expression on different occasions for different situations, or kinds of situation. The different uses of 'played tennis' to represent tennis playing on different days would be represented by different first-order predicates, and the fact that the different acts predicate the "same" feature of objects on different occasions will be hidden from view. This limitation isn't so important for statements about the present, or about a timeless realm like that of ideal mathematical objects. But we can't easily use assignments of objects, *n*-tuples, and sets or collections of them to provide a general theory of the truth conditions of representational-stage statements.

A semantic account which assigns things or *n*-tuples of them to predicates, even if the predicates get different objects in different worlds, doesn't explain how a true propositional act "fits" that part of the world that makes it true. A single statement can be made true by different situations, but situations don't "show up" in such an account. Predicate expressions in propositional representing acts are not used to identify or pick out or represent objects or *n*-tuples. They are used to represent situations (arbitrary situations of a kind), where these are something different from *n*-tuples. A statement representing a particular object as ϕ, for example a statement representing Peter as owning a car, can be made true by more than one situation. A semantic account assigning car owners to a predicate '*C( )*' and Peter to '*p*' will get the truth value of '*C(p)*' right, but it won't show how a statement representing Peter as owning a car gets fastened to the world. Standard semantic accounts are unrealistic when it comes to explaining the truth conditions of actual natural-language statements. They provide little help for coming up with a theory of truth conditions for a natural language.

The abstract level at which they aim has led logicians to adopt a too-simple paradigm for accounts of truth conditions. A complete and realistic account of truth conditions for a natural language must be grounded on a comprehensive and thorough understanding of semantic structure. The truth conditions of a statement are what the world must be like if the statement is true, and depend on connections between linguistic acts and objects in the world. This means that a satisfactory treatment of truth conditions will to some extent have the character of a metaphysical or ontological theory. It won't be a complete or detailed theory, for it only makes explicit what our linguistic practice assumes. Neither will it be a speculative theory. The world the language-using subject encounters in experience is the world he, in part, constitutes; it has the conceptual structure he provides. (It is a speculative task to complete the theory incorporated in our linguistic practice.)

To give the truth conditions of a statement, one should "follow" the semantic structure of that statement. In a statement like this:

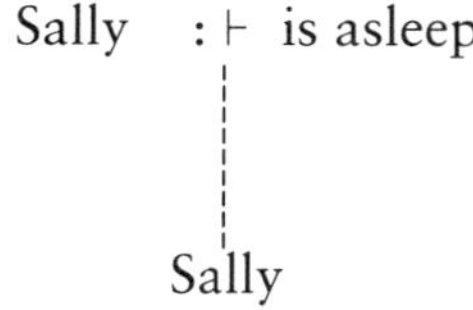

the act of using 'Sally' identifies Sally, who is in the world. The act acknowledging Sally to be asleep is an attempt to identify a particular event of Sally's sleeping. The truth conditions for a particular acknowledging act, and hence statement, of this kind are that the person Sally fell down on a certain occasion and that the speaker who has identified Sally exploits connections to the event in question to identify it. A full account of truth conditions should spell out the criteria for someone's falling down. To explain the truth conditions for a natural language, we won't employ the interpreting functions found in logic. The fundamental attending acts are themselves like "functions" from the world to the objects they identify. The acts that aren't fundamental and are relevant to truth conditions can be compared to functions from the values yielded by the fundamental acts, or to functions from the fundamental functions themselves.

There are serious (conceptual) difficulties in developing a realistic account of truth conditions for identifying-stage sentences. One source of difficulty is illustrated by a statement like:

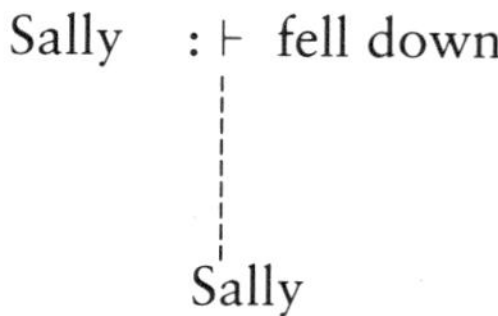

The speaker's identifying Sally makes her the initial object for a functional truth-condition account. But he doesn't simply acknowledge

Sally to have fallen down, he acknowledges her to have fallen on a particular occasion. His acknowledging act is not one that can correctly be performed for Sally on other occasions, or for other people on other occasions. And his act of acknowledging Sally to have fallen on that occasion can't be performed by other people, because they won't be connected in the same way to her fall.

To give a functional account of truth conditions, it isn't sufficient to have a "fell down" function. There must be as many such functions as there are occasions on which someone is in a position to acknowledge a particular person to have fallen down. There can't simply be one function for each fall that Sally took; for each fall, we need a function for each person in a position to identify that fall. The difficulties in developing an adequate realistic account of truth conditions make the logician's approach seem pretty attractive.

6. The Things There Are

The language user provides conceptual structure to the world he experiences. New discoveries and new information lead him to introduce additional structure, additional "locations," and give him additional clusters of connections to exploit in attending to objects. The language learner enriches his world as he becomes more proficient linguistically. Though, in principle, different language users can have their world in common, such a world would remain one which they, in part, constitute. And, in practice, different language users inhabit different worlds of experience. This claim that language users contribute conceptual structure to the different worlds they experience is not intended as a metaphor. It isn't that people actually experience the one real world with its own structure, but that if often *seems as if* they inhabited different worlds which they organize themselves. If there is a "real" world, a world of "things in themselves," behind/in addition to the worlds that subjects experience, the objects of that world are not seen, heard, felt, in experience.

That subjects provide conceptual structure to the worlds they experience explains how it is that experience provides propositional knowledge. In acknowledging/judging Muppet to be a dog, the child is not abstracting a form or essence from his experience. Neither is he comparing an idea to an independent and autonomous experience. He is using the word/concept *dog* to organize his experience. Dogs now constitute a category, a scattered part of the world to which he can attend. The criteria he employs are not criteria for being a dog—there are no criteria for that, in contrast with the case of being a Republican. (Being a Republican is something one does on purpose.) The 'dog'-criteria are for *correctly acknowledging* an object to be a dog. These criteria are open to being enlarged or supplemented as knowledge develops. When they are, additional structure will be introduced to the world. The child needs some innate skills to learn and use language, but the conceptual structure he introduces first is learned. Human beings are also able to invent new concepts to structure their worlds.

Experience is the arena where language users (concept employers) constitute their worlds. But not from scratch. Language users find themselves experiencing qualitied and spatiotemporally organized worlds. They introduce, first, perceptual structure and, then, conceptual structure. The worlds that language users organize are not infinitely plastic. These worlds could be organized differently from the ways they actually are organized, but not all organizational schemes are adequate. Anything doesn't go. Our use of language to organize our worlds makes it possible to obtain knowledge of these worlds. But we can never know everything about the world as presently structured, and the organization we have so far provided is always inadequate. More structure is wanted, and the structure we now have is in need of adjustments or repairs.

The language learner whose progress we are tracing can use expressions to attend to objects in the world, to acknowledge objects to be this or that, and to mark his acts to make certain features explicit. Sophisticated language users like ourselves can perform other kinds of acts than these, but the fundamental kinds of acts we have isolated will take a person pretty far. Many classical discussions of language—for example, Aristotle's—don't appear to take account of different kinds of acts than our fundamental acts.

The objects to which a subject attends, parts of the world of his experience, have various features at various times. An object doesn't exist without its features, it can't. (But, of course, it might exist without this or that particular feature.) A subject can't visually or tactually attend to an object apart from its features. (We never attend to an object in sense experience apart from *some* of its features.) It seems that, strictly speaking, the sensing subject is always aware of situations/events, of objects-being-ϕ. But once the subject learns to use language, he can attend to objects apart from their features. The subject attends to/identifies objects he isn't currently perceiving via connections linking him to those objects. Being connected to a speaker in certain ways is a feature of an object, but in exploiting this connection, the speaker need not attend to it. Attending to objects apart from their features is mentally separating the objects from the features, a form of abstract thought. But we are not simply separating in thought what isn't separate in reality. We are actually introducing the distinction between the object and its features to the world of our experience. This contributes to efficiency in thought and communication, for the abstractly conceived objects are convenient pegs around which to organize knowledge and belief, and are well suited to be the targets of different peoples' identifying acts.

In employing words to acknowledge objects to be this or that on particular occasions, language users provide themselves with resources for attending to scattered parts of the world. Whether these scattered parts are collections or lumps, they are somewhat abstract. A collection of objects is constituted by someone considering those objects together. The objects in a collection will be situated with respect to one another in various ways, as well as having features which vary from element to element. In attending to the collection, we ignore or abstract away from the situations and features. In this respect, a collection of sheep is different from Farmer Brown's flock of sheep even if the collection contains exactly the sheep in his flock. The flock is constituted by legal relations giving Brown title to the various sheep, by spatial relations linking the sheep, by "kinship" relations linking ewes and lambs, and so on. The flock of sheep is a structured whole, but the collection is simply constituted by those sheep considered together. Farmer Brown's flock of sheep "supports" different collections. There is the Farmer-Brown's-sheep part of the world, which waxes and wanes along with the membership of Farmer Brown's flock. It can go out of existence at one time, and be rejuvenated later. Unlike the flock, the collection has no spatial arrangement and isn't owned by Farmer Brown. Another collection is constituted by the sheep in Farmer Brown's flock at present. That collection currently coincides with the collection of sheep in his flock. But if Farmer Brown's flock gains new members or loses old ones, the collection of sheep in the flock will no longer coincide with the collection of just the sheep that were in the flock prior to the change. (The collection of just those sheep can outlive changes in Farmer Brown's flock, but it goes out of existence when one of its members dies.)

A scattered "lump" of quantities of stuff is also abstract if the spatial and other relations linking the quantities are left out of account. Consider a lump of butter that is softened, pressed in a lamb mold, and chilled, yielding a butter lamb like those sold in Polish markets at Easter. If we attend to just the quantity of butter, and ignore the organization (the shape), we are focusing abstractly on a part of the world—which gives us an abstract part of the world. This quantity of butter, with its shape, constitutes the butter lamb. The quantity considered independent of the shape is not the lamb, and doesn't coincide with it. The scattered butter part of the world is constituted by all the quantities of butter there are, considered apart from their shapes, spatial positions, and so forth.

By providing the resources to attend to objects apart from their features and, particularly, to attend to collections and scattered "lumps," language enables us to achieve general knowledge. To know about dogs or cats or water, we must be able to attend to collections and to scattered lumps. We have no other resources for doing this than linguistic/conceptual resources. These resources not only make knowledge possible, but also serve to constitute the objects of knowledge.

Although I have talked freely about objects and their features, from the language learner's perspective there are so far no features—if we understand these to be properties and relations. Instead there are objects and objects-being-featured. An object being featured is a *situation*; some situations are events. The whole world is an enormously complex situation. To understand the ontology accessible to a language user who can perform only the fundamental kinds of acts we have discussed, we will investigate his conceptually structured world of experience. It isn't entirely easy to isolate the right ontology, for we must avoid being misled by our own greater linguistic proficiency, and by our knowledge of the theories developed by various philosophers, logicians, and linguists (among others).

7. Situations

The world is constituted by various objects and situations—situations are themselves objects; an object is anything a language user can attend to and identify. Not all objects are situations. Objects are locations, for we identify them on the basis of connections linking us to them (they are situated with respect to us). This use of 'location' is still the broad one, for while a spatial position like the corner of Elmwood and Highland avenues is a location, so is a particular person like George Washington.

To get a clearer perspective on the ontology introduced by the fundamental linguistic acts, I will develop a system of notation for labelling situations. This notation will only be schematic, since I am not trying to come up with a system of labels we can actually employ for situations in our daily lives. When the speaker acknowledges Sally to have fallen:

Sally : ⊢ fell down
¦
Sally

his acts "express" two functions: (1) A Sally-attending function which, applied to the world, yields the person Sally. Let *W* be the world and σ be Sally. I will use the speaker's expression to express this function:

$$Sally(W) = \sigma$$

(2) A fell-down-on-a-particular-occasion function. The occasion in question is the occasion when Sally fell, not the occasion when the speaker performed his acknowledging act. I will use the speaker's expression for his act, but this isn't adequate. The same expression might be used on different occasions to deal with different occasions. This is not like the name 'Sally' being used for many different girls and women—in that respect the name is simply ambiguous. But 'fell down' isn't ambiguous when connected to different falls. The acknowledging criteria remain the same. I will use the speaker's expression with a subscript to express his function:

$$Fell\text{-}down_k(\sigma) = ?$$

The particular subscripts employed have no special significance. In case Sally did fall down on the occasion under consideration, the question mark should be replaced by a label for that situation of Sally falling down. In case it wasn't Sally who fell down then, or if no one fell on that occasion, the question mark will be replaced by '∅' to indicate that the function yields no value for Sally as argument.

We need expressions for the objects which are elements of situations. I will use lowercase Greek and Latin letters. I will use capital Latin and Greek letters to complete the situation label. So if Sally did fall down on the occasion in question, we could use something like '*[σ F]*' to label the situation. But the same capital letter might be used for falls on different occasions. So the label should be like this: *[σ F_k]*. Square brackets bound all situation labels.

A label '*[σ F_k]*' has some resemblance to a sentence of a logical language, but that resemblance is misleading. For 'F_k' is not a predicate; the label isn't true or false. The system of notation does allow labels for nonsituations—for example, if μ is Mary, then '*[μ F_k]*' is a label for a situation that didn't occur. But the system of notation is not a language, it is a device for gaining understanding of situations. To give an account of truth conditions, only labels for genuine situations will be employed. In the label '*[σ F_k]*,' the expression 'F_k' is not a predicate and doesn't label a property. The expression 'F_k' simply labels the situation '*[σ F_k]*.' It labels that situation abstractly and uninformatively; such expressions will not be employed either alone or enclosed in brackets as official situation-names.

If *[σ F_k]* is a particular event of Sally's falling down, and 'F_k' labels that same event, it might seem that no expression other than a label for Sally can be combined with 'F_k' to yield a genuine-situation label. For example, we don't label anything if we write '*[μ F_k]*.' We might have additional labels for Sally, say '*a*', and then write '*[a F_k]*' to label *[σ F_k]*. But this difference between '*[a F_k]*' and '*[σ F_k]*' is of no interest. However, suppose Sally is at the moment the most popular girl on her block (among whatever population). She hasn't always been, and she won't continue to be the most popular. The phrase 'The most popular girl on that block' is not a name for Sally. This expression labels an independent location in the world. At the present time, this location coincides with the Sally location. If we use 'π' for the most popular girl location, then '*[π F_k]*' labels *[σ F_k]*. The two labels '*[π F_k]*' and '*[σ F_k]*' are importantly different; that they label the same situation reveals that on the occasion of the fall, the Sally location coincided with the most popular girl location.

In using the English phrase 'the most popular girl on the block', a speaker might attend either to the most-popular-girl part of the world ("The most popular girl on the block is Sally now but it used to be Margaret") or to the part constituted by the girl who is most popular

("The most popular girl on the block wasn't always popular"). In the system of notation, one part-of-the-world label can't be used in these two ways. If π is a label for the most-popular-girl location, then it isn't used for Sally (except incidentally).

A situation label has the form:

$[\alpha\ \Phi_1]$, $[\alpha\ \beta\ \Phi_7]$, $[\alpha\ \beta\ \gamma\ \Phi_2]$, and so on.

A single situation can have different labels because different parts of the world coincide at a time, so that each part figures in the same situations at that time. But there are other ways for a situation to have different labels. If a speaker performs these acts:

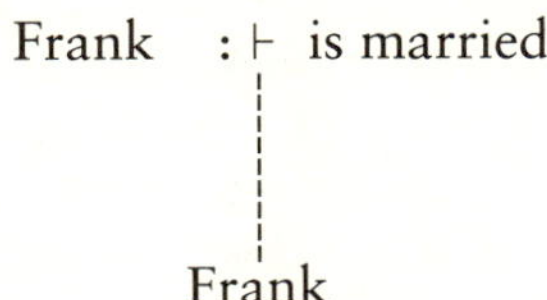

and Frank *is* married, to Kathy, then the speaker has identified the situation of Frank's currently being married. Suppose we label this situation with: $[f\ M_i]$. The acknowledging criteria for 'married' require that Frank be married to his wife. A speaker is not in a position to acknowledge Frank to be married unless he can exploit a connection to the present situation of Frank being married to Kathy. (Though he need not know Kathy's name.) But the speaker who performs these acts:

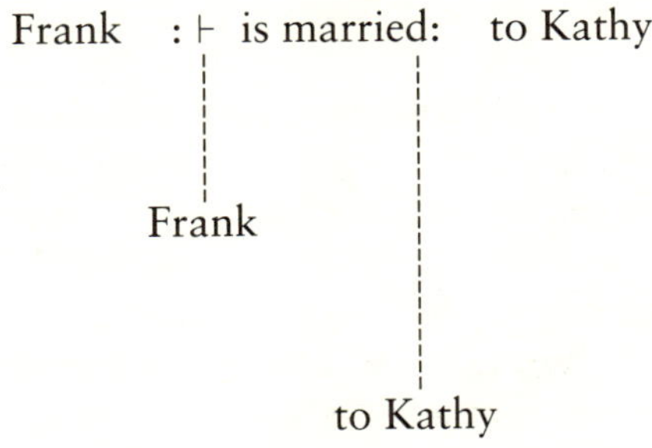

must be connected to the same situation. His acknowledging act (and his statement) have the same truth conditions—they identify the same situation—as the first speaker's act. But if we use '*[f k* N_p*]*' to label the second statement's situation, both expressions label a single situation. We shall say that the label '*[f* M_j*]*' is more abstract than '*[f k* N_p*]*', because it shows less detail. We can't avoid having abstract labels for situations in our notational system, because identifying acts are often abstract, and we may have no more information than such an act reveals. And a situation which has a certain degree of complexity according to what we know now may turn out to have more complexity when we acquire additional information.

Since labels for situations may be abstract, there are certain things that labels don't automatically reveal. One of these is the multiplicity of the situation: the number of distinct objects that are situated in that situation. The Frank-being-married situation *[f* M_j*]* looks like a one-object situation, but this is the same as the Frank-being-married-to-Kathy situation *[f k* N_p*]*. If we understand 'married' to be used here for normal monogamous marriage, our semantic knowledge allows us to determine that the being-married situation is an essentially two-object situation. However, if we correctly acknowledge John to be Megan's father:

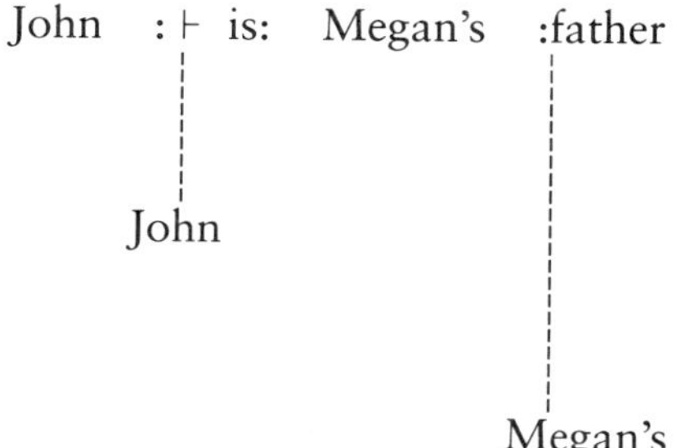

in this fashion, we can label the corresponding situation: *[j m* F_r*]*. But it is much less clear how many objects this situation contains. Is this label complete with respect to components, or does it abstractly label the situation constituted by John, Megan's mother, Megan, and all her siblings? Since it is semantically and physically necessary that there be a mother if John is to be a father, the more adequate analysis will provide a place for Megan's mother. It is less easy to decide about Megan's sister and brothers. The expression 'is . . . father' doesn't require their existence, but it "allows" for them. A world with a mother-father-child situation for each child seems less tidy that a world with only one mother-father-children situation. The latter situation is required in any case, and it bears an entailment-like relation to the mother-father-single-child situations. This example seems to me to reveal a respect in which the ontology embedded in our language is incomplete or indeterminate. A metaphysical theory might be developed which eliminates this incompleteness. Further developments of our ordinary conceptual framework could decide the issue. Or I may simply be wrong in thinking the question to have no determinate answer—a better understanding of our linguistic practice might lead me to favor one side or the other. If there is a right answer at present, this is solely a matter of current linguistic practice. There is nothing else that can be discovered about the world that would settle the matter.

We can't always determine the multiplicity of a situation from one of its labels. The label will also often fail to reveal whether the components of a situation are themselves situations. And labels provide uncertain information about the arrangement or order of components. The Frank-being-married-to-Kathy situation *[f k* N_p*]* is surely the same as the Kathy-being-married-to-Frank situation *[k f* N_p*]*. And this is no different from the Frank-being-husband-to-Kathy situation *[f k* H_s*]*. Though if we reverse the first two "names" in this last expression, we get an expression '*[k f* H_s*]*' for which there is no answering situation. Certain situations have no privileged order among their elements—no element is first, none is second, and so on. In the married couple situation, there are two parties and two *roles*: the husband role and the wife role. By convention, we use temporal order in spoken expressions to identify specific roles. In 'Frank is husband to Kathy', the first-place position indicates the husband role, and the last-place position the wife role. Neither role is "prior" to the other. While married couple situations seem to be inherently orderless, not all situations are. But even essentially ordered situations often lack first, second, and so on elements. Nick's standing between Jorge and Sarah is surely no different that his standing between Sarah and Jorge.

Although situations like the batter hitting the ball are momentary, not all situations are like this. A situation can last a short or a long time. And the objects that are situated are not "frozen" in that situation. Situations develop. World War II was a long-lasting situation/event that involved an enormous number of elements. These elements weren't just personnel, countries, weapons, and so forth; the larger situation was also constituted by smaller situations such as skirmishes, battles, landings, and campaigns.

Situations are themselves situated with respect to objects of all kinds. A situation may be witnessed by a person, caused by another situation, and take place at the same time as still another. As time goes by, a particular situation may acquire relations to new situations that occur. But once a situation is temporally related (situated with respect) to another situation, their temporal relation doesn't change. Situations are temporal locations. Earlier I suggested that not all situations are temporal locations, and used the word 'event' for those situations that are temporal locations. That suggestion now seems unsound. The situation of *A* occurring before *B* that I used to motivate the distinction is abstractly described. The actual situation will have *A* and *B* precisely situated temporally—*A* isn't simply prior to *B*. The particular situation of *A* occurring bears a precise temporal relation to the particular *B* situation. The larger situation includes events *A* and *B*, but may include no events between *A* and *B*. Gappy situations/events can't easily be given precise dates, but they do provide reference points with respect to which other situations/events can be identified.

8. Some Morals

We have followed the development of a language learner from the perceptual but prelinguistic stage to her use of language to identify (or attempt to) objects and situations. The language user in the purely identifying stage uses expressions for objects which are constitutents of her experience and for objects related to the objects of experience in ways she understands (and exploits). The language learner does not simply encounter the world of experience. She constitutes this world (in part) by contributing perceptual and conceptual structure. This world itself develops and changes as she acquires more linguistic/conceptual skills. At the purely identifying stage, both language and the world of experience incorporate the ordinary conception of experience and its objects. The language learner couldn't learn to use language in an identifying way, or to think propositionally, on the basis of some other conception. But at this point, it is more appropriate to speak of the ordinary conception, first, of the objects of experience and, subsequently, of the experience of them. For it is objects which have first claim to the language learner's attention. Her focus on the external world precedes her understanding of herself.

That language users provide conceptual structure to the world of experience explains how it is that experience provides us with propositional knowledge. No Aristotelian abstraction nor Cartesian innate ideas can do the job. But we apprehend the concepts which we introduce and use successfully to organize experience. We are aware of our own intentional activity and the concepts we use to organize the world and our experience of it.

The use of language is purposive, intentional activity. It cannot be reduced to, or explained in terms of the mechanical causal order. Nor are purposive and intentional features the "magical" accompaniment to a causal order which is, on its own terms, complete and self-sufficient. The causally organized world of experience is our invention, our creation. We introduce the organization to make sense of things, and to get along. The organization which depends on our concepts and our intentional activity can't supplant such activity and rule out either the possibility or the importance of acting intentionally.

Chapter 9

Representing: *The Fundamentals*

1. Explicit Iconic Representing

In this book we have introduced and developed a new conception of representing. This led us to distinguish representing from identifying, and to realize that either one of representing or identifying can take place apart from the other. We have further developed the conception of identifying in combination with an analysis of intentional and linguistic acts. Now we will focus on representing once more, to determine how representing shows up in propositional thinking and the use of language. I will focus on *explicit* representing, where a subject uses an object, the *representation*, of which she is consciously aware, to become representationally aware of a further object or objects. If there is such a thing as *nonexplicit* representing, it takes place when a subject uses a representation without being consciously aware of that representation; the subject becomes representationally aware of an object or objects without being aware of the representation she uses for doing this. Since the present chapter is almost exclusively concerned with explicit representing, I won't keep saying so. I will normally just talk about representing, and expect everyone to realize that I mean explicit representing.

An image doesn't represent an object because it resembles that object, nor does it represent for any other reason. An image doesn't represent "by itself" at all. Rather than being a feature of the image, *representing is what we do with the image*. To use an image to represent objects is to be (become) representationally aware of those objects. The image's being similar to objects doesn't constitute its representing the objects, but its similarity to objects makes it seem natural for us to use the image to represent objects of the kind it resembles.

Directly iconic representations resemble objects of the kinds they are used to represent. Looking at a photograph of some people is similar in important respects to looking at people. A painting of a man on a horse looks something like a man on a horse. In any iconic representing, the viewer (the subject) interprets perceptible features of the representation to become representationally aware. In directly iconic representing, the perceptible features are the same as or similar to the features of the objects of representational awareness. To use an indirectly iconic representation to become representationally aware of its objects, some additional knowledge is needed to properly interpret features which don't look like the features they represent. This additional knowledge may be knowledge of conventions, as with halos in paintings. But we might also use the rings in a photograph of a cut tree trunk to become representationally aware of the age of the cut tree at the time it was cut. In this case, the additional knowledge concerns natural regularities.

Perceiving an image is different from using that image to become representationally aware of objects. There is no reason to think that every animal that can perceive an image can also use the image to represent. Using an image to represent must also be distinguished from perceiving the image and mistaking it for an object of the kind it is used to represent. That an animal can be fooled by a picture or a mirror is no sign that the animal can use images to (explicitly) represent. It is our newly developed conception of representing that allows us to characterize the difference between animals that can and that can't use images to represent. If images represented intrinsically, the failure to "grasp" their representing would be difficult to understand. But we can now envisage the possibility that some animal that sees the picture is unable to use that picture to become representationally aware of objects. The new conception presents us with a new topic for empirical investigation: determining which animals and which kinds of animals are able to use images to represent objects. However, it isn't so easy to think up tests to determine if an animal can use an image this way.

I conjecture that for an agent to carry out explicit representing, that agent must be self-conscious. For to use a picture to represent, the agent must distinguish the picture from what it is a picture of. Which requires that he distinguish seeing the picture from being representationally aware of its objects. But then he must be aware of seeing the picture. Which is to be aware of himself seeing the picture. If I am right about the self-consciousness, and if some animals are not self-conscious, then those animals are not capable of using an image to become representationally aware of objects.

Explicit representing may require self-consciousness, but there is no reason for thinking the agent using an image to become representationally aware is acting intentionally. (Unless all self-conscious agents act intentionally.) An agent that can act intentionally can intentionally use pictures to represent objects. This only requires that he be aware of what he is doing and intend to be doing it. Intentional activity can be routine and automatic, it isn't always the product of deliberation and choice. But intentional activity is conceptual—the agent needs some conception of his actions to intend them. Not all purposive agents must act intentionally. And it isn't obvious that a self-conscious purposive agent needs to be an intentional agent. However, it is directly iconic representing that may not be intentional. Indirectly iconic representing requires knowledge extraneous to the representation, and it is hard to understand how such knowledge could be available to other than intentional agents.

Even though it need not be intentional, directly iconic representing seems to be purposive. It is characteristic of purposive activity that a complete description of the activity in terms of features pertaining to the causal order will fail to reveal its purposive character. But an iconic representation can be completely described without revealing it to be a representation. That a picture is a picture—that it is suited to be used to represent, is not a fact of the causal order. The purpose for using a picture to represent is presumably *to become representationally aware of the picture's objects*. A variety of further purposes might be served by the representing.

2. Portraying Objects

Representational awareness is not relational. It is always of arbitrary objects of this or that kind, for representational awareness is a state or condition of the representing subject (agent). But the painting which is used to provide representational awareness of an arbitrary short dark-haired man can also be used to identify Napoleon. The viewer who both uses the painting to become representationally aware and uses it to identify Napoleon is not simply performing two unrelated acts. Using the painting as a representation allows the viewer to direct her attention to the object in the world. But the viewer needs independent knowledge (about Napoleon or about the artist and his probable intention) to allow her to exploit a connection in directing (transforming) her representational awareness so that it constitutes attending to Napoleon.

The verb 'represent' is commonly used both for representational awareness of arbitrary objects ("This picture represents a man on a horse") and for identifying ("This picture represents George Washington crossing the Delaware"). This practice is convenient, for we often want to talk about both at once, but this practice is also confusing. I will sometimes talk this way when speaking/writing informally. But, strictly speaking, a picture is only used to represent arbitrary objects of a kind. For a technical term to replace the informal use of 'represent', I will make use of 'portray'. If someone uses a representing act to identify a particular object, she has *portrayed* that object. She can only portray a real object, but she can portray that object *as* doing or being things it doesn't or isn't. One can portray Napoleon riding either an arbitrary or a particular horse. We can use a picture to portray Cornwallis surrendering to George Washington at Yorktown. We have portrayed the historical event of Cornwallis' surrender. We can also portray Cornwallis surrendering at Miami Beach, in which case we have not portrayed a historical event.

When an image like a photograph is "of" a particular situation/event, the representational awareness of every object "in" the picture will be directed toward actual objects in the world, so that each object-part of the picture is used to identify an object in the actual situation. Doing this requires the viewer to have independent access, or connections, to those objects. He exploits these connections to direct his awareness to the objects he intends. Portraying the identified objects in a situation of a kind is not sufficient to identify the actual situation. He must also exploit a connection to that situation when he uses the image to identify the situation. (In the case of a photograph, this will normally be a causal connection.)

In the strict sense, we can only identify a real object—a real person or place or situation. However, in a slightly relaxed sense we *can* identify fictional characters and situations. Sherlock Holmes isn't (wasn't) real, but he has a sufficiently objective status that different people can talk and think about him. We can portray Sherlock Holmes as pursuing a criminal. When we wish to be really careful, we will distinguish fictional-identifying from plain identifying, and fictional-portraying from plain portraying. But we can normally just use 'identifying' and 'portraying' for both kinds of cases, since the context will make clear whether we have the fictional variety in mind.

When someone uses an image to become representationally aware of objects, this need not be intentional activity. But identifying and portraying are intentional. To identify a particular object, a person must intend that object. The subject's *intention for* her attending act is that she be attending to just that object. Here is where what is intentional in the *on purpose* sense "underwrites" the intentionality of thought directed to specific objects.

3. Symbolic Representing

With an image, someone can represent without identifying. And with language it is possible to identify without representing. But both images and words can be used to identify and represent at the same time. When language is used to represent, this is not iconic representing, for it isn't perceptible features of expressions that get interpreted. Intentional features associated with expressions at the identifying stage of language use are interpreted to symbolically represent arbitrary objects of various kinds.

But how does a language learner progress from the purely identifying stage of language use to the representational stage? This move is of great importance, but it needn't be marked by an event of epic proportions. The language learner who can use expressions to attend/identify and to acknowledge is in a position where she can reflect on her identifying use of expressions. If she can acknowledge Nancy to be sleeping:

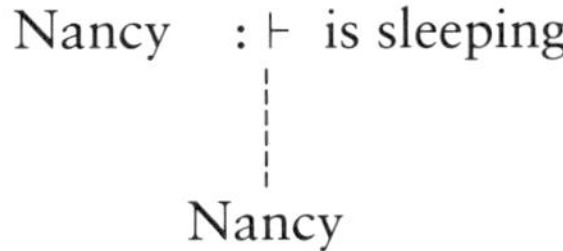

she has the materials she needs to think of what it is to be sleeping, without acknowledging anyone to be sleeping. To use the expression 'is sleeping' while thinking of what it is to be sleeping is to be representationally aware of an arbitrary person as sleeping. Each language learner must discover propositional representing for herself, but everyone seems to, though I think that some people take to propositional representing less readily than others.

The sentence 'Nancy is sleeping' can be used to acknowledge Nancy to be sleeping on some particular occasion. The same sentence can be used in a representational-stage fashion. An act of identifying Nancy can be combined with an act representing an arbitrary person (or animal) as currently sleeping. These two acts together portray Nancy as sleeping. When the two acts are performed, neither act enables the other. Nor is the representing act enabled by some other, preliminary, act. Each act is an independent act, but they have a common purpose, *to portray Nancy as sleeping.*

The act of portraying Nancy as sleeping is complex, and is constituted by the two component acts whose purpose "defines" it. But this is different from the earlier complex acts like Chuck's turning on the lights:

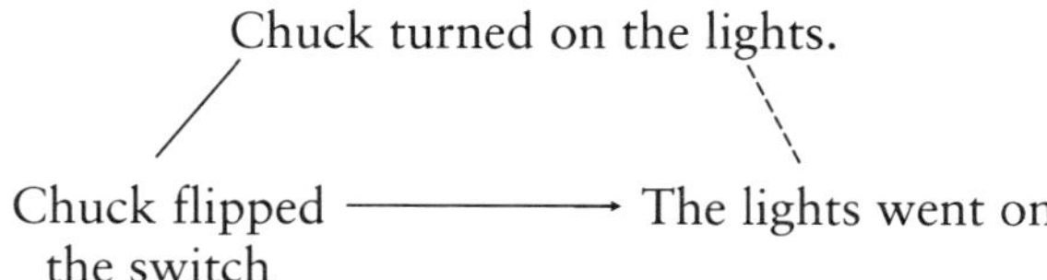

In the earlier example, the complex act was constituted by a completeable act and a completing event brought about by the completeable act. In the present case, the component acts initiate no causal sequences. Both the act of identifying Nancy and the act of representing an arbitrary object as sleeping are completeable, but they don't point toward a completing event. They point toward, and complete, one another. I will represent the acts like this:

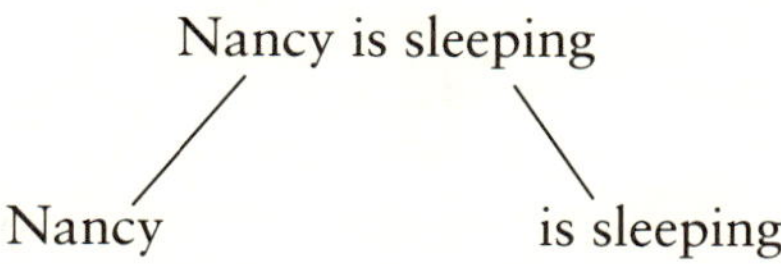

The component acts, with their common purpose, constitute the complex propositional representing act. Because predicate expressions are used to represent arbitrary objects being or doing this or that, I commonly use variables in the diagrams to call attention to the arbitrary objects involved:

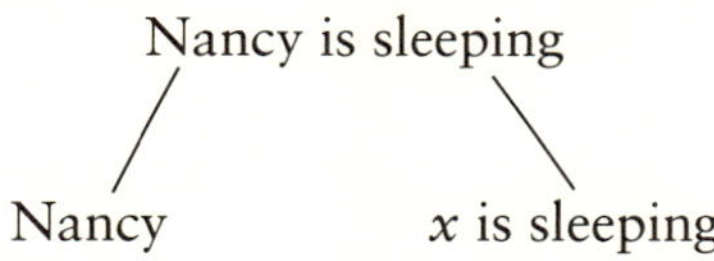

The variables are simply part of the apparatus of the diagrams, they aren't regarded as expressions in the language used to perform linguistic acts.

When an image is used to identify an object, representational awareness of an arbitrary object of a kind is directed toward an actual object of that kind. This requires the viewer to exploit his independent access to the object in "transforming" his awareness to constitute identifying. The representational awareness provided by symbolic representations is not sensible or sensual, and can't be transformed in the same way as the awareness of an image. A representing predicative act is "transformed" by combining it with independent identifying acts to portray particular objects as one thing or another. But the basic predicative act will not be transformed in this way to identify a particular situation. Instead a propositional representing act which portrays actual individuals will portray them in a kind of situation. Propositional representing includes both acts performed with predicates, and the complex acts which unite predicate acts and identifying acts. Although a completed propositional representing/portraying act (i.e., one performed with a complete sentence) will not be used to identify a situation, these acts can *correspond* to one or more situations. This corresponding is "external" to the representing, for it isn't what the language user *does* with expressions.

To understand judgments/assertions made with propositional representing acts, we should consider acknowledging acts once more. An acknowledging act has the force of an assertion, while a merely attending/identifying act does not. A simple acknowledging act is true if it identifies an actual situation. But while an acknowledging act is propositional, situations don't have a propositional character. The same situation can be identified by an acknowledging act and by a mere identifying act. In addition to acknowledging Nancy to be sleeping on a given occasion, the speaker might acknowledge her sleeping to be sound like this:

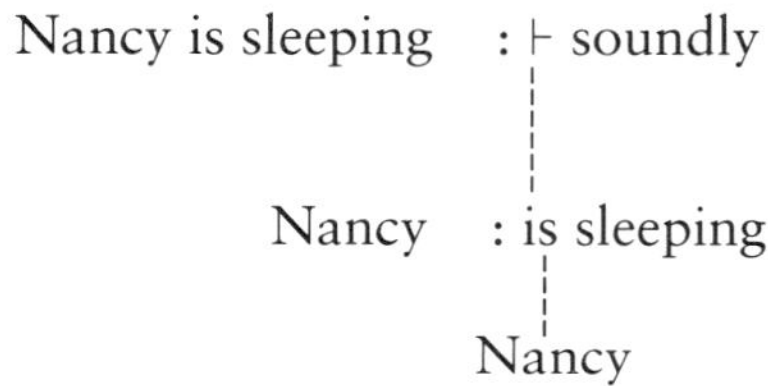

This statement might answer a question how Nancy, who is ill and is known to be asleep at the present time, is sleeping. The intermediate-level act uses 'is sleeping' to attend to the event of Nancy's current sleeping, but this is not an acknowledging act, and isn't true or false. The speaker assumes that Nancy is sleeping, and uses the act identifying her current sleeping situation to "set up" the acknowledging act.

It is only some form of acting (such as thinking) which has a propositional character. A true judgment does not reflect an independent propositional situation. What qualifies an acknowledging act for truth if it succeeds and falsity otherwise is its *point*: to hit the same target as the preliminary attending/identifying act. In performing an acknowledging act, the language user is making a point of correctly applying the acknowledging criteria to the object or objects.

The truth conditions for acknowledging acts are quite different from those for propositional representing acts. A true acknowledging act performed with a sentence like 'Nancy is sleeping' doesn't just correspond to a situation in the world, it identifies that situation. But a completed propositional representing act is true just in case it has a suitable correspondence to a situation or situations in the world. The statement:

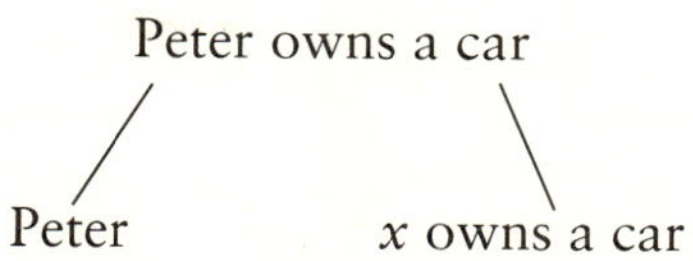

may correspond to different situations, since Peter may own several cars. Any one of those corresponding situations is sufficient for the statement to be true. Someone accepting a propositional representing act is committed to the act's having real counterparts. A person can perform a propositional representing/portraying act and accept it all at once:

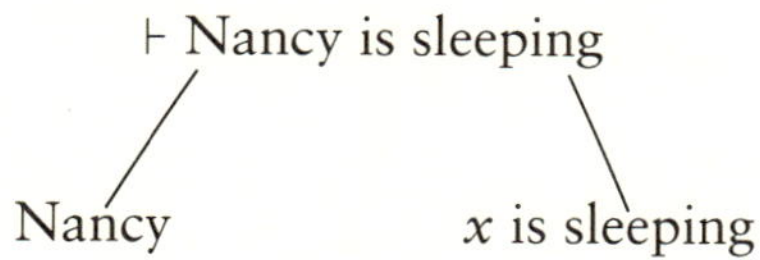

If it is true that Nancy is sleeping, then this act corresponds to a single situation in the world. We might also use the sentence 'Someone is sleeping' to represent an arbitrary person as now sleeping. Such an act will normally correspond to many situations.

Someone in a position to acknowledge Nancy to be sleeping, who has learned to use expressions to represent propositionally, can also portray Nancy as sleeping, and accept this. And the person entitled to accept an act portraying Nancy as sleeping should be in a position to acknowledge her to be sleeping. So how do the acts differ? The acknowledging act is in some respects more demanding than the propositional representing act. To acknowledge Nancy to be sleeping, the speaker must direct her attention to the particular event of Nancy's current sleeping. She must exploit connections she knows about which link her to this event. This requires her to think of how she knows Nancy to be sleeping, to consider the basis for her acknowledging act. If she currently sees Nancy to be asleep, or saw her sleeping a minute ago, her acknowledging doesn't demand much effort. But if she must remember what Nancy told her, or must think about what Nancy customarily does at this time, then her acknowledging may demand greater attention on her part. In contrast, to portray Nancy as currently sleeping, the speaker need only attend to Nancy and think about what it is to be asleep, to be sleeping at the present time. She can accept the act portraying Nancy as sleeping without much effort if she simply remembers having reason to accept it—without rehearsing the reasons. This suggests that in *coming to* a belief about Nancy's current condition, it will be common to acknowledge her to be asleep. But in reporting or recalling this belief, it will be more common to portray Nancy as sleeping, accepting the portrayal.

Propositional representing acts are normally accepted without using any words to mark this. But a speaker can also provide a "performative" prefix like 'I claim' or 'I assert'. A speaker might use 'I claim that Nancy is sleeping' like this:

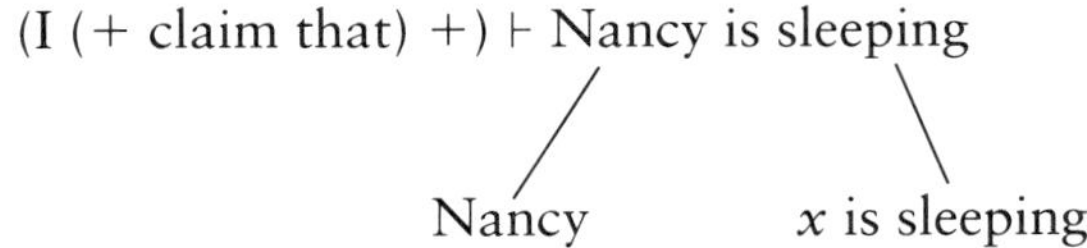

or like this:

(I (+ claim) +) ⊦ (that +) Nancy is sleeping

Nancy   *x* is sleeping

The speaker gives a special character to her act of attending to herself; The prefix act with its character makes explicit the force of the utterance. In the second diagram, the 'that' serves to make explicit the propositional character of the act portraying Nancy as asleep.

At the representational stage of language use, propositional negation is possible. Someone could deny that Nancy is asleep like this:

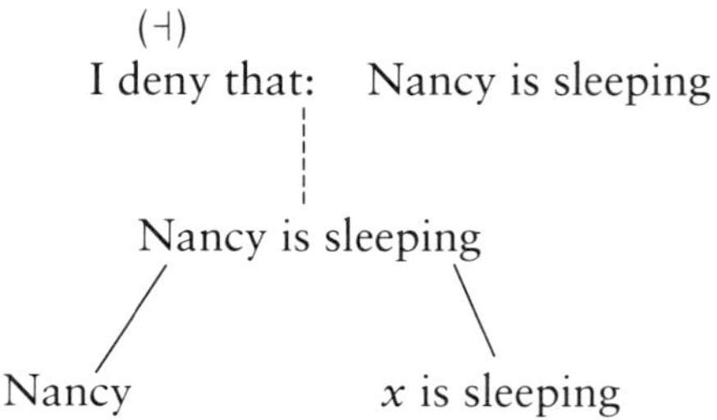

The propositional act which portrays Nancy as sleeping is not accepted. It is an enabling act which "sets up" the use of 'I deny that' to reject the portraying act. The sign of rejection/denial in parentheses above the prefix indicates that it is the prefix act which serves to reject the propositional act.

Another way to deny that Nancy is sleeping is like this:

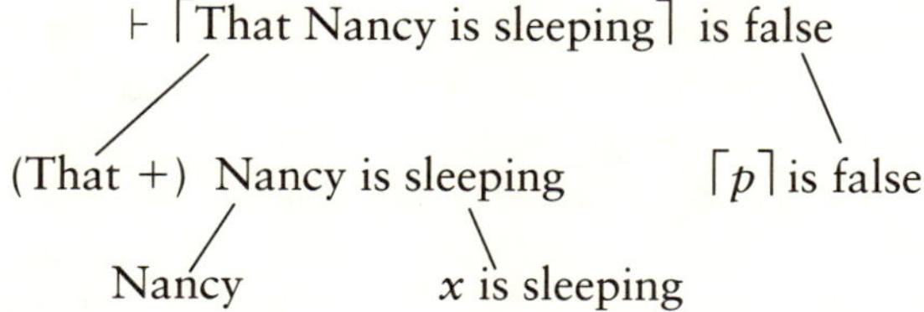

The predicate 'is false' is used to represent an arbitrary propositional act as false. The corners indicate that it is a propositional act rather than a nonlinguistic situation that is represented as false. The total propositional act does not combine an identifying act and a representing act. The act that is said to be false is actually present as a component of the total act. Although the component act is *presented* rather than identified, we will still describe the total act as *portraying* the component as false.

It sounds better in English to make the denial like this:

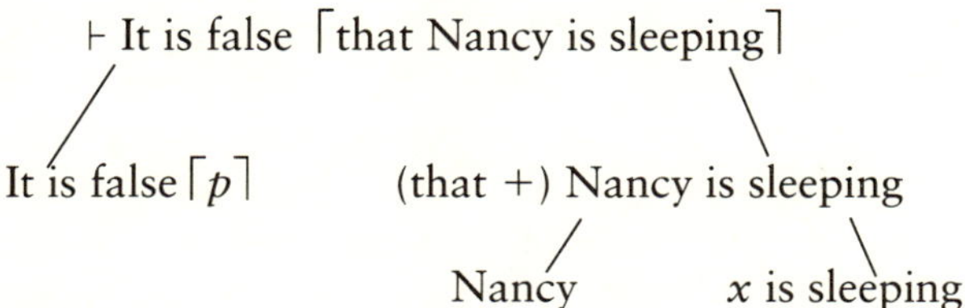

In this diagram, the prefix is used as a unit. A more thoughtful use has 'It' behaving like a variable marking the place of an arbitrary propositional act:

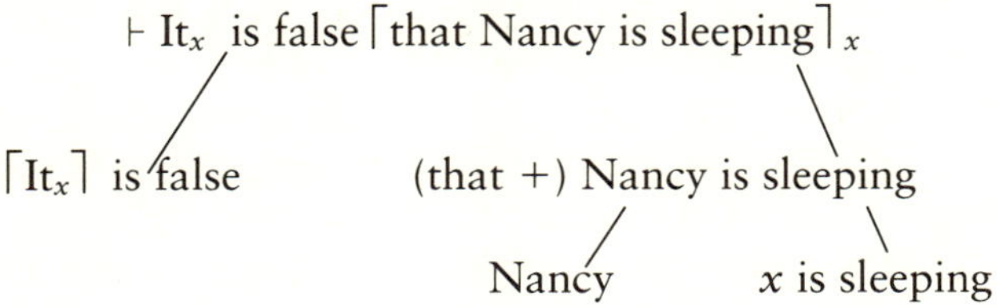

The propositional act "binds" the pronoun 'It'. The propositional act "counts" as filling the place of the pronoun 'It'. The subscripted 'x's indicate the link between the pronoun's place and the propositional act.

4. Commitment

The language learner who can use expressions to attend to/identify objects and to acknowledge objects to be this or that, but not to represent symbolically, is in the *purely identifying stage of language use*. It is necessary to be in this stage before a person learns to represent with expressions. First the child learns to use 'dog' to acknowledge objects to be dogs, and to attend to particular dogs and groups of them, as well as to the collection of all dogs. With respect to such acts, we can say that the word has (plays) an *identifying role* in the language (in our linguistic acts). The identifying role of a word may involve feature criteria like having a certain appearance or yielding a specified outcome in a given test. This role may involve inferential ties between acts of using this word and acts of using others. The identifying role is what gets interpreted when the expression acquires a representing use.

The language learner/user who performs propositional representing acts is in the *representational stage of language use*. The language user in this stage doesn't stop using expressions to perform attending and acknowledging acts, he simply performs representing acts in addition to identifying acts. I don't know how long someone must be in the purely identifying stage of language use before he catches on to using expressions to represent propositionally. It may be different for different people. It may also be that a language learner will quickly learn to use some expressions to represent propositionally, but will not routinely use all predicate expressions this way. He might find propositional representing difficult, and for the most part limit himself to attending and acknowledging acts.

The ability to make and to recognize valid inferences, and to carry out reasoning "in one's head" is more important with the use of language to represent than with the purely identifying use of language. In using a predicate to acknowledge an object to be ϕ, one need only apply ϕ's criteria to the object. Even though an object which satisfies ϕ's criteria also satisfies ψ's criteria, this may not be evident to someone at the identifying stage. However, to represent an arbitrary object as ϕ and an arbitrary object as ψ, one must reflect on what it is to be a

ϕ and to be a ψ. Such reflection will assist the language user to notice the entailment.

The entailment at issue here is *basic* entailment, which is based on *commitment*. Portraying an object α as scarlet, and accepting this, will commit a person to claiming that α is red. A statement "α is scarlet" basically entails the statement "α is red." If the concepts of scarlet and of red were learned independently at the identifying stage, and had exclusively appearance criteria, a competent language user might acknowledge an absent object to be scarlet without being committed to acknowledge that object to be red. The ability to correctly acknowledge objects to be scarlet and to be red does not require that one "see" the connection between these concepts. However, an identifying-stage language user could be *taught* to use a "scarlet"-acknowledging act as a sufficent condition for a "red"-acknowledging act; this instruction would generate a commitment from "scarlet" acts to "red" acts for that language user. At the representational stage, instruction is not required. For the language user with the concepts of scarlet and of red, the "scarlet" acts inevitably call for the "red" acts.

I have used the word 'commitment' in connection with linguistic acts and other intentional acts, but this is likely to be misunderstood. For 'commitment' is often used for various sorts of moral obligation, which I don't intend. It is common to hear of people making a commitment to one another in marriage or other "romantic" situations, where this commitment involves obligations and responsibilities. Someone who has promised to perform act *X* might be described as having a commitment which entitles the promisee to demand that she do *X*. But the commitment that concerns me does not involve owing anything to anyone. This commitment is too fundamental to be reduced to, or explained, in terms of other fundamental features. I can only attempt to draw attention to this feature, which is familiar to everybody, with my remarks. I can also characterize this feature, but not in the manner of a definition by genus and difference employing concepts at least as fundamental as the concept of commitment.

This commitment is not a form of obligation. But the commitment is to perform an action. People sometimes speak of being committed to the truth of some proposition, but this is not my sort of commitment. One can be committed to perform an acknowledging act, or to accept a propositional representing act, but one can't simply be committed to the truth of a claim. Commitment is constitutive of all intentional acts (I didn't understand this when I wrote *Using Language*). To intend to do something is to be committed to doing it. If I make a decision in advance of the action decided on, my decision will commit me ahead of time. But I am also committed while I am carrying out the act. Although commitment is a feature which "ties" an agent to an act, an agent who doesn't "honor" a commitment is not for that reason culpable, though he may be irrational.

A person is committed to doing the things she does intentionally. Performing one intentional act can also commit a person to performing others. If Jenny decides this afternoon to study tonight, her decision this afternoon commits her to the later activity of studying. A person who decides to do one thing can also be committed by that decision to doing others. If Jesse decides to dive off the high board, he is committed to diving. He is also committed to walking over to the ladder, to climbing it, and to walking out on the diving board. But decisions aren't the only acts that commit a person to performing other acts. Promises commit, and generate obligations as well. Acting with a certain purpose can generate commitments to perform further acts, even though no event can be identified as a decision to perform those acts. In playing tennis, I might serve to my opponent's backhand, in order to get her to either miss the ball or return the ball to a place where I can easily hit it out of her reach. My serving action commits me to moving toward the position to which I expect her backhand shot to go.

Some commitments are to performing an action come what may, while others are commitments to perform actions if/when certain kinds of occasions arise. I may decide on Tuesday to have dinner at a particular restaurant on Saturday, and make a reservation. I am simply committed to eating there at eight Saturday night. However, commitment isn't compulsion, and it won't *force* me eat at the restaurant on Saturday. I can change my mind before eight p.m. arrives on Saturday. I may forget about my decision, and my reservation. Although I may not honor it, the commitment to eat at the restaurant is a come-what-may commitment. I might also be committed to shut the upstairs windows if it rains. I won't have an occasion to honor this commitment until it rains when I am home.

Commitment is both characteristic and constitutive of intentional acting. Particular acts have particular commitments. Certain kinds of acts have characteristic commitments. If we portray someone's coat as scarlet, and accept this, we are committed to portraying-accepting it as red, and also to acknowledging it to be red. This is not a come-what-may commitment. We are committed to the red-acknowledging act only if the question of the coat's being red comes up, and we choose to speak/think about the matter at all. Even if we don't give the matter any attention, and so don't honor our commitment to acknowledge the coat to be red, we are come-what-may committed to not denying the coat to be red. For a commitment to consistency is fundamental to all judgmental acts. It makes no sense, and is strictly irrational, to both acknowledge an object to be ϕ and deny it to be ϕ (at the same time, in the same respect). The reason that one must learn both to acknowledge and deny—why a child can't be taught to perform only acts of acknowledging objects to be ϕ—is that acknowledging is constituted both by the commitment to be acknowledging and the commitment to not deny. One can't understand acknowledging unless he understands denying, and vice versa. A person can vaccillate between acknowledging and denying. A person can even be inconsistent, usually on different occasions, so that the inconsistency isn't apparent. But to be inconsistent is to be doing something wrong in the sense of "incorrect." In such a case, one's linguistic acts are defective.

Although I am speaking of commitment as a relation between intentional acts, and shall continue to speak this way, commitment is not a relation. For if *X* is related to *Y* by genuine relation *R*, then *X* and *Y* must actually exist. A child can't really own a make-believe horse. A person can't see an object that isn't there. But doing *X* can commit a person to doing *Y*, even though the person, who did *X*, never does *Y*. It is a feature of some acts to commit their agents to performing other acts—other kinds of acts, not other particular acts. Commitment is a feature of acts, not a relation between acts. But commitment-in-general is a determinable feature. Particular acts are characterized by commitments to perform determinate kinds of acts. Commitment is an example of what I have elsewhere (in *Using Language*) called an *intentional relation*. Intentional relations are not relations at all; they are relation-like properties by which an object is "pointed" toward a kind of object that may not actually be there.

All intentional acts, and so all linguistic acts, are characterized by commitments. Any act acknowledging α to be ϕ commits the language user to not rejecting ϕ for α. Some predicates are learned as alternatives to one another, so that, for example, acknowledging an object to be red commits a person to denying it to be green. Accepting certain statements can establish other inferential commitments; so can instruction, either in school or by means of the dictionary. At the purely identifying stage, statements generate commitments to (making) other statements. At the representational stage, statements generate still more commitments. When a person learns to use language to represent, when she becomes adept at using language this way, her inferential skills should very much increase. She can now "see" a variety of connections which were not evident before. She is committed by the connections, and they enable her to enlarge her knowledge simply by thinking.

Using language to represent gives rise to additional inferential skills. This use of language also makes possible new concepts and kinds of concepts. When language is used to represent, we can portray a situation (we can portray objects as situated a certain way) without taking a stand as to whether such a situation is actual. Hypothetical reasoning is possible at the representational stage of language use, but not before. Propositional negation becomes available. And so does propositional disjunction; someone can accept a claim that *A* or *B*, where *A* and *B* are propositional portraying acts, without knowing which is right. The use of quantified phrases to represent arbitrary objects of a kind also becomes possible when language is used to represent.

Acknowledging criteria associated with a predicate are intentional features that get interpreted once language is used representationally. But commitments associated with a predicate are also intentional features. At the representational stage, new commitments are "established," so that expressions acquire more intentional features. Such intentional features make it possible to introduce new kinds of conceptual framework.

At the purely identifying stage, characteristically logical concepts are essentially systematic. When someone denies α to be ϕ, she isn't identifying a negative situation. There are no negative situations. She rejects the use of ϕ for α, because the way α is *rules out* the (correct) use of ϕ for α. To be able to reject predicates for objects, a person must recognize certain concepts to be incompatible with others. Similarly, there are no universal situations—no situations of all ϕ's being ψ's. The concepts involved in categorical judgments owe their significance to systematic relations to other concepts. But at the identifying stage, concepts for objects are independently significant. This is no longer a requirement at the representational stage. Systems of expressions (concepts) can be introduced with inferential ties that play crucial roles in interpreting the expressions. Essentially systematic concepts (for objects) are possible once symbolic representing is customary.

5. Other Philosophers' Views of Language

Early philosophical discussions of thought and language seem to have been primarily concerned with propositional thinking of the 'to be' variety and with language used in a purely identifying way, though this isn't how the philosophers conceived of these matters. The idea that there are three basic mental operations, and that judgment is the fundamental kind of propositional thinking reveal a focus on the 'to be' form of thinking. And Aristotle's remarks about language, as well as his logic, are directed toward language used in a purely identifying way. Hobbes' views about insignificant speech and "empty" terms, found in *Leviathan*, are most appropriately (and kindly) interpreted with respect to language used to attend/identify and to acknowledge. He got things wrong, but his mistaken claims are linked to the correct understanding that one can't identify an object that isn't there. Acts like these:

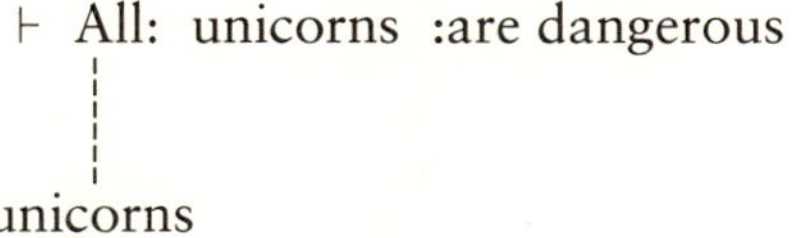

don't fail simply because the acknowledging act is incorrect. The initial act of attending to the collection of unicorns in the world fails to be an identifying act; it doesn't provide a target to be acknowledged to be wholly dangerous. The difference between this failure and the failure of the following acts:

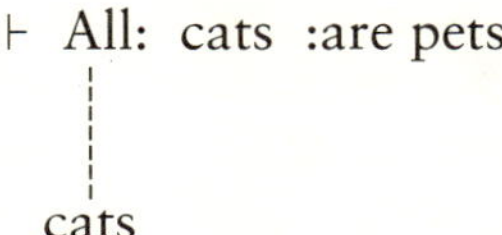

could easily seem to be a difference between nonsense and a significant but mistaken judgment.

Rationalist philosophers were impressed with the systematic character of concepts and conceptual frameworks (but without being explicitly aware of the frameworks), and with the inferential possibilities that these frameworks provide, though these philosophers tended to downplay the importance of language. The emphasis on clear and distinct ideas and clear and distinct propositions reveals a confused awareness of symbolic (propositional) representing. Frege was the first to successfully produce the logic (*a* logic) for the language used representationally, but he wasn't entirely clear about what he had accomplished. His inability to countenance hypothetical reasoning is a sign that he was still thinking of linguistic acts in an identifying-stage way.

Other philosophers than Rationalists have responded to the representational use of language. I remarked earlier that the Frege-Searle account of descriptions and names understands us to use these expressions to represent individuals rather than to "make contact" with them. The idea here is that we construct an elaborate picture of the world. The picture is separate from the world, and merely corresponds to it—or not, as the case may be. Any connections between the world and our picture of it are causal, and these connections are not part of the picture. This view is based on a misunderstanding of representing, and fails to distinguish representing from identifying. It also fails to understand in what correspondence consists.

We can regard the linguistic representing acts that we accept as constituting an elaborate picture of the world. But it is a picture we use to portray the world, and our portraying depends on acts which exploit connections in the world to identify objects in the world. When we portray α as situated by ψ with respect to β, and α *is* situated like that with respect to β, then our propositional representing act is true. The propositional act is not true because it already corresponds to the situation. For correspondence, like similarity or *taller than*, is not a relation that independently situates objects in the world. We can *establish* a correspondence by linking the propositional act to a situation which we identify. The propositional representing act is true because it is possible (in principle) to establish a correspondence linking the act to the situation. Even the truth of the propositional representing act depends on our being able to identify situations, not simply on there being situations.

The view of representing that I have associated with the Frege-Searle account of descriptions is similar to the view implicit in the writings of Jerry Fodor. The controversy about whether, or to what extent, a person's beliefs are all in her head is a conflict between an attempt to construe beliefs as pictures cut off from the world and claims that connections to the world characterize the contents of beliefs. That the connections are essential is an essential feature of the present account of representing and identifying. But these connections are often misunderstood, and explained in terms of causality rather than intentionality.

6. Beliefs

The ordinary conception of sense experience and its objects is in corporated in the language we speak. The purely identifying stage of language use is inconceivable, impossible, without the ordinary conception on which it depends. We are in engaged in developing and amending this ordinary conception, but we are not prepared to recognize a chasm, or gulf, between experience and its objects, or between our beliefs and their objects.

From the present perspective, there are different classes of beliefs to consider in relation to the world. Our conceptual frameworks incorporate constitutive principles which are numbered among our beliefs, whether or not we have thought about them or articulated them. We use conceptual systems to give structure to the world of experience. The fundamental principles of the frameworks, which we believe, determine how the world is. Although the idea that our concepts impose structure on our world is not a feature of the prephilosophical ordinary conception, we have incorporated the feature in our modified conception because we can't otherwise make sense of the way knowledge and belief are based on experience.

Our conceptual frameworks give structure to the world of experience, but they may do this in an unsatisfactory, unsuccessful fashion. The world of experience, as we have organized it, may be incoherent. Our conceptual frameworks, our fundamental theories, may need to be modified, or replaced by entirely new conceptions. The beliefs which are constitutive of our current frameworks are not independent of the way the world is, but they may turn out to be independent of the way the world comes to be at a later date. However, this independence is unrelated to the independence imagined by the "all in our heads" theorists.

Given our conceptual frameworks, we have beliefs about particular objects/parts of the world, and about groups, collections, and kinds in the world structured by our concepts. These are beliefs "within" a conceptual framework rather than beliefs constitutive of the framework. These beliefs don't determine how the world is, for we can have and do have false beliefs of this kind. But we must determine the status of such beliefs. A person may actually perform and accept a propositional act, either an acknowledging act or a propositional representing act. If she hasn't changed her mind and hasn't forgotten her act, we will count the act she performed/accepted as one of her beliefs. If she acknowledged Nancy to be sleeping at 7 a.m. this morning, she believes Nancy to have been sleeping then. If she portrayed Nancy as sleeping at 7 a.m. this morning, and accepted this, she believes that Nancy was sleeping then. But a person can also be readily disposed to perform and accept a propositional act if the occasion arises, and be committed to doing so by her (other) beliefs and actions. Even though she hasn't actually performed it, we count the propositional act she is disposed to perform (and accept) among her beliefs. (Even the acts she has performed and neither forgotten nor recanted are dispositional, for she will be disposed to perform/accept them another time, if an appropriate occasion arises.)

For those of her beliefs which are dispositional, a person presumably has materials stored "someplace" which she makes use of in performing/accepting the propositional acts that constitute her beliefs. As a heuristic model, we might think of this "internal encyclopedia" as a group of sentences. These aren't the sentences she would use to perform the acts she is merely disposed to perform/accept. The sentences would instead be records of propositional acts she has actually performed and accepted, and records of other acts of hers that commit her to performing/accepting propositional acts. These sentences would provide a basis for deriving the new propositional acts. But the sentences need to be accompanied with cues which indicate the structures of the acts to be performed with the sentences. The sentences we read in books don't have enough internal cues to determine the entire structures of the linguistic acts we perform in reading. Punctuation and syntactic features provide some cues. But the text itself has a context, and the organization of sentences within a text provides further context for determining what speech-act structures are appropriate in reading the sentences. If the material in the internal encyclopedia was just a group of sentences not incorporated in texts, then the sentences would need additional cues, perhaps on the order of the diagrams we have been using.

However, the internal encyclopedia consisting of sentences or sentential diagrams makes a poor model of a person's beliefs. We normally provide the detailed structures of our linguistic acts on the basis of features of the circumstances in which the acts are performed, as well as on the basis of features of the expressions used. The detailed structures of past propositional acts (and of propositional acts describing other kinds of past acts) aren't worth preserving; this would be inefficient. It is better to think of the stored materials as internal representations of truth conditions. They would be something like internal Venn diagrams or internal graphs/diagrams/networks of the sort developed by researchers in artificial intelligence. These internal diagrams might be used to represent in a way that seems more iconic than symbolic, and would be such that propositional information can be extracted from the diagrams in forms other than those in which it was entered. (As in the case of Venn diagrams. Once the premisses of an AAA syllogism in the first figure are "entered" in the diagram, the conclusion can be "read out" of the diagram.) An even more elaborate model might be imagined in which the believing subject doesn't always possess internal representations. Instead she possesses a device which produces internal representations when she needs them. However, we don't presently need to consider such a model.

Although stored materials are probably essential to a person's having the beliefs she does, these materials do not by themselves constitute her beliefs. For it is these materials *plus* the ability and the dispositions to use them to perform/accept propositional acts that constitute her beliefs. The materials are stored but the ability to use them is not. It doesn't even make sense to suppose that this ability could be stored "someplace." The ability that counts here is not the ability to use the stored materials to formulate sentences. The important ability for using stored materials to express belief is the ability to perform propositional acts. The stored materials are simply instruments which the knowledgeable agent employs to come up with the right expressions and use them to perform propositional acts. Computers are also instruments that can be used to obtain expressions that may be used to perform propositional acts. Computers enhance the abilities of knowledgeable agents, but don't possess those abilities.

The internal materials used in formulating one's beliefs don't constitute those beliefs, but both the internal materials and the ability to use them might be construed as being "in a person's head." This doesn't indicate that beliefs not constitutive of conceptual frameworks are "cut off" from the external world. For part of the language user's ability is to use stored materials to identify objects in the world. The stored materials are not themselves connected to the objects, but the language user knows how to "make contact" by exploiting connections which exist apart from what is in the head. It is possible for someone to attempt to identify an object and fail, either because the connection he exploits doesn't link him to the object he expects, or because he thinks there is a connection when there is none. The failure of such identifying attempts undermines any acknowledging acts based on these attempts. If all a person's identifying and acknowledging acts were in his head, then all his identifying beliefs would be mistaken. It is no different when symbolic representing acts are combined with identifying acts to yield complex acts portraying particular objects as one thing or another. These propositional representing acts are clearly connected to objects in the world. Any such acts that were accepted but were all in the person's head would be mistaken.

Chapter 10

Representing:
Logical Differences between The Two Stages

1. Entailment and Reasoning

In this chapter, and in chapter 11, I will explore the difference between the purely identifying use of language and the representational use. Even though, in fact, children may be relatively quick to use expressions to represent propositionally, we will consider the position of someone able to use expressions only for attending/identifying and acknowledging, not for representing. And we will determine how much sense such a person can make of his world. Then we will consider what becomes possible once he enters the representational stage.

This exploration of the two stages, and of the two uses of language, is important for understanding propositional thinking and its connection to experience. The purely identifying stage of language use "incorporates" and requires the ordinary conception of experience and its objects. But at that stage Descartes' Problem cannot even arise. The understanding of concepts and conceptual frameworks that is only available at the representational stage is needed even to formulate the problem, and to appreciate its importance. An adequate solution to the problem requires that we use language representationally.

This understanding of the differences between the two stages of language use is a consequence of the new conceptions of intentional acts and their structures, of representing, and of identifying, that we have introduced and developed. The conception of intentional acts was initiated in my *Using Language* (1984), and was not there associated with Descartes' Problem. But the present account of representing and identifying, and its links to the earlier treatment of intentional acts and structures, were undertaken in response to the Problem. However, our understanding of propositional thinking and the two kinds of linguistic activity shed light on a number of philosophical issues and problems not immediately linked to Descartes' Problem. This provides reason for an increase of confidence in the present account.

In this chapter, I will consider the logical systems that fit the two stages of language use. As a first approximation, syllogistic logic is a logic of identifying-stage statements, while propositional and quantificational logic are suited to the representational stage. Commitment "relations" are different at the two stages. The fundamental entailment relation, unqualified, or *basic* entailment as opposed to "qualified" relations like *truth-conditional* entailment, is derived from commitment. A specific sort of acknowledging act entails those (kinds of) acknowledging acts to which the language user is committed by the first act. A propositional representing act entails those propositional acts which one is committed to accept by accepting the first act. Basic entailment is different from truth-conditional entailment. For example, the speaker who acknowledges α to be φ is committed to acknowledging herself to believe α to be φ, but α's actually being φ doesn't satisfy the truth conditions of a statement that the speaker believes this. (Austin [1975] used 'implication' for the relation between *P* and 'I believe *P*', and used 'entailment' for what may be truth-conditional entailment. But he seems to have thought that *P* can't both entail and imply *Q*; which is a mistake.)

P may basically entail *Q* even though satisfying the truth conditions for *P* doesn't automatically satisfy the conditions for *Q*. At the purely identifying stage, the reverse can also happen. That α is φ can necessitate α's being ψ without there being an entailment from the 'α is φ' statement to the 'α is ψ' statement. Let me discuss this with respect to a contrived and artificial example which has the virtue of being simple. Consider the three expressions 'triangle', 'three-sided', and 'plane figure'. These are understood to be used for figures which are physical objects, figures constituted by masses of chalk on blackboards and masses of ink on pages of books. We can imagine that someone has learned to use 'triangle' strictly on the basis of the appearance of objects correctly acknowledged to be triangles. His acknowledging test for 'triangle' is to look at an object, trying to detect the triangle "look." We will also imagine his acknowledging criteria for 'plane figure' to be exclusively appearance criteria. For 'three-sided' his test involves both appearance (for the sides) and counting.

Whenever our language learner is in a position to acknowledge a perceived object to be a triangle, he can also acknowledge the object to be three-sided and to be a plane figure, and conversely. But he has not been taught to use his acknowledging an object to be three-sided and his acknowledging it to be a plane figure as jointly providing a basis for acknowledging the object to be a triangle. He has no verbal criteria for acknowledging objects to be triangles, only appearance criteria. The language learner may never have remarked the coincidence of the triangles and three-sided plane figures in his experience. He may not know or believe that all triangles are three-sided plane figures. He doesn't need to know this to use the expressions correctly in talking about objects in the world of his experience. Indeed, if he has relied exclusively on appearance criteria for using 'triangle' and 'plane figure' (which is extremely unlikely), it isn't clear how he *could* learn that all triangles are three-sided plane figures. For the learner isn't yet in a position to reflect on what it takes to be a triangle. Such reflection leads to the representational stage of language use. At the stage we are speaking of, for our imaginary language learner, there is no basic entailment from acknowledging an object to being three-sided and acknowledging it to be a plane figure to acknowledging it to be a triangle. The language learner can separately acknowledge an object's being all three things. But he isn't equipped to reason from the two acknowledging acts to the third.

The speaker whose only criteria for 'triangle' and 'plane figure' are appearance criteria, and who acknowledges some object to be a triangle, is not committed to acknowledging the object to be a plane figure. But this can change. The language learner can be taught additional criteria for 'triangle', either in school or by a dictionary or other source. Once he learns that being a plane figure and having three sides are jointly sufficient (as well as separately necessary) for being a triangle, then he has acquired additional commitments. It will now be the case that acknowledging an object to be a triangle commits him to acknowledging it to be a plane figure. He still won't reflect on what it is to be a triangle, and "unpack" his reflection. Being able to do this is the skill that so excited the Rationalist philosophers, and probably Plato as well; it lifts the language learner/thinker to a new "plane." Our language learner has simply been taught to connect these specific kinds of acknowledging acts. He need only remember the new acknowledging criteria for 'triangle', not think of the property *being a triangle*.

What is unrealistic about the imagined language learner is the words I have chosen. A child *might* be taught to use 'triangle' for perceived figures. He wouldn't learn 'plane figure' this way. And from the very start, it would be normal for the language teacher to call attention to triangles having (needing) three sides. While the examples aren't realistic, the learner's initial vocabulary will surely start by having exclusively appearance criteria. He will later be taught additional criteria for certain expressions. Most of us never get beyond appearances for colors and color terms. But lots of words are initially learned on the basis of verbal explanations. New words can be introduced to the language on the basis of such explanations. However, when a word which began its "life" with one set of criteria is later provided with new criteria, this might be due to rational inferences carried out by language users in the representational stage of language use. They could teach new criteria to those language users still chained in the "cave" of the identifying stage, without requiring the cave dwellers to ascend to the representational stage.

A *rational inference* is one based on commitment relations which the inferrer recognizes. At the purely identifying stage, the rational inferences "available" to one person may not be available to a different person. For many inferences will be based on commitments that have been taught to the language user. Different people who have roughly the same vocabularies might simply have been taught different commitments. One of them may associate three sets of criteria with expression ϵ, while the other has been taught fewer, or different, sets. People also differ in their ability to remember what they have been taught. The identifying-stage language learner who understands 'scarlet' and 'red' may not know that whatever is scarlet must be red.

Upon learning that Mary has purchased a scarlet jacket, he may be unable to acknowledge her jacket to be red until he actually sees it. Though if he is able to produce an internal (or external) scarlet image, that might enable him to infer the jacket's being red in advance of seeing it.

At the purely identifying stage, whatever satisfies the criteria for ϕ may necessarily satisfy the criteria for ψ, without ϕ-acknowledging acts being linked by basic entailment to ψ-acknowledging acts. But at this stage, there are certain kinds of acknowledging acts that basically entail further acts, without requiring additional information. To understand these, we need to remember the inescapable commitment to consistency. Acknowledging an object to be ϕ commits the language user to not denying that object to be ϕ, and if someone acknowledges an object not to be ϕ, she is committed to not acknowledging it to be ϕ. These commitments don't quite satisfy our definition of 'basic entailment', but they are entailment-like. And an act acknowledging some object to be ϕ does (basically) entail an act denying that object to be not ϕ.

There are no negative situations, only negative linguistic acts. Our conceptual frameworks are essentially systematic with respect to affirmation and denial. Some negative acknowledging acts (attempt to) identify actual situations, but indefinitely:

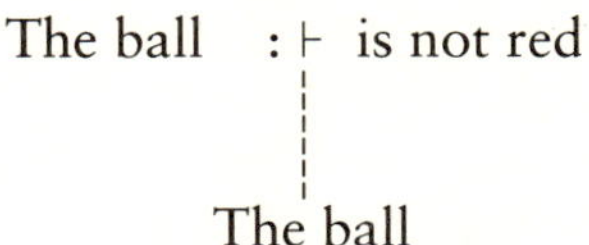

Some negative acts don't even make an identifying effort:

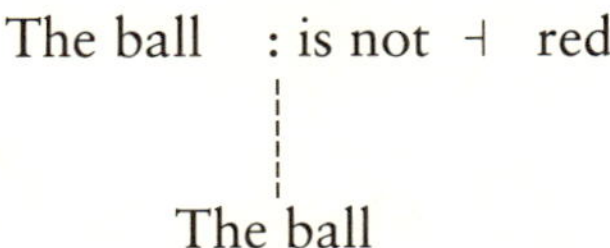

The second statement merely rejects the acknowledging use of 'red' for the ball. (The first statement also rejects the acknowledging use of 'red', but, in addition, the language user is attending to the situation of the ball's being the color it is.)

If there are no negative situations, what can make a denial successful, or correct? We have spoken of criteria associated with an expression as if objects either do or don't satisfy the criteria, and we passively observe which is the case. But this conflicts with the idea that we actively use language to give structure to the world of experience. We should conceive acknowledging criteria associated with expression ϕ as a procedure which we try to carry out on an object, or with respect to an object. If we succeed in carrying out the procedure, then ϕ is correctly applied to the object. But if we are unable to carry out the procedure, if we are blocked in carrying out the procedure, we can correctly reject the acknowledging use of ϕ for that object. It isn't that we deny the object to be ϕ because it isn't ϕ; that would be to explain our failure by appealing to a negative situation in the world. Instead the object isn't ϕ because we can't correctly acknowledge it to be ϕ. The object is, on its own, something other than ϕ. This other is what blocks our applying the criteria.

An object isn't simply not red. It is a different color than red. In denying the object to be red, we aren't recording a negative feature of the world. We are recording a failed attempt to apply the criterial test for red—we simply can't see the object as red. Failure isn't just the absence of success. It is a distinctive (kind of) experience, of which we are aware. But we need to distinguish two sorts of failure here. A person can try to do something without success, even though that something is not impossible to do. She can also try to do something which is strictly out of the question, something which it isn't possible to do. Let us call these *mere* failures and *decisive* failures. The failure which licenses a denying act must be a decisive failure, not a mere failure, and the language user must be aware of this decisive character.

To correctly acknowledge an object to be ϕ, a person must identify the situation of the object being ϕ. (If the acknowledging act is situational, and if the object being ϕ is a simple situation. Otherwise, things are more complicated, but that does not affect the contrast being drawn.) Identifying may not be justified, for the language user may be taking an unreliable person's word for the object being ϕ, but there is no correct acknowledging without identifying. In contrast, a speaker might correctly but capriciously deny an object to be ψ—he might do this without properly applying ψ's criteria. We need some expression to characterize the difference between the responsible and irresponsible cases of denying an object to be ψ. In the "responsible" cases, the language user experiences a decisive failure in applying ψ's criteria, or he takes someone's word for it, where the someone has experienced decisive failure.

The truth conditions of an identifying-stage denial are modal. For an object to be not-ϕ it must be impossible to correctly carry out the ϕ-procedure with respect to the object. For the ball to be not red it must be impossible to correctly see the ball as that color—it must be impossible to correctly acknowledge the ball to be red. The world of experience which we organize with our concepts has a modal character which we discover but don't supply. Possibility and impossibility are fundamental modal features. There are some things we can do, and others we can't. This is *de re* rather than *de dicto* modality. Being correctly acknowledged to be red is impossible for the ball (correctly acknowledging the ball to be red is impossible for us). In responsibly denying β to be ϕ, there is no need for the language user to perform an identifying act. However, she must exploit connections to a decisive failure to apply the ϕ criteria to β. If she does this, she has *registered* the modal feature of its being impossible to correctly acknowledge β to be ϕ.

The truth conditions of a denial are modal, but the denial is not itself a modal statement. The denial is true just in case carrying out a certain procedure is impossible, but the denial does not report or describe this impossibility. The denial itself has the character of a rejection or a refusal. Which is why it makes no sense to both acknowledge and deny a single object to be ϕ—one can't both do and refuse to do something at the same time.

We know there is a difference between something's being the case and its being believed to be the case. When a language user makes a statement or is committed to making it and is aware of the commitment, that statement is *in force* for the language user. If the statement acknowledging an object to be ϕ is in force for a particular language user, that statement will have inferential consequences, but these consequences are incidental to the acknowledging act. In making denials, and in making other kinds of statements of interest to logicians, the language user is more concerned with linguistic acts and their features than with situations and theirs. Such a statement's coming to be in force creates a network of commitment relations that didn't exist previously. The "point" of making such a statement might be to establish this network rather than to report modal features of the world.

2. Universal Inference Principles

In acknowledging an object to be ϕ, a person establishes a commitment to not deny the object to be ϕ. Denying an object to be ϕ commits someone to not acknowledging the object to be ϕ. These commitments are constitutive of the inferential meanings of acknowledging and denying acts, but they are negative. When someone acknowledges *A*'s to all be *B*, this establishes positive commitments. The consistency requirements for universal acknowledging acts are more complicated than for acts acknowledging particular objects to be something. It isn't consistent to acknowledge *A*'s to all be *B*, and to deny a particular *A* to be *B*. It isn't even consistent to decline to acknowledge a particular *A* to be *B*. Of course, α could be an *A* without our knowing this, but we can't consistently acknowledge α to be *A*, acknowledge *A*'s to all be *B*, and deny or decline to acknowledge α to be *B*. Having acknowledged all *A*'s to be *B*, acknowledging α to be *A* commits me to acknowledging α to be *B;* I can rationally infer α to be *B*.

It is important to distinguish statements acknowledging a collection to be this or that from statements concerning a group. A collection is constituted by someone's attending to it; an expression is used as a reference point to attend to those objects that can correctly be acknowledged with the expression—with the expression as conventionally used. A group is constituted by objects organized into a structured whole; it has an independent standing, and can simply be identified (by exploiting connections linking the language user to the structured whole). We will begin by considering universal statements about collections.

In this statement:

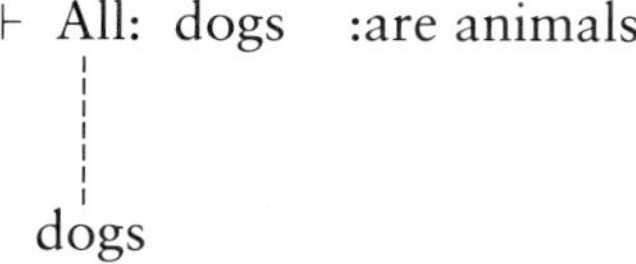

the speaker uses 'dogs' to attend to, to identify, the collection of dogs. The speaker doesn't exploit particular connections leading to particular dogs. Collections don't have the right standing to be connected to speakers and ordinary objects.

To identify the collection of dogs, the speaker uses the 'dog' acknowledging practice of her linguistic community as a reference point. She attends to the collection of those animals that have been and could be (could have been) correctly acknowledged to be dogs. The collection is abstract because it is identified (primarily) with respect to a linguistic practice. The attending/identifying act also has a modal character, for the speaker identifies the collection of animals that *could* correctly be acknowledged to be dogs. The collection of dogs hasn't got a nonlinguistic or nonconceptual status. This collection waxes and wanes through time, containing now these dogs, now those. No collection currently contains all dogs from all times, though the single collection of dogs, at one time or another, contains every dog. When the language user attends to the collection of dogs, she attends to the dog part of the world.

We have represented the speech-act structures of universal statements, but we don't fully understand these statements. For there are no independently existing collections to be identified, or independent universal situations. These statements are like negative statements in having modal truth conditions which are not the "subject" of the universal statement. To correctly acknowledge all dogs to be ϕ, it must be impossible to both correctly acknowledge an animal to be a dog and correctly deny it to be ϕ—it must be impossible to correctly deny a dog to be ϕ.

Both denials and universal judgments about collections of objects have modal truth conditions. These are not "possible worlds" modalities. To deny α to be ϕ is not to rule out α's being ϕ in some "other world." The present conceptual "family" involves what I have called *relative metaphysical* possibility and necessity (and impossibility). Something is relatively metaphysically possible if it is not "ruled out" by present and past states of the world—it is possible *relative* to present and past states of the world. One unusual thing about the possibility and impossibility associated with negation and universality is that what is or isn't ruled out is the *correct* performance of certain kinds of act, not simply the performance of the acts.

Someone correctly acknowledging *A*'s to all be ϕ has not made a modal statement, nor has she encountered or recognized a universal situation. Acknowledging all *A*'s to be ϕ either *establishes* a commitment relation or reflects a previously established commitment relation. The relation is from performing an *A*-acknowledging act to performing a ϕ-acknowledging act. A universal judgment introduces additional commitments, providing additional conceptual structure to the world of a person's experience. The acknowledging act is an organizational move.

An act acknowledging *A*'s to all be ϕ is true if it isn't possible to correctly acknowledge an object to be *A* while denying it to be ϕ. For the language user's acknowledging act to *register* this impossibility, she must encounter it for herself or rely on the testimony of someone who has. If correctly acknowledging an object to be *A* is one of the language user's criteria for (correctly) acknowledging the object to be ϕ, and the language user realizes this, she has registered the impossibility. It might also be that someone in the representational stage recognizes that *A*'s criteria include those for ϕ. That person's recognition will allow him to instruct identifying-stage language learners that all *A*'s are ϕ. The identifying-stage language learner will register the impossibility of correctly acknowledging an object to be *A* while denying it to be ϕ via her links to her instructor—without "seeing" the impossibility for herself.

However, not all correct universal statements are conceptually necessary. It can be legitimate for someone to make a universal judgment which doesn't register a modal feature. If, given the objects in the world, it isn't possible to correctly acknowledge an object to be *A* while denying it to be ϕ, but no universal judgment has been made, the universal statement isn't "already" true. The statement can't be true until it is made. Nor should we say that the truth conditions are satisfied before the statement is made. If it isn't possible to correctly acknowledge an object to be *A* and deny it to be ϕ, the world is "receptive" to a correct universal acknowledging act. But commitment isn't created by the modal features that support a universal judgment. Commitment must be established by intentional acts. Someone who makes a universal judgment as a conjecture, perhaps as the conclusion of an inductive generalization, establishes the commitment relations. The commitment relations are objectively incorrect if it is possible to correctly acknowledge an object to be *A* while correctly denying it to be ϕ. Otherwise the judger introduces additional conceptual structure to the world of her experience. Once the judgment becomes entrenched, it organizes the world of the judger's experience, and provides her access to the impossibility which her judgment can now register.

Even when an object can be correctly acknowledged to be *A* but not φ, the language user acknowledging *A*'s to all be φ introduces additional conceptual structure to the world of his experience. But his universal judgment makes his world incoherent, in need of repairs. The easiest repair may be to drop the universal judgment. An alternative possibility is to reconceive *A*'s or φ's, so that the universal judgment remains while the counter-example disappears.

Since there is no propositional negation at the purely identifying stage, there are no statements to the effect that it is false that all *A*'s are φ. But one person can object to, and reject, another person's universal statement. There are three general sorts of objection. The speaker might attempt to acknowledge *A*'s to all be φ when there are no *A*'s. To criticize the statement for this shortcoming, the identifying-stage speaker might perform these acts:

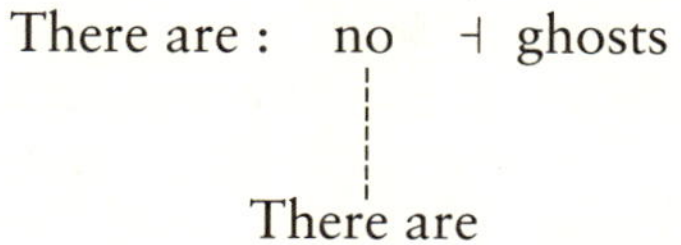

The speaker rejects the acknowledging use of 'ghosts' for objects in the world.

The second type of objection has the critic granting that there are *A*'s, but claiming that not all of them are φ. She could make this objection with the following statement:

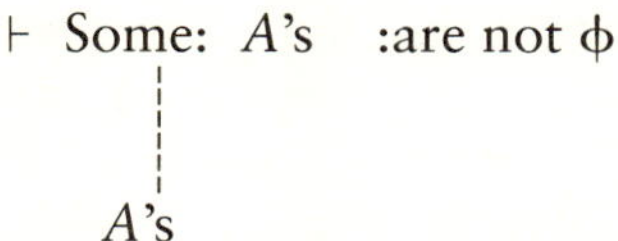

The third type of objection doesn't concern existence or truth conditions. The speaker can also be criticized for lacking justification to establish a commitment from *A*-acknowledging acts to φ-acknowledging acts. To back up this sort of criticism, it is sufficient to show that for all anyone knows, some *A*'s might not be φ. This third critic is supporting the option of declining to acknowledge the *A*'s to all be φ.

Imposing conceptual structure on the world of experience produces situations of objects being this or that. These situations exist whether we are aware of them or not. And they are all positive; there are no situations of objects not being one thing or another. The situations which have existed and which currently exist determine some things to be the case (to have been the case, to be going to be the case), leave some things open, and rule other things out. Its being possible for α to be ϕ is not a situation. What is required, what is open, and what is ruled out constitute the modal character of the world. Once we introduce conceptual structure, we find the world to have a modal character. We introduce additional modal characteristics by introducing additional conceptual structure.

An inference principle links linguistic acts of certain kinds to a further kind of linguistic act. The inference-principle statement to the effect that all dogs are animals links 'dog'-acknowledging statements to 'animal'-acknowledging ones. When language is used representationally, it is easy to state inference principles by representing arbitrary statements of certain kinds being linked to an arbitrary statement of a further kind. But at the purely identifying stage, a person cannot represent an arbitrary object as a dog or perform an arbitrary dog-representing propositional act. Universal statements make use of the resources of the identifying stage to present inference principles nonrepresentationally.

In providing conceptual structure to the world, we distinguish "essential" from "accidental" concepts. An object is essentially a dog or a human being, and accidentally a pet or a philosopher. This distinction affects our understanding (and performance) of universal judgments. If ϕ is an essential concept, and α is a ϕ at one time, then α will be ϕ throughout its existence—at least, α will be ϕ throughout if α is the right kind of object. For Jane's pet might be an animal throughout its existence, though it is a dog at one time, and a rabbit at another. Our ordinary conceptual framework also provides for *fundamental real objects*. A particular dog or a particular rabbit is a fundamental real object, but the Jane's-pet part of the world is not. Jane's pet is different animals at different times: now a dog, now another dog, now a rabbit. The distinction between accidental and essential concepts, and the understanding of which are the fundamental real objects, may in some way reflect features of experience, but they are primarily apprehended through features of language. We simply learn to distinguish a part of the world which is the same cat at different times from a part which coincides now with one cat, now with another.

Besides universal judgments about collections identified with respect to an acknowledging expression/practice, there are universal judgments about groups identified via connections to the speaker. I can identify the coins in my pocket by exploiting connections linking me to those coins; I can similarly identify the planets in the Solar System. And I can directly acknowledge such a group to be one thing or another—as opposed to accomplishing the acknowledging by establishing a commitment. In acknowledging the coins in my pocket to all be quarters, I am simultaneously applying the one expression to each coin. This universal acknowledging act has the force of a conjunction. It also commits me to acknowledging a particular coin (in my pocket) to be a quarter, because the second acknowledging act will merely repeat a "component" of the first. In *The Logic of Scientific Discovery*, Popper appears to have confused the distinction between a total-collection acknowledging act and a total-group acknowledging act with the distinction between law-like and accidental generalizations. The two distinctions are distinct.

Universal acknowledging acts about a collection are based on commitments which they either reflect or establish. But how are we to understand acknowledging acts performed with sentences such as the following?

> Almost all *A*'s are ϕ
> Most *A*'s are ϕ
> Many *A*'s are ϕ
> Some *A*'s are ϕ

If there were degrees of acknowledging or degrees of commitment, we might try to describe this acknowledging act:

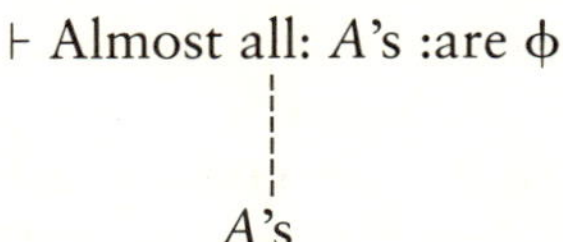

as either establishing/reflecting a commitment from acknowledging an object to be *A* to a strong but not full acknowledging of the object to be ϕ, or establishing a strong but not complete commitment to acknowledging the object to be ϕ. However, both commitment and acknowledging are all-or-none phenomena. There is no partial acknowledging act or partial commitment, though a person can have different degrees of confidence in her acknowledging act, and can be more or less willing to abandon an acknowledging act in the face of evidence to the contrary.

When someone acknowledges *A*'s to almost all be ϕ's, or to be mostly ϕ, or often ϕ, or sometimes ϕ, there are no collection-situations which could ground these judgments when correct. For these judgments to be correct, the world must have one or another modal character, though the person who performs the acknowledging act isn't attending to that character. To understand what he *is* doing, we must look at another feature than commitment. Consider a decision about a future goal to be achieved. This decision can commit us to perform some action or other, without committing us to perform a specific action. For there may be alternative paths to the goal. When we choose one means to our end, we become committed to using that means. The decision about the goal didn't commit us to using that means, but it did *authorize* our using it. One intentional act can authorize another, to a greater or lesser extent. If one act we perform authorizes another, we are not automatically entitled to perform the other. There may also be considerations that tell against performing the action. The end must justify the means, but it (usually) can't completely justify them.

When we carry out practical reasoning to determine what decision to make or what action to perform, our reasons won't usually commit us to a certain action. But they will authorize our decision (or action) to a greater or lesser extent. Similarly, an inductively satisfactory argument from premisses we accept may authorize our accepting the conclusion, without committing us to this. We must distinguish authorizing from enabling. If one act enables another, where both are actually performed, there is a structural relation between the acts. Neither commitment nor authorization is structural. When performing *A* enables *B*, it may be that the goal *to perform B*, or *B*'s goal, authorizes performing *A*. It won't in general be the case that an enabling act authorizes the act which it enables.

To acknowledge *A*'s to almost all be ϕ is to report or establish a very strong authorization from acknowledging an object (a fundamental real object) to be *A* to acknowledging it to be ϕ. Acknowledging α to be *A* will provide very strong support for acknowledging α to be ϕ. But the latter acknowledging act will be optional, not required. The almost-all authorization is correct if the probability of *A*'s being ϕ is very high. Probability, like possibility, is a modal feature which we find to characterize the world of experience.

Someone who is strongly authorized to acknowledge α to be ϕ and, on that basis, does so, is employing a weaker sort of criteria than the person who makes α pass ϕ's authentic test. But if the authorizing relation is correct, and if α is really ϕ, the acknowledging agent has identified the situation of α's being ϕ. This is more risky than acknowledging acts based on applying the expression's criteria directly to the object.

Judging *A*'s to almost all be ϕ is establishing or reporting a very strong authorization from acknowledging an object to be *A* to acknowledging it to be ϕ. Judging *A*'s to be mostly ϕ establishes/reflects a strong authorization. Judging *A*'s to often be ϕ establishes/reflects a weak authorization. While judging *A*'s to be partly ϕ establishes/reflects a very weak authorization; it is simply that the possibility of acknowledging an *A* to be ϕ cannot be ruled out. There is only one type or degree of commitment; this is the basis for deductively correct arguments. Authorization ranges from very strong to very weak.

3. Developing Syllogistic Logic

Although universal statements about collections are inference-principle statements, they don't by themselves give rise to syllogistic logic. To develop syllogistic logic, a person must be in the representational stage of language use. There are two respects in which syllogistic logic is beyond the scope of the purely identifying stage of language use. The first is that the basic entailment relations, the commitments, characteristic of syllogistic logic are not "inevitable" at the purely identifying stage. Just as it is possible for a person to understand and be able to use 'triangle', 'plane figure', and 'three-sided' without being committed to acknowledge three-sided plane figures to all be triangles, so it is possible for someone to acknowledge the *A*'s to all be *B*'s and the *B*'s to all be *C*'s, without being committed to acknowledge the *A*'s to all be *C*'s.

Among actual, reasonably sophisticated language users, there is no one who fails to use language representationally to at least some extent. The basic entailment relation from the premisses of an AAA syllogism in the first figure (Aristotle's "perfect" syllogism) to its conclusion will be recognized by virtually everyone. But our imaginary language learner who is still in the purely identifying stage is not, simply by making the premiss statements, committed to making/accepting the conclusion. The purely identifying-stage language learner who acknowledges the collection of *A*'s to all be *B*'s is committed, once he acknowledges α to be an *A*, to acknowledge α to be a *B*. If he also acknowledges the collection of *B*'s to all be *C*'s, he is further committed to acknowledge α to be a *C*. So for every object β, his acknowledging β to be an *A* will commit him to acknowledging β to be a *C*. In the reasoning that we have just (now) carried out, we have represented an arbitrary object α as being acknowledged to be an *A*, and by reflecting on this and on the universal statements, have realized that acknowledging α to be an *A* will commit a person to acknowledging α to be a *C*. The representing and the reasoning we have carried out are unavailable at the purely identifying stage.

The inferences/arguments characteristic of syllogistic logic do exemplify truth-conditional entailment. Satisfying the truth conditions of the premisses of an AAA syllogism in the first figure does "automatically" satisfy the truth conditions of the conclusion. At the representational stage of language use, there is also basic entailment from the premisses of the correct syllogisms to their conclusions—our awareness of this basic entailment is what reveals the truth-conditional entailment to us. The theory/system of syllogistic logic codifies inferences and arguments which contain identifying-stage statements, but the consistent identifying-stage language learner is not required by his very use of the language to accept these inferences. He can perfectly understand the premisses and conclusion of a valid syllogism without being committed to the conclusion by making/accepting the premisses. Someone who conceived language and linguistic acts in terms of identifying-stage concepts, but who found himself reflecting on certain kinds of linguistic acts (and so was using language representationally), might be amazed to realize that certain statments "demand" others—to realize that the first statements couldn't be true unless the others were true as well. This awareness exceeds the resources of the purely identifying stage, and could seem somehow miraculous or divine.

The characteristic inferences of syllogistic logic are not automatically "validated" at the purely identifying stage. But some basic entailments do characterize identifying-stage statements. One is the commitment from acknowledging α to be ϕ to denying α to be not ϕ. Another is the commitment from acknowledging α to be an *A* and acknowledging *A*'s to all be *B*'s, to acknowledging α to be a *B*. However, even the systematic study of these entailments exceeds the resources of the purely identifying stage.

It is one thing to begin with:

Socrates is a Greek.
All Greeks are mortals.

and rationally infer:

Socrates is a mortal.

It is something else again to understand that acts of these sorts:

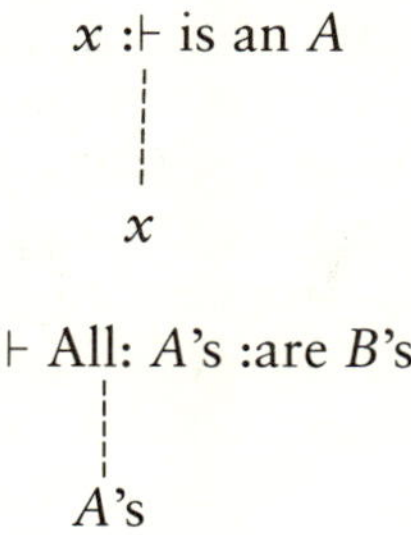

will commit a person to acts like these:

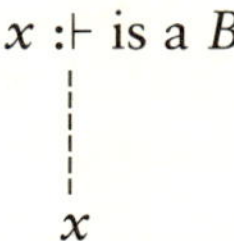

The developer of a systematic logical theory must reflect on what it is (what it means) to acknowledge an object to be this or that, and to acknowledge a collection to be wholly this or partly that. He must use actual or schematic expressions to become representationally aware of arbitrary acts of attending and acknowledging. This provides him with the insight by which he "sees" that acknowledging acts of certain kinds will generate commitments to further acknowledging acts. Since one must use language representationally even to codify/capture the basic entailments generated by the identifying use of language, it is easy to understand how the logical theorist would "detour" through representational-stage statements to find additional basic entailments linking identifying-stage statements.

Even though someone must advance to the representational stage of language use to create a science of logic, this logic could be taught to students in the purely identifying stage, without moving the students beyond that stage. With respect to the basic entailments generated at the identifying stage, the students can be taught new ways to recognize these and "follow" them. They can be taught to use certain syntactic characters as criteria for distinguishing valid from invalid arguments. They can be taught to use certain combinations of semantic structures and syntactic characters as criteria. Nothing about the purely identifying stage of language use prevents a speaker from being aware of semantic features of her own acts and the acts of others. She is aware of performing certain semantic kinds of acts, and of using expressions which are of this or that syntactic kind. The language user who infers or argues for herself, as opposed to considering the inferring or arguing of others, attempts to follow the commitments of her own acts. She doesn't need to study logic to do this, but this study may supply her with additional criteria for commitment and authorization, and so facilitate her reasoning. With respect to the arguments of others, which involve acknowledging acts the student isn't inclined to perform for herself, the study of logic enables her to evaluate the arguments without considering in detail the commitments generated by the various acts performed in the course of the argument. In addition, the identifying-stage logic student can be taught to make new commitments, including the commitments characteristic of syllogistic logic.

Students of syllogistic logic can be taught rules for determining which syllogisms are valid. They can be taught to disqualify syllogisms that commit the fallacy of undistributed middle, or which have a negative premiss but not a negative conclusion. These fallacies can be identified on the basis of syntactic criteria. Students can also be taught rules for constructing proofs from hypotheses (i.e., rules for constructing deductions) without regarding these proofs as genuine inferences. To suppose something to be the case in order to examine its consequences, someone must use expressions to represent. At the purely identifying stage of language use, one can acknowledge an object to be ϕ, deny the object to be ϕ, or decline to acknowledge or deny the object to be ϕ. But he can't suppose the object to be ϕ, for supposing requires a person to be representationally aware of an arbitrary situation of a kind. However, a student can be taught rules for writing sentences in order, which sentences might be used by someone in the representational stage to make an argument. The student learns only that being able to construct a suitable sequence of sentences provides an additional test for validity. He can do this without "seeing the point" of the sequence of sentences.

A genuine inference or argument requires the person who makes it to understand what she is saying or thinking, and to recognize how this commits her to additional linguistic acts, which she then performs. Making and recognizing commitments is constitutive of intentional activity. These are also fundamental; they can be noticed and characterized, but not explained in a reductive fashion. The identifying-stage language learners who are taught criteria for evaluating arguments without thinking through the arguments, or are taught to make new commitments on the basis of tests which don't involve the insight that this statment must be accepted once those statements are accepted, are students who are "missing the point" of logical theory. They rely on memory of various tests to evaluate arguments and to reach conclusions of their own, but they don't really understand what they are doing. Many students in my own logic classes are like this. I try to force them to understand, to think through the procedures we employ, and to recognize commitments generated by an understanding of linguistic acts, but students often succeed in the courses by simply memorizing techniques for manipulating expressions.

Aristotle used language to represent when he invented logic. He carried out rational inferences and constructed rational arguments. Like my own students, many of his followers/successors misunderstood what Aristotle was up to. The medieval logic rhymes "Barbara, Celarunt, . . ." show a concern merely with the outward form of Aristotle's deductions/reductions. Aristotle established the validity of less than "perfect" syllogisms by reducing them to perfect syllogisms. In my colleague John Corcoran's terminology, Aristotle provided cogent deductions to demonstrate the validity of syllogisms that may not have been cogent. If an argument-sequence is valid, the "gap" between premisses and conclusion may be so great that a person doesn't recognize that the premisses "demand" the conclusion. A cogent argument sequence is one where the gap is small enough for a person to see that accepting the premisses commits her to accepting the conclusion. (But what is cogent for one person may not be cogent for someone else.) The medieval rhymes allowed students to recognize valid syllogisms, and even to imitate Aristotle's deductions, without understanding the deductions. Someone who understood what Aristotle was doing would want to construct new deductions, and not simply to reproduce Aristotle's performance.

Descartes' criticisms of logic (particularly in *Rules for the Guidance of Our Native Understanding*) reveal that in his time logic was at least popularly understood to yield results which don't require much thought. Criteria based on the syntactic features of sentences were substituted for understanding (and performing) linguistic acts, and uncovering commitment relations. Descartes derided the value of logic for discovering truth, for the inferences sanctioned by his own method were to demand hard thinking and close attention to ideas rather than attention to syntactic features of expressions. Even today, logic books which cover syllogistic logic frequently give the impression that the rules of distribution and negation provide a sufficient account of validity in syllogisms.

4. Conditional Statements

Statements involving propositional negation and propositional disjunction are not "available" at the purely identifying stage of language use. For such statements contain a propositional component which is performed without at the same time being accepted or rejected. In a statement involving propositional negation like this one:

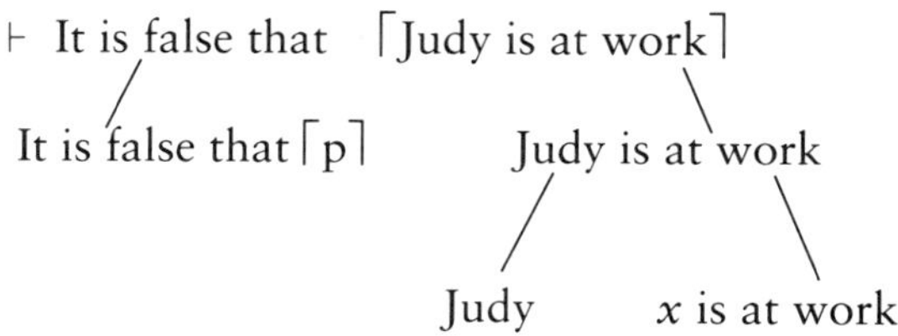

the propositional act is first performed without being accepted or rejected, and then denied. (This is semantic or structural priority, not temporal priority.) And a propositional disjunction only claims that at least one (or exactly one) of two propositional components is true without coming down in favor of either.

It might seem that conditional statements are also unavailable at the purely identifying stage, but in fact these statements can be made at the identifying stage. For conditional statements need not contain force-neutral propositional components.

Let us first consider a conditional directive: "If it rains, close the windows." Without the conditional prefix, the sentence 'Close the windows' might be used to direct the addressee to close the relevant windows. I represent a directive act like this:

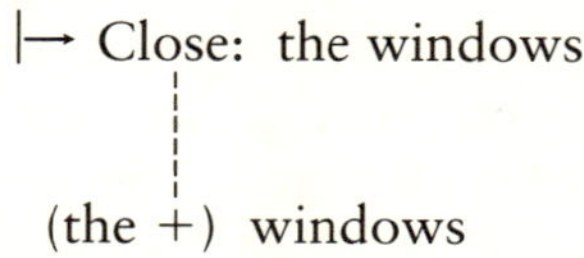

The symbol '|→' indicates the directive force of the act. It is a command, not a request. The speaker identifies the (relevant group of) windows as a reference point, which enables her to use 'Close' to direct the target to close them. This directive act is an identifying-stage counterpart to an acknowledging act. But it isn't an attempt to identify a situation. It is rather an attempt to get a situation to occur. The speaker performs this directive act in order to get the addressee to do what is wanted. But the addressee is supposed to carry out the order intentionally. The speaker is trying to get him to accept a commitment to close the windows and to act with this (to fulfill this) commitment.

The directive act is directed to an addressee. He is the target of the directive act in the same way that an object is the target of an acknowledging act. An alternative representation for the directive act is the following:

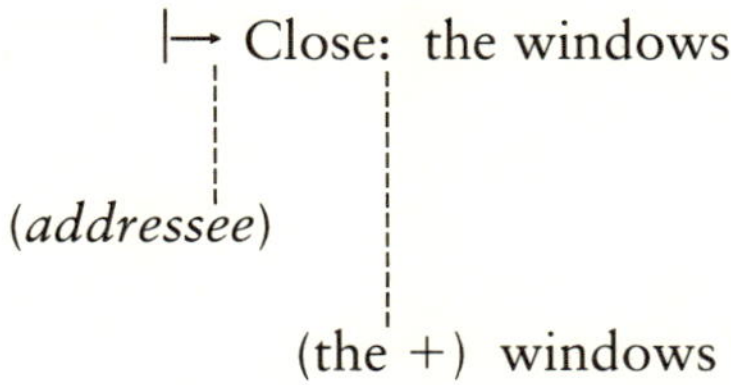

The italicized expression in parentheses is not said or thought by the speaker. It is our word for the person to whom the speaker attends, the person whom she targets. I will usually simplify directive diagrams by omitting to name the target, but the speaker's attending to the target definitely figures in her command.

The condition of the conditional command is not a propositional act. It does not represent the weather as raining (or represent the present situation as a rainy situation). This is instead a provisional attending act. To provisionally attend to a particular object or to an arbitrary object/situation of a kind is to be on the lookout for the object or situation. One does this in learning to use language—the student is tested to see if she understands 'yellow' by being directed to point to yellow things. The teacher uses 'yellow' to provisionally attend to a yellow object in order to get the student to, first, provisionally attend to a yellow object (the student uses the teacher's expression to do this) and, subsequently, actually identify one or more yellow objects. To be on the lookout for an object or situation, it isn't necessary to represent the object or situation, one is simply prepared in case such an object/situation turns up. The provisional attending act of looking out for rain enables the sentence 'shut the windows' to be used to conditionally direct the addressee to shut the windows. The point of the conditional command is to get the addressee to establish a commitment relation linking acts of acknowledging it to be raining to acts of closing windows.

The sentence 'It is raining' is an idiom for acknowledging the current circumstances to include rain falling. The whole sentence is used as a unit. I will represent the acknowledging act as follows:

$\vdash$ It is raining

No linguistic act enables this acknowledging act. When an expression is used to perform a provisional attending act, I will enclose the expression in lower "corners." So in the conditional directive "If it is raining, shut the windows," I will represent the provisional attending act like this:

$\lfloor$ It is raining $\rfloor$

The whole conditional directive is represented:

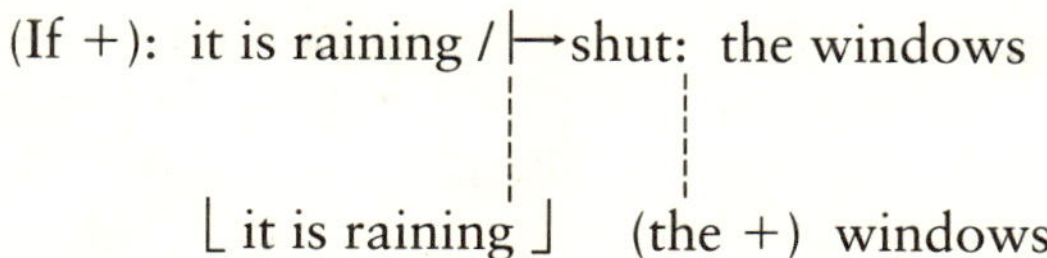

The provisional attending act enables the conditional directive. The reference point act is also an enabling act for the conditional directive. The *target* of the conditional directive is the object of the speaker's attention, but no word is used to express or perform this attending. The conditional directive is performed with 'If . . . shut.' The 'If' is used to make explicit the conditional character of the directive. Conditional acts are marked with a slant line—this takes the place of one colon in other representations of enabled acts.

Consider the conditional directive "If Tom comes on the porch, lock the door." This might be performed as follows:

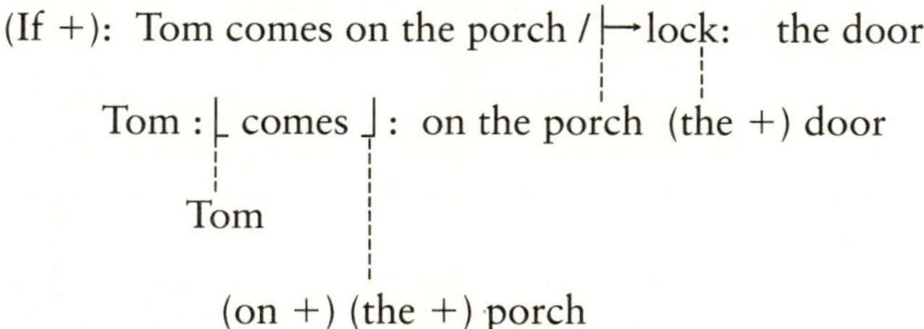

Here Tom and the porch are actually identified; this isn't provisional. What is provisional is Tom's coming on the porch.

Conditional acknowledging acts can be represented in a similar way. The sentence 'If Tom wins the race, then Rosemary will be pleased' might be used like this:

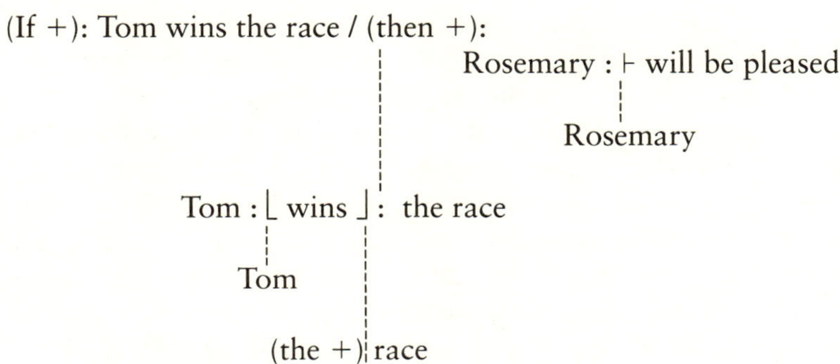

Provisionally attending to Tom winning the race enables the act acknowledging Rosemary to be pleased on the condition of Tom's winning. The conditional acknowledging act is performed with 'If . . . , then . . . will be pleased.' The two words 'If' and 'then' serve to make explicit the conditional character of the acknowledging act. The conditional statement serves to establish or report a commitment from acknowledging Tom to win (to have won) the race to acknowledging Rosemary to be pleased on the occasion of Tom's winning.

A conditional statement is an inference-principle statement. For such a statement to be true, it must be impossible to both correctly perform the antecedent's acknowledging act and correctly deny the consequent's predicate to apply to its target. The statement above is correct if it is (and will be) impossible to both correctly acknowledge Tom to have won and correctly deny Rosemary to be pleased on that occasion. (This doesn't mean there isn't a world where Tom wins without Rosemary being pleased; it means that it isn't possible to correctly carry out these acts in our world.) A conditional statement is neither true nor false until it is actually performed. Once performed, it is true if, and only if, either there is (and will be) no actual situation corresponding to the provisional attending act or there is an actual situation for the consequent.

A speaker might capriciously perform a correct conditional acknowledging act. A more responsible speaker will *register* the modal feature which constitutes the conditional's truth conditions. To register this feature, the speaker must be aware of the connection from the antecedent's acknowledging act to the consequent's. He could do this if he knew the antecedent act to have no actual counterpart, or he knew the consequent's acknowledging act to be correct, or he recognized an already existing commitment from antecedent to consequent, or he established the commitment by deciding to do *B* if *A*. He would also register the impossibility if he relied on the testimony of someone with such knowledge. Even if the language user makes a correct conditional statement and registers the appropriate modal feature, her conditional acknowledging act may not be justified. She might, for example, be relying on the testimony of someone who isn't trustworthy.

Since there is no propositional negation at the identifying stage, the language learner at this stage can't negate a conditional propositional act. But he can object to someone else's conditional statement. If he knows α to be ϕ while β isn't χ, he can tell this to someone who makes a conditional statement "If α is ϕ, then β is χ." Conditionals are commonly criticized for being unjustified. Someone making this criticism may inappropriately use the word 'false', but the point of the criticism is that the speaker had no business making the conditional statement. The speaker had no business establishing a commitment from α's being acknowledged to be ϕ to β's being acknowledged to be χ. If α is known not to be ϕ or β is known to be ψ, then the commitment connection would be harmless—and pointless. The conditional assertion is most in order when it isn't known whether α is ϕ and isn't known whether β is ψ. In those circumstances, it is appropriate to challenge the conditional by showing that for all one knows, α might be ϕ without β being ψ.

The antecedent of an identifying-stage conditional statement can't be another conditional, for conditional statements are full-fledged illocutionary acts. But the consequent of one conditional can contain another:

> If Tom wins the race, then if Dan comes in second,
> our team will win the meet.

Here the conditional assertion that our team will win is simply subject to two conditions.

Earlier we considered a statement "The first person on Mars will be an American" made by a speaker who isn't sure there will be a person on Mars. She means "The first person on Mars, if there is one, will be an American." Her statement can be analyzed as a "condensed" conditional:

The first person on Mars / $\vdash$ will be an American

$\lfloor$The first person on Mars$\rfloor$

(The entire structure isn't shown here. The provisional attending act would normally have additional structure.) The acknowledging act is conditional on there being a first person. The speaker is reflecting/establishing a commitment from using 'The first person on Mars' to perform an identifying act to an act acknowledging the identified person to be an American.

Just as syllogistic logic is grounded in identifying-stage statements, though it uses the resources of the representational stage, so there could be a logic of identifying-stage conditionals. Perhaps part of Stoic logic should be understood this way. The principle Modus Ponens is actually an identifying-stage principle, for this principle merely "unpacks" the commitment established by conditional statements. But Modus Tollens depends on representational-stage resources. To see that acknowledging β to be Ξ on the condition of α being ϕ and denying β to be Ξ require that α not be ϕ, one needs to be able to suppose that α is ϕ and then realize that this would lead to contradiction.

5. The Logical Limits of the Identifying Stage

Identifying-stage negative statements reject the acknowledging use of a predicate with respect to one or more individuals. In propositional negations, someone can reject an entire propositional representing act. At the representational stage, it is also possible to portray an individual as not being something or other. The sentence 'Kevin is not a military officer' might be used this way:

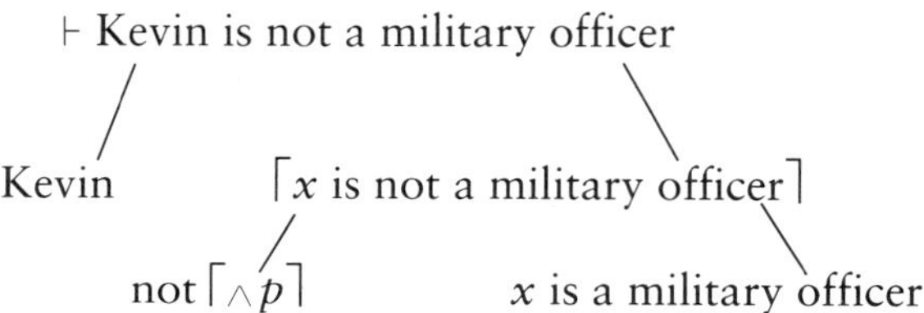

In this diagram the 'not⌈∧*p*⌉' represents an arbitrary propositional act as false, or ruled out (by the way things are). The "spike" indicates that 'not' will be placed within the propositional expression. The complex act:

⌈*x* is not a military officer⌉

not⌈∧*p*⌉ *x* is a military officer

doesn't represent a propositional act as false. Instead it represents an arbitrary object *x* as one for which the predicate '*x* is a military officer' is false (as one for which the *predicative act* is ruled out).

An internal 'not' can also be used to portray a specific propositional act as false:

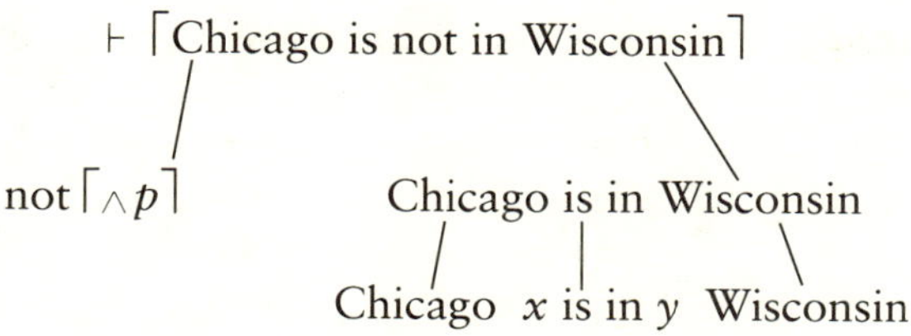

Although propositional disjunctions require the resources of the representational stage, many uses of 'or' can be accommodated at the purely identifying stage. The sentence 'Henry is an Episcopalian or a Presbyterian' might be used like this:

Henry : ⊢ is an Episcopalian (+ or +) a Presbyterian
Henry

The 'or' is used to make explicit the disjunctive character of the acknowledging act.

But how are we to understand this disjunctive character? If Henry is correctly acknowledged to be an Episcopalian or Presbyterian, then it must be possible (in principle) to correctly acknowledge him to be an Episcopalian or to correctly acknowledge him to be a Presbyterian. If ϕ and ψ are acknowledging expressions, we could have disjunctive acknowledging criteria such that one first applies the ϕ criteria to an object α, and if α passes the ϕ-test, then α is acknowledged to be ϕ or ψ. If α turns out not to be ϕ, or if the ϕ-test proves hard to apply or is inconclusive, one applies the ψ criteria to α; if α passes that test, then α is acknowledged to be ϕ or ψ. And α is denied to be ϕ or ψ just in case α fails both tests. But if this is how disjunctive predicates were used, no one would acknowledge α to be ϕ or ψ unless she knew which predicate applied to α. (Though if ϕ applied, the test wouldn't be continued to find out about ψ.) While disjunctive predicates could, in principle, be used with such disjunctive criteria, and may sometimes actually be used like this, we don't normally use the predicates this way. One rarely acknowledges α to be ϕ or ψ when she knows α to be ϕ or knows α to be ψ. Disjunctive acknowledging is most in order when a person doesn't know which of the two acknowledging acts would be correct.

A disjunctive acknowledging act is indefinite. Someone might acknowledge α to be ϕ or ψ if the acknowledging criteria for the two expressions have something in common, and whatever satisfies the common part must satisfy the remaining criteria of one of the two expressions. This would allow someone to determine α to be ϕ or ψ without determining which it is that α is. Or someone could have an indefinite memory of just which α is—she once knew, but now can't remember. Similarly, a disjunctive acknowledging act can be made on the basis of a decision narrowing a wide range of choices to two. Someone decides for now to do *A* or *B*, postponing the final decision until later.

There are no disjunctive situations. The language user who knows which disjunct is correct might perform a disjunctive acknowledging act to indefinitely identify a certain situation. The person holding out two hands can acknowledge the prize to be in one hand or the other, and the chooser will get the prize only if he selects the correct hand. In such a case, the prize-holder may actually identify (attend to) the situation of the prize being in her left hand, though she does this in such a way as to keep her audience in the dark. However, ordinarily the language user performing a disjunctive acknowledging act is not in a position to exploit connections linking her to a particular situation. She acknowledges at least one of the disjoined expressions to be applicable to the target. (She acknowledges at least one of two kinds of acknowledging acts to be correct for the target.) So the truth conditions for the disjunctive acknowledging act are modal. The language user who performs a correct disjunctive acknowledging act will register the modal feature if she successfully applies criteria which require at least one of the disjoined predicates to apply. The point of the disjunctive acknowledging act is to establish/reflect a commitment to whatever consequences the acknowledging acts have (would have) in common. If Henry is either Episcopalian or Presbyterian, then he is Protestant.

Identifying acts can be disjoined like this:

```
Rich :(+ or +): Sheila : ⊦ won the prize
                         ¦
                         ¦
                Rich (+) Sheila
```

Here the two identifying acts jointly enable the acknowledging act. The two targets constitute a collection acknowledged to be such that at least one member won the prize—it is partly a won-the-prize collection. The 'or' makes explicit that the acknowledging act is disjunctively predicated of the joint target. The '(+)' between 'Rich' and 'Sheila' indicates that the two identifying acts are combined to identify the combination of Rich and Sheila.

It is also possible to use the phrase 'Rich or Sheila' to indefinitely identify one of the two. In such a case the speaker knows which one won, but may be withholding this knowledge from her audience. She uses the disjunctive phrase to attend to just one of the two people. If she did this, she might make this statement:

```
Rich  or Sheila  : ⊢ won the prize
       |
       |
       |
Rich (+ or +) Sheila
```

The 'or' makes explicit the indefinite character of the identifying act.

A sentence like 'Rich or Sheila knows the answer' can be used to say either that at least one knows the answer or that they both know the answer. The following statement:

```
Rich  : (+ or +) :  Sheila : ⊢  knows the answer
                             |
                             |
                             |
                        Rich (+) Sheila
```

means that at least one of the two targets knows the answer. But in other circumstances, the same sentence could be used to say they both know—anyone who wants the answer can get it by asking either Rich or Sheila, it doesn't matter which. When the sentence is used with the "both-and" meaning, it might be used this way:

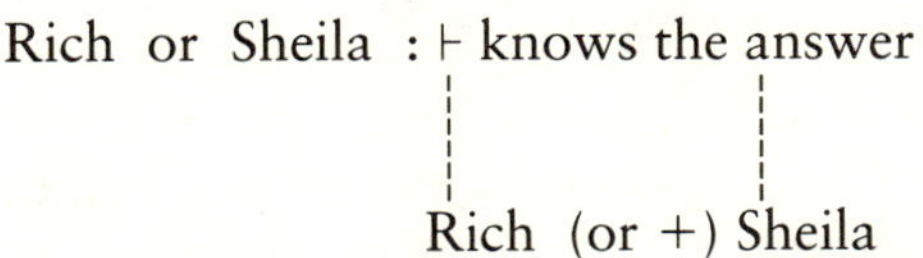

The one acknowledging act applies separately to each of Rich and Sheila. The 'or' is used to give a special character to the act of identifying Sheila. The 'or' emphasizes the interchangeableness of the two identifying acts in this situation.

At the purely identifying stage, it is sometimes possible to use 'or' to link sentences, if this is done with sentences used to talk about the same object. As well as saying "Henry is an Episcopalian or a Presbyterian," the speaker might use 'Henry is an Episcopalian or he is a Presbyterian' like this:

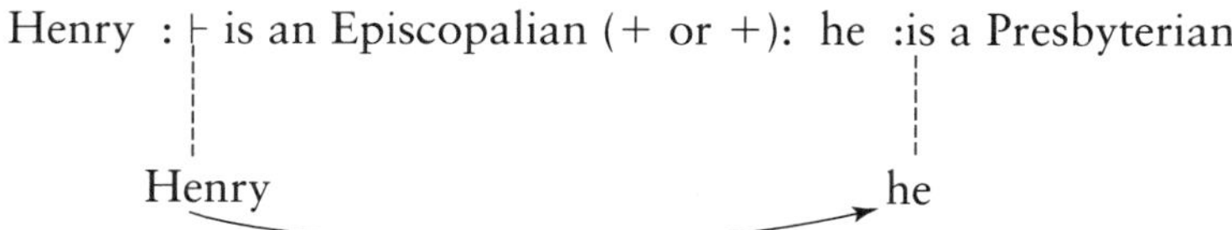

Henry is identified and reidentified, but is only once acknowledged, disjointly, to be either an Episcopalian or a Presbyterian. The looping arrow indicates that the pronoun 'he' "borrows" the identifying (attending) performed with 'Henry.' Statements applying different predicates to different objects cannot be disjoined at the purely identifying stage, for the predicates couldn't in such a case be used to perform acknowledging acts. To use the sentence 'Either Dagwood is working hard or Mr. Dithers is out of town' to make a statement, one needs to use and understand each component sentence, and claim that at least one of the propositional acts is true.

The sentence above could also be used to perform a propositional representing act:

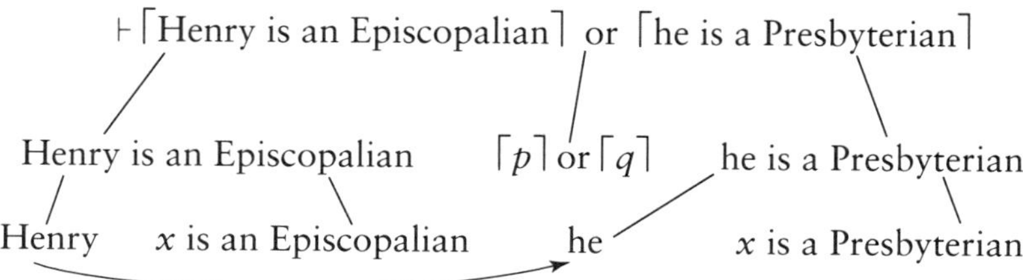

The pronoun 'he' is still used *repetitively*, to "pick up" the identifying performed with 'Henry.' For a disjunctive propositional act like this to be true, at least one of the disjoined propositional acts must be true. In some such cases, the truth of one disjunct rules out the truth of the other. In portraying an arbitrary one of two propositional acts as true, and accepting this, one licenses inferences to consequences common to both propositional acts. To accept the disjunction is to accept what the two disjuncts "share." This idea is captured by the inference principle sometimes called *disjunction elimination*. The opposite principle, *disjunction introduction* (which is often called *addition*), is licensed directly by the truth conditions of the disjunctive statement.

Conjunctive statements can easily be accommodated (performed) at the purely identifying stage. For example, we might have this structure:

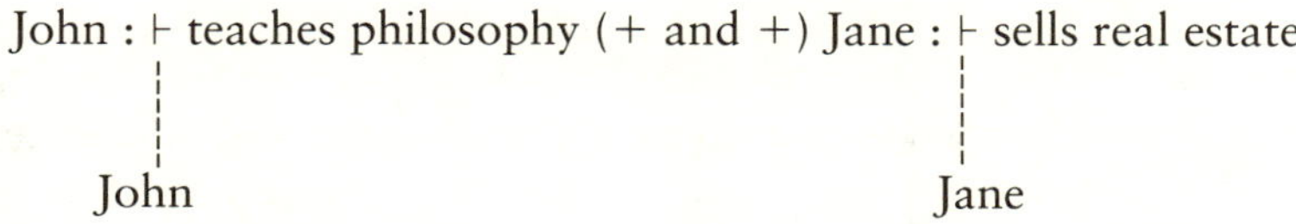

The 'and' simply makes explicit that the two acknowledging acts are intentionally performed in tandem. And 'and' can be used at the identifying stage to connect expressions shorter than sentences. Here:

Peter : (+ and +) : Newton : ⊢ are philosophy professors

Peter Newton

there are two identifying acts, and one acknowledging act which "covers" both targets. The 'and' gives a special character to the acknowledging act, making explicit that the act applies to both Peter and Newton.

The sentence 'Ted is an architect and a Presbyterian' could be used to perform these acts:

Ted : ⊢ is an architect (+ and +) ⊢ a Presbyterian

Ted

The one identifying act provides a target for two acknowledging acts. In this case, 'and' is used to make explicit that the two acknowledging acts are jointly applied to the one target. Being an architect is one thing, being a Presbyterian is something else. The conjunctive predicate is not used to identify a conjunctive situation, for there are no conjunctive situations. Instead the speaker separately identifies (or tries to) two situations.

The sentence 'Frank and Kathy are married' is ambiguous. It could be used to perform these acts:

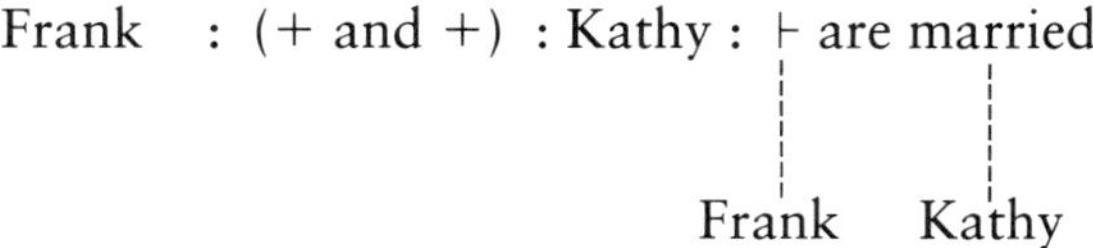

which acknowledges both Frank and Kathy to be married persons, but they need not be married to one another. The sentence can also be used like this:

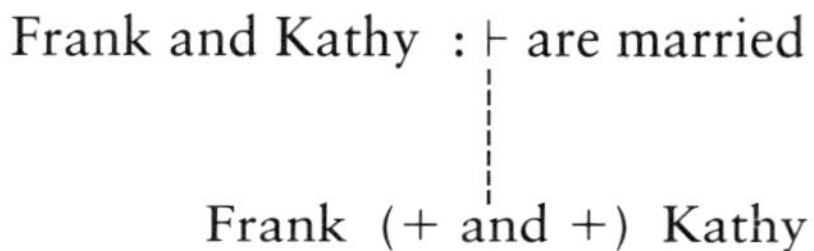

This acknowledges the couple Frank-and-Kathy to be a married couple. Here, the 'and' makes explicit that the two identifying acts, together, identify a couple (a group, not a collection). Note that the ambiguity of 'Frank and Kathy are married' is missing from 'Both Frank and Kathy are married.' This last sentence calls for the following structure:

(Both +): Frank : (+ and +): Kathy : ⊢ are married

Frank Kathy

At the representational stage, someone can conjoin two assertions:

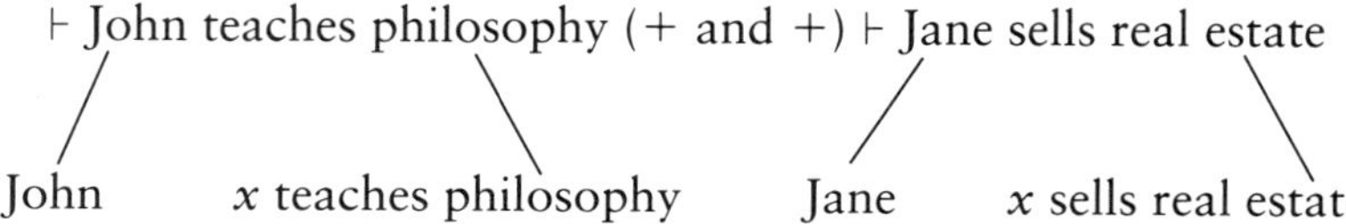

It is also possible to perform one accepting/asserting act for the two propositional acts:

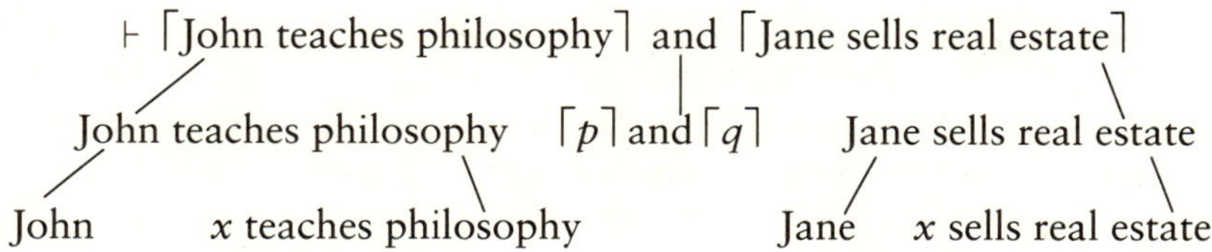

In this case, 'and' is used to represent an arbitrary propositional act p and an arbitrary act q as both true. This assertion emphasizes that both components are true, in contrast to the first statement(s) where the primarily focus is on the separate propositional acts.

At the representational stage of language use, the condition of a conditional statement can be a propositional representing act rather than a provisional attending act. This changes the structure of conditionals. At the representational stage, we can perform a conditional propositional act without accepting/asserting that act. We can just consider it. We can incorporate it as a component in a more complex propositional act. At the representational stage, a whole conditional propositional act can be accepted, as opposed to having the consequent conditionally accepted. For example, the sentence 'If David stays home, the party will be a success' might be used as follows:

⊢ If ⌈David stays home⌉ / ⌈the party will be a success⌉

If ⌈p⌉ / ⌈q⌉ David stays home (+) the party will be a success

David x stays home (the +) party x will be a success

I have retained the slant line as a sign of conditionality. The two propositional acts are intentionally performed "in tandem," and this is marked by the '+' in parentheses. This is different from the disjunctive and conjunctive examples considered earlier. In those cases, two "separated" propositional acts were combined with the disjunctive or conjunctive expression. Here the two propositional acts are performed and considered together prior to representing one as conditional on the other. This treatment is necessary in order to accommodate some cases where pronouns in the consequent are governed by expressions (acts) in the antecedent. We appear to consider the propositional acts as representing a common "scene" before we represent one as conditional on the other.

For propositional act *Q* to be conditional on propositional act *P* is for there to be a correct commitment from accepting *P* to accepting *Q*. Such a commitment might be due simply to the conventional criteria associated with the two acts. It might be due to conventional criteria together with other commitments the speaker has made (by accepting certain propositional acts, making certain decisions, or performing other relevant actions). Otherwise, a commitment can be established by accepting the conditional act. (Accepting the conditional act either establishes or reflects a commitment from antecedent to consequent.) But one can represent *Q* being conditional on *P* even if *Q* isn't. For the commitment from *P* to *Q* to be correct, it must be impossible to correctly accept *P* while correctly denying *Q*.

The conditional propositional representing act is false if either there is no commitment from the antecedent to the consequent or it is possible to correctly accept the antecedent and deny the consequent. Since the commitments generated by accepting a certain propositional act vary from one person to another, a particular conditional propositional act might be true for one person and false for someone else. If it is possible to correctly accept the antecedent and reject the consequent, the conditional is false for everyone. If it is impossible to do this, the conditional is false for those speakers for whom there is no commitment from antecedent to consequent. For such a person, the conditional can change from being false at time t to being true at time $t + k$, should that person establish a commitment from antecedent to consequent.

Syllogistic logic cannot be systematically developed by a person unless she is in the representational stage of language use, but syllogistic logic concerns identifying-stage statements. At the purely identifying stage, these statements have truth-conditional consequences which they may not basically entail. At least, not everyone at the identifying stage must be committed to the truth-conditional consequences of a given statement. However, at the representational stage, a language user will be able to trace commitments from the identifying-stage statements to their consequences. (The truth-conditional entailments will also be basic entailments.) Syllogistic logic can be taught to identifying-stage students without moving them beyond that stage.

Modern propositional logic is essentially a representational-stage study, for it deals with propositional representing acts and their semantic relations. However, classical proposition logic is inadequate in the sense of being incomplete. For this logic is exclusively concerned with truth-conditional concepts: with truth-conditional entailment and truth-conditional consequence. It does not recognize basic entailment (which is a kind of "absolute" deducibility) or explore the relations between basic entailment/consequence and their truth-conditional counterparts.

And classical modern logic presupposes the existence of abstract, timeless propositions just waiting to be apprehended/expressed, although the real bearers of truth and falsity are propositional acts, which don't exist unless someone performs/makes them. We can represent a statement—an arbitrary statement of a kind—which no one makes, but that statement (statement-kind) depends for its "existence" on our representing activity. The misguided acceptance of abstract, timeless propositions has had many unfortunate results. One of these is the misunderstanding of truth conditions for conditional propositions (propositional acts). If these must be timelessly true or false, then their truth or falsity must be independent of whether anyone accepts them. But conditional statements are inference-principle statements that are "in force" only for those who have made the right commitments. Our improved understanding of language and propositional representing acts doesn't discredit modern propositional logic, but it opens the way to more comprehensive and more adequate logical theories.

6. Indefinite Phrases

At the purely identifying stage of language use, an indefinite phrase can be used to identify a particular object:

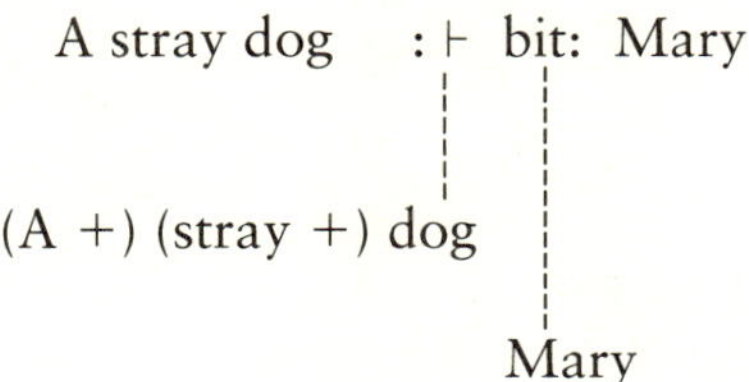

The speaker uses 'dog' to attend to a particular dog. Her use of 'stray' doesn't help her to identify the dog, but it does make explicit (it *reveals*) something relevant about the dog. (The speaker could also use 'stray dog' as a unit.) She has identified the particular dog indefinitely, because she hasn't enabled her audience to independently identify the dog. They must use the phrase to attend to whatever dog is the object of the speaker's attention.

An identifying-stage language user can use an indefinite phrase to perform an acknowledging act:

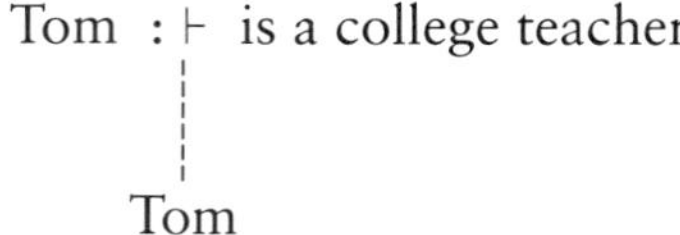

An indefinite phrase can also be used with a different auxiliary to perform an acknowledging act:

Dan : ⊦ (has +) a car

Dan

In acknowledging Dan to have a car, the auxiliary 'has' gives a special character to the acknowledging act. It marks the temporal location of the situation that is being identified, and it marks the car-acknowledging as of the car-linked variety.

It is possible to use a form of 'to have' to indicate how individuals are situated with respect to one another:

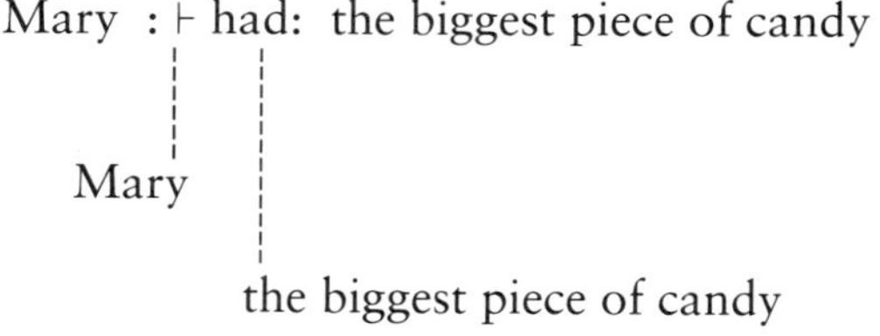

But this is unusual. The *having* that is common to having a piece of candy, having a mother, having a car, having a good time, and having the measles is difficult to discern. The verb 'have' ('to have') is an auxiliary, without much content of its own. When combined with an indefinite phrase, it forms a particular kind of expression, associated with a particular kind of acknowledging criteria. For George to have a mother is not for him to be situated by owning with respect to his mother; it is for him to be "mothered." But, clearly, if George has a mother, then he is linked to her by the child-mother connection. Knowing that George has a mother enables a language user to identify George's mother by exploiting his connection to George and the son-mother tie linking George to George's mother. This is possible at the purely identifying stage.

At the purely identifying stage, an indefinite phrase can be combined with a verb in a way we have not previously considered. If we try to understand the sentence 'Jorge speaks Spanish', we can see that it would not be used for a situation linking two objects. The same verb 'speaks' can be used with different languages. But Spanish, French, Korean, and so on are not parts of the world to which someone can attend. The sentence would not be be used like this:

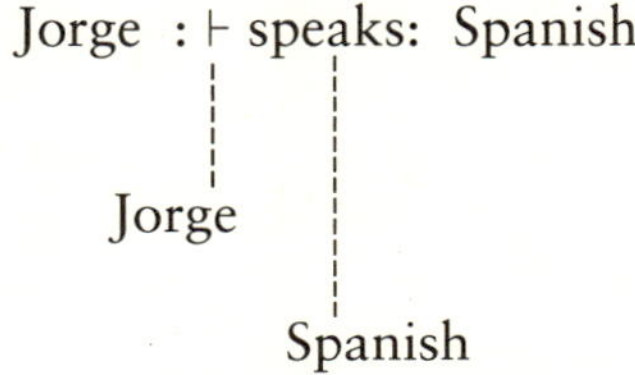

Instead, 'speaks' is an incomplete acknowledging expression. In the context of considering languages one might speak, the acknowledging criteria associated with 'speak' are incomplete, or determinable. These criteria are further specified by indicating the language. In these acts:

Jorge : ⊢ speaks (++ Spanish)

Jorge

the word 'Spanish' is used to give a special character to the acknowledging act performed with 'speaks'. This is unlike cases where the character conferred simply makes explicit a feature the act independently has. Here the character-giving act contributes a semantically important feature to the character-receiving act. It completes or determines that act. To signal this kind of case, a '+ +' is enclosed in the parentheses.

An indefinite phrase can also be used in this new character-giving way. Such a use can be accommodated at the identifying stage:

Dan : ⊢ owns (+ + a car)

Dan

The phrase 'a car' is used to further specify the kind of owning Dan does.

The quantificational use of expressions, and the use of pronouns and variables "bound" by quantified phrases, is possible at the representational stage of language use, but not at the purely identifying stage. An expression used quantificationally represents an arbitrary object, either a completely arbitrary object or an arbitrary object of a kind. The sentence 'Some person is sleeping' might be used to acknowledge an indefinitely identified person to be sleeping:

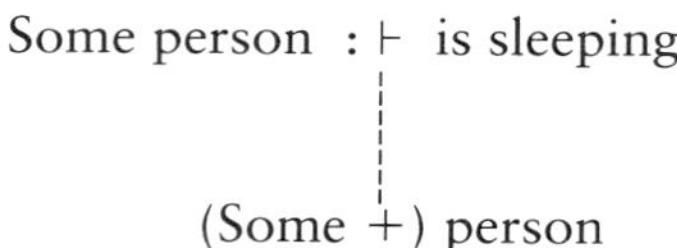

It might also be used to portray that person as sleeping:

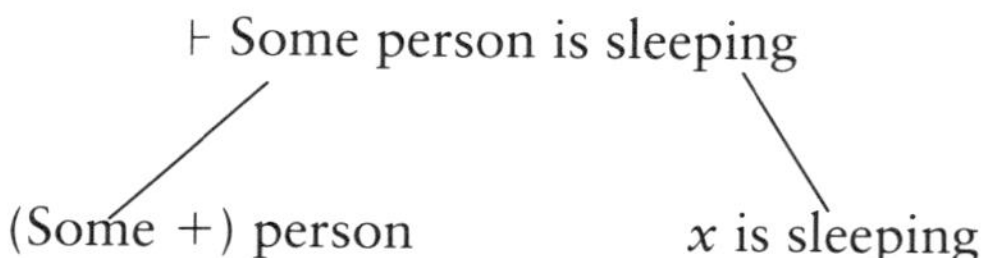

The phrase 'some person' can also be used to represent an arbitrary person—either an arbitrary member of a contextually determined collection, like the people in this hotel, or a completely arbitrary person. This is the *quantificational* use of the phrase. In the two diagrams above, the phrase is used to identify some one person. The shape of the diagram when the phrase is used quantificationally is the same as the shape of the lower of the two diagrams above. I will introduce a notational device to indicate that the indefinite phrase is used quantificationally:

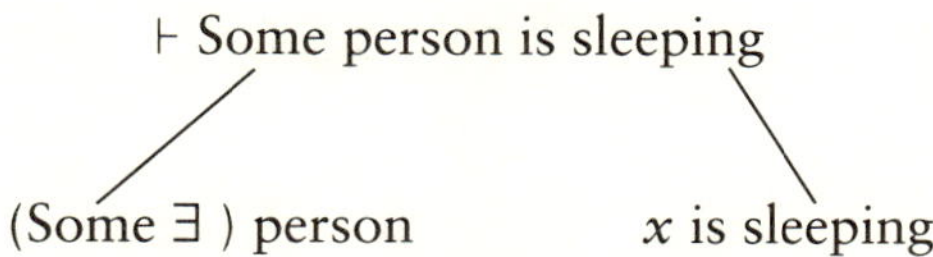

In the lower left act, 'Some' is used to make explicit the quantificational character of the representing act. To indicate this, I use '∃' instead of the customary '+'; the logical symbol indicates the character that 'Some' makes explicit. If the propositional act were performed with 'Someone' rather that 'Some person', I would use this diagram:

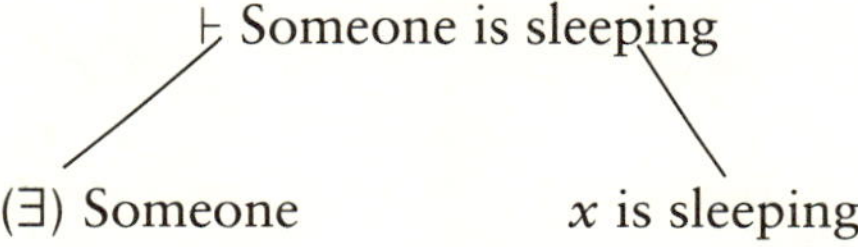

Indefinite phrases can also be used quantificationally:

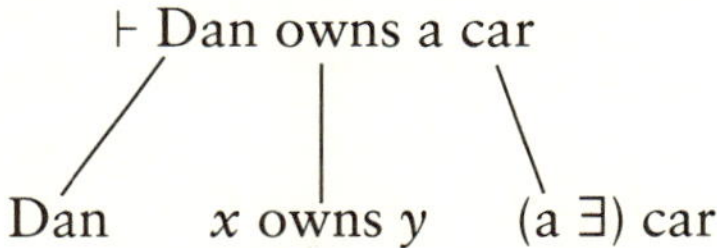

Dan is represented as owning an arbitrary car. The difference between this statement and the following:

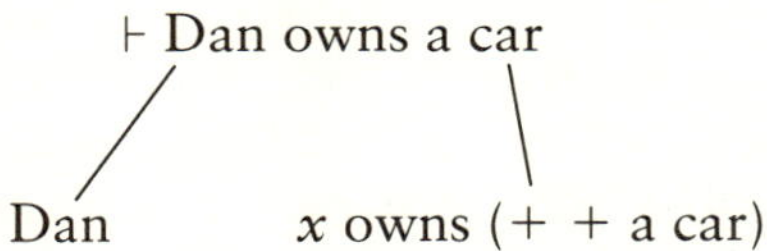

is slight. In the first statement, the speaker gives some thought to the car Dan owns, while the second statement is concerned only with car-owning.

A statement formed with an indefinite phrase or a 'some'-phrase used quantificationally—like the statement that Bill owns a car—is true just in case it is possible to establish a correspondence between the statement and suitable objects and situations. The statement:

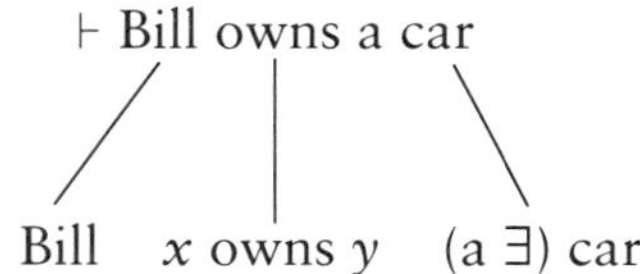

is true just in case it is possible (in principle) to exploit a connection to identify a car for which the predicative act performed with 'Bill owns *y*' is true. So the statement is true just in case there is a car such that Bill owns it. But normally, in making a statement containing a quantified phrase, a speaker isn't claiming that there is a corresponding object, though he is committed to such a claim. He will make the quantificational claim as a way of sanctioning inferences to statements that would be entailed by any statement concerning a specific object. If Bill owns a car, then we can infer the consequences of an arbitrary statement characterizing Bill as owning some particular car.

We use propositional representing acts to build up a picture, or a set of pictures, of the world. The complex picture or set of pictures is detailed and specific in some parts and general or indefinite in others. The picture/set is connected to the actual world by various identifying acts. For a portraying act to be true, it must be possible to establish a suitable correspondence between that act and objects and situations in the world. But accepting the act—accepting the act as true—is different from claiming that the act is true. To accept the act is to place it in one's "authentic" world picture, with the presumption that it belongs there. (Although accepting the act is not claiming that the act is true, accepting the act commits one to the claim that it is true.) Some acts belong because they portray specific objects and situations to which they can be made to correspond. Others belong because they sanction correct moves or because they indicate a negative or indefinite feature that the authentic pictures properly possess.

7. Government and Binding

There are (at least) three logically important uses of pronouns. A pronoun is used *repetitively* if it is used to repeat a different act, and could without loss be replaced by the expression being "repeated." The repetitive use of pronouns is available at the identifying stage:

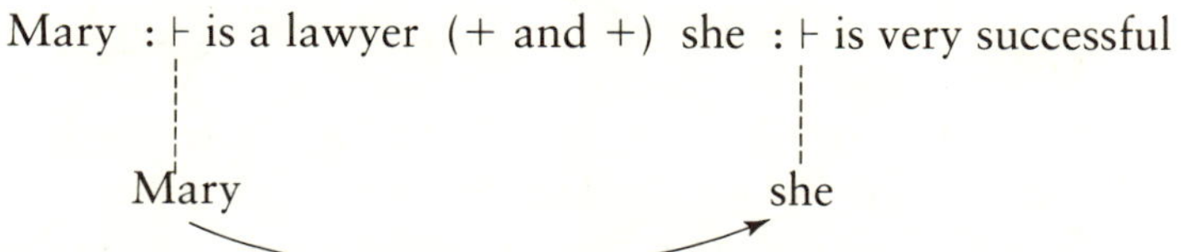

The arrow from the expression being repeated to the repeating pronoun signals the repetitive use.

Pronouns are also used repetitively in propositional representing acts:

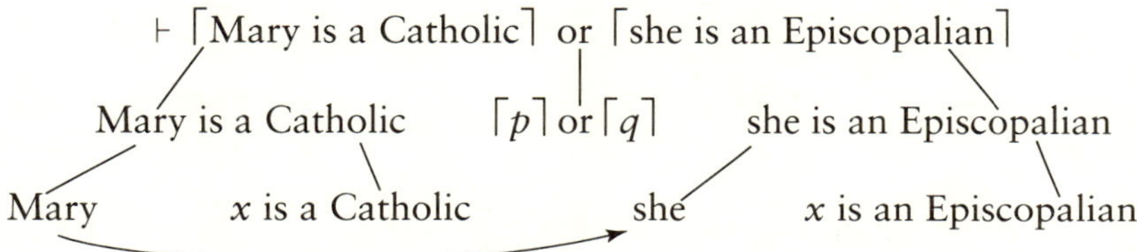

Repetitive pronouns need not repeat a single expression or phrase. Consider the (polite) directive "If you have a quarter, please put it in the parking meter":

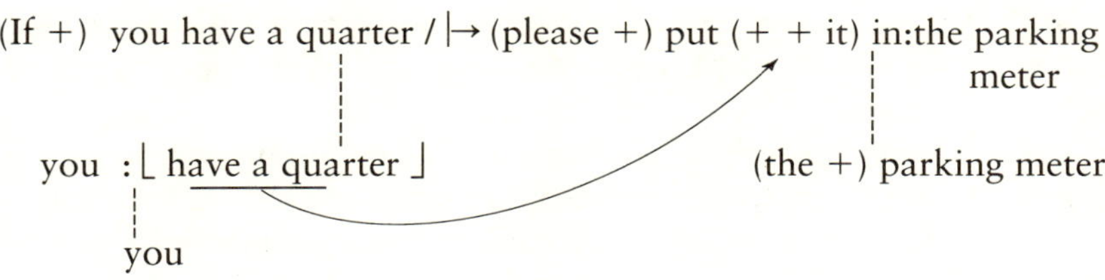

To a "fan" of first-order logic, this directive poses a puzzle. For 'a quarter' will be interpreted quantificationally, and construed as the antecedent of 'it'. The whole directive will be interpreted as having the sense of "For every quarter that you have, put it in the parking meter." But it is obvious to any English speaker that the addressee is not being told to put all his quarters in the meter. The directive is to the effect that if you have a quarter, then put it (i.e., a quarter that you have) in the meter. The "every quarter" reading isn't available at the purely identifying stage. But even for a language user in the representational stage (as all of us are), that would be a bizarre reading. In the directive above, 'it' isn't simply taking the place of 'a quarter'. The directive is not "If you have a quarter, please put a quarter in the parking meter." It is "If you have a quarter, please put a quarter that you have in the meter." The pronoun is "repeating" a phrase adapted from the antecedent of the conditional. The line drawn beneath the phrase 'has a quarter' and attached to the base of the arrow indicates that the whole provisional act serves as antecedent to the pronoun.

Conditional propositional acts also use pronouns repetitively. The sentence 'If Dan meets a pretty girl at the party, he will invite her to the dance' might be used like this:

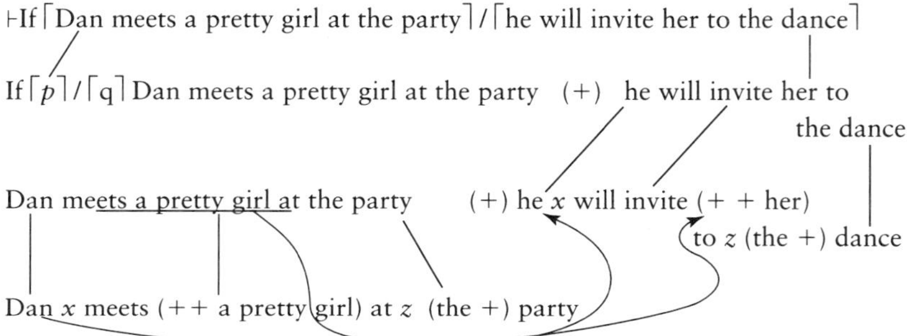

Even if Dan meets several pretty girls, he need invite only one to the dance for the statement to be correct. Dan will invite a pretty girl he meets at the party.

The *reflexive* and the *redirective* uses of pronouns are only possible at the representational stage of language use. When an expression used quantificationally is related to a pronoun in the way a first-order quantified phrase is related to a variable it binds, the pronoun is used *reflexively*. I have chosen this expression because the use is characteristic of reflexive pronouns. But reflexive pronouns are not always used reflexively, and other pronouns can be used this way. The sentence 'Judas killed himself' would normally be used to make a statement in which 'himself' is used reflexively. The basic structure of this statement is:

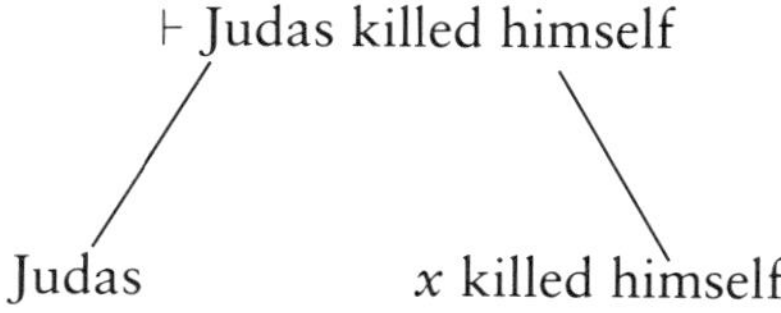

The sentence would not normally be used like this:

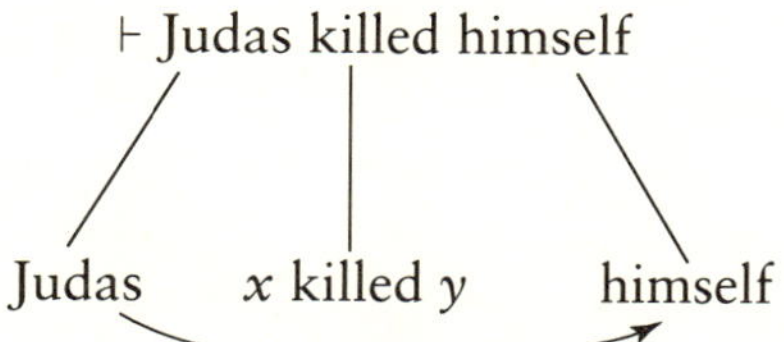

For '____ killed himself' is an intelligible lexical unit. It can be predicated of different males without changing the meaning of the predicative act—the pronoun 'himself' is not used to identify now this man, now that one. The predicate '*x* killed *y*' is used to represent an arbitrary individual *x* (an arbitrary person or animate object) as having killed an arbitrary individual *y*. The reflexive pronoun 'himself' is used to tie together the two empty spaces in the predicative act (and to restrict the predicative act to males), so that the two places can be simultaneously "occupied" by a single expression (a single identifying act). A fuller representation of the statement will be:

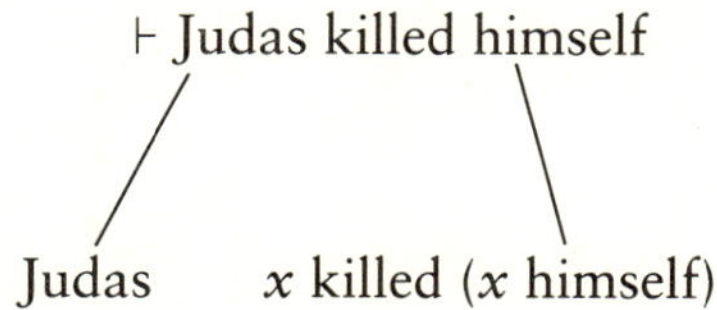

Rather than using '+' to indicate the special character conferred by the reflexive pronoun, the variable '*x*' is put in its place. This indicates that the pronoun 'himself' will be "bound" by whatever expression replaces the initial occurrence of '*x*.' Sometimes I find it helpful to indicate the change brought about by using the reflexive pronoun with a diagram like like this:

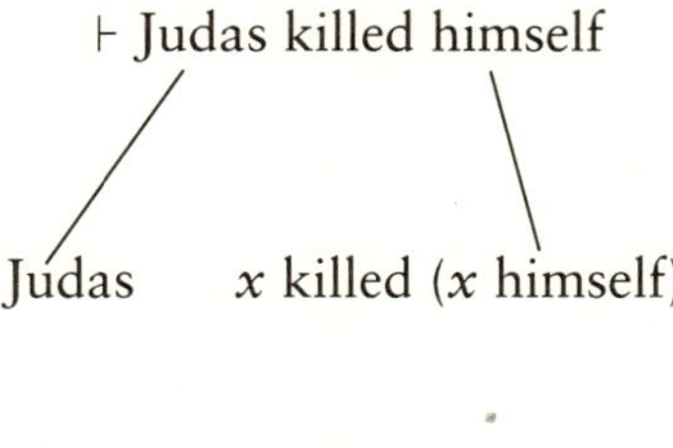

x killed *y*

At the lowest node, the predicative act is represented with distinct variables. When the reflexive pronoun is used to give a special character to the predicative act, the result is a predicative act in which one expression can simultaneously fill two places. In the expanded diagram, there is no line between the lowest node and the node immediately above it. Both nodes represent the same act, once without its special character and once with it. There is no structural relation to be represented.

A pronoun used reflexively doesn't have an antecedent in the same sense that a pronoun used repetitively or redirectively does. For the reflexive pronoun is logically prior to the speech act which "binds" it. (Remember, logical priority is different from temporal priority. Logical priority is indicated by the bottom-to-top organization of the tree-structure diagrams.) A pronoun used reflexively contributes its "significance" to a predicative act before the act which "binds" that pronoun takes effect. A pronoun used reflexively just marks the place that is to count as being filled by a speech act performed in a different "location." Pronouns used reflexively don't demand quantificational acts; the pronouns can be bound either by an identifying act (as above) or by a quantificational act:

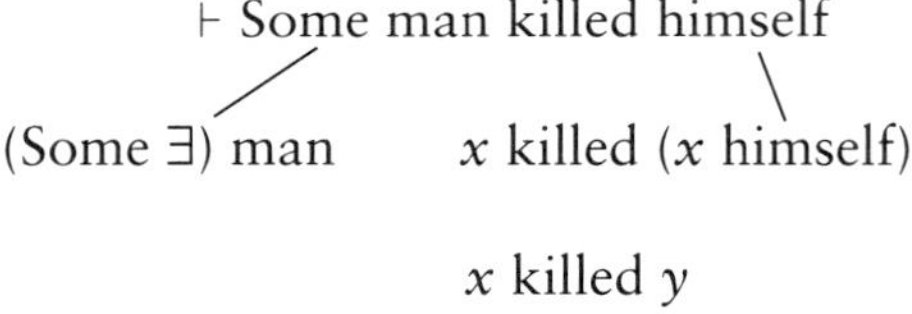

In English, quantificational acts normally occur "inside" statements rather than at the front, as in a first-order language. We say "Bill owns a car" rather than "For some car, Bill owns it." But we *can* say the latter:

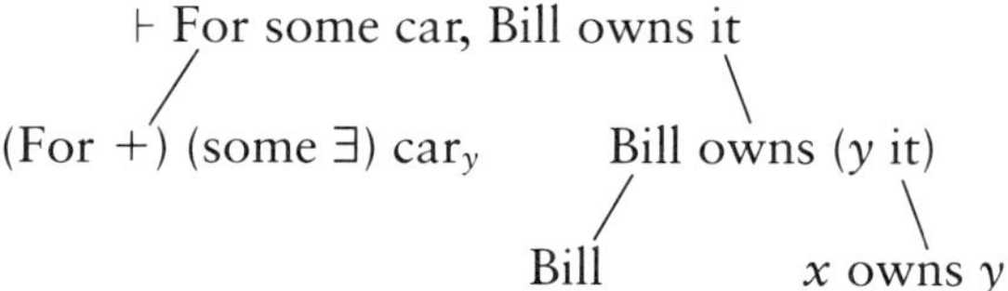

In this statement, the pronoun 'it' is used reflexively, even though the pronoun does not serve to link two argument places in the predicative act performed with '__ owns __.' The pronoun used reflexively marks the place to be "filled" by a quantified phrase occurring elsewhere. The variable '*y*' in parentheses indicates the reflexive character of the pronomial act. The subscript '*y*' attached to the prefixed phrase indicates the position that phrase is intended to fill/cover. The propositional act represents an arbitrary car as owned by Bill. This is different from representing Bill as owning an arbitrary car, for the acts represented above give more prominence to the arbitrary car than to Bill. (The word 'For' gives a special character to the prefix act, highlighting the prominence of the act.)

The reading "For some car" is preferable to the customary reading "There is a car such that." And for a first-order sentence:

$(\exists x)C(x)$

the reading "For some object *x*, *x* is *C*" is preferable to "There is an object *x* such that *x* is *C*." With the preferred reading, the quantificational use of the phrases comes naturally—this is the use where the phrases are used to represent arbitrary objects of a kind. The reading "There is an object *x* such that . . ." expresses the idea of correspondence—of a correspondence between the representing act one performs and objects and situations in the world. Just representing an arbitrary object is simpler and more direct than representing an object and commenting on the representing.

Consider the statement "If a man eats meat, then he is not a vegetarian." In this statement (in the statement that would be made with the displayed sentence), the pronoun is not used repetitively or reflexively. Instead it is used *redirectively*. This pronoun is governed by the phrase 'a man', which is used quantificationally. The whole conditional statement has a general or universal significance: no man who eats meat is a vegetarian. The conditional statement represents one propositional act as conditional on another. The 'if'-clause statement is easy enough to represent:

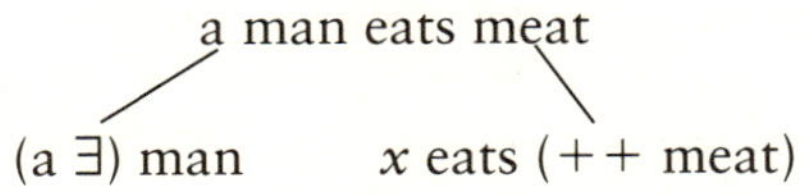

a man eats meat

(a ∃) man *x* eats (++ meat)

The indefinite phrase is used to represent an arbitrary man. The predicate expression is used to represent an arbitrary object (perhaps an arbitrary animate object) as a meat eater. Both component acts are performed in order to represent an arbitrary man as a meat eater. But the consequent propositional act cannot be independently represented. For the pronoun 'he' is not used to perform an independently significant act. This pronoun cannot be replaced by some other expression to obtain an independent and equivalent propositional act.

In performing an act representing one propositional act as conditional on another, it is important that the two component acts be performed and considered "in tandem." With the present example, this is a two-step procedure. The first step combines two representing acts:

a man eats meat (+) ⌜*x* is not a vegetarian⌝

(a ∃) man *x* eats (+ + meat) not ⌜∧*p*⌝ *x* is a vegetarian

The left act represents an arbitrary man as eating meat. The right act is a propositional act, but not a complete propositional act. It represents an arbitrary individual as not being a vegetarian. This act is incomplete because the '*x*' marks a space that needs to be filled in order to satisfy syntactic requirements. (The sentence 'Something is not a vegetarian' can be used to represent an arbitrary individual as not a vegetarian and this propositional act will be complete. It isn't simply the representing of an arbitrary individual that makes the act represented above incomplete.) The incomplete propositional act is one component of the complete act represented here:

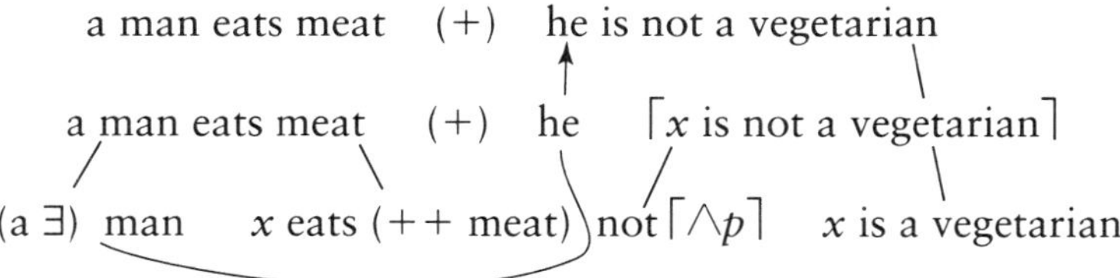

Initially the indefinite phrase 'a man' is used to represent an arbitrary man in order to represent an arbitrary man as a meat eater. This phrase is subsequently *reused* in order to represent that same arbitrary man as not being a vegetarian. Its initial purpose directed the indefinite act to the left propositional act. The pronoun serves to further direct the same indefinite act to the right propositional act. The pronoun serves to *redirect* the indefinite act (but without "disturbing" its original direction). The two propositional acts represent an arbitrary man as, jointly, eating meat and not being a vegetarian. The redirective use of the pronoun is signaled by an arrow from the antecedent, through the pronoun, to the representing act to which the antecedent is being redirected as a component. The arrowhead does not point to the pronoun, but to the act of which the redirected act is a component. (So the antecedent act is a component of both propositional acts.)

The conditional statement establishes a commitment from the left propositional act to the right act:

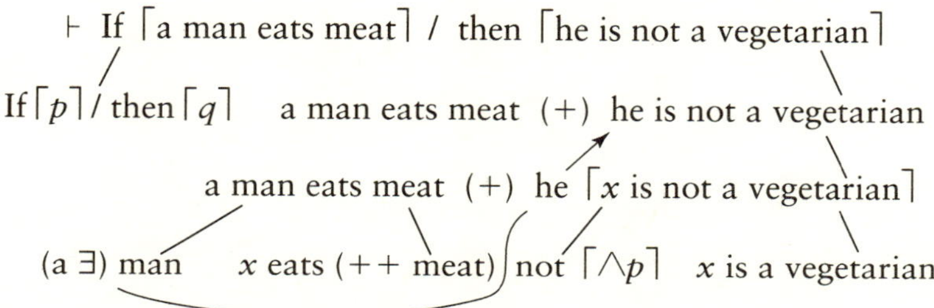

This does not establish an inferential connection between an act of accepting the 'if'-clause propositional act and an act of accepting the consequent act. For while the 'if'-clause act could be accepted, the consequent act cannot—it isn't independently significant. This conditional statement represents a general commitment relation, and establishes a basic entailment from one kind of statement to another kind. Accepting any statement which represents a particular man as eating meat will commit the speaker to accepting a statement representing the same man as not a vegetarian.

A quantified phrase can *bind* a pronoun used reflexively, and *govern* a pronoun used redirectively. We have no special terminology for the relation between its antecedent and a pronoun used repetitively. For a phrase to bind a pronoun used reflexively, the pronoun must be within the scope of the phrase, where scope is understood in terms of speech-act structure. A quantified phrase can govern a pronoun used redirectively, even when the pronoun is outside of the (normal) scope of the phrase.

8. Universally Quantified Phrases

Universally quantified statements are similar to universal collection-statements in establishing/reflecting inferential connections. The sentence ‘Every dog has four legs’ could be used to establish/reflect a basic entailment. The entailment is from identifying a dog to portraying (and accepting this) the dog as having four legs. So from the statement that every dog has four legs and this statement:

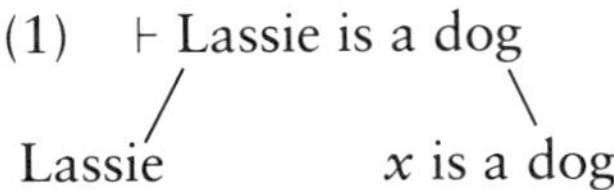

the following could be rationally inferred:

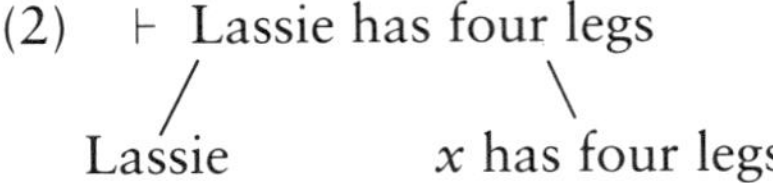

Statement 1 isn’t simply an act of identifying a dog. The statement identifies Lassie and portrays Lassie as a dog, accepting this. The statement is to the effect that in identifying Lassie one has identified a dog. So that the inference principle established by the universal statement has application, and commits the speaker to statement 2.

I will represent a statement made with ‘Every dog has four legs’ like this:

⊢ Every ⌜⌜dog⌝ has four legs⌝

Every ⌜*m*⌝ / ⌜*f(m)*⌝   dog   *x* has four legs

The expression ‘Every’ is used to represent an inference from an arbitrary nominal act to an arbitrary predicative/propositional act as being correct. I will use ‘*m*’ and ‘*n*’ as common-noun variables, and ‘*f*’, ‘*g*’, and ‘*h*’ as predicate variables. Propositional and predicative acts are generally of the same kind, but I use these predicate variables to indicate the incomplete character of a predicative act. The slant line in ‘Every ⌜*m*⌝ / ⌜*f(m)*⌝’ indicates the inferential character of the universal expression. This line is not inserted in the upper node, because an ‘every *m*’ phrase can occur at different places in a sentence, and there is no convenient and uniform way to incorporate slant lines in the sentential expression. The inference principle that is established is from “dog” acts to “dog having four legs” acts, so the upper corners enclose both expressions.

The sentence 'Steve knows every girl in the freshman class' might be used like this:

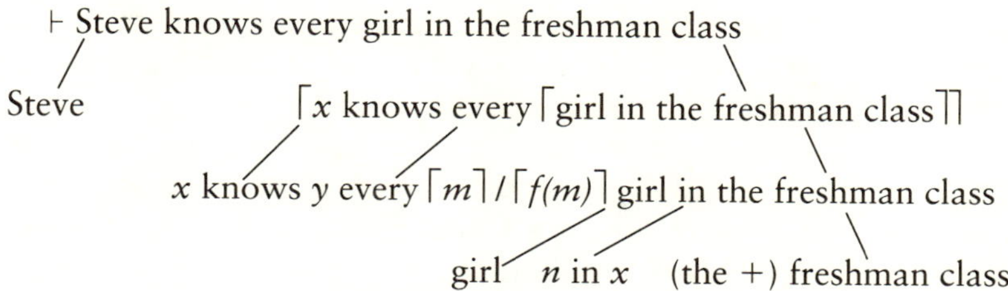

The predicative act ⌈*x* knows every ⌈ girl in the freshman class⌉⌉ represents an arbitrary individual (person) as one for whom the inference from being a girl in the freshman class to being known by that individual is correct.

A complete propositional act formed with 'every' represents a kind of correct inference: an inference from one kind of act to another. It represents an (arbitrary) inference from an arbitrary identifying act to an arbitrary predicative/propositional act. The "Every dog has four legs" statement above represents as correct an inference from an arbitrary dog-identifying act to an arbitrary act of accepting a has-four-legs propositional act for the identified dog. These inference-principle statements are not "about" the expressions used. Any dog-identifying act that is known to be such commits the speaker (who has established the inferential connection) to a has-four-legs act. And if there are other expressions than 'dog' for picking out dogs, the inference principle "covers" them as well. For it isn't that 'dog' acts lead to 'has four legs' acts. It is dog-identifying acts that lead to acts of portraying-and-accepting the dog as having four legs.

Both conditional and universal statements are inference-principle statements. But there is an important difference between the two. Conditional statements have a propositional 'if'-clause act and a propositional consequent act. They authorize (and represent) inferences from one kind of propositional act to another. Universal statements don't connect two propositional items. They connect a nominal to a propositional act. This feature of universal statements accounts for the existential presumption of most universal statements. In a statement made with 'If someone jumps off the roof of this building, she will be killed', there is no indication that the speaker thinks someone *will* jump. But with 'Every person who jumps off the roof of this building will be killed', there is at least a strong suggestion that someone will jump. A person can represent a kind of propositional act without expecting that someone will perform and accept an act of that kind. It (normally) seems pointless to represent a kind of identifying act unless one thinks there are/will be acts of that kind.

The universal quantifier 'every' can be attached to a complex noun phrase containing indefinite phrases which govern pronouns in the predicative act to which the quantified phrase is attached. For example, in the statement one would make with 'Every man who knows a ballerina admires her'. This statement will authorize inferences from identifying a ballerina and identifying a man who knows her to portraying-and-accepting the man as admiring the ballerina. In combining the 'every' act with the nominal and predicative acts, there is a kind of "delay" involved. The act performed with 'man who knows a ballerina' is combined with the act performed with '*x* knows *y*', and the indefinite phrase is then used to govern a redirective pronoun. The overall statement is like this:

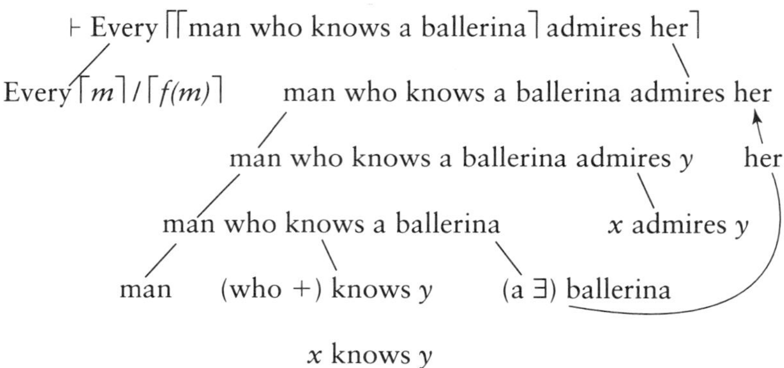

The word 'man' is used to represent an arbitrary man, in order to represent an arbitrary man with the feature of knowing an arbitrary ballerina. And this act is performed in order to represent an arbitrary man who knows a ballerina as admiring an arbitrary individual. Which is done in order to represent an arbitrary man who knows an arbitrary ballerina as admiring that ballerina. The last predicative act is one of two (immediate) inputs to the complete propositional act. In combining the predicative act with the universal quantifier act, the nominal component of the predicative act is distinguished from the completed predicative act, to represent an inference from the one to the other.

Although modern logic is concerned with representational-stage statements, it tells less than the whole story about these statements. In many cases, standard logical languages fail to adequately represent the semantic structures of natural-language statements. Logical-language sentences often represent statements which are imperfect approximations to natural-language statements. And the logical theories fail to accommodate basic entailment in addition to truth-conditional entailment. One result of this is an inadequate appreciation of the significance of various completeness and incompleteness results. However, I will save the further discussion of these topics for another occasion. This book is already long enough.

9. Some Paradoxes

Understanding the difference between the purely identifying and the representational stages of language use, and situating discussions in a speech-act framework provides the resources to resolve some problems posed by self-referential statements. We will consider the simple Liar Paradox first, and begin by looking at statements which can be made at the purely identifying stage. These are statements where the speaker acknowledges the very statement she is making to be false. Self-referential statements are not out of the question. A speaker can certainly focus on what she is presently doing, and acknowledge this to be something which it is. She can acknowledge herself to be thinking or writing or dancing. She can acknowledge her present statement to be in English, and deny her present statement to be in French.

So what about acknowledging her present statement, the very speech act/activity she is performing, to be false? She can't do it. Acknowledging is always sincere, and the speaker must be aware of what she intends to be saying. At the purely identifying stage, a speaker can't suppose that something is so, and by considering the propositional act without endorsing it, be drawn into endorsing it. If she performs the propositional act at all, she is acknowledging that very acknowledging act to fail in its attempt to be an identifying act. She can't sincerely, and seriously, and knowingly do this. Perhaps St. Paul was only aware of the purely identifying use of language, which would explain why he missed Epimenides' point. (Alan Anderson comments on St. Paul's obtuseness in his introduction to Martin 1970.)

Consider a somewhat more complicated version of the Liar. Jim says, "The next statement Doris makes will be true." Before Jim can get in another word, Doris says "The last statement Jim made was false." They don't make the statements in each other's presence, because Jim's statement would be unmotivated, while Doris couldn't knowingly acknowledge Jim's statement to be false. But suppose Jim admires and respects Doris, and has great confidence in both her truthfulness and her accuracy. Jim's comment is made to Richard when Doris is not present. Jim actually says, "Doris is truthful and accurate. She never gets things wrong. Why I am absolutely confident that the next statement she makes will be true." Doris, who has a low opinion of Jim, makes very different remarks to Margaret. "Jim is such a stupid dishonest man. He never speaks the truth." She pauses, then immediately after Jim makes his remark, says, "I'm sure the very last thing he said was false." In this scenario, both speakers have performed genuine acknowledging acts. What can we say about the truth or falsity of their acts?

The interrelatedness of the two statements keeps either one from being true. Each speaker is trying to identify a situation that would exist only if his/her acknowledging act failed to identify a situation. The acts can't succeed by failing. They simply fail. It doesn't make any difference whether we describe their acts as false, or simply settle for *untrue*. We can (we *could*, if our story were true) correctly acknowledge their acts to be false, or untrue, because their acts, and their failure, are objective features of the world. We can exploit connections to the failed acts, and the situation of their failing, in ways that the speakers, at the times of their statements, cannot.

10. Truth Conditions

Before discussing paradoxical acts at the representational stage, we must devote some attention to the truth conditions of statements and propositional acts. A simple acknowledging act is true if it identifies a situation. But the denials, disjunctive acknowledging acts, and inference-principle acknowledging acts made at the purely identifying stage are not intended to be identifying acts. In denying Seattle to be in Oregon:

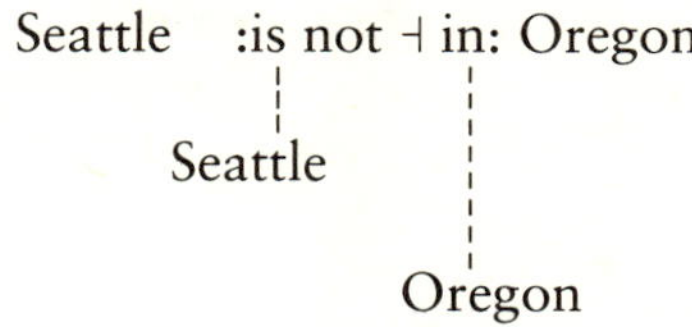

the speaker rejects using 'in Oregon' to perform an acknowledging act for Seattle. She is not identifying Seattle's being in Washington. Her acknowledging act is true if it isn't possible to correctly acknowledge Seattle to be in Oregon. Her statement can be true even if it doesn't register this modal feature. She could register it by trying to apply the "is in Oregon" test to Seattle, and failing decisively. (She might look up information in an encyclopedia, or use a map, or travel through Oregon and Washington. She could take someone's word for it, if they registered the modal feature.) Her denial is true if it is possible (in principle) to register the modal feature which answers to that denial.

With propositional representing/portraying acts, correspondence rather than identifying is the key to truth. However, correspondence is not a relation that either obtains or not, independently of anything we do. Correspondence must be established. But the word 'establish' can suggest proof or justification. In the present context, these suggestions are misleading. Someone might establish a correspondence between a simple propositional act, like this:

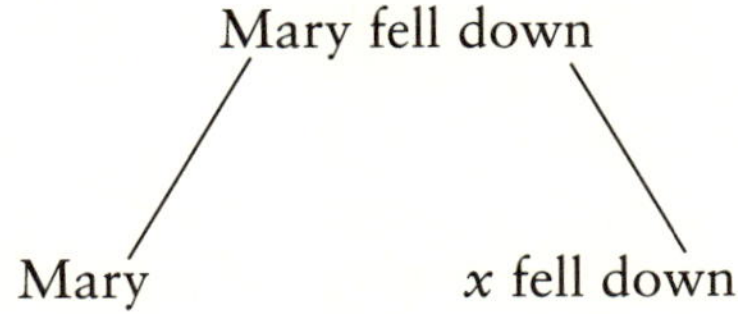

and the situation of Mary's falling down on a particular occasion, by identifying that situation. (But this identification may essentially rely on someone else's testimony.)

A propositional representing act is true if it is *possible* to establish a correspondence between that act and the world. It must be possible to correctly establish a correspondence, and this correspondence must "respect" any identifying acts which are elements of the propositional representing act. (So we can't correctly make the propositional act portraying Mary as falling down correspond to Chicago's being in

Illinois.) Someone who correctly establishes a correspondence between a propositional act and the world has *verified* the propositional act. A propositional act will be false if it isn't possible to verify it.

If someone portrays a propositional act *A* as false:

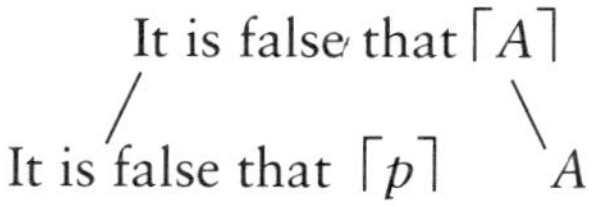

```
            It is false that ⌜A⌝
              /              \
It is false that ⌜p⌝           A
```

the propositional act is actually present to the speaker (an instance of the *A*-kind of propositional act is present). Suppose *A is* false. Then its being impossible to verify *A* is a modal feature of the world. To register this modal feature, the speaker can do something which reveals the act *A* to be unverifiable. She establishes a "correspondence" between the negative propositional act and the world by registering the modal feature. One can similarly establish a correspondence to verify a disjunctive propositional act or a quantificational propositional act.

A true propositional act portraying objects $\alpha_1, \ldots, \alpha_n$ as ϕ might correspond to a single situation linking the objects to one another. But the act might also correspond to a situation containing more than *n* objects, or to a complex of situations such that not all the objects are ingredients of any one simple situation. Semantic structure won't reveal everything there is in the situations that are represented/portrayed. However, it is the propositional acts, including incomplete predicative acts, for which correspondences to the world are established. These correspondences ultimately fasten on situations and complex situations, not on sets or collections of objects and *n*-tuples.

The possibility and impossibility relevant to truth conditions for representing acts are *relative metaphysical possibility* and *impossibility* (and *necessity*). As we conceive the world and its development in time, the present and past are completely fixed or determined. With respect to the future, some things are determined and some things are open. At a given moment, there are various alternative next moments. For each of these, there are further alternative next moments. And so on. What is now determined is now relatively metaphysically necessary. As time passes, more and more things become determined, but new alternative possibilities keep opening up.

What is determined is also possible, but the contingent possibilities, the open possibilities, are not now determined; however, some currently contingent possibilities will become determined, and others will become impossible. (And some present open possibilities will continue to be open in the future.) There are some objectors to our customary understanding of relative metaphysical possibility and necessity. A determinist does not believe there are open possibilities. For him, whatever is possible is also determined (and conversely). The determinist has greatly simplified the ordinary conception. In the opposite direction, there is a way of interpreting some puzzling features of quantum physics, so that it isn't correct that the past and present are completely determined. On this understanding, the world at present contains some indefinite or determinable features that don't concern the future—an object can presently be *A* or *B* without being either, say. It isn't clear to me whether this understanding makes sense, or how it might be consistently developed. And there is no plausibility to determinism. So I will at present stick with the ordinary conception of relative metaphysical possibility and necessity.

To say that it is possible to establish a correspondence between some propositional act and the world is to say that the way the world is now determines that saying certain things will be true and others false. It is (in principle) possible to now (and in the future) establish a correspondence between certain propositional acts and the world; it is now and will continue in the future to be impossible to establish a correspondence between other propositional acts and the world. But this makes trouble for some propositional acts concerning the future. It is Aristotle's Sea Battle dilemma. So long as our propositional acts concern the present and past, they will be true or false. For a claim about an already determined future event, a correspondence can (in principle) presently be established or else a correspondence is and will be impossible. But if it isn't now determined that a sea battle will occur next week, and this isn't precluded either, then it isn't possible to now establish a correspondence. It is now possible that a correspondence can be established in the future, but this is no sign that the sea battle prediction is true. For it is also now possible that a correspondence will later on become impossible to establish.

We might choose to use 'true' so that the Sea Battle propositional act isn't now true or false, though in the future such a propositional act will be one or the other. But this decision would put us at odds with ordinary usage, and nothing is lost by staying with ordinary usage. So we will say that a propositional representing act is true if either it is now (permanently) possible to establish a correspondence between that act and the world or it will in the future become (permanently) possible to establish such a correspondence. A propositional representing act is false if it is now (permanently) impossible to establish a correspondence or in the future it will become permanently impossible to do so. The Sea Battle prediction is already true or false, though we aren't now in a position to verify the prediction or its negation.

11. The Paradoxes Again

At the representational stage, we can perform propositional acts which aren't at the same time accepted. We can perform the following, for example:

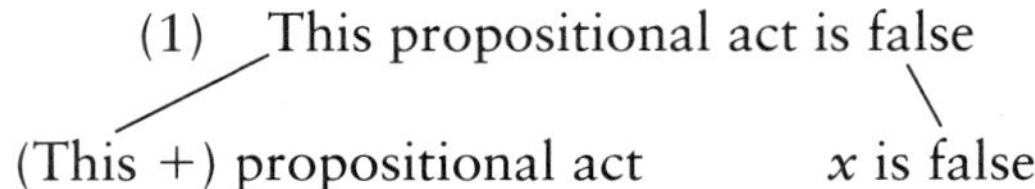

For the present, we shall consider propositional acts of particular people, performed at particular times and places. So I have performed one propositional act in producing the sentence (and diagram) above, and each reader performs a distinct act when she reads the sentence. Each of these propositional acts which has the structure I have indicated will portray itself as false. Upon considering such acts, we realize that none of them can be verified. For if any such act were true, it would also be false. Any attempted verification must fail.

So propositional act 1 is false. Suppose we represent the act just performed like this:

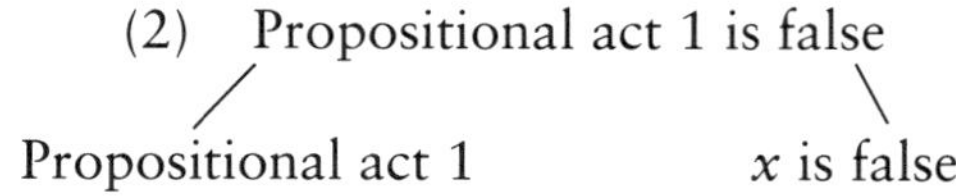

Since it is in fact impossible to verify (1), and we can determine this to be the case, propositional act 2 is true. Indeed, we have verified propositional act 2. (Each of us has verified her own propositional act 2.) But propositional acts 1 and 2 portray the same object as having the same property; how can one act be true and the other false? The answer to this isn't complicated. In performing propositional act 1, each of us creates a new object having the modal character of being impossible to verify. This provides a target for propositional act 2. Propositional act 2 "stands" apart from (1), but it isn't in a different language.

The truth of propositional act 2 doesn't "carry back" to (1). We can't perform (1) over again. If we use the same words to perform an act with the same structure, we will obtain propositional act 3, which will be a new impossible-to-verify propositional act. That propositional act 1 is impossible to verify is the permanent status of propositional act 1. We can't verify the act by failing conclusively to verify it, we can only verify a subsequent claim that it is unverifiable.

Things are somewhat more complicated if we consider propositional-act types rather than actual propositional acts. Suppose we consider (and perform) the following propositional act, propositional act (*a*):

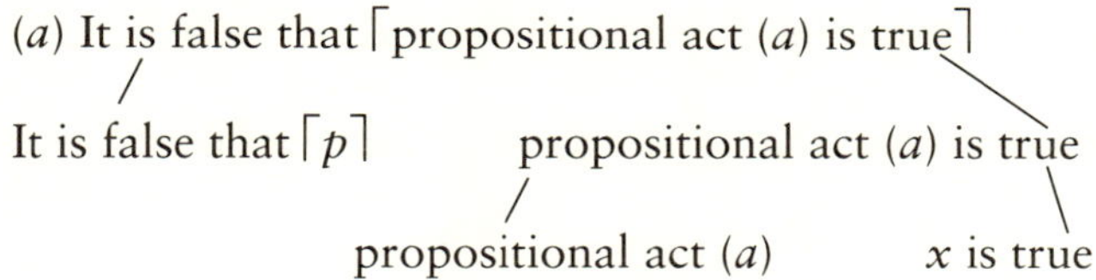

Propositional-act types are repeatable (we can perform more than one propositional act of the same type), so we can consider a deduction made with such acts. We will begin by supposing a propositional act. Suppositions are a kind of illocutionary act. If we begin with a supposition, and infer a further propositional act, that act may also have the force of a supposition. But when certain suppositions lead to others, we can sometimes infer an assertion.

To begin with, suppose that propositional act (*a*) is true. Then it is false that propositional act (*a*) is true. (We have inferred the further supposition that it is false that propositional act (*a*) is true.) Since we have just inferred (and performed) propositional act (*a*) with the force of a supposition, we can infer that propositional act (*a*) is true. Again our conclusion has the force of a supposition. We can clearly continue this deduction cycle indefinitely.

We can understand that propositional act (*a*) can't be verified. It is false. But how can we say this without committing ourselves to accepting propositional act (*a*)? In making the claim

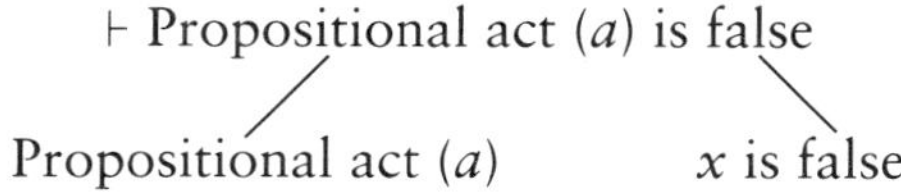

we haven't performed propositional act (*a*). We have performed a different, true, propositional act. Accepting this true act doesn't commit us to accepting a false one. However, it is even possible to use the sentence 'It is false that propositional act (*a*) is true' to make a true claim. For in identifying an object, we exploit a connection linking us to the object we intend. No matter what expression we use, we can intend the propositional act (*a*) other than the very act we are performing. We can say "It is false that propositional act (*a*) is true" and mean *the propositional act (a)* performed with other sentences *(other sentence tokens) than this one.*

However, act types are not genuine objects. To say that a propositional-act type is false is to say that acts of that type are all false. Let us consider a more perspicuously formulated propositional act:

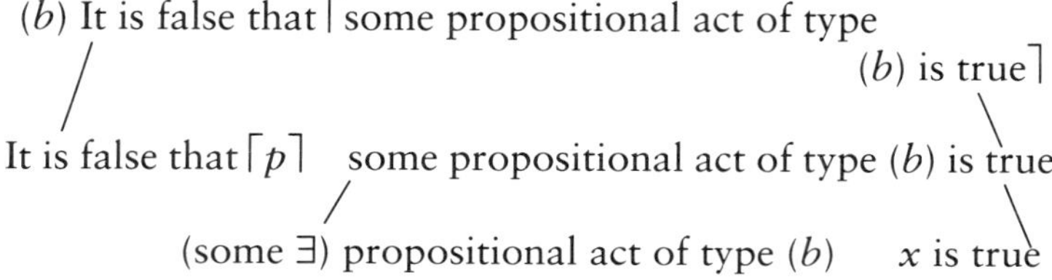

Suppose that some propositional act of type (*b*) is true. In that case, we can infer the consequences of an arbitrary such act's being true. Which means that we can perform a type (*b*) act (an actual, particular type (*b*) act) and treat this as representative of an arbitrary type (*b*) act. (Much as we can draw a particular triangle and use it as a representative triangle.) So it is false that some propositional act of type (*b*) is true. But then the (immediately) preceding act is false. Which means it isn't false that some propositional act of type (*b*) is true. And so on, and on.

We can see that the initial supposition, and its type (*b*) consequence are false. All instances of the initial supposition are false, and all type (*b*) propositional acts are false. A type (*b*) propositional act portrays a different propositional act as false, and that different act *is* false. But the type (*b*) act can't be verified, so it is false as well. We can attend to a particular propositional act of this sort:

Some propositional act of type (*b*) is true.

/ \

(Some ∃) propositional act of type (*b*) *x* is true

and acknowledge it to be false without performing a type (*b*) act. We can portray such a propositional act as false by means of propositional acts which aren't type (*b*) acts, and safely accept these portrayals. Making a "safe" statement to the effect that the propositional act represented by the diagram above isn't true doesn't commit us to making a type (*b*) statement. It is certainly possible (and, I think, common) to accept incoherent commitments. But we needn't accept incoherent commitments in the present case. We can recognize that a propositional act can't be verified without performing such an act ourselves.

The various "paradoxical" propositional acts are false, but certain attempts to say that they are false won't work, by virtue of being paradoxical themselves. And some propositional acts which portray paradoxical propositional acts as false are false themselves. The paradoxical propositional acts and statements aren't destructive of our ordinary conceptual frameworks, and admitting them as significant elements of the very language we are speaking doesn't commit us to accepting incompatible propositional acts. But the paradoxical statements and propositional acts do impair our ability to formally characterize logically true propositional acts and logically valid inferences. For example, if we suppose a propositional act *A*, and correctly infer a negation of *A*, we can be confident that *A* is false. But some attempts to characterize *A* as false may themselves be false. In the example considered earlier, we infer "It is false that statement (*a*) is true" from "Statement (*a*) is true." By what (once) seemed an unexceptionable inference principle *negation introduction*, one would infer, as an assertion, "It is false that statement (*a*) is true." So that inference principle leads us astray when applied to the case at hand.

Similarly, the law of excluded middle is true, it we understand this to be the claim that every significant propositional act is either true or false. But if we take the law of excluded middle to claim that every significant propositional act or its formally characterized negation is true, then paradoxical propositional acts will provide us with exceptions. The paradoxical statements/acts defeat certain formal characterizations of logically true statements and logically valid inferences. But it is the formal principles which must "give" in these cases. The formal principles characterize logically true statements and logically valid arguments in terms of certain kinds of verbal formulations, and are not the source of truth or validity.

However, formal principles are necessary for the systematic codification of necessary truths and correct inferences. Since codification is one of the main goals of logic, as well as an important source of genuine understanding, it is no wonder that logicians limit their attention to domains of statements/propositional acts which either don't contain paradoxical propositional acts at all, or which contain some device for isolating paradoxical propositional acts so that they don't affect or infect the nonparadoxical acts. These paradoxical items are not illicit in themselves, but they impede the logician's pursuit of his own (appropriate) goals. And the paradoxical propositional acts are not of great theoretical interest. They have the character of aberrations or amusements, without playing an important role in our linguistic practice.

It is essential to the present treatment of paradoxes of self-reference that we understand these to concern actual speech acts. Propositional acts, like people, occur in space and time. The truth of a statement or a propositional act depends on what some person does or could do; it is not a timeless feature of a timeless abstract entity. A theorist who conceives linguistic items to express abstract, impersonal concepts and propositions, which exist with their various features in some kind of splendid isolation, cannot find my treatment of the paradoxes acceptable. For such a theorist, a paradoxical proposition isn't an item which comes into existence at a given time and in so doing creates a new situation to talk about. From the abstract proposition point of view, if a paradoxical proposition were legitimate in any sense, this proposition would have eternally been numbered among the significant propositions. The paradoxical proposition would be "on all fours" with other propositions which denied the paradoxical proposition to be true. And this would explode the eternal class of significant propositions. From the abstract-proposition perspective, the paradoxical propositions must be declared illicit. They violate some essential requirement of significant propositions. In spite of the fact that we understand them perfectly well.

Chapter 11

Representing:
Transcending Identifying-Stage Limitations

1. Propositional Experience

In this chapter, we will continue to explore the new possibilities for experience and thought that are opened up at the representational stage of language use. This will enable us to understand how Descartes' Problem comes to our attention, and how we can solve it. In addition, our exploration will touch on several more-or-less independent issues, including the nature of mathematical objects.

Learning to use language to identify objects in the world of experience, to acknowledge them to be this or that, and, finally, to represent/portray them as this or that changes the character of experience. A person comes to have *propositional experience.* Other philosophers have spoken of propositional experience. A person doesn't just see, she sees *that.* But the philosophers who speak of propositional experience have not been able to explain in detail what it is to have such experience. I shall here endeavor to provide such an account.

Upon learning to use language, the child can attend to a portion of his experience, and acknowledge that portion to be blue, or green, or a cat. He can identify a particular object like his mother, and acknowledge her to be sitting down, or smiling, or whatever. To begin with, the language learner will say or think words in the presence of the appropriate objects. But as he gains proficiency in using language, he will be able to see things to be familiar objects, and to see things to be of this or that kind without producing any words.

He can recognize that part of the world of his experience to be Mama without a word. He can wordlessly see the door to be open or the lights to be on. I will use the expression 'take to be' to label what amount to nonverbal acknowledging acts. The child takes that object to be his mother. He takes the door to be open and the lights to be on. The preverbal child can see his mother without employing or possessing concepts. It requires concepts to see that person to be his mother, to take her to be his mother.

To perform a verbal identifying act, one produces a word and uses the word to attend to an object by exploiting connections one knows about. To perform a verbal acknowledging act, one is attending to an object or objects and applies an expression to the object(s), employing criteria associated with the expression. The verbal acknowledger succeeds in applying the criteria to the object, registering his success by saying/thinking the expression. The connection between the expression used and the criteria employed is arbitrary, conventional. The same criteria might have been associated with a different expression; in the future they may actually come to be associated with a different expression. The proficient language user is able to hold the expression apart from the criteria; he can apply the criteria without saying the word. But he will be disposed, and committed, to produce the expression should the occasion arise.

In experience, a person doesn't need to use words to notice or attend to an object or a part of the world. Noticing an object activates the person's linguistic skills and dispositions. Although she is aware of the objects she notices, and will be acting intentionally when she notices them, this noticing will not normally be an enabling act/activity. For while noticing does enable further acts, an enabling act is one whose agent intends for it to be enabling. A person *can* scrutinize an object to determine what it is; her scrutiny is intended to make recognition possible. But most of the time, things catch our attention, we simply fasten on them without intending to make some further activity possible. In any case, noticing an object does make it possible to apply various criteria to the object. We see the object to be brown, shaggy, a dog. We are prepared to produce the words if someone asks us, but usually no one does. We merely take the object to be brown, shaggy, and a dog.

Propositional acts performed with expressions, even propositional acts performed at the purely identifying stage, can be quite complicated. For example, the sentence 'Diana is playing tennis with Kathy' might be used like this:

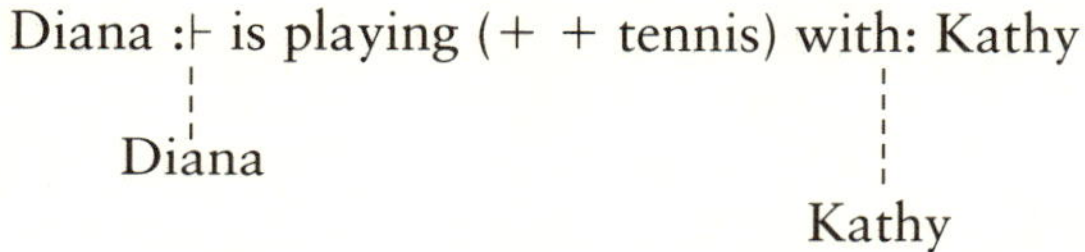

Propositional acts of taking to be don't have elaborate structures. They need not be "supported" by enabling acts. And they won't have component acts performed to give special characters to other components. Someone might see Diana and take her to be playing tennis without noticing who her opponent is. But if he attends to both Diana and Kathy, taking Diana to be Diana and Kathy to be Kathy, he will simply take the two of them to be playing each other. He won't use one as a reference point and make the other his focus. And he won't perform a determinable act of taking them to be playing, and determine this with a further tennis-specifying act, he will simply apply his tennis-playing criteria to what they are doing. (Someone who was unfamiliar with tennis could see the two women and take them to be playing a game without taking them to be playing tennis.)

And a person will customarily perform many acts of taking to be at the same time. Both a picture and an experience are worth a thousand words. A speech act necessarily has a temporal order, which allows different components and different enabling acts to make different contributions to a complex act or statement. But a person can perceive different objects and situations at once. Acts of taking to be don't have the temporal structures of speech acts, though, of course, a person has successive experiences and takes them to be successive. Acts of taking to be are much easier to perform than speech acts, since the energy and effort required to produce words are not expended.

One must actively employ criteria in taking things to be one way or another. We aren't simply presented with experience, and passive before it. We work over experience to provide conceptual, propositional structure. But merely applying criteria is much easier than applying criteria and producing words. We can at once perform several acts of taking to be, though we can only say one thing at a time.

Language users have propositional experience, but not all their experience is propositional. For propositional experience occurs against a background of other experience. We surely see and hear and feel more things than we notice or attend to. It is the things we attend to that we take to be this color or that shape or a dog running toward us. I can see a person without noticing the clothes they are wearing or the color of their eyes. When I think of friends and acquaintances who are not present, I often have a difficult time saying which of them wear glasses and which don't. I don't attend to every feature of the objects I attend to. And those objects I attend to are surrounded by objects and situations that I experience without noticing. I can bring my attention to bear on these objects, and so experience them propositionally. But many objects come into and pass out of experience without being taken to be anything.

It may seem odd to describe any kind of experience as intentional. For experience, including propositional experience, is usually involuntary. Experience doesn't result from deliberation and choice; the most we can do is choose to put ourselves in position to have one kind of experience rather than another. We can't help experiencing the things that come before our eyes and ears. We can't even refrain from having propositional experience. Once we have the relevant concepts, we must experience an object we notice to have some of its apparent features. We can't help seeing what kind of object is before us. Once we have learned to have propositional experience, our having it is habitual, and inescapable. Similarly, we can't help understanding what someone says to us in our own language. Most of us can't help reading expressions before our eyes. (But dyslexic persons often have difficulty reading, and will run their eyes over written expressions without using these expressions to perform linguistic acts.)

Voluntary and deliberate acts are intentional, but the converse isn't (always) the case. Habitual, involuntary acts can be intentional, if they are purposive acts one is aware of performing and intends to be performing, acts which owe their essential character to the agent's conception of what she is doing. The general goal to be achieved by propositional experience is making sense of the world, including ourselves. We have a fundamental need to make sense of things, and the imposition of conceptual, propositional structure contributes to satisfying this need. We are certainly aware of the objects we notice, and we are aware of noticing them. We intend to attend to these objects. And we employ and apply concepts when we take objects to be this or that. So our awareness of seeing an object to be of a kind is awareness of employing the concept of that kind, but we don't usually realize this. We can be aware of seeing the animal to be dog without knowing that we are employing the concept of a dog.

We don't simply find conceptual structure in experience, and somehow pull it out. Nor do we bring concepts to experience, and find them fitting an independently given world of objects. Instead we introduce conceptual structure to experience, and we modify this structure (these structures) over time to make ever better sense of things. Once the world of experience has been conceptually organized, this world can seem to be an independent domain which simply yields its forms to our attentive gaze. For propositional experience doesn't require us to use words, either out loud or in our heads. When we perceive things to be this and that, but without saying so, we can easily think we are finding how things are apart from any activity on our part. However, we are acting when we perceive things propositionally. Our very experience is judgmental; there is no gap to be bridged between experience and knowledge/belief. Seeing really is believing.

To better appreciate the intentional, propositional character of the experience of taking things to be one thing or another, it will be helpful to develop notation for representing acts of taking to be. If Jane takes the object before her to be a dog, I will represent Jane's act like this:

(*that*) ⊢ (*is a dog*)

The italicized expression in parentheses aren't used by Jane. *We* are using them to represent Jane's acts. The word '*that*' in parentheses represents Jane's attending to the object before her. The assertion sign signifies that Jane's act is a taking-to-be. And '*is a dog*' in parentheses represents her act of taking the object to be a dog.

2. Perceiving Representative Objects and Their Features

People at the representational stage of language use continue to take objects to be this or that. They do this without reflecting on what it is to be this or that. But at the representational stage, it becomes possible to perceive *that* something is the case. When she uses a predicative expression to represent an arbitrary object as having a certain property, the language user interprets the predicate and its associated intentional features. In propositional perception, there is no interpretation. Rather than using 'x is scarlet' to become representationally aware of an arbitrary object as scarlet, the perceiver is aware of an actual jacket as scarlet. When someone is representationally aware of an arbitrary object as having a property, she focusses on the property rather than the object. In perceiving an actual object as having a property, a person also focuses on the property at the expense of the object. She perceives the jacket as a representative scarlet object, as an instance of something scarlet. The propositional perception is different from the preconceptual perception organized by percepts. Someone preconceptually perceives an object as representative—as one of those things. But she does not distinctly attend to both the object and its feature.

Our conception of properties and relations derives from the representational use of language. At the purely identifying stage, a person identifies objects of various kinds, including situations. She is aware of objects with features, and uses the features in applying acknowledging criteria. But she can't conceive of objects and their features as distinct "components" of the "total" objects. Properties and relations are not a new or extraordinary kind of object which ordinary objects own or possess. In talking as if they were objects—abstract objects which ordinary objects exemplify, in which ordinary objects participate—we are attempting to accommodate properties and relations in an identifying-stage conception. However, they don't fit. A property is how an object is (can be) characterized. Being red is how the ball is, colorwise. A relation is how objects are with respect to one another; it isn't a further object through which they are linked. As Frege understood somewhat dimly, representational predicative acts reveal the characters of properties and relations. For properties and relations are "created" by predicative representing acts, to be counterparts of the acts. Frege didn't understand that these acts also provide representational awareness of objects, albeit arbitrary ones. But we can't adequately conceive or represent features apart from featured objects. It is our representing arbitrary objects as this or that which makes clear that properties and relations can be shared; an arbitrary object can be any object.

At the purely identifying stage, in the conceptually-structured world of experience, objects are one thing or another. One or more objects having a certain feature(s) constitute a situation. A successful acknowledging act might identify a single situation. But there isn't a single situation for every correct acknowledging acts. Some such acts identify complex situations, or complexes of situations, although the agent need not know the complex details. We can't simply "read off" the make-up of the world from our true statements. But there *is* a property or relation for each open predicative act. Properties and relations weren't in the world of experience from the beginning. The representational use of language gives us our conception of properties and relations, and introduces this conceptual structure into our world. These features don't all "generate" situations, though some of them do structure single situations.

Learning to use language to represent gives us our conception of properties and relations, and allows us to perceive that things are propertied and related. When someone conceptually perceives an object as representative—when she perceives that the object is whatever, she perceives it as a sample of objects of that kind. A sample isn't just one of many objects of the same kind. It is an object one uses to understand what it is to be of that kind. Representative perception is probably important to aesthetic appreciation, both of nature and of works of art. And representative perception figures in certain mathematical proofs. Someone regards a representative object as an arbitrary object of a kind, and "manipulates" it to discover features that must characterize all objects of the kind. By investigating one triangle, we learn about triangles in general.

Acts of taking to be are represented by placing an assertion sign '⊢' before an italicized predicate expression in parentheses, and after an italicized expression which labels the target of the act of taking to be:

(*That*) ⊢ (*is a triangle*)

This representation has some analogy to our representation of acknowledging acts. To represent an act of perceiving that something is the case, I will use an assertion sign to the left of both the labelling expression and the predicate expression:

⊢ (*That*)(*is a triangle*)

One both attends to the particular object and to the object as representative; these are two "moments" of a single act.

When someone perceives an object, and takes the object to be ϕ, the perception is direct. If the taking-to-be is correct, she perceives the situation of the object being ϕ. The criteria for being ϕ may be in some sense inferential. Perhaps for an object to be (correctly) acknowledged/taken to be ϕ, it must first be acknowledged/taken to be both ψ and Θ. Even so, one simply perceives objects to be ϕ. Representational-stage propositional perception isn't inferential either. A person can directly see that the grass is green or the apple is ripe. However, if the apple turns out not to be ripe after all, she only thought she saw that it was ripe. There is no convenient locution for propositional perceptions that may or may not be correct. When she thought she saw that the apple was ripe, she did see the apple as a representative ripe fruit, but she was mistaken in doing so. She may have correctly seen that the apple was dark red, which is ordinarily a reliable sign of being ripe. But she need not have *inferred* the ripeness from the color. She simply saw the apple that way.

All propositional perception is direct. A judgement can be based on—inferred from—propositional perceptions, but the inferred judgment is not a perception. However, what one person infers, another may simply perceive. Seeing that the corn is withered, Morgan may infer that the corn has received insufficient moisture. Roger may just see the corn as representative of corn which has received insufficient moisture.

3. Weights and Measures

The conceptual structure we introduce organizes the world of experience. But given this conceptual structure, we simply find certain things to be the case. The objects of various kinds, and the situations into which they are organized are objective features of the world of experience. Some true acknowledging statements identify situations in the world. Others, like negative and universal statements, have modal truth conditions. The truth of such statements depends on the world of experience possessing certain modal features. A true acknowledging act which is "properly" carried out will register these features. The truth of propositional representing acts depends on correspondence. In the simplest case, a propositional representing act is true if a (suitable) correspondence can be established between that act and a situation in the world. For other propositional representing acts, the correspondence will link propositional acts to modal features that get registered.

But these remarks do not accommodate comparison judgments. A comparison judgment acknowledging one object to be taller than another, or similar in color to another, or older than another, does not attempt to identify an independent situation. In comparing two objects, one of them can be used as a standard for assessing the other. The sentence 'Sheila is taller than Dan' might be used like this:

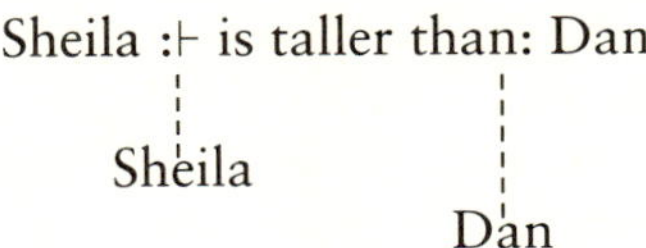

This diagram has the same shape as one which represents a statement acknowledging Sheila to be next to Dan. But in the 'next to'–statement, Dan would be identified as a reference point. In the 'taller than'–comparison judgment, Dan is identified as a standard for assessing Sheila's height. The same sentence could be used to make a statement in which the roles are reversed:

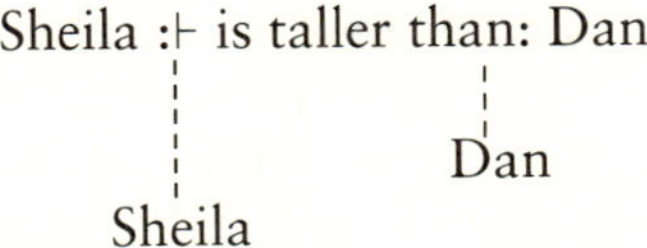

I have been using 'acknowledge' as a technical term, since what counts as acknowledging for me would not always ordinarily be regarded as acknowledging. The principle difference so far is that ordinarily one can acknowledge only what is true, while on my usage acknowledging can be false. Another difference is that ordinary usage suggests that what is acknowledged to be the case must be the case antecedent to one's judgment. But I will use 'acknowledge' for both situational and comparison judgments. Sheila can be acknowledged to be taller than Dan.

Statements which give the results of counting and measuring have the character of comparison judgments, even when no comparing takes place. The truth of this statement:

My right hand :⊢ has five fingers

(My +) right hand

depends on a situation or situations involving my hand with its fingers. But there is no special numerical situation—there is simply my hand and the fingers. The numerical judgment has the "after the fact" character of comparison judgments. Once the conceptually structured world of experience is available, we use numerical concepts to classify situations on the basis of numerical similarity.

But how is the numerical case different from the statement that the car is blue? For the car isn't simply blue, it is a specific shade (of blue). Don't we also use the concept *blue* to class together objects or situations on the basis of a similarity? We do, but both the concept of blue and the concept of a specific shade of blue are color concepts. The world of experience is structured by color concepts, and general concepts simply give us tools for abstract and incomplete identifications of situations. In contrast, numerical concepts are not actually constitutive of situations, but are used to classify antecedently available situations. However, if numerical concepts were to play a fundamental and constitutive role in some well-established, accepted physical theory, this would provide grounds for counting at least some numerical judgments within the framework of that theory as situational judgments. The boundary between situational and comparison judgments is not a chasm, and is not fixed once and for all, for all time.

Ordinary measurement statements are comparison statements:

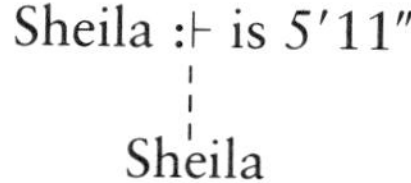

Sheila is just who she is, and fills her part of the world. In measuring her height in feet and inches, we are applying our measurement concepts to the antecedently given situations, and are not discovering an antecedently given numerical dimension of Sheila.

As well as making comparison judgments at the purely identifying stage of languages use, we can also make comparison judgments which are representational:

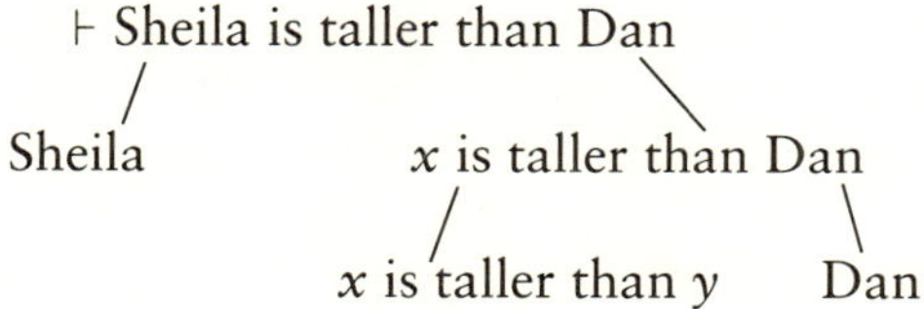

Sheila is represented as being beyond Dan with respect to height; Dan is portrayed as the standard of measurement.

In the following comparison judgment:

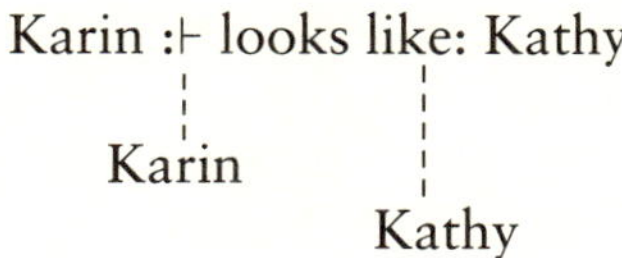

Kathy is the appearance standard with respect to which Karin is judged.

Situations are positive. There are no negative situations, no situations of an object not having a feature or several objects not being organized a certain way. But it is certainly true that there are features an object doesn't possess and arrangements that a group of objects doesn't exemplify. The things that objects are, the positive situations that exist, provide the basis for the things that objects aren't. This ball being red is the basis for the ball's not being blue, or green, or brown. Its being red *precludes* its being some other color. While it is red, it is impossible for the ball to be some other color. (But it isn't impossible for it to *become* some other color.) The ball being red is a positive situation, an existing situation. For the ball not to be green is for green to be impossible for the ball (at this time). This is a modal feature of the ball.

The modal features an object possesses are objective. A feature ϕ is necessary or contingent for a given object, possible or impossible for it, either at a certain time, or permanently. Becoming ϕ is also necessary or contingent, possible or impossible for an object. An object's possessing a modal feature is not a situation—it isn't being *called* a situation. But the modal features an object possesses are grounded in situations in which the object is an ingredient. That a person has studied French, and spoken French, and has certain "French" information stored in her memory is what grounds its being possible for her to speak French. But while modal features are grounded in actual situations, they don't reduce to those situations. The world is dynamic. Things happen. And more things can happen than will happen.

The objective modal features which depend on existing situations are *metaphysical* modal features. A feature ϕ is *relatively* metaphysically necessary for an object or objects at the present or in the future if past and present states of the world—past and present situations—determine that the object(s) is (are) or will be ϕ. A feature is relatively metaphysically possible for an object if past and present situations don't preclude its being or becoming ϕ. Relative metaphysical modalities are relative to a given time, and are determined by the whole world up to that time. *Absolute* metaphysical modality depends on objects or situations considered in relative isolation. The question of whether it is possible for a dolphin to survive out of water is a question about absolute metaphysical possiblity. We are not concerned with this dolphin or that, and what is determined or open for particular dolphins. We are asking if the natures of dolphins and water and air are such that surviving out of water isn't precluded for dolphins. We can similarly say that a particular person who has learned to ride a bike, has ridden successfully in the past, and has suffered no disabling physical changes, is able to ride a bike in the absolute metaphysical sense of 'possibility', even if circumstances conspire to prevent that person from having an opportunity for bike riding—even if God decides to allow no bike riding opportunities to come that person's way. Bike riding will be absolutely metaphysically possible for the person even if it is relatively metaphysically impossible.

Propositional acts, whether they are acknowledging acts or representing acts, are objective elements of the world. As such, they possess metaphysical modal features. If an acknowledging act is true, it is (relatively) metaphysically impossible for that act to be false. If it is false, then it is metaphysically impossible for the act to be true. Similarly, a true propositional representing act is one for which it is or will be possible to establish a correspondence to the world. But propositional acts also possess epistemic modal features. A propositional act is *relatively epistemically possible* if its being true isn't ruled out by present knowledge. This might be a particular person's present knowledge, or a particular community's. And there are different senses of 'know' and 'knowledge', giving different concepts of relative epistemic possibility and different sorts of relative epistemic possibility. Instead of there being a single concept, there is a *family* of concepts of relative epistemic modality. A concept of necessity and its corresponding concept of possibility constitute a *modal concept pair*. So there is a family of relative epistemic modal concept pairs. (There are also families of absolute and relative metaphysical modal concept pairs, and of absolute epistemic modal concept pairs.) A propositional act is relatively epistemically necessary if it is basically entailed by current knowledge.

A propositional act is *absolutely epistemically possible* if its truth isn't ruled out by its very meaning—that is, if it isn't inconsistent or self-contradictory. A propositional act is absolutely epistemically necessary if it is analytically true. (But logical truth is also a member of the family of absolute epistemic necessity.) Corresponding to the four families of modal concept pairs are four families of concepts of probability. A feature is relatively metaphysically probable for an object, to a greater or lesser degree, if past and present states of the world determine a tendency for the object to possess/acquire that feature. A feature is absolutely metaphysically probable for an object of a kind if objects of that kind possess an objective tendency to have or acquire the feature. A propositional act is relatively epistemically probable if current knowledge provides a high degree of support for the propositional act. A propositional act is absolutely epistemically probable if the meaning of such acts is such that they possess a degree of inherent likeliness. These concepts also apply to propositional experiences. An object seen at a distance might properly be taken to be very probably a dog. The propositional act of taking the object to be a dog would be absolutely epistemically probable.

Fundamental situational judgments attempt to identify situations. Other types of acknowledging acts, such as negative and universal acknowledging acts, are concerned with acts themselves. A negative acknowledging act rejects the acknowledging use of an expression for some object. A universal acknowledging act establishes a commitment from one kind of acknowledging act to another. The truth of such acts depends on certain features being present, on certain acts and combinations of acts being impossible. These modal features are grounded by nonmodal situations which the world contains.

Correct comparison judgments must also be grounded by situations in the world. But the grounding situations will not be comparison situations. However, we do need to make a space for comparison situations. Someone comparing objects in this or that respect will *constitute* a comparison situation. But the comparer is an element of this situation, together with the objects she compares. And her comparison may be accurate/correct or not. When Joe is correctly judged to be taller than Rita, the comparison constitutes/establishes an *ordering* of the two in terms of height. An incorrect comparison will be a failed attempt to constitute an ordering. A correct comparison might also establish a measurement or a similarity. Before anyone compares Joe and Rita in terms of height, it is possible to do so (at least in the absolute metaphysical sense, and undoubtedly in the relative metaphysical sense as well). It isn't possible to correctly judge Rita to be taller than Joe or the same height as Joe. Joe's being taller than Rita is originally a modal feature of the two of them. When someone correctly compares the two with respect to height, a possibility is realized, and this actualization has features that any correct comparison must have. An actual ordering situation has come into existence.

Truth as correspondence, which is characteristic of the representational use of language, is a modal feature. For correspondence, like similarity, is not a feature which structures situations encountered in the world. Correspondence must be established by a propositional act linking the propositional representing act to an appropriate situation or feature in the world. The truth of a propositional act for which no correspondence has been established consists in the present or future possibility of establishing the correspondence.

4. The Holism of the Representational Stage

Characteristic (nonlogical) concepts of the purely identifying stage of language use are independently significant. Feature criteria for fundamental identifying-stage concepts are appearance criteria or involve detectible features of a person's "inner life." Some concepts will have alternative criteria, and some criteria will have an inferential character. For example, one criterion for correctly acknowledging a figure to be a triangle is that the figure have the triangle "look." Another criterion is that the figure be correctly acknowledged to be a plane figure and correctly acknowledged to have three sides. When a concept has alternative criteria, some will be the basic criteria associated with the concept when it was first learned, and others will result from subsequent education.

Inferential connections and inferential moves can be taught to identifying-stage language users. But except for connections established by "logical" statements like universal and conditional inference-principle judgments, the language user won't "see" that when certain statements are true, then certain further statements must also be true. He won't see that satisfying the criteria for certain concepts "automatically" satisfies the criterion for a further concept. Such recognition is characteristic of representational-stage language use.

At the representational stage, a language user becomes aware of inferential connections that weren't apparent previously. They weren't connections at all from an identifying-stage perspective. These newly evident connections are additional intentional features associated with expressions, and they contribute to the meanings of representational-stage concepts. But these new connections will at first be regarded as less fundamental than the identifying-stage criteria of concepts, and identifying-stage intentional features associated with expressions. The picture is that expressions or concepts have fundamental criteria associated with them, and that inferential connections are less fundamental consequences of the fundamental criteria. Most language users at the representational stage probably retain this picture. However, for reflective language users, the significance of identifying-stage concepts undergoes a radical change at the representational stage. Inferential connections become as important to the significance of these concepts as their original criteria. To begin with, stuff is salt if it has a certain look and taste, and similarly for water. Subsequent conditions require that salt dissolve in water, that water dissolve salt. But these are less fundamental. At the representational stage, what it is for stuff to be salt or water depends on a network of connections linking a host of concepts. Conceptual frameworks that are essentially classificatory at the purely identifying stage of language use can be transformed at the representational stage to constitute essentially systematic frameworks. At the representational stage, it is also possible to develop new conceptual frameworks that are essentially systematic from the outset.

We can characterize the difference between the purely identifying stage of language use and the representational stage in terms of holism. But there are different sorts of holism. If we consider holism with respect to knowledge and belief, then holism claims that a person's knowledge/belief consitutes a system, or several systems, and that a single belief or piece of knowledge can't be evaluated independently of the system to which it belongs. This may be interpreted as the modest claim that giving up one belief will require a person to give up or modify other beliefs. Such holism is not controversial, and is characteristic of the identifying stage.

Holism with respect to knowledge and belief may instead be understood as a claim like Quine's, that a single belief or belief candidate cannot be independently tested. Instead of testing a single belief, one must test a whole system of knowledge/belief. A belief which appears to be supported, even conclusively supported, by the evidence can always be undermined by modifying background beliefs in one's system. A belief which appears to have the evidence against it can be saved and secured by suitable modifications to background beliefs/principles.

This stronger holism is not characteristic of knowledge/belief at the purely identifying stage. Acknowledging criteria allow a language user to consider objects and groups of objects one at a time in determining whether to acknowledge an object to be ϕ or several objects to be ψ-situated with respect to each other. One expression may be used to give the acknowledging criteria for another, but the acknowledging criteria for expressions at the identifying stage must be traceable by a finite number of steps to appearances, self-conscious awareness, and actions. This is true even for expressions/concepts which are introduced by language users at the representational stage of language use, and taught to identifying-stage language users. It requires a representational-stage language user to invent and develop number theory, or to develop postulates about the existence and character of atoms and their components, but school children can be taught about numbers and atoms while in the purely identifying stage. They won't get the opportunity to acknowledge an object in experience to be a carbon atom, but they can acknowledge objects to contain carbon atoms.

But how can a single acknowledging or denying act be independently authorized? Consider a woman who acknowledges an object in experience to be green. She uses appearance criteria on the object—it looks green to her, and this is enough. We can imagine a variety of circumstances in which the object wouldn't really be green. These won't be circumstances in which the language user is confused about the criteria associated with 'green'. The troublesome cases are those where the conditions in which the language user perceives the object distort the true color. Perhaps there is something wrong with the language user's eyes, or her neural functioning, or the light in which she sees the object. So her acknowledging act presumes or presupposes normality claims about the circumstances in which she perceives the object. If she questions some of those claims, she won't be entitled to acknowledge the perceived object to be green.

When the acknowledging criteria associated with an expression are appearance criteria, these criteria are only appropriate or applicable under certain normality conditions. Given some reason for thinking conditions to be abnormal, it is an error to uncritically apply the criteria. But the application of the criteria in apparently normal conditions does not depend on a "suppressed" premiss that conditions are normal. The correct application of the criteria depends on the conditions being normal, but not on anyone's thinking or saying so. At the purely identifying stage, beliefs face the tribunal of experience one at a time, not en masse.

In addition to holism concerning knowledge and belief, there is a holism with respect to meaning. This is usually associated with expressions. Holism denies that expressions have independent or "atomic" meanings. On a holistic view, the meaning of a given expression is its "place" in a system of meanings, or a system of meaningful expressions. One consequence of a holistic view is that words can't be learned, or understood, one at a time. A person must master a system of expressions to understand the individual members of the system. Since I have given up the idea that words have meanings, I need to explain meaning holism in a different way. A holistic view should claim that a linguistic act doesn't have meaning in isolation, independently. To understand the meaning of a given linguistic act, one must understand the acts to which this act commits the speaker, and the acts that are incompatible with this act, and so forth. One doesn't understand what it means to acknowledge an object to be scarlet unless she knows that the speaker is committed to acknowledge the object to be red, and colored, and to reject acts acknowledging the object to be blue, green, purple, and so on. One can't *just* know what it is to be scarlet.

At the purely identifying stage there are some kinds of acts that have somewhat holistic meanings. Inference-principle statements are essentially bound up with commitment relations linking kinds of identifying and acknowledging acts. To understand an act acknowledging dogs to all be animals, one must understand the commitment from acknowledging Rex to be a dog to acknowledging Rex to be an animal. But while a person may have established a commitment from "scarlet"-acknowledging acts to "red"-acknowledging acts, this won't affect her ability to perform and understand "scarlet"-acknowledging acts. She can independently understand such acts. The primary acknowledging criteria associated with "scarlet" are appearance criteria.

Meaning holism *is* characteristic of acts of symbolic representing performed by reflective language users. To represent an arbitrary object as a triangle, a person will understand the connection between being a triangle and being three-sided, and between being a triangle and being another sort of plane figure. The network of semantic relations linking the different (kinds of) acts characterizes the language user's representational awareness. This network is interpreted to constitute the awareness. Holism with respect to knowledge and belief is also characteristic of the reflective representational use of language. Accepting one propositional act will "amount to" accepting a collection or system of such acts. To portray an object as scarlet, and accept this, a person must *mean* that the object is red and colored, that it isn't blue, green, or invisible. She must also mean that the object will present a characteristic appearance in normal circumstances.

In acknowledging or taking a jacket to be scarlet, a person employs criteria without reflecting on the criteria or their conditions of applicability. When these criteria are properly applied in suitable circumstances, the acknowledging/taking to be is correct. Otherwise it isn't. The judgment's being correct *depends* on things being so, but it *doesn't* depend on other judgments being correct. Even though the person who takes the jacket to be scarlet is committed by that to taking the circumstances of vision to be normal. In judging *that* the jacket is scarlet, a person "places" a propositional representing act in her "authentic" system of representations. She in effect places the consequences of the representing act in her authentic system. Each element of the system depends on other elements of the system. This is true even for the propositional experiences characteristic of the representational stage. Experiencing the jacket as a representative scarlet object, perceiving that the jacket is scarlet, requires some awareness of what it is to be scarlet. One is aware of the criteria for acknowledging an object to be scarlet, and the circumstances necessary for employing them. The correctness of the perceptual judgment depends on the correctness of judgments which it entails. We can only appraise one element of the system of representations against the background of the others. It is the whole system which must be determined to be adequate or inadequate.

It isn't really correct to say that representational-stage knowledge and beliefs confront experience as a corporate whole. For there is no opposition between experience and belief. Representational-stage knowledge and belief include and incorporate propositional experience. But the success of one's representational-stage knowledge/beliefs, including experience, must be assessed as a whole. In contrast, acknowledging acts, acts of taking to be, and attempted identifying acts performed at the purely identifying stage can be assessed one at a time. Someone who makes an identifying-stage judgment is operating within a conceptually structured world of experience. But from this perspective the person is not in a position to reflect on or think about conceptual structure. He is not in a position to challenge the conceptual structure within which he operates. The conceptually structured world of experience is simply a given.

In an identifying-stage judgment, there are conditions under which it is appropriate to apply acknowledging criteria associated with an expression. In applying the criteria, a person needn't think about or represent these conditions. The conditions are simply objective features which do or don't obtain. Representational-stage judgments about perceived objects entail both propositional perceptions (in suitable circumstances) and judgments about the conditions under which perceptions occurred. The entailed consequences form part of the content of the original judgment. In principle, we can accommodate nearly any propositional representing act by making suitable adjustments to our other beliefs. In practice, our skills and dispositions, as well as our habitual practices, constrain our judgments. We simply can't make the adjustments required to accept just any propositional representing act.

Representational-stage judgments can depend on (potential) judgments about the circumstances we are in. But representational-stage judgments can also depend on judgments/principles concerning fundamental features of a conceptual framework—these are fundamental features of the world of experience. It is possible to encounter anomalous perceptions which can't be accommodated in an accepted conceptual system or world. From the identifying-stage perspective, perceived objects will be acknowledged or taken to be this or that without difficulty. Any anomalies will reside in the commitment relations which have been established, and will simply show a need for adjustments to these relations. From the perspective of identifying-stage judgments, a new world is inconceivable. But from the representational-stage perspective, anomalous experiences call the world of experience into question. The experiences may turn out to be only apparently anomalous, if a way to accommodate them in established conceptual frameworks is discovered. If the experiences are genuinely anomalous, a new world must be devised. The new and old worlds will be incommensurable.

Using language in a purely identifying way is a necessary preliminary to using language to represent. Identifying is in this sense more fundamental than representing. But the use of language to represent provides a new perspective on the world and our knowledge of it. The representational use of language makes possible systematic scientific knowledge. It makes possible a scientifically organized world of experience, and gives us new access to ourselves and our role in creating this world. The representational use of language is essential for understanding the world as opposed to merely classifying the things in it.

5. Pretending

In the course of writing this book, I have been developing, or articulating, new conceptual frameworks. This is an essential part of adding to our knowledge of the world. The production of new conceptual frameworks takes place all the time in science, and in most other fields (like jurisprudence, religion, and literary criticism). Some conceptual frameworks are simply invented, and imposed on the world of experience. Other conceptual frameworks are implicit in our practice, and must first be uncovered, then further articulated. An adequate framework for subatomic particles needs (needed) to be made up. But someone engaged in intentional activity must have some conception of what she is doing. This conception may not be fully explict. It may not be entirely accurate. And it certainly won't be complete. But ferreting it out is an essential preliminary to fixing it up.

The conceptual framework for propositional thinking and propositional experience, together with the framework for understanding linguistic acts, is implicit in the thought, experience, and linguistic activity. But this doesn't mean that everyone already possesses such concepts as *identifying*, *acknowledging*, and *taking to be*. All language users perform acts of identifying, acknowledging, and taking to be, and have some conception of what they are doing when performing these acts. But to identify mother, or Sally, or the house on the corner, a person needn't possess the general concept *identifying*. In using 'mother' to identify his mother, a language user is employing the concept of this mother. (He uses 'mother' to express this concept.) He is aware of using 'mother' for his mother, and can use the word itself to label the kind of act he is performing. The language user is aware of performing a "mother" act in which he focuses on his mother. The language user will have concepts of "mother" acts, of "Sally" acts, and of "the house on the corner" acts. These are all identifying acts, but the language user won't know this. *We* know it, because we have developed or articulated the conceptual framework for linguistic acts. We have based this framework on our understanding of the acts we all perform with language; this framework provides room for concepts we already possessed—like "mother"-act concepts—and introduces concepts for kinds of acts we find ourselves performing.

Developing even an implicit framework is a trial and error procedure. We can't simply reflect on our practices and run up against the appropriate concepts. We must invent or adapt expressions to label/characterize the acts we perform, and try using these frameworks to make sense of our practices. Because these practices themselves are accessible in a way that subatomic particles are not, we can actually "measure" the fit between our conceptual framework and our conceptually structured activity. We can determine that the concepts are adequate to our practices—though there will probably always be room for improvements to the conceptual framework.

The status of the conceptual framework developed to deal with representing isn't so easy to pin down. Not all representing is intentional, though some of it is. Symbolic representing is intentional, for in this representing it is intentional features that get interpreted. Indirect iconic representing is also intentional and conceptual to some degree. When a person interprets the halos in a painting as indicating that the person represented is holy, the interpreter must possess the concept of being holy, and somehow bring that concept to bear in viewing the painting. But directly iconic representing doesn't seem to be either intentional or conceptual. At least, it needn't be. Looking at the image is similar to looking at the image's objects, and one just finds herself being able to employ her percepts to organize her awareness of the objects "in" the picture. Since directly iconic representing is not a conceptually structured activity, we can't immediately ascertain that our concept of using an image to become representationally aware of arbitrary objects as this or that fits the activity we engage in. If representing were conceptually transparent, it probably wouldn't have proved such a hard nut for philosophers to crack. But we do have a kind of "direct" access to representing and representational awareness. We can determine that the present conception, though incomplete, accommodates the elements we know about.

One respect in which the conception of representing is incomplete is the treatment of representational awareness. We don't quite know how to think about this awareness. In order to get a better "grasp" of what goes on in representational awareness, we can either introduce new concepts linked in ways we specify to the concepts currently available, or we can look for some familiar phenomena that can be used as a model to shed light on what we don't understand. We can combine these approaches, of course, but we can only carry out one strategy at a time. I have at present no ideas about new concepts which further articulate/develop our conception of representing. So I will look for a familiar model. Consider directly iconic representing, where the image resembles its object. Awareness of the colored and shaped image resembles awareness of a similarly colored and shaped object. The perceptual organization that the subject contributes allows her to perceive the image itself as a part of this world. But she also supplies perceptual structure to the represented object. Representational awareness of an object isn't genuine awareness of an object. Being representationally aware of an arbitrary object is only something *like* being actually aware. It is also something like *pretending* to be aware of an actual object.

Being representationally aware of an arbitrary object of a kind is not a case of pretending. But the concept of pretending seems close to what we need to understand representational awareness. We do not possess an adequate conception of this awareness, though the awareness itself is quite familiar. To come up with an adequate conception, we must introduce new concepts and stretch old ones. But we need some source of ideas for how to do this. With pretending, we distinguish pretending which aims to deceive from pretending which is a kind of play. The nondeceptive pretending is the one to look at. A person can pretend that some object is what it isn't. She can pretend that this toy is a car. She can also pretend that she is, or is doing, what she isn't. She can pretend to be driving the toy car. She can pretend to be a racecar driver.

For conceptually endowed agents, pretending is conceptual and intentional. To pretend to be a nurse, a child needs to have the concept of a nurse. But a prelinguistic child should be able to pretend with respect to percepts. He might pretend to fall down, or to be hurt. It doesn't require concepts to use an image to represent, but the conceptually endowed agent will take objects in pictures to be this and that. With directly iconic representing, a person does something like pretending to supply perceptual and conceptual structure. He isn't "really" doing this because there aren't *really* objects "in" the picture. Pretending requires self-consciousness. The pretender must be aware of the difference between the way things really are and how he is pretending they are. The person who uses an image to become representationally aware must also be self-conscious. He must be able to provide perceptual structure in a "nonserious" way, and be aware of doing so. The ability to pretend—better, the ability to do whatever it is that "underlies" pretending—is a fundamental and irreducible ability of agents who self-consciously use images to become representationally aware of objects.

We have propositional experience of ourselves and the world around us. We see this to be a door, that to be a window. We know ourself to be worrying about unpaid bills, and to be walking across the room. We also have propositional representational awareness. Looking at this picture is like looking at a blonde woman in a blue dress. We "pretend" to see an object with certain features, and this allows us to *take* the object *to be* a blonde woman in a blue dress. But just as we aren't really aware of a woman, we aren't really taking either the painted image or the "pretended" object to be a woman in a blue dress. It is more "pretense." This "pretense" is natural and unforced; there is little apparent difference between taking a real object to be a woman and taking a represented object to be one. And we can not only "take" a represented object to be a woman, but we can also "see" this object as a representative object—as an arbitrary woman or an arbitrary woman of a certain type.

When someone uses an image to become representationally aware of objects, and "transforms" this awareness so that she identifies actual objects, portraying them as something or other, there is no pretense in the identifying. She is now "pretending" to perceive the identified objects, and to perceive them as whatever. Real objects can be portrayed as anything one likes—the portraying does not commit the viewer to believing the objects are as portrayed. But the viewer can take the image to be accurate in one or another respect, and use the image and her representational awareness as an occasion for taking the real objects portrayed to be as the image shows.

With features of a picture, like halos, that represent indirectly, the perception of those features isn't like perceiving what they indicate. Looking at a painting of figures with halos is like looking at people with lighted circles above their heads. But if one understands how to interpret the picture, she is simply representationally aware of people, and uses the halos as providing grounds for "taking" those people to be saintly, or holy. A picture with halos represents in a way that is only slightly indirect. Consider a wholly indirect iconic representation, a graph showing the sales of trucks during the month of November. Looking at the graph has very little in common with looking at trucks being sold. One can hardly be said to be doing something like pretending to look at truck sales. Instead, we use the graph to "pretend" to take truck sales to be as represented. If the graph is also used to identify actual truck sales, this "pretended" taking to be is cashed in for the real thing. But we "understand" the graph, we are aware of what is being represented, quite independently of whether it has a real counterpart.

Symbolic representing is also nonperceptual. Saying or thinking 'is red' isn't much like perceiving a red object. Someone who uses 'That apple is red' like this:

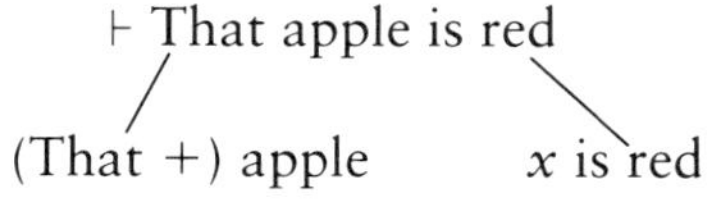

to portray a particular apple as red is not "pretending" to perceive the apple as a representative red object. In using the predicate 'is red', the language user considers what it is to *be* a red object, not what it is to *see* one. To symbolically represent an arbitrary object as red, to be symbolically representationally aware of an arbitrary red object, is to do something like pretending *to be* such an object. Understanding what it is to be ϕ is understanding this "from the inside." To symbolically portray an object as ϕ is like playing the ϕ-role on behalf of the object. It isn't pretending, but it is importantly like pretending.

6. Telling Stories

Pretending, or something like it, is important for storytelling and other fictional narratives. John Searle (1989) pointed this out, although his account isn't based on the present analysis of speech acts. He focuses on pretended assertions rather than pretended identifying and acknowledging acts, or pretended acts of accepting a propositional act. In writing a work of fiction, the author pretends to identify some objects, and may actually identify others. Arthur Conan Doyle pretends to identify Sherlock Holmes and Dr. Watson in his stories. He actually identifies London, and England, and a host of other genuine objects. The author performs some genuine acknowledging acts and some pretended acknowledging acts. He actually accepts some propositional representing acts and pretends to accept others. To provide a thorough and comprehensive account of fictional discourse, it would probably be helpful to introduce some notation to our diagrams to indicate pretended acts. But I won't do this now, for I am not after such a thorough and comprehensive account. I will instead represent acts of claiming that Sherlock Holmes lived in London like this:

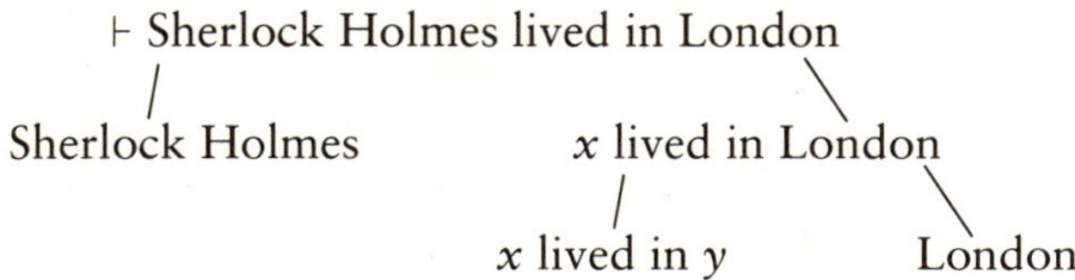

just as I would represent acts of using 'Arthur Conan Doyle lived in London'.

In writing a fictional narrative, the author pretends to identify characters and events that don't really exist. But the activity of writing (and publishing) the story creates a status for the characters and events. They become objective fictional characters and events. Other people can identify them, and can make both true and false statements about them. Identifying a fictional character with objective status is still pretending as compared to identifying a real object, but it is a different kind of pretending than the author engaged in when making up the character. When someone tells us about a real person whom we haven't heard of, we become able to identify that person, exploiting connections that lead from us, via our informant, to the intended person. When someone makes up a story about a fictional character and tells it to us, we are linked to the narrator in the same way we are linked to the person who tells us genuine news. If we repeat the fictional story to another person, that person will be linked to the author via us, and can exploit this connection to identify the fictional character. To identify a real object, we must exploit connections linking us to the object. To identify a fictional character, we must still exploit connections, but they need only link us to some authoritative presentation of a narrative about that character.

When Arthur Conan Doyle made up Sherlock Holmes and told stories about him, his pretended identifying acts gave an objective fictional status to Holmes and Watson and the other characters. The author's original acts had no real targets. Once the original stories were available, their existence/presentation provided an objective, real target for later identifying acts, even those by Arthur Conan Doyle. But the target is a narrative, not persons. Arthur Conan Doyle had the authority to create new "official" adventures for Sherlock Holmes, but no one else did/does. If our practices were different, there might be an authoritative storytelling branch of society, empowered to extend the accounts of previous authors. There have certainly been a large number of new Sherlock Holmes stories in recent years, but as things stand, none of them can achieve a canonical status.

The truth about a fictional character depends on what is actually written down or stated in the official canon. Plus whatever is entailed by what is written down/stated. Plus certain "default" assumptions. Unless told otherwise, we can assume that people in the Sherlock Holmes stories are like the rest of us in most respects. Sherlock Holmes must have had a mother, who had a mother of her own, and that mother (grandmother) also had a mother. This great-grandmother isn't mentioned in any Sherlock Holmes story, but we can assume, by default, that there was such a woman. We also know as a matter of logic, that this great-grandmother either had blue eyes or eyes of some other color. But we can't go farther than this. There is no fact of the matter about the actual color of the great-grandmother's eyes.

7. Mathematical Objects

The discussion of fictional statements and fictional realms has a lot of bearing on mathematics. If no language users had ever advanced beyond the purely identifying stage of language use, then language users might have introduced numerical expressions, and used them for counting and measuring objects, but those language users wouldn't have talked or thought about numbers. For numbers are fictitious objects, and the realm of numbers is a fictitious realm.

At the purely identifying stage, one can acknowledge a group or collection to have *n* members, to have fewer than *n* members, or to have more than *n* members. Most of us have two hands and ten fingers. There are more than one million people in the world, but fewer than ten billion. One can also use numerical expressions to acknowledge objects to be so long or so old or so heavy. These numerical expressions are not being used to identify numbers. They are instead used to acknowledge objects, including groups and collections, to be of certain kinds.

If all language users had somehow gotten stuck at the purely identifying stage, they would have developed numerical expressions for counting and measuring things. They would also have developed techniques for calculating. Two things of a kind and three more make five things of that kind. Seven and five make twelve. Three nonoverlapping groups/collections of seven objects make up a collection of twenty-one objects. So long as the language users didn't reflect on what it is to be a two-membered group or a five-membered group, which would involve using language representationally, they would use trial and error methods to develop techniques for calculating. Actually bring together two objects and three more, and count the result. And presume that the result obtained for these five objects would also hold for other groups of two and three. As calculating techniques became more complicated and more sophisticated, it would be natural to manipulate numerical expressions to obtain results. Instead of considering what you get when you add five eggs to seven different eggs, deal with the expressions 'five' and 'seven' alone—better yet, devise techniques for manipulating numerals like 'V' and 'VII' or '5' and '7'.

Knowing addition and "times" tables, being able to add, subtract, divide, and multiply, and to apply the results in practical matters requires only skills for manipulating marks. There is no need to think about numbers as opposed to numerals. There is no need to admit numbers as objects in this world or some other.

Once the numerical counters, measurers, and calculators learn to use language representationally, they won't automatically find themselves contemplating numbers as opposed to numerals. Using language representationally does make it possible to represent an arbitrary three-membered collection and an arbitrary (disjoint) two-membered collection, and just "see" that the resulting collection must have five members. One is no longer limited to trial and error methods for developing techniques for calculation. One can now make rational inferences to discover numerical features of objects and the numerical results of calculation.

When calculation is carried out with numerical expressions alone, and language is used representationally, it is quite natural to think of the numerical expressions as names for some kind of objects. (It will also be easy—natural—to confuse the numbers with numerals; these are numeral types, not tokens.) But the move from "Three objects plus two more objects makes five objects" to "Three plus two is five" is momentous. It is a move from the real world of experience to a fictitious realm of abstract objects. It is a move from a world which is probably finite to a world which is most certainly infinite. Our procedure for producing numerals is endless in the sense that, however far we go, it is possible to go farther. At any given time there will be a greatest numeral produced to that point, but a greater numeral can be produced at a later time. The procedure for producing numerals is potentially infinite. We can use language representationally to represent, for an arbitrary numeral, the procedure for obtaining the next numeral and also the next numeral itself. When we construe numbers as abstract individuals existing independently of us, we can represent an infinite collection of numbers. Our representation won't have infinitely many elements. For the natural numbers, we need only represent one or more initial numbers, and represent the "transition" from an arbitrary number to its successor. For other types of numbers, we represent some individual numbers, and then represent how, for arbitrary numbers, other numbers are situated with respect to them. We have transformed the representations of potentially infinite procedures for producing numerals to representations of an actually infinite realm of numbers.

A person needs to be in the representational stage of language use to make up numbers, and to develop number theory. She needs to be in the representational stage to represent "pure" geometric figures, and to develop geometry. But mathematics can be taught to students in the purely identifying stage without moving them out of that stage. The student can be taught to count, so that she can proceed indefinitely, without understanding that her counting procedure is potentially infinite. She just knows how to produce the next numeral, given any numeral—she doesn't understand that this is what she can do. The student can also be taught to identify numbers without representing them. She identifies them in the same way she can identify Sherlock Holmes: with respect to authoritative sources of information about numbers. The student can be taught that there are an endless supply of numbers without really understanding this. One must be able to represent an arbitrary successor for an arbitrary integer to grasp the infinity of the natural numbers.

Some of the puzzles that Wittgenstein poses in *Remarks on the Foundation of Mathematics* depend on his (and our) looking at mathematics from the standpoint of an identifying-stage language user. How can we be justified in correcting the numeral producer who counts past one million in a nonstandard way? We don't simply want to say that the aberrant counter isn't proceeding the way we would. We want to say that he is mistaken. But at the identifying stage, we can know how to count without being able to represent our procedure. This leaves us with no resources to challenge the counter who produces 1,000,003 as the numeral succeeding 1,000,000. Wittgenstein simply failed to understand how we use language. We can by finite means represent the potentially infinite procedure for counting, and can also represent the infinite sequence of natural numbers. With respect to these representations, the aberrant counter is mistaken. He has failed to produce/identify the successor to 1,000,000.

At the representational stage of language use, it isn't necessary to invent numbers or ideal geometric figures or sets. But their invention is a great convenience to mathematical studies. For theoretical purposes, we could hardly get along without them. Recognizing abstract mathematical entities very much simplifies the development and presentation of mathematical theories. But this important practical reason for postulating fictitious mathematical entities is no reason for regarding these entities as genuine elements of the world of experience or any other real world. In a similar way, fictional narratives certainly play an important role in our culture. They may be practically important for our understanding one another, and the world. But their characters and events are nonetheless unreal—their *fictitious* characters and *fictitious* events aren't real.

Fictional realms are always incomplete. There will be statements about these realms that are neither true nor false. This can also be a problem for mathematical statements. Since temporal relations don't intrude in the realm of mathematics, it is easier to tell a complete story about numbers than it is about Sherlock Holmes and his ancestors. But given the mathematical story "in effect" at a given time, there can be statements whose truth value is objectively undetermined. If this is discovered, the official story can be enlarged to provide values to these statements. But such enlargements need motivation. Why, for example, did negative and complex (imaginary) numbers come to be accepted? They were controversial in the nineteenth century, and are taught in grade schools today. And what about the Axiom of Choice? How should we decide whether or not to make it part of the story of sets? I don't know the answers to these questions. But I do know that the realm of mathematics isn't extended on the basis of explorations in some platonic universe. We instead enlarge our official stories for some reasons that seem good to us.

Chapter 12

Knowledge and Certainty

1. Justifying Belief

Simple acknowledging acts attempt to identify situations or to constitute certain sorts of situations. Other acknowledging acts establish/reflect commitments, reject certain predicative acts, or make/reflect commitments common to disjoined predicates. In performing any acknowledging act, a language user is trying to get things right. (All acknowledging acts are sincere.) But for nonelementary acknowledging acts, the truth conditions are modal. So in performing those acknowledging acts, a language user is trying to register modal features. It is possible to perform a true nonelementary acknowledging act without registering these features, but such an acknowledging act is true "by accident." In performing acknowledging acts, a person exploits connections to certain objects and situations, including situations of conclusive failure to apply acknowledging criteria to objects. The language user who succeeds in identifying situations, constituting comparison situations, or registering modal features gets things right nonaccidentally.

Propositional representing acts represent/portray objects as possessing features, including modal features. These acts are true or false, depending on whether or not they can be verified. Verification also depends on exploiting connections, identifying situations, and registering modal features. Ordinarily, a person who accepts a propositional representing act will think he has verified the act. (But we must not confuse verifying the act with proving it. We can verify the act without being at all justified in accepting it.) For we don't accept propositional acts capriciously. One can't simply believe whatever he wants to believe.

A person's beliefs include her current propositional experiences—her acts of taking to be and her acts of perceiving objects as instances of kinds. They include those past propositional experiences that she remembers and is committed to reaffirming, as well as any acknowledging acts she is currently performing or propositional representing acts she is currently accepting. Her beliefs also include acknowledging acts that she is readily disposed to perform and is committed to perform, so long as she is readily disposed to recognize the commitment, and propositional representing acts that she is readily disposed to accept and is committed to accept. So beliefs are partly occurrent, mostly dispositional. However, the relevant dispositions are to perform propositional acts, and are not simply dispositions to act as if certain propositions were true.

Someone's propositional experience takes place "within" a conceptual framework. The propositional experience presupposes the framework and the principles which govern the framework. The experience is justified with respect to the framework if it properly employs the criteria associated with the framework and its concepts. But the framework itself might be inadequate or even incoherent. If so, the propositional experience which is justified with respect to the framework might be unjustified in a larger sense. However, someone whose experience is taking place within a conceptual framework is not likely to be giving any thought to the adequacy or inadequacy of the framework. For example, he may unreflectively take these events to be a case of witchcraft, and try to identify the person responsible. In his world this may *be* a case of witchcraft, although *we* are confident that such a world cannot be sustained.

In addition to beliefs constituted by her propositional experience, and beliefs about remembered past experience, a person will have occurrent and dispositional beliefs that are not about experience. These may be based on experience. A person may judge or be disposed to judge familiar objects that are not present to be one thing or another, relying on the memory of experiencing the objects. Someone can accept information from other sources (other people, newspapers, books, etc.), and use this as a basis for additional judgments. The beliefs obtained in this fashion may be about specific objects, or they may be general. Determining whether, and to what extent, such beliefs are justified is a difficult matter; but these beliefs are certainly indispensible in practice. A person can also obtain beliefs by figuring things out for herself. She believes what she has already figured out and what she is readily disposed to figure out, so long as she is committed to accept it.

There are various kinds of justification, or standards for justification. I will loosely distinguish and characterize three *levels* of justification. A belief is *strongly justified* if its justification guarantees its truth—a strongly justified belief must be true. Classical philosophers thought mathematical knowledge is strongly justified. Some propositional acts are simply "seen" to be true—someone's grasping their evident character is sufficient to strongly justify his accepting the propositional acts. Other strongly justified propositional acts are deduced from strongly justified propositional acts by deductions which are evidently correct. A belief might be strongly justified with respect to a conceptual framework which may or may not be correct or adequate.

In considering what beliefs are justified, it is important to understand that it is actual linguistic acts which are justified or not. If Sara acknowledges Jim to be tall, her act might be justified. She will be justified or not when she accepts a propositional act portraying Jim as tall. If Sara has not thought about Jim's height, but her justified beliefs commit her to accepting that Jim is tall, we should not say Sara *would* be justified in accepting this. The best we can do is claim that Sara *could* be justified in accepting it. To actually be justified she must make the judgment, and must reach the judgment by appropriate means, such as a rational inference following correct commitments from justified beginnings.

Inferences as well as beliefs can be justified. A rational inference traces commitments. But some commitments may be faulty. An unsatisfactory conceptual framework can sanction unreliable inferences, although these will be correct with respect to that framework. Other commitments are simply established by the language user. He may decide to perform certain actions in the future. His decision to act can justify him in inferring that he will act, and that various consequences of his act will occur. He may also accept a conditional or universal propositional act. Such acts may reflect commitments already in force, but they can also establish commitments. These commitments can be objectively incorrect. (They can make his world incoherent.) But if the commitments are established by justified judgments, then they are correct, not faulty. In addition to making rational inferences, a person may make inferences based on authorization rather than commitment. Such inferences aren't being counted as rational inferences, but they can produce justification if their authorization is correct.

Justification for belief can be inferential, but it can also be immediate. From within a given conceptual framework, there are correct and incorrect ways of applying the concepts to experience. Someone might, for example, be immediately justified in taking a certain animal to be a dog. A person could also be immediately justified in accepting a statement which formulates a principle constitutive of a conceptual framework she occupies.

It is conceivable that a person could be strongly justified in accepting a conceptual framework. This might be relative justification, if the person is justified in accepting this framework because she recognizes its relation to another, accepted framework. The justified framework might be a consequence of the other framework, or it might simply be clear that the justified framework, like an arithmetic framework, has applications to the other framework. We can also understand the claim that a person is "absolutely" strongly justified in accepting a conceptual framework, even if no one ever is in such a position. An absolutely justified framework would presumably be applicable to oneself and his intentional acts, rather than to external objects.

For there is an important difference between conceptual frameworks for external objects and conceptual frameworks for ourselves and what we are up to. When conceptual frameworks for external objects are applied to experience, they are (partly) constitutive of the world of experience. They can't be measured against independently experienced objects, but must be judged on the basis of their success in organizing the world and making sense of it. But that we are actively engaged in constituting the world of experience is a fact about us that we need to understand, and this fact is not constituted by our conception. Our conception of what we are up to does characterize and so constitute our intentional activity. But there is an objective fact of the matter about what we are doing, and both our conceptions and beliefs can be more and less adequate to the way things are. What we think we are doing is what we are trying to do, but we might really be doing something else.

The second level of justification is *simple*, or *plain* justification. A simply justified belief might turn out to be untrue. Plain justification will always presuppose one or another conceptual framework within which a person is operating. But even within a framework, with respect to that framework, a plainly justified belief can turn out to be untrue. A person can be plainly justified in taking this object to be yellow or that animal to be a cow. (Even someone who correctly applies a concept's acknowledging criteria to an object can obtain incorrect results.) A person who accepts a conclusion reached by tracing sanctioned commitments from plainly justified premisses will also be plainly justified. It is characteristic of a plainly justified belief that a person couldn't have correctly declined to accept it. The person was either committed to accept it, by an evident commitment, or else the correct employment of certain concepts "called for" the belief to be accepted.

A belief is *weakly* justified if it is authorized but not required, and is accepted on the basis of its authorization. One might be plainly justified in taking the distant object to probably be a horse. She will be only weakly justified if instead she takes it to be a horse.

If a belief isn't about current or past experience, it may be obtained (or obtainable) by an inference. But not all such beliefs are inferential. For I am restricting inferences to those acts where a person proceeds from propositional premisses to a conclusion which these (are thought to) support. A person might use information at her disposal to reach a belief without carrying out an inference in my sense. A person who knows α to be three-sided and a plane figure might judge α to be a triangle without taking another look at α. She doesn't first say/think α is three-sided and α is a plane figure, and then proceed to judge that α is a triangle. She simply realizes that α's satisfying the criteria for being a plane figure and the criteria for being three-sided are sufficient for α's being a triangle. Although her belief wasn't acquired inferentially, we don't distort her procedure very much if we provide an inferential reconstruction of it.

2. Explanations

The concepts and conceptual frameworks we employ give structure to the world of our experience. Once the world is conceptually organized, it contains situations to be identified and portrayed, and its objects have conceptual modal features. Within a conceptual framework and a conceptually structured world, statements have objective truth conditions. True acknowledging acts identify objective situations and register objective modal features of things. True propositional representing acts can be made to correspond to the world (they can be verified).

From the perspective of a conceptual framework, from *within* a conceptual framework, statements are justified or not. Justification conditions for statements within a framework will ordinarily be determined by the particular framework involved, though there may be certain kinds of justification that hold for all frameworks. (For example, a person who begins from justified premisses and, relying on justified inference principles, rationally infers a conclusion will be justified in accepting that conclusion.) It is not clear that there is a sense in which we can be said to be justified in accepting fundamental conceptual frameworks. We can understand what is meant by a claim to be strongly justified in accepting a framework, but it is doubtful that anyone is strongly justified. The weaker sorts of justification could only apply to one framework with respect to another.

For someone's acquisition of a belief to be justified, her experience and her other justified beliefs must require or authorize her to hold the belief, and she must be aware of this. But it can be legitimate to acquire a belief in the absence of justification. We have a need to make sense of ourselves and our world, and we can satisfy this need on occasion by adopting a belief in order to explain some phenomena or solve some puzzle. Explanations can sometimes be justified by inference. But some explanatory hypotheses are formulated and accepted solely to provide the desired understanding. If such a hypothesis is to be worth anything, it must be clear initially that the hypothesis does explain what needs explaining. (This doesn't mean that the hypothesis must be the true explanation, but only that we must recognize that if the hypothesis were true, it would provide a satisfactory account.)

It is frequently claimed that hypotheses can and should be tested by the hypothetico-deductive method.

It would ordinarily be foolish to simply accept the first explanatory hypothesis one dreams up. A satisfactory explanation must not only explain what we wish to understand, but it must also be consistent with what we know and believe, and must not raise problems more difficult than the one it solves. A satisfactory explanatory hypothesis needs to be consistent with our experience—with our experience so far, and with the experience we will subsequently have. It makes clear sense to check to see if the hypothesis's consequences are consistent with new experiences as well as old ones. But if our checking doesn't turn up any barrier to accepting the hypothesis, if our tests corroborate the hypothesis, we haven't provided positive support for the hypothesis. We haven't justified our accepting the hypothesis. Nonetheless, there is nothing unreasonable about accepting such a hypothesis. It often makes good sense to do so.

Some writers have spoken of an inference to the best explanation, and use this expression to label our accepting a hypothesis merely because it explains what we want to have explained. But their usage is at odds with my employment of 'inference' (and also 'argument'). To accept an explanation because it is an explanation, and superior in some ways to the alternatives we have thought of, is not to provide any support for the explanation. In such circumstances, we have no satisfactory premisses providing reasons for thinking the explanation true. Although information available to us doesn't "call for" the explanatory hypothesis, and doesn't justify our accepting that hypothesis, it can nonetheless be perfectly appropriate for us to do so.

Our basic epistemic "task" is *not* to discover the truth about things. Our task is *to make sense of our experience and its objects*. We need to make both theoretical and practical sense of things. To make practical sense, a person needs to accept goals and values, and to live a certain kind of life. In this book, I am primarily concerned with making theoretical sense. I have no space for discussing our practical concerns. Theoretically, we understand what truth is well enough to know that a true account will provide the best possible explanation for what we don't understand. But we often lack direct access to the truth about what needs explaining. When we accept a hypothesis that has been corroborated, and have no additional grounds for thinking the hypothesis true, we are not accepting the hypothesis because it is probably true, or likely to be true. We accept it because doing so contributes to satisfying our need to make sense of the world.

An explanatory hypothesis that concerns a particular situation or event will be true or false independently of its being accepted. Suppose Frank accepts the hypothesis that Jones committed a certain crime, but Frank has no evidence for this hypothesis. Frank is not justified in accepting the hypothesis. In fact, Frank is motivated by his dislike of Jones. Although Frank may feel he is entitled to his opinion about Jones, and even that he is authorized to accept the hypothesis, Frank is mistaken. He should not have accepted the hypothesis. On our story, Frank didn't look for evidence that might be available, and he didn't attempt to corroborate the hypothesis. If he had done these things, and found nothing to authorize his rejecting the hypothesis, it might then be legitimate to accept the hypothesis, though this wouldn't be sufficient for a court of law. Adding the hypothesis to his stock of beliefs wouldn't affect the fundamental character of any of Frank's conceptual frameworks.

The case is somewhat different with a universal hypothesis, say the hypothesis that every *m* is ϕ. Accepting this hypothesis establishes a commitment from *m*-identifying acts to judgments that the *m*'s are ϕ. Someone might accept the hypothesis without justification and not be subject to criticism. If it genuinely isn't possible to identify an *m* while correctly rejecting an act portraying the *m* as ϕ, then her conception of the world of experience has been correctly altered. Otherwise, the universal judgment is objectively incorrect, though it might subsequently be rendered correct by other conceptual changes.

An act accepting an explanatory hypothesis which isn't justified by experience or inference may acquire a justified status. To the extent that the explanatory hypothesis constitutes a modification of an existing conceptual framework, it will become involved in the standards of justification for that framework. Although one wasn't initially justified in accepting the hypothesis, that hypothesis has become justified. But only with respect to the framework which it helps to constitute, for accepting the hypothesis may change the framework for the worse. While it is desirable to have justified beliefs, it is easy to overrate the importance of justification. Things would be different if we could provide a kind of absolute justification for our theories/conceptual frameworks about the external world of experience. But no objective situations determine our fundamental conceptual frameworks and theories to be correct or incorrect. Indeed, a new theory/framework may even be incompatible with the world of experience; our current world may falsify the proposed theory/framework. The new theory will make good sense of our experience or not. It may simply be a good start at making sense, which good start will need to be further revised and refined. But the theory isn't a good or poor match for the independent, objective world of experience. An accepted theory/framework supplies conceptual structure to the world of experience. A proposed theory/framework is a proposal to reconstitute and reorder that world. The only basis for accepting a theory/framework is that it seems to make good sense of the world of our experience, or it promises to do so. This cannot be counted as evidence in its favor.

However, there is a difference between theories/frameworks for the external world, and theories/frameworks for ourselves. That we contribute conceptual structure to the world of experience, and so are partly constitutive of that world, is an objective feature of ourselves. We constitute our actions by performing them. For intentional acts, our concepts of what we are doing characterize what we are doing (by characterizing what we are trying to do). Still, an intentional act can have features in addition to those we are aware of, or intend.

In this book I have been developing a new theory/conceptual framework for thought and action. I am not "teasing" this account out by making an analysis of existing concepts and systems of them. At least part of the time I have been thinking up new concepts governed by new principles, and have presented these as a way of understanding ourselves, our experience, and our conceptual and intentional activities. Although this account is brought forward to make sense of ourselves, it is not constitutive of ourselves and what we are up to in the same way that concepts of external objects are constitutive of them. Our activity, whether it is merely the perceptual organizing of experience, or is conceptual and intentional, is an element of the world of our experience. Although we contribute this element, our contribution is what it is no matter how we think of it. We find that we are acting and have acted, and try to devise an account which captures and illuminates our activity.

An account of the self and its intentional activities will not be constitutive of the self and these activites. It is objectively correct or objectively incorrect. This exempts the account from the cycle that Kuhn has described for knowledge of those objects we constitute. Although it isn't strictly necessary, we expect a period of normal science to end in crisis, and be followed by a period in which the old order is overthrown and a new order established. This leads to a new period of normal science, to be followed by a new crisis. And so on, perhaps indefinitely. We don't have access to independent objects of experience, whose features we try to ascertain. We do, however, have access to ourselves and what we are doing. We are not independent, of course, but there is an objective fact of the matter as to our role in the world of experience. There is a chance that we will get things right about ourselves in such a way that new information or new experience won't overthrow what we have accepted. Of course, it is also possible that an entirely satisfactory scientific theory might be developed, one that could subsequently be expanded and perhaps modified in small ways, but never overturned. But with the scientific theory, there is no way to examine both the theory and its object, to assess the fit between them.

We have a privileged access to our experience and our intentional activity. But this doesn't make it easy to understand how things are with us. We can't by reflection "read" the true account out of our self-conscious experience of ourselves. Just as in the case of our knowledge of the things we partly constitute, we must think up theories/conceptual frameworks and try them out. However, by virtue of our self-conscious awareness, we can see "from the inside" whether such a theory adequately explains what we are doing. Still, being adequate to what we have so far noticed, or pondered, is no guarantee of overall adequacy. The experience of adequacy "so far" is no guarantee of real adequacy.

Our privileged access to ourselves, our experience, and our intentional activity does not provide a royal road to an adequate theory of ourselves and our activity. But the different status of the knowledge of ourselves and the knowledge of physical objects, including our own bodies, is surely responsible for the belief that the mind is distinct and perhaps separable from the body. Since bodies are partly constituted by ourselves and our conceptual activity, how could the self, the mind, be dependent on them?

3. The Structure of Knowledge: Explanations and Reports

Just as we distinguished different concepts of entailment, so we find there are different concepts of analyticity. A propositional act of the true or false variety is *basically* analytic if performing the act commits a person to accepting it. This description/definition is most appropriate for propositional representing acts, for it is propositional representing acts that can be performed without being either accepted or rejected. An acknowledging act will be basically analytic if the performance of the act "certifies" the correctness of the act. (There is no question of our not accepting our own acknowledging acts; an acknowledging act has the status of a sincere assertion.) A propositional act is *truth-conditionally* analytic if its truth conditions can't fail and couldn't have failed to be satisfied. Either sort of analytic propositional act will be true when viewed from the perspective of the conceptual framework within which it is framed. But a propositional act that is analytic with respect to a defective framework may also be defective.

I think it likely that all truth-conditionally analytic propositional acts are basically analytic. But the converse isn't true. (This is parallel to the relations between the two kinds of entailment.) If this sentence:

> The statement I am currently making is in English.

is used to perform a propositional act, the act will be basically analytic. Making (and understanding) the propositional act requires that one accept it. But if we understand the truth conditions of such a propositional act to be that the speaker is at the time of utterance saying something in English, these truth conditions don't *have* to be satisfied. For nothing requires that the statement actually occur. Hence, the statement is not truth-conditionally analytic. A more interesting case of a basically analytic statement which is not truth-conditionally analytic is Descartes' *cogito*:

> I am thinking, I exist.

The truth conditions are that the speaker is at the time both thinking and existing. But he could probably exist without thinking, and he could certainly fail to exist. The truth conditions could fail or could have failed to be satisfied.

Neither concept of analyticity is the concept that Kant had in mind. Kant's analytic judgments/propositional acts were a subdivision of *a priori* propositional acts. An *a priori* propositional act is one that reflects or registers features of a conceptual framework within which it is "framed". Some *a priori* propositional acts seem trivial or empty—they express principles governing merely classificatory conceptual frameworks (or principles governing the merely classificatory portion of an essentially systematic framework). The trivial *a priori* propositional acts are analytic in Kant's sense. His synthetic *a priori* propositional acts express principles governing essentially systematic frameworks. These are frameworks linking a number of inferentially related concepts. A fundamental concept in such a framework can't be given an adequate explicit definition in terms of the other fundamental concepts. And it can't be deleted without "damaging" the other concepts. An essentially systematic framework may be applicable to the world or part of the world, but when it is, a person will be unable to conclusively determine, even in principle, that a fundamental concept applies to a particular situation. Each particular judgment depends on or presupposes others that haven't been made.

Propositional acts that are analytic in Kant's sense are both truth-conditionally and basically analytic. But Kant's synthetic *a priori* propositional acts will also be analytic in both senses. However, a propositional act which is basically analytic may not be *a priori*. For some basically analytic propositional acts owe this character to the circumstances of their utterance or occurrence. These acts will not simply reflect features of a conceptual framework. When someone speaks/thinks an instance of Descartes' *cogito*, her propositional act is basically analytic. It isn't *a priori*. That is part of the reason why the *cogito* was attractive to Descartes. It provided an indubitable truth about existence, one which wasn't a merely conceptual (*a priori*) truth.

Although Descartes was a Rationalist with a capital 'R', he didn't hold that metaphysics (the *Meditations*) was (entirely) *a priori* knowledge. He didn't hold that physics or the essential part of physics was (entirely) *a priori*. Mathematics *is a priori*. But metaphysics and the general part of physics that includes the laws of motion depends on basically analytic propositions of both the a priori and the non–*a priori* varieties. And once a person turned her attention to more detailed physical phenomena, she couldn't find satisfactory explanations either by appealing to *a priori* principles or by deriving the phenomena from metaphysical foundations. Instead she needed to formulate hypotheses that are consistent with fundamental physical principles and which account for the facts that can be observed.

For Descartes, systematic knowledge of nonpurposive items is explanatory. And knowledge of different areas has roughly the same explanatory structure. Descartes didn't consider a deductive system to provide an ideal for knowledge. Descartes thought of knowledge as problem-oriented. One starts with something that needs to be solved, or explained. Then she looks for fundamental propositional acts and principles that will allow her to deduce an explanation. This is the pattern with mathematics. But in mathematics the fundamental propositions and principles are *a priori*. The pattern of explanation is the same in metaphysics, though the fundamental propositions and principles are basically analytic, and only some of these are *a priori*. Physics also employs this pattern of explanation, only now the fundamental propositions and principles from which an explanation is deduced include *a priori* truths, basically analytic propositional acts, and empirical hypotheses. It is the deductive structure of these explanations which underlies the mechanical conception of causality, in contrast with Aristotle's concepts, including his concept of efficient causality. From Descartes' perspective, nonpurposive explanatory knowledge (and belief) has the same deductive structure, no matter what kind of propositions and principles are employed.

It was the Empiricists who drove a wedge between *a priori* and other kinds of knowledge. They failed to understand/appreciate the systematic character of the conceptual frameworks/theories employed in mathematics. (Kant was right that mathematics is synthetic *a priori* in his sense.) For the Empiricists could only accommodate the purely identifying use of language and the merely classificatory conceptual frameworks associated with the identifying use. But they did recognize the explanatory structure/character of mathematical proofs and solutions to problems. And they insisted that our knowledge of the world of experience does not have this character. We are passive recipients of experience of the world. Our knowledge can only report and summarize what goes on, though our summaries involve an element of (inductive) risk.

Empirical knowledge is a report, not an explanation. But one displays cleverness in formulating especially succinct and comprehensive summaries of what takes place, and this can provide empirical knowledge with a systematic organization, allowing certain parts to be deduced from others. The deductive structure gives empirical knowledge an organization similar to that given to systems of *a priori* knowledge, but the empirical knowledge remains nonexplanatory. Fundamental propositions and principles are not being used to provide understanding of less fundamental consequences derived from them. In the Empiricist scheme, it is the consequences that are fundamental, and the succinct summaries merely organize this foundation.

From the present perspective, Descartes's understanding of systematic, nonpurposive knowledge (and belief) is the correct one. This knowledge aims at explanation, not at succinct and elegant reports. These explanations appeal to fundamental principles and propositions to explain what is less fundamental. The explanations have a deductive or statistical structure where the more fundamental support the less fundamental which they explain. With *a priori* knowledge, fundamental principles and propositions are *a priori*. With other knowledge, only some fundamentals are *a priori*. However, as knowledge develops, what was once a matter of hypothesis and conjecture can acquire an *a priori* status. This will not make these propositions secure, for apart from mathematics, which is directly concerned with fictitious items (though these must reflect features of the world of experience), *a priori* principles and propositions have an empirical character. They are constitutive of conceptual frameworks and theories which we deploy to organize and make sense of the world. They can turn out to be incoherent or unsatisfactory in other ways. In which case we will amend or replace them. *A priori* propositions are not immune from criticism.

Perhaps some *a priori* propositions are or should be immune from criticism. If there are such, I don't know which propositions they are. It certainly isn't true that philosophical propositions have this character, or should have it. Nor is there reason for philosophy to be especially concerned with basically analytic propositions. Although Descartes had high hopes for these propositions (propositional acts), his hopes appear to have been groundless. Scrutinizing such propositional acts as the *cogito* won't take us very far.

Not all knowledge is systematic and explanatory. Indeed, not all systematic knowledge is explanatory. Some knowledge does consist of reports; these may be expressed succinctly, in a systematically organized fashion. Such knowledge depends on the conceptual frameworks within which it is formulated, and will include or presuppose *a priori* principles. But this knowledge is characteristically different from *a priori* knowledge systematically presented. For *a priori* knowledge is explanatory while reports are not. Succinct reports are also different from explanatory knowledge that isn't (yet?) *a priori*. Knowledge isn't usefully subdivided into *a priori* and empirical knowledge. The basic contrast is between explanatory knowledge and reports. Explanatory knowledge is further subdivided into the *a priori* and the non–*a priori*.

Nonpurposive explanatory knowledge (and belief) has a deductive or statistical structure, where the more fundamental both logically supports and explains the less fundamental. We also have explanatory knowledge which is purposive or intentional. In this knowledge, we explain actions by appealing to purposes, intentions, goals, and structures. What does the explaining need not provide logical support to what gets explained. Much explanatory knowledge combines purposive and nonpurposive explanations. It is difficult to have a comprehensive body of explanatory knowledge which is entirely purposive, for purposive activity usually exploits the causal order. Purposive and causal explanations will normally be inextricably intertwined.

I have a much less clear perspective on systematic and explanatory purposive knowledge than on systematic and explanatory knowledge that isn't purposive. The purposive knowledge hasn't been fully understood or carefully surveyed. In this book I have been giving a purposive account of thought and action, especially linguistic action. This account provides analyses but not (in general) predictions. Being in a position to make accurate predictions has been thought to be an important goal of systematic scientific knowledge; it has sometimes been taken to be the most important goal. The position of this work is that making sense of the world and our experience of it is the most important goal for systematic explanatory knowledge. Accurate predictions are a useful byproduct of successful causal explanations. They are not the reason why we seek such explanations, but are one sign that we have found them. Purposive and intentional explanations give us understanding, but only let us know what to expect in general, not in detail. Purposive explanations make sense of what comes first in terms of what is supposed to come after.

4. Knowing

In one sense, we know objects which we are currently experiencing, or which we have experienced and still remember. This is knowledge by acquaintance in (pretty much) the ordinary sense of 'acquaintance'. (The acquaintance admitted by Bertrand Russell has no place in the present scheme of things; his acquaintance is grounded by his conception of experience and its objects.) Our presently experiencing an object allows us to direct our attention to it, to directly (perceptually) attend to it. We can also use an expression or image to attend to an absent object which we have experienced, and can remember. This attending will also be considered direct, for it does not employ intermediate objects. We simply find that we can directly attend to some absent object, exploiting our connection to past experience. We cannot explain this by appealing to stored materials, for no such materials can establish links to the past. (Direct attention is not self-certifying. We may falsely "remember" an experience we didn't have. And for most objects we attend to directly, we also have indirect connections we can exploit.)

The objects we identify on the basis of reading or hearing about them, or through some inference, are objects we attend to indirectly. These objects are situated with respect to ourselves via intermediate objects, and we exploit a chain of connections in attending to them. In order for someone to exploit such a chain in identifying an object, the person needs some knowledge or awareness of the connection. But what sort of knowledge is this? If it is knowledge by acquaintance in our modest sense, then we will have to allow language users the experience of connections linking objects that are out of reach. That isn't possible, so some other explanation is wanted. A person requires propositional knowledge/belief to attend to objects indirectly. Someone can directly attend to an absent but previously experienced friend. Even if she has never experienced the friend's mother, she can indirectly attend to the friend's mother. Her attending to her friend and her possessing minimal biological information allows her to attend to the situation of her friend's having a mother. And this gives her access to the mother in that situation, for the situation of her friend's having a mother is the situation of her friend's having *this* mother.

In attempting to identify an object, a person can make a mistake. For she must identify or be disposed to identify the relevant situations linking her to the identified objects. She can't simply believe there is a situation of a certain sort—such a belief would involve the representational use of language. She must actually exploit particular situations. (But she can identify/exploit a complex situation or complex of situations without being able to supply the details.) If her attempt to identify an object essentially and crucially depends on a false belief, her attempt fails. Her attempted identifying act is unsuccessful and incorrect.

If we restrict our attention to propositional knowledge, there are different sorts of knowledge or different senses of 'knowledge'. Scientific knowledge is what is accepted by the normal science of a given time. Scientific knowledge changes. We generally acquire more of it as time goes on, but we occasionally give some up. Perhaps some accepted scientific "knowledge" turns out to be false by the very standards in effect when it was accepted. Experiments may have been carried out improperly, or someone may have made incorrect calculations or even lied. That seems better described as a case of false scientific beliefs than as false knowledge. The interesting case is where a scientific theory is overthrown and replaced by a more successful one. At the time when it was in power, the overthrown theory provided conceptual structure to its world. The theory corresponded to the world it helped constitute. In retrospect, from the perspective of its successor, the overturned theory is false. But it wasn't false while it was accepted. The scientific knowledge of a given time won't be false, but it may become unacceptable.

Let us consider a more humdrum sort of knowledge, knowledge in the *ordinary* sense. Even here, there are different concepts of knowledge, relative to different concepts of justification. Knowing something "for sure" is knowledge that is strongly justified. The knowledge which philosophers have tried to capture with the characterization justified true belief is knowledge which "might not have made it." This is *simple*, or *plain* knowledge, and requires plain justification. Beliefs which are only weakly justified are not ordinarily considered to be knowlege. I am weakly justified in believing my lottery ticket isn't the winner, but I don't *know* this. Both for sure and plain knowledge are relative to a conceptual framework whose principles are not questioned. Within such a framework, the formulation of the framework's principles can be evident, and strongly justified. However, we are presently more interested in knowledge that isn't either *a priori* or analytic.

Consider simple knowledge. Is such knowledge adequately characterized as simply justified true belief? To answer this question, it is helpful to distinguish identifying-stage knowledge from representational-stage knowledge. If an acknowledging act is simply justified, it might be false. But a simply justified acknowledging act which identifies a situation will be true, and not by accident, which makes it a convincing candidate for knowledge. An acknowledging act with modal truth conditions might be true by accident. In that case, the acknowledging act does not register modal features. If it does register these features, and is justified, it seems to constitute knowledge.

The truth of a propositional representing act is independent of its being or having been verified. And a propositional representing act can be true by accident. Even a propositional representation which is believed with (simple) justification can be true by accident. But in such a case, the believer has not verified her justified true propositional representing act. For propositional representing acts, truth and simple justification are necessary but not (jointly) sufficient for simple knowledge. The additional requirement is that the propositional representing act be verified (by the knower). The verification actually establishes a correspondence between the propositional act and the world. In verifying a propositional representing act, a person will either identify situations or register modal features. This can't be successfully accomplished by accident. We should note that on this account of knowledge, a person is in a position to know that he knows something. (This is dispositional, which keeps the regress from being vicious.) But he can also think he knows something when he doesn't.

I have provided the sketchiest of accounts for simple knowledge. It might be interesting to try to flesh out the account, and to deal with difficult cases and possible counter-examples. But I don't regard this as an important task. For simple knowledge is not a permanent accomplishment. Knowledge is relative to conceptual frameworks and the theories these incorporate. If a conceptual framework proves to be inadequate, this can undermine what is known within the "confines" of that framework. A correct characterization of knowledge will appear more important to a view that recognizes only one fundamental conceptual framework. This could be a view like Empiricism, which thinks the conceptual framework is supplied by experience, or it could be a view holding the framework to be innate. For such a view, what is known can be known once and for all. Since knowledge is permanently valuable, there will be good reasons to precisely determine what is required for something to be known. However, from the present perspective, it isn't worth going to a lot of trouble to provide this determination.

5. Certainty

We believe things with more and less confidence. Our belief that *A* may be hesitant, while we are completely confident that *B* is true. If acknowledging acts and acts of accepting propositional acts were matters of degree, then the degree to which we acknowledge α to be φ might be the degree of confidence we have in α's being φ. But acknowledging/accepting is an all or none affair. Someone either acknowledges α to be φ or she doesn't; she either accepts or doesn't accept that α is φ.

A person who doesn't believe that *A* may have some inclination to believe it. Her inclination can be strong or weak. She can also be strongly or weakly authorized to accept that *A* (is true)—*A* is more or less probable for her. And a person who does believe that *A* may be more or less willing to abandon her belief in the face of evidence to the contrary, or even in the face of phenomena that could be more easily explained/understood if *A* were false. Someone's degree of confidence that *A* (is true) can be identified either with her willingness to accept *A* or with her reluctance to abandon her commitment to accepting *A*. In the first case, her confidence in *A* is independent of her believing *A* and also independent of *A*'s being true. In the second case, her confidence depends on her belief, but is independent of *A*'s being true.

People frequently use the words 'certain' and 'certainty' to express great confidence. Thus a person who is certain that *A* must actually accept that *A*, and have great confidence in the evidence which he finds to strongly support *A*. Someone who is certain in this sense may be mistaken. However, philosophers (and others as well) have sometimes used 'certain' to signal a propositional act whose very performance makes the truth of the act apparent to the performer. This might be a propositional act which is immediately certain: in (thoughtfully) performing the act, its truth is apparent to the performer. A propositional act could also be mediately certain. If the act is reached by an inference which is certain to be correct from premisses which are certain, it will be mediately certain. For propositional acts to be mediately certain, inferences as well as propositional acts must be capable of being certain. When a judgment or inferential move is certain in this sense, there is no chance that the judger/inferrer is mistaken.

This philosophical sense of 'certain' is associated with strong justification and knowledge "for sure." I am using 'justify' in such a way that a person who is justified in believing *A* is a person who believes *A* and is justified in doing so. To say that Bill is justified in believing *A* is different from saying that Bill would be, or could be, justified in believing *A*. These latter formulations are ambiguous. Bill *would be* justified in believing *A* if

1. Bill does not believe *A*, but has sufficient information to allow him to be justified in coming to believe *A*.

or

2. Either Bill is actually justified in believing *A* or else Bill doesn't believe *A*, but has sufficient information to allow him to be justified in coming to believe *A*—this second understanding is appropriate only if the speaker doesn't know whether Bill believes *A*.

These matters are further complicated by our dispositional understanding of belief. When a person is readily disposed and committed to accept a propositional act, but has not performed and accepted the act, he believes it. But this belief is not yet justified. We can only say it would be justified. Even this formulation needs clarification. A person who is in a position to accept a propositional act with justification might nonetheless accept the act without justification. For a dispositional belief to be one which would be justified we will insist that the subject be committed to accept the belief and that, further, he be readily disposed to accept it with justification. For a person to justifiably come to believe *A*, he must be aware of being justified, though this awareness need not be propositional. (He need not explicitly take himself to be justified; his awareness of what he is doing is sufficent to enable him to take himself to be justified.)

For a person to be philosophically certain that *A*, the person must actually be thinking and accepting *A*, and must be strongly justified in the accepting. Even if nothing were certain in this sense, it would not be illicit or incoherent to speak of this kind of certainty. But many judgments are certain. We can have certain knowledge of *a priori* propositions from within the framework with respect to which they are *a priori*. With respect to the ordinary conception of experience, I know that sensory awareness of an object guarantees the existence of the object. Perhaps I can't know for certain that I am having sensory awareness (I might be hallucinating instead), but I can be sure about some of the features of the awareness. Descartes was certain that a cause must possess at least as much reality as its effect. However, knowledge that is certain with respect to a conceptual framework may not survive the rejection of that framework. This is a very poor sort of certainty.

All propositional acts employ concepts belonging to a conceptual framework. But some propositional acts can survive the demise of their conceptual framework. Different frameworks may accommodate propositional acts of essentially the same kind. If we begin with the ordinary conception of sense experience, according to which we directly see distant objects and events, and then modify this to have us directly seeing sights and indirectly seeing the objects and events which produce them, many judgments will be unaffected by the modification. There are some true and certain judgments that will remain true and certain no matter how we change our conceptions. We can know for certain that we are having experience, and what are some of the characters of this experience. Perhaps we cannot be certain of seeing a blue ball, but we can be certain of having an experience which is blue-ball-like. And we can be certain we are taking there to be a blue ball. In general, we can be certain of what we are intending to do. Sometimes we can be certain of what we are doing. We may not be certain that we are walking across the room, for this depends on perceptions that may prove unreliable. We can be certain that we are thinking about Chicago, or about philosophy. We can be certain that we believe one thing or another. We can be mediately certain that 3 divides 81 exactly.

It may be that all "absolute" certainty comes down to awareness of ourselves, of our experiencing and our acting. We can be sure that any adequate conception of ourselves and what we are up to will allow us to be certain that our experience at a given time has features which we detect, that we intend whatever it is we do intend, and that we exist whenever we think we do. It is certainly more plausible to explain certainty in terms of awareness of what we are up to than to drag in such features as clarity and distinctness. (Descartes' appeal to what we clearly and distinctly perceive or recognize was a move made in desperation. Nothing about a genuinely certain judgment is illuminated by this appeal. But he had to say something—which then acquired a life of its own.)

It is certainly possible to develop a system of certain knowledge, where this is certainty with respect to a conceptual framework. Mathematics has traditionally been conceived this way, although much (most?) mathematical knowledge falls short of certainty. The "idea" is that one *can* be certain of mathematical knowledge, although we don't always make the effort that being certain requires. Descartes thought certainty important, and described a strategy for swiftly surveying lengthy proofs to ensure that one had certainty from beginning to end. But mathematical knowledge can be satisfactory without being certain. We need not be certain when we remember being certain. And we don't count on certainty when we achieve results and write them down. Doing proofs in mathematics or logic, we will surely be certain of now this, now that. We ordinarily make no special effort to retain this certainty, so as to be certain of everything at once. We *couldn't* be certain of everything at once. Our past results are not so precarious as to require this anyway—there are no Cartesian demons trying their best to deceive us.

Absolute certainty, certainty that isn't relative to one or another conceptual framework, doesn't appear to add up to a systematic body of knowledge. Interestingly enough, Descartes was aware of the difference between certainty with respect to a conceptual framework and absolute certainty, though he conceived these differently than we have. And he believed that absolute certainty does yield a system of knowledge. When Descartes imagined that an evil demon might have produced us and be doing his best to deceive us, Descartes imagined that we might even be deceived about mathematics. Descartes didn't understand that conceptual frameworks are artifacts, and that one can be developed to replace another. He thought we are innately endowed with a fundamental conceptual framework, which we can develop further. But the evil demon might as a dirty trick have provided us with a conceptual framework which doesn't "fit" the world we actually inhabit. Our certain mathematical judgments might accurately reflect principles of our innate conceptual framework, but fail to have application to the real world. Descartes' argument to show that this hasn't happened was intended to be an argument containing only absolutely certain judgments and relying exclusively on absolutely certain inferential principles. Descartes' argument didn't succeed, for he made use of causal principles that are certain only with respect to a conceptual framework. Or so it seems to us—for Descartes must have had some reason to judge the causal principles to be absolutely certain.

From the present perspective, Descartes was mistaken. Absolutely certain knowledge exists, but it doesn't add up to anything. There is no reason why it should, in science or philosophy or anywhere. We must actively make sense of ourselves and our world. The world isn't revealed to us. It makes no sense to hold out for certainty. Acquiring and developing knowledge is a trial and error procedure. We can always do better than we have done so far.

Chapter 13

A Solution

1. Another Look at the Conceptions of Experience

In this chapter, I will further develop the new conception of representing to provide a solution to Descartes' Problem. But I must confess that I find this solution somewhat disappointing. It is, as one reviewer of this manuscript remarked, rather "thin." The solution doesn't tell us all that we would like to know. It doesn't give us the key which simply opens one door after another. What the solution does is provide a general conceptual framework within which we can operate. This framework is what we need to make sense of experience and the access it provides to the real world. But the framework is in need of further development. Instead of being the final step on our journey of self-exploration, it is simply the beginning of a new enterprise. While explanation must come to an end somewhere, there is no reason to think that the account in this chapter, and this book, is as far as we can go.

Let us begin this chapter by reflecting on the ordinary conception of sense experience and its objects. The ordinary conception is characteristic of the purely identifying stage of language use. However, with respect to this stage, it is more appropriate to speak of the ordinary conception of the world of experience, and of our experience of the world. For the primary focus at the identifying stage is on the objects rather than on our experience of them. The purely identifying stage of language use requires that we have direct access to some objects and situations, and indirect access via these to others. We can also directly attend to ourselves and our activities. Language users at the identifying stage are not self-consciously aware of using concepts to provide structure to the world of experience, though this is what they do. The understanding that this is going on requires a representational-stage perspective.

At the purely identifying stage, nonlogical concepts are, in principle, independently significant. Nonlogical conceptual frameworks are merely classificatory. The ordinary conceptual framework for the world and our experience of it includes concepts and criteria for objects encountered in experience and for objects linked to experience, it includes concepts and criteria of seeing, hearing, feeling, remembering, thinking, and so forth. These criteria ultimately come down to appearances, to the characters of our various experiences (including the experience of thinking).

Inferential connections that are established at the purely identifying stage are subsequent to the fundamental concepts and their acknowledging criteria. Inferential connections are not, in general, constitutive of significance. Although, for example, dissolving in water comes to be a necessary condition for being (correctly acknowledged to be) salt, this behavior isn't conceptually essential to salt. Salt just happens to dissolve in water. At the purely identifying stage, many causal connections amount to nothing more than regularities. (But there will be concepts whose fundamental acknowledging criteria involve characteristic behavior in specified circumstances.) When the language user learns to use language representationally, and takes up this practice in earnest, inferential connections can acquire a fundamental status and become constitutive of significance. Inferential connections can become conceptual necessities, although we continue to allow for the possibility of merely accidental regularities.

The ordinary conception of experience and its objects which is characteristic of the purely identifying stage is, at that stage, a merely classificatory framework. At the representational stage, it can be transformed into an essentially systematic framework, which is what allows us to amend, or even replace, this framework. At the purely identifying stage of language use, fundamental acknowledging criteria come down to features we learn to detect in experience. Once language learners progress to the representational stage, they acquire no reason to challenge the ordinary conception. Language learners will not think that objects aren't where we perceive them, and more or less as we perceive them. We have learned to accommodate sticks in water and square towers at a distance, as well as circular objects seen at an angle. We can correct some appearances with others. For the ordinary conception is a robust conception, and handles ordinary experience pretty well.

Using language representationally makes it possible to transform the signficance of certain concepts so that they become essentially systematic. This has happened to the ordinary conception of experience, though it may have taken a new conception of physical processes to bring this about. The mechanical conception of physical processes is a development of the ordinary conception of the objects of experience, and our experience of them. But the mechanical conception is an essentially systematic framework. Adopting this conception isn't simply a matter of knowing how to make certain machines, or how to exploit some natural processes. Neither is it a matter of knowing how to use such words as 'cause' and 'effect'. The mechanical conception is actually a developing theory/view of the world. It organizes the concepts of things currently understood. We have concepts of some things and the way they behave. Light does this, that, and the other. Light *is* the stuff that does this, that, and the other, as well as exhibiting other essential behavior not yet understood. The mechanical conception of physical processes is a systematic conception of the processes currently understood, and a strategy or way of approaching those processes not yet mastered. The mechanical conception is not so much a view of what the world is like as a demand about the way the world shall be understood. It is a systematic framework which at a given time organizes a number of concepts, but which perpetually makes allowance for the addition of new concepts.

Applying the mechanical conception to the workings of our bodies provides the opportunity to rethink the ordinary conception of experience. Ordinarily, we directly see some things, feel others, and hear still others. We now have occasion to recognize that these are different modalities of sensory awareness, and to notice a systematic interrelationship between such awareness and its objects. If we acknowledge ourselves to experience sensory awareness, we are committed to admitting the existence and presence of an object of this awareness. Not only does the awareness depend upon objects, but there is also dependence in the opposite direction. Objects don't need to be sensed if they are to exist, but acknowledging criteria are not criteria for *being* objects. The acknowledging criteria for the concept of a dog are criteria for *correctly acknowledging* an object to be a dog. With respect to the ordinary conception, our being able to think and talk about objects in the world essentially depends on our having sensory awareness of objects in the world. Once the ordinary conception is reconceived from a representational stage perspective, the concepts of awareness and of its objects are systematically interdependent. But at that point the mechanical conception of physical processes drives a wedge between sensory awareness and external objects. This provides the opportunity to make changes to the way we conceive experience and/or its objects, and requires us to do so.

2. A False Start

We have not responded to Descartes' Problem (or Problems) by abandoning the ordinary conception of experience and its objects, and coming up with a replacement. Instead we have adopted Kant's strategy, and revised and further developed the ordinary conception of experience. But we have incorporated this revised conception in a larger conception of thought and language use. Within this larger framework, we recognize that the objects of experience, and indeed, the whole world of experience, are not independent objects to which we have been granted access. We are partly constitutive of the world of experience, by providing its conceptual structure. This conception of thought and experience provides a new understanding of propositional thinking, both the 'to be'-variety and the 'that'-clause variety, and a new understanding of linguistic and mental acts. By developing this revised conception, and reflecting on its "fit" with our experience and our intentional activity, especially our linguistic activity, we can see that an attempt to simply abandon the ordinary conception and "start over" must fail. For the language we speak and the linguistic acts we perform owe their significance to the ordinary conception they incorporate. This is not a ladder we can climb and kick away, for there is nothing to lean the ladder on, nothing to step onto from the ladder. If we give up the ladder, we fall to the ground.

But Descartes' Problem is still a problem. Our strategy has not so far led to a solution or a resolution. If we experience the different parts of our bodies, and we use our bodies to experience the things around us, then if our bodies work the way we think/know they do, our experience can't provide us with direct access to our bodies and the things around us. Which consequence undermines experience, thought, and language.

In attempting to solve Descartes' Problem, we are not in the position of developing a conceptual framework/theory which imposes conceptual structure on a previously unformed reality. There is a fact of the matter about ourselves, our experience, and our intentional activity. We must be able to establish a correspondence between the account we come up with and the independent reality constituted by our experience and our activity. This reality is inescapably active and intentional. It can't be reduced to the mechanical causal order which we intentionally constitute. A possible solution, one that is initially attractive anyway, is to place the active self outside the world of experience. Although we are partly constitutive of that world, we don't need to be in it. This solution would require a rather drastic change to our conception of thought and experience. For as we currently have it, the subjects of experience do belong to the worlds they experience. We feel headaches in our heads, and tickles on the soles of our feet. We see with our eyes, hear with our ears, and feel things from the outside with our hands, feet, and whole bodies.

Kant adopted this solution to Descartes' Problem. Given this solution, we really have bodies, but we aren't "in" them. We constitute all physical objects, including our own bodies, "from the outside." Although we don't see things when it is completely dark or when our eyes are closed, we aren't seeing with or "through" our eyes. Our visual experiences are simply correlated with our eyes being open and aimed in a certain direction, as well as with light being available to our eyes. Instead of classifying sense experiences on the basis of the sense organ we employ, we just have qualitatively different kinds of experience. Some experiences are characteristically visual, while others are characteristically auditory, or tactile. If we took this approach, we could continue to *say* we see with our eyes, but change our understanding of what this means. This would minimize the apparent disagreement between the new understanding and the ordinary conception, but such a change could only be motivated by an intent to "cover up" a difficult feature of the new conception. As we ordinarily conceive things, our eyes give us access to the objects we see. We see with and through our eyes.

On the solution being considered, not only don't we sense with our sense organs, but we don't think with our brains. It is our conceptual activity that constitutes neural activity, and not the other way around. But this solution isn't satisfactory. The first, and most fundamental problem with the solution is that it simply isn't believable. We just *can't* be on the outside, looking into the world of experience. This first objection is nothing like a proof that the proposed solution is incorrect. But a satisfactory solution has to be consistent with our awareness of ourselves and what we are up to. Even apart from its intuitive lack of appeal, this solution can't be developed to account for all the things that need explaining. For the solution would encompass our actions as well as our bodies. The self will operate on the world of experience, but not in it. However, we certainly are participants in the world of experience. We move our arms and legs, we walk around in the world we see and hear and feel. Our purposive and intentional acts are performed "side by side" with the mechanical causal order. We intentionally perform action *A*, and by means of *A* intentionally cause *B*. Although the solution which removes the self from the world of experience is not satisfactory, there is a respect in which this solution is on the right track. For it is true that the world of experience isn't the last word, or world. We are constituting this world (in part), but we aren't in the same sense constituting ourselves; we only constitute ourselves in the Existentialists' sense, by choosing and acting. We can't be elements of the world of experience "on all fours" with the elements we constitute.

We not only conceive ourselves to be actively experiencing objects from within the world of experience, but we conceive other people to be members of the same world. We conceive ourselves and others to be living and acting in the world of experience. If we were constituting the world of experience from outside, then the same must be true for other people. We could only infer their existence from the similarity between their bodies, and bodily behaviors, and our own. But this is a ludicrous proposal. We don't infer the existence of others, we simply encounter those others.

If we were outside the world of experience, and acted outside that world, we would have the task of "squaring" our actions with what takes place in our worlds. This might lead us to talk of two "stances" or two perspectives. The events in the world of experience, from the "inside" perspective, might get causal explanations, while our extraterrestial activity would be purposive and intentional. And somehow our bodily movements would instantiate both the causal and the intentional orders. This might be appealing to someone inclined to identify the world of experience with the causal order, who thinks that all events in the world must receive causal explanations. But such a view is neither reasonable nor plausible. There is no hope of reconciling causally produced bodily motions with the intentional actions we carry out. We move our arms and our legs, they aren't moved for us. We act in the world of experience to achieve goals in the future, our bodies aren't simply pushed along by events in the past.

3. Nonexplicit Representing

To solve Descartes' Problem, we must take seriously the mechanical understanding of physical causality, applied to the workings of our own bodies. External objects interacting with our bodies produce neural events which are the crucial items for sensory awareness. Various events taking place within our bodies also produce neural events. As well as "hosting" these neural events, we also experience sensory awareness, which is nothing like the neural events. To solve Descartes' Problem, we must account for the relation between the events and the awareness. We are not consciously aware of the events in their neural capacity. We don't feel things happening in our heads when we look around us. So we don't use the neural events to carry out explicit representing. However, in discussing representing, we allowed for the possibility of nonexplicit representing. With explicit representing, we interpret objects and features of which we are consciously aware to become representationally aware of further objects. In nonexplicit representing, we are not consciously aware of the representation. We shall understand sensory awareness to be nonexplicit representational awareness constituted by interpreting certain neural phenomena. So the awareness of our bodies and external objects that we "enjoy" in sensory awareness is actually representational awareness. It is because we are not aware of the neural events and our interpreting them that we can think of our bodies and the objects around us as actually present to us in experience. But objects of representational awareness are not really objects. External objects are real, but we are not really, directly, aware of them. The world of experience is not the real world. (However, each of us is a real component of her own world of experience—representational awareness of her body and other bodies is "continuous" with her plain awareness of herself and her activity. And each of us is a real component of the real world.)

Someone who balked at admitting nonexplicit representing, but who accepted the (updated) mechanical conception of the physical world, and who agreed about the importance of neural events for experience, might either identify sensory awareness with the neural events, or claim that sensory awareness is a somewhat mysterious condition caused by the neural events. Such a person would claim that *experiential* awareness should be distinguished from representational awareness, for representational awareness is an activity and experiential awareness is not. Experiential awareness entirely belongs to the causal order. However, that person's account cannot be sustained. Explanations must surely come to an end someplace, perhaps at puzzling facts about how the world happens to be. But it makes little sense to identify sensory awareness with neural events. That is like identifying apples with oranges, or kangaroos with grasshoppers. The firing of neurons and whatever else goes on in our heads is nothing at all like being aware of dogs, cats, and tin cans. Awareness is awareness *of*, and neural events are not about anything. It is equally unsatisfactory to think that sensory awareness is a distinct something caused by the neural events. The causal order has no space to accommodate this mysterious something. It is our operating on (with) the events in our heads that constitutes awareness.

The causal advocate would have us being patient receptors of experience, not active producers of it. But an experience that was simply given to us would not take us beyond ourselves. We would be left seeking regularities in a welter of sense data. Instead we are actively aware of the world of experience and its various parts, and we actively transform this world and our experience of it by introducing conceptual structure. If we were passive recipients of the initial experience, we would be in no position to act on this experience, and transform it. We could at most actively develop views about experience. We would never achieve the kind of views we actually hold.

The understanding that sensory awareness is really representational awareness allows the present theory to accommodate the interesting kinds of examples that Dennett discusses (Dennett 1992; Dennett and Kinsbourne 1992; among other places). Just as an ordinary picture only gives some of the details of an actual scene, so neural events might be "gappy" in various ways, and still be interpreted to provide "smooth" awareness of objects in space and time. We interpret whatever material we have to work with, but gappy material need not lead to gappy interpretations.

4. Experience We Can't Help Having

We actively interpret neural items to constitute sensory awareness. But we aren't aware of the neural items, though we are, in a way, aware of our interpreting. For our interpreting the neural items is what constitutes sensory awareness. We are both aware of the objects of sensory awareness (i.e., we are sensorily, representationally, aware of objects) and aware of being sensorily aware. This interpreting activity must be purposive, but it isn't intentional. Although we may sometimes intend to be having sensory awareness, this intention isn't necessary. And sensory awareness doesn't require its subject to have a conception of this awareness—the awareness can take place without any concepts at all.

If sensory awareness is purposive, there must be a purpose of or a purpose for this activity. The purpose need not be one of which we are aware, it certainly is not a purpose that we consciously select. Some purposive activity might not be conscious activity. Some might be conscious but entirely "automatic." Relative metaphysical possibility and necessity are linked to what is determined. What past and present states of the world determine to be the case is relatively metaphysically necessary. (The necessity is relative to the present.) As we ordinarily conceive of this, all present and past states or situations are completely determined, but in the future some things are (already) determined, while others are open possibilities. Some things that are now determined in the future owe this determination to the causal order. Past and present causes determine that future effects will occur. But the very idea of determination is not essentially linked to causality. Things can be determined without being caused to be that way. A nonconscious or an "automatic" purposive activity would be like this. The interpreting activity that constitutes sensory awareness is automatic, we can't help doing it. The interpreting activity must satisfy an instinctive need. And we must be determined to satisfy it as we do.

But if we are determined to interpret neural events to constitute sensory awareness, why should this awareness receive a purposive rather than a causal explanation? We understand how, in the causal order, the past drives and determines the future, to a greater or lesser extent. But in the purposive order, a future goal calls forth activity to achieve that goal. Present activity is explained in terms of what is supposed to follow. How can it make sense to think of a future goal as determining a present action?

It may be in the very natures of salt and water that salt will dissolve in water. The nature of electrons may determine how electrons travel through space. These are certainly causal matters. It can also belong to the nature of a purposive agent to have certain needs, some instinctive goals. The nature of the agent may determine that in specified kinds of circumstances, the agent will act to achieve this or that goal. The way the agent acts to achieve the goal may also be determined without being caused. We insist that these facts and features belong to the purposive rather than the causal order, because the two orders are distinct, and the causal order will not accommodate either goals or purposes. But these are not cases where the future determines the present. At present the agent's very make-up, its nature, determines the agent to have certain goals and to act in a certain way to satisfy those goals. We understand the agent's activity in terms of the goals, but the agent presently has those goals. It is their accomplishment which is in the future.

With respect to the causal order we think the past is, in many cases, completely determining the future. Where the causal laws are statistical rather than invariable, we still think of the past as determining the future to some extent, and what is determined extends to the very small details of what takes place. When a purposive agent is determined to have a goal, and to act in a certain way to achieve that goal, we do not expect what is determined to extend to the very small details of what happens. Instinctive needs and goals can often be satisfied in various ways. The kind of act that an agent is determined to perform is determined with respect to the goal of the act. If what seemed to be purposive activity was completely determined, in all its details, this would provide us with a reason to reclassify the activity, transferring it to the causal order. (But we are not in a position to know just what is determined and what isn't.)

Although a purposive agent might have some flexibility in carrying out an action it is determined to perform, this flexibility should not be confused with freedom of the "free will" variety. If an agent which is determined to perform a certain kind of action performs one particular action as opposed to others it might have performed, this action may be free in some suitable sense of 'free'. But for an action to be an instance of free choice or free will, it must be an intentional action which the agent is not determined (in advance) to perform. The agent's undetermined choice to perform the action, which may not be distinguishable from the action itself, must be what determines that such an action is performed.

It isn't sufficient to characterize this freedom in terms of what might have been otherwise. That is simply the absence of determination. Freedom requires understanding, which the agent herself uses as a basis for determining the action she performs. According to Kant, the issue of whether people (sometimes) act freely is one of the Big Three of philosophical issues. It doesn't seem that important to me, or that difficult. There is no one who doesn't conceive himself as free when he is in the course of deliberating about a decision he must make. Can everyone really be misguided on this score? It provides neither guidance nor comfort to the deliberator to tell him that both his deliberating and his eventual decision/action have been determined in advance. Such a view can only provide consolation when one's choices turn out badly, and this is small comfort. That someone can understand freedom and raise questions about it is sufficient evidence that he can act freely. For to understand what it is for an intentional act to be an open possibility—to be possible without being determined—a person must have experience of such possibility. Someone who considers the question of freedom is acting intentionally when she does this. Her thinking isn't caused. If she makes the question of freedom her own (as opposed to merely reading or hearing about the question), she is acting freely when she ponders the question, and when she answers it—no matter how she answers it.

5. What We Can Be Made Of

I don't directly see the real desk which is front of me, or feel it, but I am representationally aware of a tan desk with a beige top and a hard surface. The actual desk supports my real right arm, while there is no desk that I see and feel. The seeing and feeling are real—I am really interpreting neural events to constitute this awareness. The representational awareness of a tan desk is simply a kind of representational awareness; the awareness doesn't relate me to anything, real or otherwise. But in the world of experience, the arm I see and feel is my arm. It is a particular arm rather than an arbitrary arm, and I can move it as well as experience it. Although the ordinary conception misleads me into thinking that experience puts me in touch with real objects, I must actually use experience to get at the real objects. When I move my right arm and look in that direction, I am wrong to think I see the arm moving but I am not wrong about moving the arm. Moving the arm causes neural events which I interpret to provide representational awareness of an arm in motion. The arm I see isn't the arm I am moving. So I can be really aware of moving my right arm without really being aware of the arm moving. Still, I manage to use my awareness of a moving arm to direct my attention to the arm that is really in motion.

I am not directly aware of my body, but only representationally, sensorily aware of a body. However, I am not representationally aware of a self, I am directly aware of myself and (some) things I am doing or trying to do. When I am aware of myself moving my right arm, it is conceivable that I am not moving my arm. Perhaps I have representational awareness of a moving arm, though the real arm isn't moving. In any case, I am genuinely aware of myself trying to move the right arm, and also aware of being sensorily aware of a moving arm. When I am thinking about something, I am aware of this, and of what I am thinking about. A recalcitrant body can't undermine this awareness.

Descartes thought the difference in status between the awareness of the self and the awareness of bodies showed that we are even better placed to investigate and understand the self than we are to explore our bodies and the things around us. He also thought he had good reason to contrast his immaterial mind/self with his extended material body. But while we are certainly aware of what we are doing or trying to do, this awareness doesn't appear to provide us with knowledge of what the self is "made of." Our conception of the self is of an active subject of experience. This active subject might have (or be) immaterial, "spiritual" components. Then again, it might not. Though I agree with Chomsky that there is no real content, or point, to materialism now that the views of matter found in the early mechanists and Descartes have been abandoned. On my own conception, my self is the whole "package" that constitutes me, whatever this turns out to be. So my self is not a component of the "larger" me, it *is* the larger me. What I am made of surely has considerable bearing on what I am and can do. I don't expect to find out much about what I am made of by exploring mental and linguistic activity.

6. Pretending and Imitating

To be representationally aware of a horse is not to be related to a horse, to either a real horse or a horse of another color (status). To be representationally aware of a horse is to have a horse-kind of experience. We could express this adverbially, and speak of experiencing horse-ly, or of being horse-representation-ally aware. But this adverbial locution is not illuminating: it does not help us understand representational awareness. And we do need help here. Although representational awareness is familiar to everyone, we do not have an adequate conception of this awareness. Representing is most commonly conceived as a relation, which it is not. We simply don't know how to handle nonrelational awareness. As a start, I have proposed that we think of being representationally aware of a horse as involving something like pretending. Looking at a picture of a horse is something like pretending to be directly aware of a horse. Using a predicate to represent an arbitrary horse is something like pretending to be a horse. Our concept of pretending is one of the few familiar concepts that are useful for giving us an orientation for thinking about representing, and this can start us on the path to an adequate account of representing.

The pretending that is relevant is not pretending that aims to deceive, as when someone commits the offense of impersonating a police officer. It is instead the pretending involved in children's play, or in dramatic performances. Although being representationally aware of a horse is something like pretending, representational awareness is more primitive, more fundamental, than pretending. This more primitive activity underlies, or is a prerequisite for pretending. Instead of thinking of being representationally aware of a horse as standing in some kind of relation, we can think of this as trying to imaginatively see what it is like to be a horse. When we look at a picture of a horse, this is like pretending to be directly aware of a horse. But we never are directly aware of a horse. Our only objects of direct awareness are ourselves. Pretending to be directly aware of a horse in looking at a picture is pretending to have the relation to the horse that we have to ourselves. But this makes the pretending to be directly aware a variety of pretending to be a horse. In looking at a picture of a horse, our representational awareness is explicit, because we realize that the horse-awareness is not sensory awareness. Sensory awareness of a horse is nonexplicit, but sensory awareness is also nonrelational. Because we are not aware of the representation used to achieve sensory awareness, the precursor to pretending that constitutes this awareness must be more remote from pretending than is the activity that constitutes explicit representational awareness.

As a simplified model of sensory awareness, consider a sentient agent in some science-fiction account. This agent has a flexible sense organ which surrounds the objects to be sensed, and precisely adapts to their outer surfaces. The agent registers the shape its sense organ has assumed, without being aware of this shape. The shape taken by the sense organ is not the shape of the sensed object; the difference is as convex to concave. The sense organ has the object's shape, but from the outside. To be aware of the shaped object, the sentient agent needs to "appreciate" this shape from the object's perspective. Given the shape of the sense organ, the agent must do something like imaginatively pretend to be an object with the actual shape of which the sense organ's shape is the "reverse."

This story/metaphor has two features that are helpful in thinking about sensory awareness. The first is that the feature of the sense organ which gets interpreted is not (quite) the same as the feature it is interpreted as. In our case, we interpret neural items as objects having colors and shapes. But the neural items themselves have no colors, and their shapes are (probably) not the same as the shapes of which we are sensorily aware. We are innately and instinctively equipped with whatever we need to interpret the features of neural items as the quite different features of objects in the world of experience. A better understanding of the neural items might conceivably provide us with understanding of how the neural features can be thought of as the "reverse" of the features of which we have sensory awareness. The second helpful feature of the story is that it provides a treatment of the nonrelational awareness that is not, at bottom, adverbial. Being representationally aware of a red object is something like pretending to be a sensible red object, and is not simply a case of sensing redly. Pretending to be is object-directed, while adverbial awareness seems unable to yield awareness *of* objects.

I shall use the word 'imitate' as a technical term for the primitive precursor of pretending. The agent who interprets a painting of a red ball to become representationally aware of a red ball, or the agent who interprets neural events to become sensorily aware of a red ball, is *imitating* a red ball. It is understood that imitating in the technical sense is not imitating in the ordinary sense; similarly, ordinary imitating is not technical imitating. At present, the technical sense of 'imitate' is rather thin. The technical concept of imitating needs to be filled-in, or filled-out. What I shall have to say here is merely a beginning. Some of the meanings conventionally associated with 'imitate' are appropriate to the technical sense. In some uses, imitating is linked to pretending; the child who pretends to be grown up is imitating a grown-up. And the verb 'to imitate' seems (to me) much less "relational" than 'to represent'. If I imitate a dog, or a philosopher, there is no suggestion that this links me to some dog, or some philosopher. Even if I knew how to imitate Immanuel Kant, and did this, the imitating is all on my side, and doesn't connect me to him. In imitating Immanuel Kant, I would be imitating anyone who is/was like Kant in the imitated respects.

The present theory/conception of sensory awareness and of representing is very much "in process." This whole book is merely a beginning, it is not the end of any matter. (Though I would like it to mark the beginning of the end of misguided attempts to understand experience and thought along either Empiricist or computational lines.) But even as so far developed, this account has interesting and important consequences. One of these concerns internal images, which most people claim to experience. The present account (or approach) leaves no room for such images. In sensory awareness, we interpret neural events/states to constitute awareness of colored, shaped objects, or sounds, or warm-or-cold, hard-or-soft, rough-or-smooth objects, etc. Some neural events are interpreted to give us awareness of external images: paintings, drawings, statues.

When we imagine a red triangle, or a green circle, or a silver Mercedes Benz, we must be interpreting neural events, but not to give us representational awareness of a picture of one of these things. In imagining a red triangle, for those of us who can do it, we are interpreting neural events which we have produced to give us representational awareness of a red triangle. The difference between seeing a red triangle and imagining one is the difference between a strong, vivid, lively representational awareness and a weaker awareness. The awarenesses are the same in kind, but different in degree. In neither case does the awareness link the subject to an actual triangle or image. Descartes was right: Although there are many differences between our dreaming and waking experiences, the difference is not in the kinds of objects involved. Whether we are dreaming or awake, our awareness of objects is representational.

7. Matching

The new conception of representing that has been developed in this book makes a sharp distinction between representing, strictly speaking (which is being representationally aware of arbitrary objects), and identifying. This distinction will be invoked to explain how we get at real objects in the real world, even though we have no sensory awareness of these objects.

In using neural events and states to carry out nonexplicit representing, agents are not consciously aware of the neural items and the way the items are being used. (But using these items to represent nonexplicitly is [=] being sensorily aware.) This might seem to explain why we ordinarily take experience to provide direct and immediate access to our bodies and other objects. However, representational awareness, of which sensory awareness is a special case, is awareness of arbitrary objects of various kinds, not awareness of specific real objects. We need an explanation of how we have come to understand experience as giving us access to particular objects and groups of them. Given this understanding, we can then explain how explicit representations are used to identify particular objects. But the initial "identifying" is a puzzle.

In explicit representations that aren't used to identify real objects, we can represent a single object with different representations. In a comic strip with several panels, we see Dagwood Bumstead engaged in different activities. Successive panels are used to represent successive actions. But our use of different representations to represent/identify a single fictional character is parasitic on the use of different representations to identify a single real object. We are bringing our conceptual frameworks, including our concepts of identity, from the world of experience to the fictional world. We are treating the world of Dagwood as if it were the real world.

We do the same thing when we represent an arbitrary horse in motion, where different images represent successive positions. Even without an authoritative story about the horse (as there is an authoritative story about Dagwood), we interpret the images against the background of a fictional world (against the background of a fictional version of the real world). That the horse in this picture is the same as the horse in that picture isn't a matter of resemblance. It depends instead on the painter's or the viewer's intentions, and on the pretense that there is an independent world whose objects are to be identified by means of the images. Our use of images to identify and reidentify a single object, whether it is real or fictional, can't explain how it is that different occurrences of sensory awareness are routinely taken to be awareness of a single object.

We don't initially bring our conceptual frameworks to bear on sensory awareness, for we have sensory awareness before we learn language. Animals incapable of conceptual and propositional thinking have sensory awareness. It isn't correct to describe the owners of preconceptual experience, or the nonconceptual owners of sensory experience, as *thinking that* they experience objects in the world. Nor can we properly say they think that they don't experience such objects. These owners simply don't have propositional thoughts. But subjects of experience are not limited to representational awareness of arbitrary objects having various qualities. Like ourselves, they must direct their attention to particular objects. For it is particular objects that are dealt with in life. A nonconceptual/preconceptual subject can't use its representational awareness to identify objects, for identifying (as we are understanding it) is intentional and conceptual. We need to recognize an activity which links subjects through experience to objects in the world, which activity is more fundamental than identifying, and prior to identifying. There would be no identifying in the absence of this activity.

Representational awareness alone wouldn't lead an agent to attend to and operate on objects giving rise to the awareness. Sensory awareness must be understood as the active response to objects and events producing the neural events which, when interpreted, constitute sense experience. In producing/constituting sensory awareness, the agent is trying get at the objects which gave rise to the awareness. But what can the agent be trying to do? Whatever it is, I will use 'match' as a technical term for the activity the agent attempts to carry out. When she interprets neural events to constitute sensory awareness, the agent isn't simply watching a movie. The agent is actively trying to *match* the objects causing the neural events.

The attempt to match these objects is externally directed. This attempt takes the experiencing agent beyond herself (itself). The matching is successful to the extent that the sensory awareness "captures" the features of the objects which gave rise to it. Matching or attempting to match objects in the world is purposive. For the subjects of sensory awareness, their attempt to match objects is instinctive. They are determined by their very natures to act this way.

Once Descartes realized that internal events were the critical items for sensory awareness, he was faced with explaining how people come to believe that experience provides access to the external world. He "solved" this problem by postulating a natural inclination to believe that the experienced qualities belong to our bodies and objects around us. He didn't feel compelled to explain what leads nonhuman animals to think they are in touch with external objects, because he regarded these animals as machines which don't enjoy sensory awareness. Hobbes also found a need to explain how inner events get us thinking about external objects. His explanation was that the inner events that give us awareness are motions in an external direction. We mistakenly think we are aware of objects in the direction where the motion is "pointing." In recognizing an activity of matching, I am responding to the same problem that Descartes and Hobbes confronted. The instinctive attempt to match external objects is my "version" of Hobbes' motion in an external direction.

The agent imitates objects of sensory awareness as a way of trying to match its body and external objects. The nonconceptual owner of sensory awareness doesn't "think" the objects of sensory awareness are the ones it is trying to match. It doesn't have an opinion about the status of objects of sensory awareness. The agent simply uses the awareness to guide its attending and acting. Conceptual owners of experience are in a position to have propositional thoughts and beliefs about experience and its objects. Since we are not consciously aware of neural events we interpret to constitute sensory awareness, it is quite natural to think that sensory awareness provides direct access to the objects we try to match. It is natural to think that sensory awareness is not representational awareness, but is instead the kind of awareness we have of ourselves and what we are up to. In many cases, perhaps, sensory awareness "might as well be" direct awareness of the real objects. But the ordinary conception of experience and its objects is, after all, unsatisfactory.

8. Portraying Real Objects in the Real World

To discuss the relation between the world of experience and the real world, we will enlarge our earlier conception of portraying. So far, portraying takes place when someone uses an image of which she is aware to become representationally aware of arbitrary objects *and* also uses the image to identify an actual object or objects. The agent uses the image to portray objects which that agent identifies. This is *explicit* portraying. Only objects in the world can be explicitly portrayed in an unqualified sense. While someone can use a painting to portray Napoleon on an arbitrary horse, she can't portray the arbitrary horse. But we can, with qualification, speak of portraying fictional characters. Someone can fictionally portray Sherlock Holmes, for example.

There is also nonexplicit portraying. A subject of experience will interpret neural events in trying to match objects that caused the neural activity. In doing this, the subject *nonexplicitly portrays* the objects it is trying to match. But there must be a degree of success in the matching for portraying to occur. In a hallucination, the subject will be representationally aware of kinds of objects, but the experience doesn't match any objects well enough to portray them. Even when the subject succeeds in nonexplicitly portraying real objects, she may portray them in ways that they aren't. Portraying a ball as blue will be inaccurate portraying, if objects in the world fail to have the colors we sense. A real object *X* can be portrayed as related to another object *Y*, where there is no object of the sort *Y* should be. Although the subject has portrayed *X*, and has portrayed *X* as related to *Y*, he has not portrayed *Y*. There is no *Y*.

On our usage, representing is not a relation, but portraying is. Portraying links a subject to objects which she "gets at" by means of a representation. The distinction between explicit and nonexplicit portraying was modeled on the distinction between explicit and nonexplicit representing. Explicitly, the subject is directly and ordinarily aware of the representation she uses; in the nonexplicit case, she isn't. Nonexplicit portraying is a relation to objects responsible for present experience. This won't take us "as far" as explicit portraying based on identification of absent objects. But identifying is intentional and conceptual, while experience need be neither.

The objects portrayed in experience are constituents of the real world. It isn't clear how to describe the relation of these objects to the world of experience (to a subject's world of experience). A preconceptual/nonconceptual subject of experience will portray objects in experience, but the subject isn't (yet) capable of thinking these objects to be as portrayed, or thinking them to be not as portrayed. The preconceptual/nonconceptual subject does not inhabit a world of experience. It inhabits the real world, and uses experience to get along in that world. To inhabit a world of experience, a subject must use concepts and engage in propositional thinking.

We produce the world of experience in response to the real world to which we belong. We need to determine how we should now conceive of this world. (To begin with, we conceived the world of experience simply as *the* world. At present we need a new conception.) Either the world of experience is constituted by real objects as we portray them, so that the world of experience is after all the real world. Or the world of experience is nonexistent, make-believe, except for ourselves and our activity. However, the second alternative fails to accommodate the insight that sensory awareness is a way of matching the real world. In sense experience we portray real objects. The world of experience is the real world, but not *simply* the real world. It is the real world as we portray and conceive it.

The objects portrayed in experience are constituents of both the real world and the world of experience. In the real world, the objects may or may not be as we portray them. But the objects as we portray them are the fundamental elements of the world of experience. However, we can distinguish corrected from uncorrected experiences. When one line appears longer than another, though they are the same length, we have portrayed the one line as longer. This experience is corrected by the further experience of measuring the lines with a ruler. In the world of experience, the two lines have the same length. In the world of experience, things are as we portray them in suitably corrected experience. (Since different people inhabit different worlds of experience, different people may differ on the correction techniques they employ.) The world of experience is something like the world that is "created" in performing a play. Real actors are in the play. They often wear genuine clothes, have genuine furniture on stage, and genuinely move around. But in the play the actors are pretending to be characters other than themselves. They are pretending that the props and stage setting are different than in fact they are. In a play, an actor doesn't simply pretend to be someone else. He also pretends that the other actors are different than they in fact are. He pretends that the stage is not a stage, but a room in a house. And so on. In the world of experience, the only ones who are "pretending" are the agents who imitate objects, who portray and identify objects. The objects portrayed and identified are not playing roles. The objects are portrayed as occupying places in the world as the agents portray it.

9. The Reconceived World of Experience

Objects we portray in sense experience are only a tiny part of the real world. The conceptual structures used to build the world of experience inform our experience. These structures allow us to presently remember past experience, and to attend to and identify objects remote in space and time. The world of experience is constituted by ourselves, by the objects we portray in experience, and by the objects to which we have conceptual acccess, as we portray and conceive these objects. Our conception of ourselves and our experience also informs the world of experience. In the world of experience at a certain stage of development, we portray (have portrayed) ourselves as having direct access to the objects of experience—we portray ourselves as having direct access to objects that in fact we only portray.

The world of experience at a given time won't contain all the objects in the real world. It will only contain the objects to which our experience and our concepts give us access. If the real world contains objects of which we have absolutely no idea, then those objects don't belong to the world of our experience. We are at present unable to portray or identify them. But this can change in time. New knowledge and new concepts can introduce new objects into the world of experience. (We can overthrow the present world of experience in favor of a new one.) Although the world of experience contains fewer objects than the real world, and contains objects to which we have conceptual access but may not have portrayed either in experience or symbolically, I will informally continue to say that the world of experience is the real world as we portray it. This locution gives the right idea of the relation between the worlds.

Not only does the world of experience fail to fully capture the real world, but the world of experience can be defective in ways that go beyond being incomplete. The conceptions which give structure to the world of experience can be inaccurate or even incoherent. The world of experience can contain objects and kinds of objects not found in the real world. It is conceivable, for example, that some community's world of experience would accommodate elves and trolls. As they conceive the world and the way things work, elves and trolls play important roles. In their world of experience, it might be possible to identify a particular troll or group of them—for example, the ones that did this or caused that. If *we* are right, that community's conception is mistaken. There aren't really (and there have never been) elves and trolls. So how could members of that community identify elves and trolls? In an unqualified sense, a person can only identify a real object. But the members of that community can identify elves and trolls in much the same way that we identify Sherlock Holmes. (It is an important difference that we know Sherlock Holmes to be fictitious while the members of the community take elves and trolls more seriously.) Elves and trolls for that community have a status determined by the beliefs and conceptions of that community. Those people can fictionally identify particular elves or trolls without realizing that the identified objects are fictitious. Though the community's members can unqualifiedly portray certain real events as due to the actions of trolls, they can't unqualifiedly portray or identify the trolls.

The world of experience may be quite different from the real world, but once our portrayal and conceptions determine its character, the world of experience has an objective status. Statements are true or false with respect to this world. Acknowledging acts identify or fail to identify situations in the world of experience, they register or fail to register modal features. A statement that is true with respect to the world of experience may not really be true. (In someone's world of experience it may be true that some event was caused by magic; the event wasn't really caused by magic.) The world of experience will never *be* the real world, but the world of experience can match the real world to a greater or lesser degree. Although the world of experience will never catch up to, or exhaust, the real world, we can hope to make ever better sense of the world. Unfortunately, it is possible to make pretty good sense of things without getting them right.

At the purely identifying stage of language use, the world of experience is portrayed in (with) sense experience, and this is expanded on with linguistic attending and acknowledging acts. But no linguistic acts attempt to portray objects. At the purely identifying stage, a language learner is not in a position to understand or employ essentially systematic conceptual frameworks. At this stage, conceptual frameworks are essentially classificatory. At the purely identifying stage of language use, the ordinary conception of experience and its objects is the only conception available. This framework is essential for learning language, for the objects attended to when they are portrayed, identified when they are absent, and acknowledged to be one thing or another must be understood to be elements of experience.

At the representational stage of language use, it becomes possible to develop and deploy essentially systematic conceptual frameworks. The mechanical causal conception of physical objects and their interactions, which undermines the ordinary conception of experience, is essentially systematic. The principles governing this framework determine that from an adequate characterization of a certain kind of event, we can derive (a statement of) the consequences of the event. (The interdependence of the event and its consequences reflects the systematic character of the conceptual framework.) At the representational stage we can systematically reconceive the ordinary conception of experience. This is necessary if we are to understand how the mechanical conception poses a challenge to the ordinary conception of experience. Instead of unreflectively taking experience to give us immediate access to objects in the world, we come to appreciate that an occurrence of sensory awareness of a ϕ might occur at some "remove" from an actual ϕ.

The new conception of thinking and using language, which incorporates the (cleaned-up version of the) ordinary conception of experience and its objects, is not satisfactory. But we have now accommodated this new and enlarged conception within an even more comprehensive scheme. For the world of experience is our response to the real world acting on us, and this response portrays the real world. In this comprehensive framework, we abandon a relational understanding of sensory awareness, without abandoning either subjects of experience or a relational "access" connecting these subjects to objects in the world. I can understand that my seeing the mug on my desk is actually an experience of imitating a white mug with stains, which imitating is my attempt to match the actual mug. Although at one level I portray the mug as white, I have my doubts about the color, and am prepared to subject this aspect of the portrayal to correction. (But perhaps the mug really is white.)

10. Two Puzzles

In achieving representational awareness, a subject must "interpret" a representation. Her interpreting constitutes her awareness. But there are some cases of representational awareness where there seems to be no representation. Consider a painting of a painting, which may be of other things as well. This could even be a painting of a painting of a painting, and so on. In looking at a painting of a painting, we can often see what the painting in the painting is a picture of (if we have represented the inner painting from the front). Not only can we use the "overall" painting to become representationally aware, but we can also use the painting in the painting to become representationally aware. But that is a problem. The "overall" painting is a real object in the real world. The painting in the painting is only an object of representational awareness. But objects of representational awareness are nothing—we have only a kind of awareness, not an object with any status. How can I use a painting of which I am only representationally aware to become representationally aware of something further? An object of representational awareness isn't an object with which I can *do* anything.

The solution to this puzzle isn't difficult. A painting of a painting is a real object. The physical parts of this real object are also real objects. A portion of the overall painting is interpreted to constitute representational awareness of a further painting. This same portion is also a real painting contained in the larger painting. We interpret the little painting to become representationally aware of its objects, and this representational awareness is subsequently attributed to the painting of which we are representationally aware. (And so on, for the painting of a painting of a painting.) Our awareness of the painting's part is like the awareness of the whole painting. In each case, this awareness is transformed to give us representational awareness of objects.

Now let us consider a more serious puzzle. The solution I am proposing for Descartes' Problem involves nonexplicit representing.

Nonexplicit representing is understood on the model of explicit representing, which is our paradigm for representing. In explicit representing, we are plainly aware of an object we use to become representationally aware. But according to the solution proposed to Descartes' Problem, we are never plainly aware of images or other representations. What we took to be direct awareness of a painting or drawing is representational awareness. Except for the awareness of our selves and some of our actions, all our awareness is representational. The objects of representational awareness have no status, so how can they be interpreted to provide further representational awareness? And how can we understand nonexplicit representing on the model of explicit representing, when there is no explicit representing?

Even with respect to the ordinary conception of experience, according to which we have direct access to images and other objects, our use of an image to represent has little effect on the image. We can't wear out a picture by looking at it, or by "seeing" the scene it is used to represent. In using an image to represent, we don't do anything to the image. Instead we "transform" our awareness of the image. We progress from being aware of the image to being (representationally) aware of its object. The fact that sensory awareness is representational awareness rather than plain awareness shouldn't undermine our understanding of explicit representing. In explicit iconic representing, we transform our sensory awareness of objects to constitute new representational awareness, of further objects. This new representational awareness, explicit representational awareness, isn't sensory awareness, but only sensory awareness, or its neural underpinnings, given a further interpretation. In interpreting neural events to represent a painting, we are trying to match the painting in the world. We attend to the painting at least to some extent. The transformed sensory awareness is no longer an attempt to match external objects. The transformed awareness is detached, or "abstracted." We attend to the image when we transform our sensory awareness to become representationally aware of further objects, but we need not attend to anything further.

We will still understand nonexplicit representing on the model of explicit representing. In explicit representing we transform one awareness to constitue another. In nonexplicit representing we do something to neural events and (possibly) states to constitute sensory awareness.

Our doing this is not caused by the neural events or their antecedents, for using neural events to become sensorily aware is a purposive activity. But we are determined to do this, we can't help doing it. Perhaps we are constantly trying to constitute sensory awareness, but the sensory awareness only "comes off" when appropriate neural events occur. In that case, we don't need to explain how we (or any sentient agent) "know" when there are neural events to interpret. We are not on the lookout for neural events, we simply are always trying to interpret neural events. When they don't occur, nothing happens; when they do occur, we get awareness. It seems possible to argue that we are always aware of a body like our own, and of the way its limbs are positioned, and that we are always attending to our body and its disposition. Even if there are no times when we have no awareness, it will still be the case that we are always interpreting and trying to interpret neural events, and that this perpetual striving leads to awareness whenever appropriate neural items turn up.

An alternative understanding of the process by which neural events give rise to sensory awareness would recognize a kind of preconscious precursor to awareness. This preconscious "awareness" will register the occurrence of neural events, and then be transformed to constitute sensory awareness. The preconscious awareness would be a precursor to plain awareness (which is the awareness we have of our selves) rather than to representational awareness. To understand sensory awareness in this alternative way, we must posit both a preconscious version of awareness and a transformation of this "awareness" to constitute sensory awareness. What the preconscious awareness would be and exactly how we would transform it aren't immediately evident. The only way to improve such an understanding is to further develop our conception, and to have success with the improved conception in explaining the things we know are taking place.

11. What Do We Supply to the Real World?

We are responsible for the conceptual structure of the world of experience. We don't abstract concepts from experience. We don't come into existence equipped with a fundamental supply of innate concepts. Instead we think up concepts and use them for dealing with things. (Though others have thought up and have taught us most of the concepts we employ.) Some concepts and systems of concepts work out very well. Some don't work at all. And some are useful for a time but subsequently prove inadequate. What is the relation between the conceptual structures we introduce and the real world?

There seem to be two possibilities. The first is that our concepts, when our understanding is correct or adequate, match features which the world contains independently of us. The world of experience has a conceptual structure which we supply. If this structure captures genuine features of the world, we won't regard those features as conceptual, because conceptual features originate in the concepts an intelligent agent produces to make sense of her experience and the world in which she finds herself. A good word for the objective counterpart to an adequate conceptual feature is 'form.' But the objective forms are not like Plato's, and gifted with an existence out of space and time. Instead they are more Aristotelian, providing structure to objects and situations in the real world.

The second possibility is that the real world lacks independent features which might be captured by our concepts and conceptual structures. At least, the real world doesn't possess these features "ahead of time." For we are real components of the real world. When we introduce conceptual structure to the world of experience, we have really done this. If our conceptual structures enable us to make good sense of the real world, then these structures and our success are objective features of reality. But our conceptual structures don't match independent forms, and it is possible that different people—perhaps from different parts of the universe—might each develop theories and conceptual frameworks that succeed in making excellent sense of experience and the world, while these different people's frameworks and theories are mutually incompatible, and no tests can be performed to show that one theory/framework is superior to the others.

Even with respect to this no-form possibility there will be some things which have conceptual structures essentially. For intentional acts owe their characters to the agents' conceptions of what they are doing. And there is a right answer to a question about what act an agent performs. What is going on intentionally depends essentially on what the agent thinks is going on, and on what the agent is trying to do.

I will confess that I am a friend of the forms. But I also follow Kant in thinking we are cut off from direct access to what things are like in themselves. There is no proving that there are forms which might be captured by concepts. There is also no point in supposing that the world is form-less. We must use concepts in making sense of the world, and our practice in doing so enjoys reasonable success. We are trying to match the real world. If it is possible to do this, then forms are real features of real objects.

But even though we accept the view that there are forms in the world which we try to match or capture with our concepts, not everything which is the case is independent of us and our conceptual activity. Our intentional activity depends on us and on the concepts we have of what we are doing. Collections of objects depend for their existence when they exist on our concepts and on our acts of attending to whatever falls under a concept. Comparison and measurement situations are created/constituted by us, and are informed by the concepts we bring to them. Ourselves and our activities, including conceptual activities, constitute objective ingredients of the real world.

12. Are There Some Things We Can't Get Right?

The world of experience is the real world as we portray it. But we accept the world of experience. Initially we take it to be the real world. Subsequently we recognize it as a portrayal of something else, though we can't help believing the real world is the way we portray it. Strictly, we only portray real elements of the real world. But we will sometimes mistake "fictional" portraying acts for the real thing. From our perspective, we portray the objects countenanced by the world of experience. We are elements of the world of experience, just as we are agents in our dreams. We are directly aware of ourselves, but we also portray ourselves as this or that, as *doing* this or that. Initially, for example, we portray ourselves as directly experiencing the objects of experience. Now we know better.

If a person learns to use language representationally, and absorbs the mechanical causal understanding of physical processes, her conception of experience and its objects will become incoherent. (Actually, it is the combination of the ordinary conception with the mechanical causal conception that becomes incoherent.) We have overcome this incoherence by incorporating a revised version of the ordinary conception of experience in a larger framework. The ordinary conception characterizes our portrayal of the real world, but not our access to the real world. It is now possible while we are portraying the real world, to recognize that this is what we are doing. We no longer take awareness in the world of experience to be direct awareness of real objects. But we don't need to continually insist on the distinction.

It may be easier to correct a misconception in or of the world of experience than a misperception or misportrayal. We can't help but portray objects of experience as colored, warm, cold, sweet, sour, and so on. We apparently interpret neural events which have no color to provide sensory awareness of colored objects. But the current scientific understanding of the world gives us no reason to think that objects actually possess the kinds of colors of which we are aware. Light of specified wavelengths isn't the same as the redness we see. It could be that objects actually do have the kinds of colors we see, but that these colors either play no role in the causal order or else have effects of a kind we have not so far detected. But suppose that real objects aren't really colored. We will still portray them as colored, even though our conception of the world leads us to discount colors in things. Our conception will correct our perception.

We have no direct access to the real world, except through our selves, which are real elements of the real order. We get at the real world by portraying it and conceiving it, by constituting the world of experience. We can't reasonably expect that we will ever eliminate all misunderstandings and misconceptions. After all, we only try to make sense of things; we have no authoritative source of information as to how things really are. Even if we did eliminate all mistakes, the world of experience would never be adequate to the real world. There will surely always be more to understand than we do understand. What we don't understand must be vastly more than what we do understand.

Kant recognized a distinction between the real world and the world of experience, though he didn't use this terminology, and he didn't understand this distinction as I propose. Kant gave reasons to show that the world of experience can't *be* the real world. Trying to make this identification lands one in inescapable paradoxes, or antinomies. We ourselves have no temptation to confuse the world of experience with the real world. Even when we accurately portray and conceive the real world, our activity with respect to the world is different from the world itself. For the world of experience to actually be the real world, we would need to experience real objects directly—and we don't. But Kant's strategy in discussing the antinomies might be adapted to argue that one can never hope to match the real world with the world of experience, not even imperfectly. Kant's strategy was to show that the world of experience must have certain features that the real world can't/couldn't have. Kant's basic idea here is that the world of experience is "centered" around the people who constitute it. We begin with ourselves and "work outward." In doing this, we will never come to an end, either spatially or temporally. The very idea of coming to an end is absurd. But so is the idea of an actual infinite extent in time or space.

The antinomies Kant discussed aren't quite so puzzling, or paradoxical, as he thought. There could have been a first moment in time, for example. Or things might have always been going on. But perhaps Kant's strategy can be employed to different effect. Could there be some features of the world of experience that must misrepresent, or camouflage, features of the real world? Kant was certainly right that the world of experience is centered on us, for this world is constituted by our activity. It is unlikely that we play such a central role in the real scheme of things. Perhaps there are features which we are determined to supply to the world of experience, which features distort the real world, although we can/will never notice the mismatch. This strikes me as unlikely, but there is, in any case, no point in worrying about this possibility, since it can never come to our attention. It may also be that some features of the world of experience distort the real world, but that we can discover and (possibly) compensate for such features. Colors that we perceive/portray might be an example of such features.

Features of the world of experience that are mistaken for real features should not be confused with features that we contribute to the real world. We are real elements of the real world, and what we do is real. Some situations exist independently of us, and others depend on and involve us. When we make comparisons or measurements, we constitute comparison situations. In constituting comparison situations, we may act to obscure the pre-existing features and situations on which the comparison is based. For example, we may think that *being taller than* is a fundamental relation linking objects rather than a feature created by comparing objects, which comparisons are based on really fundamental features of things. It is also conceivable that making one kind of measurement or establishing one kind of (comparative) order precludes making or establishing another, although the "dimensions" measured or compared are conceptually distinct. This could easily be misunderstood as an "indeterminacy" which is independent of us. Such a misunderstanding would not be a case of reading an inevitable feature of the world of experience into the real world, but instead a case of improperly distinguishing what depends on us from what does not.

13. Mind and Body

Many philosophers are likely to say that what I have called Descartes' Problem is nothing but the Mind-Body Problem. It may not be the Mind-Body Problem as classically formulated, but it "amounts" to the Mind-Body Problem. However, this identification is a mistake. It is the position that Descartes developed in response to Descartes' Problem that gives rise to the Mind-Body Problem. Descartes' account of the mind, the body, and their interrelations is not simply an articulation of our ordinary conception of these things; it is not the commonsense view (it isn't just folk psychology). If the physical world is governed by mechanical causal laws, but we aren't entirely subject to these laws, then Descartes thought we must have a nonphysical component. Our nonphysical components allow us both to understand the physical world, and to intervene in that world, carrying out actions for which there is no sufficient mechanical causal explanation.

The Mind-Body Problem is the problem of understanding and explaining how the nonphysical mind is connected to the physical body. Descartes suggested that this problem must remain opaque to us, because God has failed to provide us with the innate ideas needed for understanding the connection. God apparently doesn't think we need to understand the connection, for he has given us what we need for effective and moral living. We can understand and control (to some extent) the physical world. We can understand and control ourselves. Who could ask for anything more? The Mind-Body Problem is a *problem* for Descartes because the "out" which he provided himself here is not persuasive. It isn't clear that, or how, a nonphysical mind could interact with a physical body. And it must. Events in the body cause sensory awareness, which is mental. Mental emotions have physical sources. And our mental acts, our decisions, our imaginings, have physical consequences. Our decision to pick up the fork on the table, which decision is mental, conceptual, and intentional, causes events in the brain which eventually produce a grasping and lifting of the fork with our hand.

If Descartes hadn't separated the mind from the body in his account, he wouldn't have faced his Mind-Body Problem—which is *the* Mind-Body Problem. Some other account than Descartes' may face a different problem of linking the mental and the neural aspects of our lives. That would be *a* mind-body problem, not *the* Mind-Body Problem.

The present account does not posit separate mental and physical substances, but does distinguish both awareness and self-consciousness from neural events. Items in and out of our bodies cause the neural events that matter for the sensory awareness—which awareness we mistakenly took to give us immediate access to our bodies and external objects. The neural events are not identical with the sensory awareness. The neural events don't cause the sensory awareness. Sentient subjects interpret neural events to constitute sensory awareness. They use the neural events to imitate bodies and external objects. The sensory awareness that the subject constitutes is not a further neural event. The awareness is a mental event that occurs when and where the neural events occur. It is constituted by giving a purposive direction or focus to the neural events, and need involve no changes to the neural events. (But the agent can act purposively to gather new sensory inputs or to move around. She will then be producing neural events on her own, which neural events won't be caused by external objects.)

Descartes was right in distinguishing mental events from neural ones. Identity theorists are right in not admitting mental events which are separated from neural events, which require additional "material" than neural events. An agent uses the neural events themselves to constitute sensory awareness. We not only use neural events that are provided for us by the causal order, we also produce neural events to think with. We can imagine a red circle or a yellow fire engine or the opening of Beethoven's Fifth Symphony. These imaginings are not so vivid or lively as sensory awareness due to external objects, but they are constituted by interpreting neural events, the events we produce or "perform" as the "matter" of *imaginative* sensory awareness. When we think with words, without actually speaking, we produce and interpret neural events to give imaginative sensory awareness of utterances, and further use the imaginative awareness to attend to objects, to acknowledge them to be one thing or another, and to perform propositional representing acts. In performing intentional actions which involve bodily movements, we "perform" neural events causing the movements that take place. But the thinking (and acting) which employs neural events is not thinking *of* neural events. We think *with* the events, not of them (though, of course, we can and do think of neural events).

Although the present account is not dualistic in Descartes' fashion, it *is* dualistic. The fundamental dualism is between the causal and the purposive. With respect to our mental activity, the dualism is between the causal and the intentional. It might be argued that this fundamental dualism is the operative dualism even for Descartes. Given his understanding of the physical world, matter is "lumpy" and *inert*—it couldn't *do* anything. Since we do things, the part of us responsible for intentional behavior can't be material. But the fundamental objects in space and time are no longer conceived as being either lumpy or inert. Indeed, to characterize them as material, or physical, is to provide virtually no information about them.

We find that some complex objects are living, and that either all or some living things act purposively. Some of the purposive agents act intentionally. Presumably, it is the components of a purposive agent and their organization which make possible the purposive behavior. And similarly for intentional agents and their behavior. The purposive and intentional possibilities inherent in these complex objects won't be predictable from the causal features of their components. But it is a mistake to regard this "emergence" as mysterious or unintelligible. It is no more mysterious than the fact that electrons and photons exhibit certain kinds of behavior in certain kinds of situations. Exhibiting specified behavior is part of what it is to be an electron. Similarly, it is simply a fact about the world that certain kinds of complexity lead to purposive or intentional behavior. This may or may not be an ultimate fact. Perhaps we can understand this in terms of something more basic. Or perhaps this is where explanations come to an end.

In interpreting neural events to constitute sensory awareness, the agent may or may not produce/perform additional neural events. In any case, a mental occurrence of sensory awareness is not a kind of neural event, which is a creature of the causal order. The neural events are the material of sensory awareness. In a similar way, neural events don't constitute linguistic mental acts. We produce and interpret neural events to provide imaginative sensory awareness of utterances. This imaginative awareness is constituted to perform identifying acts, acknowledging acts, and propositional representing acts. These further, linguistic/mental, acts are not constituted by further neural events, although we produce further events. The relation between neural events and the sensory awareness they are used (interpreted) to constitute, and between neural events used to constitute imaginative awareness of utterances and the linguistic acts performed in constituting imaginative awareness, has some resemblance to the relation between syntactic features of a sentence in an artificial logical language and the semantic structure represented with the sentence. In both cases, the "syntactic" is an inadequate guide to the "semantic."

The syntactic features of an artificial-language sentence are not sufficient to determine the semantic structure it represents (the structure it is used to represent). The association is conventional. The language with its syntactic features is *designed* for representing semantic structure. The syntactic features aren't needed for understanding semantic structure or for making cogent arguments. The language merely helps organize our knowledge. Similarly, the causally operative features of neural events won't determine how the events are interpreted. With respect to (plain) sensory awareness, it is likely that agents are determined to interpret events of certain kinds to constitutue sensory awareness of certain kinds of objects. If we understood both how the agent is determined to act and the neural events that occur, we could in principle say what kind of sensory awareness the agent "enjoys." Less in the way of "prediction" is possible with linguistic mental acts. The character of the neural events occurring when someone constitutes imaginative awareness of utterances and performs linguistic acts won't reveal the language being spoken. Even given knowledge of the language, the character of the neural events won't determine the complete semantic structure of the linguistic acts performed. The situation is similar when people talk out loud. We can't always tell by listening what is the semantic structure of someone's speech act. There are conventional clues and cues to structure, but they sometimes fail us.

When we think without words, there must be neural states and events available for us to interpret. We can take a perceived object—an object we match at least approximately with sensory awareness—to be ϕ without saying or thinking the expression for ϕ. The criteria for correctly acknowledging the object to be ϕ are recorded in neural items we can interpret. In taking the object to be ϕ, we do interpret them. The interpreting itself is not a kind of neural operation, but we will surely produce neural events in the course of interpreting the neural information. Activating the disposition to use the ϕ-word for the perceived object brings about a change in the neural landscape.

The difference between what we do in (plain) sensory awareness and what we do in imagination and thought is like the difference between our listening/reading and our speaking/writing. When someone addresses us, we use her words to perform linguistic acts. When we are talking, we produce-and-use the words all at once. In thinking and acting, we produce neural events (better, we purposively but not intentionally carry out neural activity) and use them all at once. We produce and interpret imaginative sensory awareness and carry out various linguistic or mental acts. In actively moving about, we produce both motion and awareness of motion. We don't need to explain how this thought gives rise to that neural event, for the thought is simply the interpreted neural event. We could wonder how it is that we can think with neural events, but explanation must come to an end someplace. We simply find that we can do this. Similarly, to move our arm intentionally, we perform/produce neural events that we know nothing of. It is simply a fact that this is how we work. It is no more mysterious than any other fact. (But in a sense all facts are mysterious. For why are things as they are instead of being some other way?)

14. Personal Identity

There are several concepts of identity. One concept concerns identifying acts with a single target. This is the Morning Star-Evening Star sort of identity. Another concept of identity is the philosopher's concept, according to which identity is a relation that everything has to itself. This "relation" does not link an object to itself to constitute a situation, but is only a relation by courtesy. There are no identity situations, and there are no difference situations either. Len's being a different person from David is not some feature of the world in addition to David being an element of the world and Len being an element. Difference is a modal feature of the world rather than being an unsaturated entity suited to constitute situations. (It isn't possible to exploit the Len connections to identify David.)

The more interesting concept, or concepts, of identity concern time. This is the identity of an object at one time with that same object at another time. A very weak or "watery" sort of identity unifies a part of the world through time, where the part is identified by its situation with respect to us or some other object. A part of the world of this kind can pass into and out of existence, and come back again. Farmer Brown's flock of sheep is such a part. The flock exists when Brown owns sheep, ceases to exist when he sells (or slaughters) them all, and comes back into existence when he subsequently acquires new sheep. The Farmer-Brown's-flock-of-sheep part of the world can contain different sheep at different times and still be the same part of the world. We don't so often use the word 'same' in connection with this sort of entity. (But we will sometimes do it. We can easily make up stories in which it would be appropriate to say that this flock of sheep is the same as an earlier flock, even though the members of the flock aren't the same.) This concept of identity also applies to the Elizabeth's-husband part of the world. Her husband may be different men at different times. We would even call them different husbands. ("Elizabeth has had seven husbands.") But the Elizabeth's-husband part of the world is the same part from one time to the next, at least for those times when Elizabeth is married.

Not every part of the world is recognized by our conceptual system as a fundamental individual. A person is a fundamental individual, while the Elizabeth's-husband part of the world is not. A nonfundamental individual can be different fundamental individuals at different times, but a single fundamental individual can't be constituted by different fundamental individuals at different times. With respect to some kinds of fundamental individuals, particularly medium-sized individuals, the kinds of objects of which we have sensory awareness, spatiotemporal continuity is an important consideration in determining that the same object exists at different times. The boat which has all its components replaced over the years remains the same boat because it is (by and large) continuous with itself from one moment to the next. In addition, the changing boat occupies the same role in the larger scheme of things. It belongs to a certain fleet owned by some company, is used to carry out certain tasks, and so on.

An example that John Pollock once talked about is a table composed of four or five separable parts. These parts are combined when the table is assembled. But when the table is taken down, the parts are stored in different locations. What is the status of the disassembled table? The answer, in part, requires a decision by us. Our conceptions of identity aren't sufficiently well-developed to give a clear-cut answer. I prefer to say that the table ceases to exist when disassembled (unlike a folding table which has been folded up). It exists anew, but is the same table, when reassembled. The continued identity of the table does not depend on its own spatiotemporal continuity, but only on the spatial-temporal continuities of its parts. If some of the parts get replaced while the table is disassembled, we have a basis for saying that the subsequently reassembled table is only partly the same as the old table. (Though if the parts get replaced while the table is assembled, as is the case with the boat, then spatiotemporal continuity considerations may dictate that the altered table is completely identical with the earlier table, though some parts are new. But continuity considerations aren't conclusive. It is still a matter for us to decide.)

Our conception of identity through time is not completely developed. It has a certain looseness which might be removed in various ways. And the conception as we now have it is not dictated by the very nature of things, so that it couldn't conceivably be otherwise. Consider the example of a worm which, if cut at an appropriate location, yields two worms. I have been told that when this occurs, there is some principled basis for claiming that one piece is the original worm, while the other is a new worm. This may be correct, the way things are with worms, but it isn't necessary apart from our present conceptual framework. It is entirely conceivable that one worm might become two, where each worm had an equal claim to being the same worm as the original. In that case we could decide that the first worm had been "extinguished," and two new worms had taken its place. We could as well decide that each worm was identical with the original worm, without being identical with each other. (Temporal identity doesn't "have" to be transitive.)

We are actually capable of getting two worms from one, but we can't do the same thing with people. However, a world in which one person can spontaneously "decompose" into two people is entirely conceivable. Each of the two subsequent people could be spatiotemporally continuous with the single original person. Each would have the same memories of the earlier single life. In such a case, it would make more sense to think of each subsequent person as the same as the earlier person, than to think of them as brand new people. As well as imagining a world where people split, we can imagine one where two people merge to become a single person. Our current concepts of identity are not "prepared" for such a world. There is nothing impossible about modifying our concepts so that one object could be identical with two different objects.

A person generally exhibits spatiotemporal continuity throughout her life. But this doesn't appear to be what is crucial for personal identity. A continuity of experience, thought, and action seems to be what really "counts" for personal identity. (On the present view, this comes down to a continuity of action.) We can imagine going to bed in one place and waking up in a different place, with a different body, and still being ourself. We would need to remember how things used to be with us, and be disposed to think and act in much the same ways as before. (The changed body, including its neural equipment, might restrict the discharge of these dispositions.) The new body wouldn't be spatially continuous with the old, yet we would be the same person. And the period between going to sleep and waking might be several years, or centuries, rather than overnight, without any existing body being us in the interval, and we would still be the same person. In the absence of either spatial or temporal continuity, a continuity of experience, thought (including memory), and action (a continuity of purposive and intentional action) would seem to provide a sufficient basis for saying that a person at one time was the same person as someone earlier.

It might be objected that while we might *call* the later person the same person as the spatiotemporally discontinuous earlier person, while we might use the same name in both cases, the two wouldn't *metaphysically* be the same person. This objection suggests that identity is a fundamental feature of the world to which we have some kind of cognitive or epistemic access, and that it makes no sense to suppose that *real* identity is somehow up for being reconstrued or reconceived. I reject that suggestion. Our only access to a feature like identity is conceptual. We try out concepts on the world. We use concepts to organize our worlds of experience, as a way of portraying the real world. The way we organize the world of experience is certainly inadequate at present, even incorrect. There may be a right, or a best, way to conceive identity, but we currently have no basis for saying we know which concept this is.

15. In Conclusion

In this book I have been trying to develop and refine new conceptions of experience, thought, and language (linguistic activity). It seems characteristic of work in philosophy to be conceptual as opposed to empirical, and my own work is typical in this regard. I have not run subjects through laboratory experiments or tracked the development of groups of children from childhood through adolescence to adulthood. But the distinction between conceptual and empirical research is not between research which is all one and research which is all the other. Any research has both a conceptual and empirical dimension. New knowledge requires new conceptions, either the further articulation of existing conceptual frameworks, or wholly new frameworks to supply a novel organization to the world of experience. A conceptual framework needs empirical data to organize, but the data may be available before the framework is developed, and be familiar and readily accessible rather than recondite. I have supported my novel conception primarily by calling attention to historical problems that it solves or explains, and by noting familiar facts that it makes sense of. These familiar facts may not be familiar to normal eighth-graders or high-school graduates. But this data hasn't been gathered using specialized tools or techniques, and hasn't been turned up for the first time by my research.

The view I have presented has not been proved beyond the shadow of a doubt. It hasn't been proved at all. What it has going for it is its success in making sense of the phenomena to which it applies. But an understanding of the view I have presented *is* sufficient to reveal the misunderstandings and misconceptions incorporated in many views of human cognition and in many research programs in cognitive science. The very idea of computers thinking, talking, or carrying out other characteristically human activities makes no sense. It isn't that some tasks are just too hard for the kinds of computers now available. Nor is there a proof that task *A* is impossible for computers in the sense that trisecting an angle with a ruler and compass is impossible for anyone. Computers are entirely creatures of the mechanical causal order. They do not and cannot function either purposively or intentionally. But we do. Other animals than ourselves certainly function purposively—computers can't even do that. Some other animals appear to act intentionally—if, for example, it is correct that gorillas can learn to use language. The causal and purposive orders are complementary, but mutually exclusive. While it might be possible to construct a machine that is able to act purposively, such a machine wouldn't be a computer. No one can program purposive behavior.

There is a place in philosophy for arguments and proofs, but I don't think this place has the highest importance. The same is true of science. The situation is somewhat different in mathematics, for mathematical statements are not, in general, about the real world. It is possible to argue for or against the claim that the mechanical causal order is complete and self- sufficient, leaving no space for a fundamental category of purposive activity. Such arguments can go on endlessly, and inconclusively. Instead of making efforts to devise new arguments in favor of the reality and irreducibility of purposive behavior, I have instead been concerned to develop systematic purposive explanations. Just as there are causal sciences, so there can be (and are) purposive sciences. The characters of the two fundamental kinds of explanation lead to different kinds of science. Purposive sciences, for example, will be much less predictive than causal sciences. The best way to "prove" that such sciences are possible is to actually develop them. Which is what I have trying to do, at least in outline.

The present view has consequences for research in cognitive science. It doesn't preclude the kinds of research that people are actually carrying out. It does deny some of this research the significance that is attributed to it. Computers are never going to carry on conversations, although they can certainly produce sentences. And they can become ever more effective mechanical versions of Venn diagrams. Researchers in artificial intelligence won't be happy to have this be the true state of things. They either want computers to be considerably more than mechanical Venn diagrams, or else they want us to be nothing more than that. But apart from hurting their feelings, the present account doesn't deny the importance of the research. Superior mechanical versions of Venn diagrams may be enormously valuable to us.

I have presented a conceptual framework and a theory of experience, thought, and language. This is a general framework which can accommodate more specific theories and conceptions. The general theory/framework needs to be supplemented with more specific theories; it needs to expanded, refined, and corrected. In addition to providing a framework for research, this theory provides directions for research, it points toward areas for investigation and suggests strategies for carrying out investigation. In the large I have provided an account of purposive and intentional activity, and of the differences between the mechanical causal order and the purposive order. I have provided an analysis of the structural relations linking intentional acts, and have applied this analysis to the further analysis of linguistic acts. This analysis of linguistic acts can be carried much further than I have done. In addition, the basic analysis of structural relations needs to be enlarged/refined and applied to other intentional acts than linguistic ones.

The account of the development of language-using skills, which involves two stages, the purely identifying stage and the representational stage, is not based on studies of children learning to speak. It rests on a "How could it be otherwise?" argument, combined with an analysis/theory of representing. This account needs to be tested empirically, and refined and corrected on the basis of empirical research. The account provides conceptual tools for assessing linguistic skills. It provides conceptual tools for specifying pedagogical goals. We want language users to use language representationally. We want them to be able to think things through in their heads, and to follow arguments they hear and read. Once we understand what this amounts to, we are in a better position to help them achieve these goals. Understanding the difference between the two stages of language use promises to be fruitful for understanding historical philosophers and philosophical controversies. Aristotle, Hobbes, and Wittgenstein seem to have confined their attention to the purely identifying stage of language use, while Plato recognized representational-stage insights and Kant noticed synthetic *a priori* judgments that can't be accommodated at the purely identifying stage. Most major philosophers seem to be right about something important, though they often misunderstand just what this is. The present account provides new tools for sorting out what they were right and wrong about.

In my own case, I am anxious to begin to develop new logical theories. In *Using Language*, I presented several formal languages intended to capture/represent features of natural languages, particularly English. I gave a treatment of the so-called "donkey"-sentences ("If a man owns a donkey, he beats it") that is superior to others I have seen, although so far as I can tell it has been entirely overlooked. But the framework developed in this book provides the resources to replace those languages by more realistic, more satisfactory ones, and to develop different kinds of logical system which more adequately represent natural-language statements. A fully satisfactory system of illocutionary logic, one which properly distinguishes propositional content from illocutionary force, can now be developed. (The illocutionary logic found in Searle and Vanderveken 1985 is not satisfactory.)

I have now reached the end of this book, for which I am quite thankful. It is much longer than I originally anticipated. I hope that it is not quite so exhausting to read as it has been to write.

References

1. Descartes' Problem

Austin, J. L. 1979. *Sense and Sensibilia.* Oxford: Oxford University Press.

Davidson, Donald. 1984. "On the Very Idea of a Conceptual Scheme." In *Inquiries into Truth and Interpretation*, 183–98. Oxford: Oxford University Press.

Descartes, René. 1967. *The Philosophical Works of Descartes.* Vols. 1 and 2. Translated by Elizabeth S. Haldane and G. R. T. Ross. Cambridge: Cambridge University Press.

Kearns, John T. 1984. *Using Language: The Structures of Speech Acts.* Albany: SUNY Press.

Kuhn, Thomas S. 1977. "Concepts of Cause in the Development of Physics." In *The Essential Tension*, 21–30. Chicago: University of Chicago Press.

Russell, Bertrand. 1972. *The Problems of Philosophy.* Oxford: Oxford University Press.

Talmy, Leonard. 1990. "Fictive Motion and Change in Language and Perception." Conference of the International Pragmatics Association, Barcelona, Spain, July.

Tarski, Alfred. 1983. *Logic, Semantics, Metamathematics*, revised edition with new introduction by John Corcoran. Indianapolis, Ind.: Hackett Publishing Company.

2, 3. The Larger Problem

Descartes, René. 1958. *Descartes Philosophical Writings*, selected and translated by Norman Kemp Smith. New York, Modern Library.

———. 1972. *The Philosophical Works of Descartes*. Vols. 1 and 2. Translated by Elizabeth S. Haldane and G. R. T. Ross. Cambridge: Cambridge University Press.

Smith, Norman Kemp. 1963. *New Studies in the Philosophy of Descartes: Descartes as Pioneer*. New York: Russell and Russell.

4. The Empiricist Response

Ayer, Alfred Jules. 1952. *Language, Truth, and Logic*. New York: Dover Publications.

Berkeley, George. 1965. *Principles, Dialogues, and Philosophical Correspondence*, Edited by Colin Murray Turbayne. New York: Bobbs-Merrill.

Hume, David. 1955. *An Inquiry Concerning Human Understanding*. Edited by Charles W. Hendel. New York: Bobbs-Merrill.

———. 1981. *A Treatise of Human Nature*. Edited by L. A. Selby-Bigge. Oxford: Oxford University Press.

Russell, Bertrand. 1972. *The Problems of Philosophy*. Oxford: Oxford University Press.

Sellars, Wilfrid. 1963. *Science, Perception, and Reality*. New York: Humanities Press.

5. Acting Intentionally

Austin, J. L. 1975. *How To Do Things With Words*. Cambridge, Mass.: Harvard University Press.

Fodor, Jerry. 1990. "A Theory of Content, I: The Problem." In *A Theory of Content and Other Essays*, 51–87. Cambridge, Mass.: MIT Press.

Hull, David L. 1989. *The Metaphysics of Evolution*. Albany: SUNY Press.

Kearns, John T. 1984. *Using Language: The Structures of Speech Acts*. Albany: SUNY Press.

Kuhn, Thomas S. 1977. "Concepts of Cause in the Development of Physics." In *The Essential Tension*, 21–30. Chicago: University of Chicago Press.

Searle, John R. 1974. *Speech Acts: An Essay in the Philosophy of Language*. London: Cambridge University Press.

6, 7, 8. Learning to Use Language

Austin, J. L. 1975. *How To Do Things With Words*. Cambridge, Mass.: Harvard University Press.

Baker, Lynne Rudder. 1987. *Saving Belief: A Critique of Physicalism*. Princeton: Princeton University Press.

Boole, George. 1958. *An Investigation of the Laws of Thought, On Which are Founded the Mathematical Theories of Logic and Probabilities*. New York: Dover Publications.

———. 1965. *The Mathematical Analysis of Logic*. New York: Barnes & Noble.

Bowerman, Mellissa and Soonja Choi. 1991. "Learning to Express Motion Events in English and Korean: The Influence of Language-Specific Lexicalization Patterns." *Cognition* 41 (1991): 83–121.

Fodor, Jerry A. 1975. *The Language of Thought*. New York: Thomas Y. Crowell.

———. 1981. *Representations: Philosophical Essays on the Foundations of Cognitive Science*. Cambridge, Mass.: MIT Press.

———. 1987. *Psychosemantics: The Problem of Meaning in the Philosophy of Mind*. Cambridge, Mass.: MIT Press.

———. 1990. *A Theory of Content, and Other Essays*. Cambridge, Mass.: MIT Press.

Jusczyk, Peter W., Angela D. Friederici, Jeanine M. I. Wessels, Vigdis Y. Svenkerud, and Ann Marie Jusczyk. 1993. "Infants Sensitivity to the Sound Patterns of Native Language Words," *Journal of Memory and Language* 32 (1993): 402–20.

Kearns, John T. 1967. "The Contribution of Lesniewski." *Notre Dame Journal of Formal Logic* 8 (1967): 61–93.

———. 1979. "A Little More Like English." *Logique et Analyse*, n.s., 87 (1979): 353–68.

———. 1984. *Using Language: The Structures of Speech Acts.* Albany: SUNY Press.

Kripke, Saul A. 1972. "Naming and Necessity." In *Semantics of Natural Language*, ed. by Donald Davidson and Gilbert Harmon, 253–355. Dordrecht, Holland and Boston: D. Reidel Publishing Co.

Lesniewski, Stanislaw. 1927–31. "O podstawach matematyki" (On the Foundations of Mathematics). *Przeglad Filozoficzny* 30 (1927): 164–206, 31 (1928): 261–91, 32 (1929): 60–101, 33 (1930): 77–105, 34 (1931): 142–70.

———. 1930. "Über die Grundlagen der Ontologie." *Sprawozdania z posiedzen Towarzystwa Naukowego Warszawskiego* (*Comptes Rendus des Seances de la Societe des Sciences et des Lettres de Varsovie*) 23 (1930): Classe 3, 111–32.

———. 1931. "Über Definitionem in der sogennanten Theorie der Deduktion." *Comptes Rendus des Seances de la Societe des Sciences et des Lettres de Varsovie* 24 (1931): Classe 3, 289–309.

Luschei, Eugene C. 1962. *The Logical Systems of Lesniewski.* Amsterdam: North-Holland Publishing Co.

Mehler, Jacques, Peter W. Jusczyk, G. Lambertz, N. Halsted, Josiane Bertoncini, and C. Amiel-Tyson. 1988. "A Precursor of Language Acquisition in Young Infants." *Cognition* 29 (1988): 144–78.

Montague, Richard. 1974. "English as a Formal Language." In *Formal Philosophy: Selected Papers of Richard Montague*, ed. Richmond H. Thomason, 188–221. New Haven, Yale University Press.

Putnam, Hilary. 1975. "The Meaning of Meaning." *Minnesota Studies in the Philosophy of Science* 7 (1975): 131–93.

———. 1988. *Representation and Reality*. Cambridge, Mass.: MIT Press.

Quine, W. V. 1960. *Word and Object*. Cambridge, Mass.: MIT Press.

Searle, John. 1974. *Speech Acts: An Essay in the Philosophy of Language*. London: Cambridge University Press.

Sobocinski, Boleslaw. 1949. "L'Analyse de l'Antinomie russellienne par Lesniewski." *Methodos* 1 (1949): 94–107, 220–28, 308–16; 2 (1950): 237–57.

Tarski, Alfred. 1983. *Logic, Semantics, Metamathematics*, revised edition with a new introduction by John Corcoran. Indianapolis, Ind.: Hackett Publishing Company.

Wood, Susan B. 1976. "George Boole's Theory of Propositional Forms." Ph.D. dissertation, State University of New York at Buffalo.

9, 10, 11. Representing

Anderson, Alan Ross. 1990. "Introduction." Martin 1990, 1–11.

Austin, J. L. 1975. *How To Do Things With Words*. Cambridge, Mass.: Harvard University Press.

Descartes, René. 1958. *Rules for the Guidance of our Native Understanding*. In *Descartes Philosophical Writings*, selected and translated by Norman Kemp Smith. New York: Modern Library.

Kearns, John T. 1978. "Three Substitution-Instance Interpretations." *Notre Dame Journal of Formal Logic* 19 (1978): 331–54.

———. 1979. "A Little More Like English." *Logique et Analyse*, n.s., 87 (1979): 353–68.

———. 1986. "Modal Semantics Without Possible Worlds." *The Journal of Symbolic Logic* 46 (1981): 77–86.

———. 1984. *Using Language: The Structures of Speech Acts*. Albany: SUNY Press.

———. 1988. *The Principles of Deductive Logic*. Albany: SUNY Press.

———. 1989. "Lesniewski's Strategy and Modal Logic." *Notre Dame Journal of Formal Logic* 30 (1989): 291–307.

———. 1993. "Church's and Turing's Theses." Technical Report 93-3, Center for Cognitive Science, State University of New York at Buffalo.

Kenney, Emelie A. 1988. "*Discovery on the Threshold: The Recognition and Acceptance of Complex Numbers*". Ph.D. dissertation, State University of New York at Buffalo.

Kuhn, Thomas S. 1970. *The Structure of Scientific Revolutions*. Chicago: University of Chicago Press.

Robert L. Martin, ed., 1970. *The Paradox of the Liar*. New Haven: Yale University Press.

Popper, Karl R. 1968. *The Logic of Scientific Discovery*. New York: Harper & Row.

Quine, W. V. 1961. "Two Dogmas of Empiricism." In *From a Logical Point of View*. Cambridge, Mass.: Harvard University Press.

———. *Word and Object*. Cambridge, Mass.: MIT Press.

Searle, John R. 1974. *Speech Acts: An Essay in the Philosophy of Language*. London: Cambridge University Press.

———. 1989. "The Logical Status of Fictional Discourse." In *Expression and Meaning*. New York: Cambridge University Press.

Smith, John E. 1981. "The New Need for a Recovery of Philosophy." Presidential Address delivered before the Seventy-Eighth Annual Eastern Meeting of the American Philosophical Association, Philadelphia, 29 December 1981.

Wittgenstein, Ludwig. 1956. *Remarks on the Foundations of Mathematics*. Edited by G. H. von Wright, R. Rhees, and G. E. M. Anscombe. Translated by G. E. M. Anscombe. Oxford: Basil Blackwell.

12. Knowledge and Certainty

Armstrong, David M. 1993. "A World of States of Affairs." Talk given to Philosophy Colloquium at the State University of New York at Buffalo, Fall 1993.

Descartes, René. 1958. *Descartes Philosophical Writings*. Selected and translated by Norman Kemp Smith. New York: Modern Library.

Hume, David. 1955. *An Inquiry Concerning Human Understanding*. Edited by Charles W. Hendel. New York: Bobbs-Merrill.

———. 1981. *A Treatise of Human Nature*. Edited by L. A. Selby-Bigge. Oxford: Oxford University Press.

Kant, Immanuel. 1956. *Immanuel Kant's Critique of Pure Reason*. Translated by Norman Kemp Smith. London: Macmillan.

Kearns, John T. 1981. "Modal Semantics Without Possible Worlds." *The Journal of Symbolic Logic* 46 (1981): 77–86.

———. 1984. *Using Language: The Structures of Speech Acts*. Albany: SUNY Press.

———. 1989. "Lesniewski's Strategy and Modal Logic." *Notre Dame Journal of Formal Logic* 30 (1989): 291–307.

Kuhn, Thomas S. 1970. *The Structure of Scientific Revolutions*. Chicago: University of Chicago Press.

13. A Solution

Chomsky, Noam. 1994. "Language and the Cognitive Revolution." Second Annual Distinguished Speaker in Cognitive Science Lecture, Center for Cognitive Science, State University of New York at Buffalo, Spring 1994.

Dennett Daniel C. 1987. *The Intentional Stance*. Cambridge, Mass.: MIT Press.

———. 1992. " 'Filling In' Versus Finding Out: A Ubiquitious Confusion in Cognitive Science." In *Cognition, Conceptual and Methodological Issues*, ed. H. L. Pick, Jr., P. Van Den Broek, and D. C. Knill, 33–49. Washington, D.C.: American Psychological Association.

Dennett, Daniel C. and Marcel Kinsbourne. 1992. "Time and the Observer: The Where and When of Consciousness in the Brain." *Behavior and Brain Sciences* 15 (1992): 183–247.

———. 1993. "Back from the Drawing Board." In *Dennett and His Critics: Demystifying Mind*, ed. Bo Dahlbom, 203–35. Oxford, UK and Cambridge, Mass.: Blackwell.

———. Forthcoming. "Seeing is Believing—Or is it?" CCS-92-4, Center for Cognitive Studies, Tufts University, Medford, Mass. In *Perception*, ed. K. Akins, *Vancouver Studies in Cognitive Science*, vol. 5. Oxford: Oxford University Press.

———. 1995. "Dismantling the Cartesian Theater." Third Annual Distinguished Speaker in Cognitive Science Lecture, Center for Cognitive Science, State University of New York at Buffalo, Spring 1995.

Descartes, René. 1897–1906. *Oeuvres de Descartes*. 4 vols. Paris: Leopold Cerf.

———. 1958. *Descartes' Philosophical Writings*. Selected and translated by Norman Kemp Smith. New York: Modern Library.

———. 1967. *The Philosophical Works of Descartes*. Translated by Elisabeth S. Haldane and G. R. T. Ross. London: Cambridge University Press.

Hobbes, Thomas. 1966. *Leviathan*. Edited by Michael Oakeshott. New York: Collier Books.

Kant, Immanuel. 1956. *Kant's Critique of Pure Reason*. Translated by Norman Kemp Smith. New York: St. Martin's.

Kearns, John T. 1984. *Using Language: The Structures of Speech Acts*. Albany: SUNY Press.

Searle, John R. and Daniel Vanderveken. 1985. *Foundations of Illocutionary Logic*. Cambridge: Cambridge University Press.

Index